CALENDAR

OF

LETTER-BOOKS

PRESERVED AMONG THE ARCHIVES OF THE CORPORATION

OF THE

CITY OF LONDON

AT THE GUILDHALL.

LETTER-BOOK L.

Temp. EDWARD IV.—HENRY VII.

EDITED BY

REGINALD R. SHARPE, D.C.L.,

LATE OF ST. JOHN'S COLLEGE, OXFORD,

OF THE INNER TEMPLE, BARRISTER-AT-LAW;

RECORDS CLERK IN THE OFFICE OF THE TOWN CLERK OF THE
CITY OF LONDON.

*PRINTED BY ORDER OF THE CORPORATION UNDER THE DIRECTION
OF THE LIBRARY COMMITTEE.*

LONDON: PRINTED BY JOHN EDWARD FRANCIS, BREAM'S BUILDINGS, E.C.

MCMXII.

ERRATA ET CORRIGENDA.

Page 121, note 4, for " 1912 " read *1911*.

Page 128, line 8 from bottom of text, for " certain butchers " read *the Fellowship of Butchers*.

Page 148, line 7 from bottom, for " Chaunce " read *Chaunte*.
Page 326, col. 2, after Stokton read *Stokdon*.

Page 328, col. 2, insert :—

Awstorp', John, 204n.

———— ———— Johanna, wife of, daughter of John Worth, 204

INTRODUCTION.

LETTER-BOOK L commences A.D. 1461 and closes in the year 1497.

Soon after the accession of Edward IV. William Dunthorn was appointed Common Clerk (*i.e.*, Town Clerk) of the City in the place of Roger Spicer *alias* Tonge, who had been discharged on account of his Lancastrian proclivities.[1] The new Town Clerk and his more famous predecessor in office, John Carpenter, had some characteristics in common. One of Carpenter's foibles was occasionally to sign official documents with his surname only. This grew into a common practice with Dunthorn and later Town Clerks, and has been continued down to the present day. Both Carpenter and Dunthorn took an intelligent interest in the City's Records, the former being responsible for the compilation of the City's customs and franchises in the well-known 'Liber Albus,' whilst the latter made a compilation, chiefly from the City's Letter-Books, known as 'Liber Dunthorn.'[2]

It is remarkable that in Carpenter's time the City's Records were not in the Town Clerk's custody, but in that of the Chamberlain. It was not until 1462, when Dunthorn had been nearly a year in office as Town Clerk, that the Court of Aldermen decreed that all Rolls and Records in the custody of the Chamberlain should be transferred to the custody of the Town

[1] "In isto comuni concilio [5 Aug., 1 Edward IV.] consideratum est et inactitatum quod Rogerus Tonge dudum communis Clericus Civitatis propter suas magnas offensiones et rebelliones erga dominum nostrum Regem per ipsum multipliciter factas et perpetratas omnino sit disoneratus ab eodem officio et quod nullo modo illud officium occupet infuturum, &c."—Journal 6, fo. 46.

[2] In November, 1474, the Court of Aldermen assigned to Dunthorn certain port dues at Sandwich, of the value of £115 3s. 3d., on the understanding that he would cause to be freshly transcribed one or two books containing the customs and ordinances of the City at his own expense. Journal 8, fo. 91.

Clerk.[1] It is difficult not to believe that Dunthorn himself was responsible for this change, as also for another order of the Court, made a few months before, which placed the clerks of the Mayor's Court, of which the Town Clerk for the time being was *ex officio* Registrar, entirely at Dunthorn's disposal.[2]

There are entries in the Letter-Book before us recording historical facts which are marred by the introduction of irrelevant matter couched in florid and pedantic language. This is no doubt due to Dunthorn's affectation, a weakness from which Carpenter also had not always been free.[3] Thus the account of the banquet given by the Serjeants-at-law in 1464 in Ely House, when Matthew Philip, the Mayor, met with such discourtesy that he refused to take the seat allotted to him, and returned in high dudgeon to his own house, is prefaced with an account of the fabulous foundation of London by Brut and a laudatory comparison of the City of London with the towns of Venice and Genoa. But apart from this, the record of the event is interesting as being an official and contemporary account. It appears, moreover, to be the only account which mentions an unsuccessful attempt made by the Serjeants to set matters right, by inviting the Mayor to attend a banquet on the following day, when they would see that due respect was paid him.[4]

---

[1] *Infra*, p. 17.

[2] *Infra*, p. 15.

[3] See Riley's 'Memorials,' p. 580.

[4] *Infra*, p. 7. Another story not complimentary to the hospitality of the Serjeants-at-law is to be found in the records of the Drapers' Company under the year 1521. The Mayor, Sir John Brugge or Bruges, who was a member of that Company, attended the Serjeants' feast that year; but although he had no cause to complain of want of deference paid to him officially, the banquet itself left much to be desired. "To show what the fare was," runs the record, "is but loss of time. I suppose that the worshipful citizens were never worse served." Herbert, 'Twelve Great Livery Companies,' i. 412. The Serjeants had little excuse for providing poor fare, seeing that the "Pastelers," or pastrycooks, were expressly forbidden to provide the fare for certain great feasts (the Serjeants' feast being of the number) without consulting the Wardens of the Pastelers' Fraternity, to the intent that the feasts should be "welle and worshipfully dressed," for the honour of the City and the honour and profit of those who had to pay for the entertainment. *Infra*, p. 311.

At another time, when recording the imposition of a fine by the Court of Aldermen on a man for marrying a City orphan without having first obtained permission of the Court, Dunthorn cannot refrain from quoting Cicero on the importance of bestowing special care upon children;[1] whilst on another occasion he quotes Seneca,[2] for the sole purpose of displaying his classical attainments. Dunthorn died in office in February, 1489-90, and was succeeded by Nicholas Pakenham, but neither the death of the former nor the appointment of the latter is recorded in the Letter-Book.

Early in the volume we find recorded the petition of the Mayor and citizens—presented, as was the custom, by the mouth of the Recorder—to the Duke of Clarence, Steward of England, for permission to perform the customary services and to receive the customary fees at the Coronation of Edward IV. (28 June, 1461). We have also the names of the thirteen citizens chosen from the leading livery companies to assist the Mayor on that occasion.[3] The proceedings are here recorded in simple terms, but when the account becomes transferred from the Letter-Book to ' Liber Dunthorn,' the Town Clerk must needs add an utterly unnecessary preface, which detracts from the dignity of the narrative.

Four years later Ralph Josselyn, the Mayor, received a writ of Privy Seal, dated from Sheen, 13 April, 1465, bidding him attend at Westminster Palace on Sunday, the 26th May, on the occasion of the Queen's Coronation.[4] This is all that the Letter-Book tells us of the matter, but if we turn to ' Liber Dunthorn ' we find the following particulars recorded, viz., that on Friday after the Feast of the Ascension the Queen came from Kingston to the Tower with a retinue of nobles ; that the King created the following knights (more correctly Knights of the Bath), viz., the Mayor, Hugh " Whiche," Thomas Cook, and John Plomer, Aldermen, as well as Henry Waver, citizen and draper (afterwards an Alderman) ; and that on the following Sunday

[1] *Infra*, p. 11n.
[2] *Infra*, p. 11.
[3] *Infra*, pp. 5, 6.
[4] *Infra*, pp. 58-9.

(26 May) the Coronation took place, the Mayor and citizens performing the customary services, and the Mayor receiving the usual fee.[1]   On the accession of Richard III. the citizens again put in their claim for service at the Coronation of the King and Queen, and their claim was again allowed.[2]

Beyond these Coronation claims, and the letter sent by the "bastard" Falconbridge to the Mayor and Aldermen in 1471 desiring permission to pass through the City with his Kentish followers, together with the reply to the same, there is scarcely an incident of national interest recorded in the Letter-Book. Even the temporary recovery of the throne by Henry VI. and the flight of Edward IV. are scarcely noticed or not at all; and the same may be said of the short reign of Edward V.,[3] the demise of Richard III., and the accession to the throne of the House of Tudor.

Again, there is nothing recorded indicative of Lambert Simnel's insurrection of 1487 (unless it be a proclamation against propagators of false "tidings and tales"),[4] and nothing relating to the Perkin Warbeck conspiracy ten years later. For such matters we have to turn to the City's Journal or Repertory[5] of the day.

We should have expected to find the Letter-Book recording frequent instances of money granted to Edward IV. by the novel method of a so-called "Benevolence." As a matter of fact we find only one mentioned, and that was a grant of 5,000 marks made by the City early in 1481, when England was

---

[1] 'Liber Dunthorn,' fos. 62 b, 63. Cf. Gregory's 'Chron.' (Camd. Soc.), p. 228; Fabyan (ed. Ellis), p. 655.

[2] *Infra*, pp. 207-8.

[3] The Journal of the day is careful to note the regnal year 1 Edward V., the election of Thomas Fitz William as City Recorder being entered as having taken place on the 19th June of that year. Journal 9, fo. 26 b.

[4] *Infra*, p. 243.

[5] Journal 10, fos. 104 b, 105, 108; Repertory 1, fos. 10 b, 13, 19 b, 20, 20 b. The series of the City's Records known as "Repertories" are concerned with proceedings of the Court of Aldermen as distinct from the Common Council, and commence in 1495.

threatened with a Scottish invasion.[1] The money, as we learn from another source, was repaid the following year.[2] Of a former Benevolence to which the Mayor and Aldermen made heavy contributions in 1475, to assist the King in his expedition against France,[3] the Letter-Book says not a word.

On the other hand, we are forcibly reminded of two calamities which befell the nation within a few years of each other. One was a scarcity of cereals towards the close of 1482, which threatened a famine in the City had not merchants been encouraged to send their grain to London by a promise that it should not be intercepted by the King's purveyors;[4] and the other was a visitation of the epidemic known as the "sweating sickness," which in 1485 carried off two Mayors and six Aldermen within a week. Thomas Hille, who was Mayor at the time of the outbreak, fell a victim to the sickness, and died on the 23rd September, and was succeeded by William Stokker, appointed the following day. Within four days Stokker himself was dead, and on the 29th John Warde was elected Mayor for the remainder of the official year. There was no Mayoralty banquet, but we are told that the Mayor attended the banquet given by the newly appointed Sheriffs, who had been sworn into office the previous day, and were to be presented before the Barons of the Exchequer on the following day.[5] Warde appears to have had but little liking for the City at any time, and the civic authorities had some difficulty in getting him to reside in London, even before the epidemic. On the 28th June the Court of Aldermen had bidden him return and reside within the City with his family, under a penalty of £500.[6] It is therefore not surprising that when the Mayoralty year expired he was not put in nomination for re-election, and Hugh Brice was elected.[7] Warde probably went back into the country, glad to get away from the pestilential City.

[1] Infra, pp. 175-6.
[2] Cotton MS. Vitellius A xvi., fo. 137. Kingsford's 'Chronicles of London,' pp. 188-9.
[3] Id., fo. 134; Kingsford, 'Chron.,' p. 186.
[4] Infra, p. 199.
[5] Infra, pp. 226-7.
[6] Journal 9, fo. 78 b.
[7] Id., fo. 89 b.

Among events of purely municipal interest with which the Letter-Book is largely concerned may be mentioned a dispute which arose in 1462 between the City and the Hanse merchants upon a claim made by the latter to a mansion over Bishopsgate, and to a right of defending the main part of the gate, including the "Portcolys," in time of war. They refused, moreover, to keep in repair a certain portion of the gate (as in duty bound under the "composition" made with the City in 1282[1]) unless their claim to the mansion were allowed. Thereupon the deed of "composition" was examined by the Mayor and Aldermen, and was found in no way to support the claims put forward by the merchants. As the gate stood in immediate need of repair, the merchants were summoned to give up the keys in order that the repairs might be carried out by the civic authorities. On their refusing to do this the Court of Aldermen instructed the Mayor to take forcible possession of the gate, and to expel the foreign merchants. This was done ; and as the merchants resolutely refused to give up the keys, new keys had to be made, and William Calbeck, a Serjeant-at-Mace, who occupied a mansion over the gate, was commissioned by the Court to execute the necessary repairs at the City's expense.[2]

[1] 'Liber Albus,' i. 485-8. We have already seen how, in consideration of the Hanse merchants having been charged with the custody and repair of Bishopsgate, they had been exempted in 1305 from the customary payment of two shillings by those passing through the gate with merchandise ('Cal. Letter-Book C,' p. 111). We have seen, too, that in 1427 a fresh settlement had been arrived at between the City and the Hanse merchants, confirming the "composition" of 1282, subject to certain payments to the Mayor and Sheriffs for the time being in money and in kind ('Cal. Letter-Book K,' p. 46). Nevertheless, disputes continued to arise throughout the reign of Henry VI., and a few years after the accession of Edward IV. it is recorded that the Easterlings (i.e., the Hanse merchants) were in debt to English merchants to the extent of £13,520. Kingsford's ' Chron. of London,' p. 180.

[2] Infra, pp. 13, 14. These proceedings, which are recorded as having taken place in March and April, 1462, appear to have been taken by the civic authorities in spite of an Order in Council issued in the previous December, to the effect that the merchants of Almaine should be permitted to enjoy all their ancient privileges for the next twelvemonth, and that none should molest them. Vide infra, p. 18, where note 1 is incorrect and should be deleted.

Although the Hanse merchants are believed to have been in occupation of the Steelyard, near Dowgate, as early as 1320,[1] they did not become actual proprietors of it until 1475, the year following the Treaty of Utrecht (20 July, 1474),[2] granted to them by Edward IV. as a reward for their assistance against Queen Margaret and the Earl of Warwick. At that time it was the property of the Corporation.[3] It was one of the stipulations of the treaty that not only the court (*curia*) in London called the Steelyard, but the Steelyard at Boston in Lincolnshire, should be confirmed to the Hansards. Towards this end the Mayor and Aldermen, on the 11th February of that year (1475), covenanted to make over the depôt to the King in "exchange" for a remission of a sum of £70 3s. 4d. out of the yearly fee ferm paid by the Sheriffs, as well as their leasehold in an adjoining tenement belonging to Elsing Spital for a similar remission of a sum of £13 16s. 8d.[4] This deed of covenant was followed a few days later by another conveying both properties to the merchants of Almaine, the one in perpetuity, the other for a term of thirty-two years,[5] and on the 12th May the Court of Aldermen agreed that the merchants should have a confirmation of their liberties under the City's Common Seal.[6]

Another clause of the treaty guaranteed to the Hanse merchants the possession and custody of Bishopsgate according to the terms of the " composition " already mentioned.

The reader is reminded that by the terms of this " composition " the Hanse merchants were allowed to have an Alderman of their own choice as of old, provided he was a freeman of the

---

[1] Stow's ' Survey ' (ed. Kingsford), ii. 319.

[2] Rymer, ' Fœdera,' xi. 792-803.

[3] It had been the mansion house of John Reynwell, Alderman and Fishmonger (Mayor 1426-7), and had been by him conveyed to the Corporation for charitable purposes (Stow's ' Survey,' ed. Kingsford, i. 234 ; ii. 320-1). It was probably

the same house as that conveyed by the City in 1464 to the "venerable" John Waldene for life, and, on his decease shortly afterwards, to his widow for a term of years. *Infra*, pp. 44, 54.

[4] *Infra*, p. 127.

[5] *Infra*, pp. 127-8.

[6] *Infra*, p. 129.

City and was presented to the Mayor and Aldermen, to be by them sworn to administer justice. At that time a foreigner, Gerard Merbode by name, was Alderman of the Hanse,[1] and in 1320 John le Long, an Easterling, held the same office ;[2] but before the end of the fourteenth century we find two City Aldermen elected in succession by the merchants to be their Alderman, one of them being the well-known William Walworth.[3]

The importance of the office of Alderman of the Hanse is illustrated by a casè recorded in the year 1344 in a series of Rolls of 'Pleas and Memoranda,'[4] preserved at the Guildhall. There we read that a London merchant had been robbed of goods to the value of £20, and had forthwith brought an action in the Sheriff's Court for damages. It happened, however, that the thief was a merchant of the Hanse, and as such was claimed by John Hamond, at that time Alderman of the Hanse as well as Alderman of the City of London, to be tried before him at the Guildhall of the Teutonics, and his claim was allowed.

In course of time the election of their Alderman passed out of the hands of the merchants into the hands of the King, who usually appointed one of the City Aldermen.[5] The Treaty of Utrecht expressly stipulated that in civil or criminal causes affecting the Hanse merchants in England the King should appoint two or more judges, who, without the formalities of law, should do speedy justice between the parties.[6]

The same year that the Hanse merchants came into possession of the Steelyard we find an ordinance of Common Council recorded in the Letter-Book which hitherto appears to have passed unnoticed. It is to the effect that thenceforth two Aldermen of the same Art or Mistery should not be nominated

---

[1] 'Liber Albus,' i. 486, 487.
[2] 'Cal. Letter-Book E,' pp. 119, 120.
[3] 'Cal. Letter-Book H,' p. 158.
[4] Roll A 5, membr. 24.

[5] See 'Cal. Letter - Book K,' p. 401 ; also *infra*, pp. 65, 161, 211, 271.
[6] Rymer, 'Fœdera,' xi. 795.

together for the Mayoralty.[1] It is not clear for what purpose this ordinance was made; the nearest parallel to it is an ordinance made in 1384 (when the election of members of the Common Council reverted from the Guilds to the Wards), to the effect that no Ward should return more than eight persons of the same Mistery.[2]

There are other ordinances recorded in the Letter-Book affecting the mode of municipal elections. Thus, in 1480, an ordinance was passed restricting the inhabitants of a Ward to the presentation of two Aldermen and no more (if any were presented) on the occasion of an election of an Alderman for their Ward, otherwise the election was to be void.[3]

Again, in 1491, the Common Council decreed that when the election of a Chamberlain took place the Mayor and Aldermen should nominate two persons for the Commonalty to select one for the office; and further, that, with respect to the election of Bridge Masters, the Mayor and Aldermen should nominate four persons for the Commonalty to select two of them.[4] The reason for these innovations is to be found elsewhere than in the Letter-Book, viz., that many "Bridge Masters" had hitherto done "litell good in thoffice," and when discharged returned only "syngle accomptes," whilst some Chamberlains had been in arrear in their accounts to large amounts of money.[5]

That the accounts, both of the Chamberlain and Wardens of London Bridge for the time being, were usually in arrear is testified by the terms of the appointment of City auditors as recorded periodically in the Letter-Book.[6] Notwithstanding these ordinances, no change in the manner of election of

---

[1] *Infra*, p. 113. Another restriction was imposed the same day on Aldermen attending elections by the Common Council, viz., that each should be accompanied by only one servant to carry his gown. *Infra*, p. 133.

[2] 'Cal. Letter-Book H,' p. 227.

[3] *Infra*, p. 175.

[4] *Infra*, pp. 279-80.

[5] Cotton MS. Vitellius A xvi., fo. 144. Kingsford's 'Chron.,' p. 196.

[6] In 1479 the Court of Aldermen had occasion to complain of the dilatoriness displayed by the Chamberlain in presenting his "grete accompte." *Infra*, p. 164.

Chamberlain or Wardens appears in the Letter-Book; but for some reason or other the election of a Chamberlain for the years 1489 and 1490 is not recorded.

Here it may be remarked, by the way, that in 1474 William Philip was elected City Chamberlain in place of Robert Colwiche, who had been annually appointed since 1463, and had recently been elected Alderman of Farringdon Without. His ceasing to be Chamberlain was probably on that account,[1] although many Aldermen had previously filled that office. From his day, however, down to 1765, when Theodore Janssen, Alderman of Bread Street Ward, was elected Chamberlain, no Alderman was Chamberlain except Sir Peter Rich, who held the office on the King's nomination in 1684 and 1688. From 1766 down to the present day Aldermen have invariably been elected Chamberlain, with the exception of Benjamin Scott (1858-92); but all of them (excepting John Wilkes, 1779-97) resigned their aldermanic gowns on their election as Chamberlain.[2]

At the present day Sheriffs for the time being appoint their own Under-Sheriffs, and this custom appears to have prevailed from the earliest times down to the year 1441, when (as we have seen) the Court of Common Council ordained that in future the Under-Sheriffs should remain in office during good behaviour, their frequent removal having caused much expense and inconvenience.[3] Their appointment then became vested in the Common Council, so far at least as concerned the Under-Sheriffs of London.

On the other hand, the appointment of Under-Sheriffs for the county of Middlesex still appears to have remained with the

---

[1] Similarly, William Purchas, or Purches, who had been City Chamberlain since 1484, resigned that office on being elected an Alderman in 1492, and was succeeded by William Milborne. *Infra*, p. 289.

[2] Whilst this Calendar is passing through the press, we regret to record the death of the Right Hon. Sir Joseph Dimsdale, Bart., K.C.V.O., who had been City Chamberlain since 1902.

[3] 'Cal. Letter-Book K,' p. 257. Cf. *infra*, pp. 35-6, 227.

Sheriffs of London and Middlesex for the time being; but the system worked badly, and those appointed proved so often unsatisfactory that in 1482 the Common Council endeavoured to raise the standard by imposing a property qualification on those seeking the office, and insisting upon those who were appointed residing continually within the City or county.[1]

Four years later (1486), the officers of the Sheriffs' prisons or Compters, known as Secondaries (or Under-Sheriffs), obtained fixity of tenure of office during good behaviour, and became no longer removable, except by order of the Court of Aldermen.[2]

Lastly, the Court of Aldermen thought fit, in 1483, to forbid any one to be elected Serjeant-at-Mace to the Mayor until he had served two consecutive years as Serjeant-at-Mace to one of the Sheriffs.[3]   This ordinance, however, was modified two years later by another ordinance, which allowed yeomen (*valecti*) of the Mayor and of the Chamber to be elected Serjeants of the Mayor and Chamber, notwithstanding any ordinance to the contrary.[4]

The Letter-Book records an interesting ordinance also made by the Court of Aldermen in 1475, prescribing the number of sessions to be held in the year for gaol-delivery of Newgate. It was to the effect that thenceforth they should be held at least five times a year—four times by the Sheriffs, and once (or twice, if necessary) by the Mayor, provided the Sheriffs held the first four sessions and the Mayor the fifth (or sixth, if need be).   The ordinance then goes on to prescribe the number of law officers, Aldermen, and jurors who should in future be invited to dinner, and the amount of money to be allowed the Middlesex jurors for their refreshment.[5]

The ancient custom of appointing special commissions of *oyer* and *terminer* and gaol-delivery (so often recorded in the earlier

---

[1] *Infra*, p. 196.

[2] *Infra*, pp. 235, 236. Cf. ordinance of 1494, *infra*, p. 300.

[3] *Infra*, p. 191.

[4] *Infra*, p. 228.

[5] *Infra*, p. 137.   Cf. Cotton MS. Vitellius A xvi., fo. 135. Kingsford's 'Chronicles of London,' p. 127.

Letter-Books) appears to be falling into desuetude,[1] and instead of gaol-delivery taking place once a year (as was usually the case under the old system), it was now to be held at least five times a year, greatly to the relief of the unfortunate prisoners awaiting trial.

At the present day, pursuant to the Act of 1834 constituting the Central Criminal Court,[2] sessions are held at least twelve times a year, or once a month, the time being fixed by general orders of the Court approved by at least eight judges of the High Court.

In April, 1479, the Letter-Book records an ordinance by the Mayor and Aldermen adjourning the sessions of all Courts held before the Mayor and Sheriffs until after Trinity Sunday.[3] We are not told the reason for this ordinance, but it was probably due to a pestilence that ravaged the City and the country between September, 1478, and November, 1479.[4]

It is to be noted that the Mayor and Aldermen, even when recorded as sitting in the *Inner Chamber* of the Guildhall, where they usually sat as a *Court of Aldermen*, are frequently described in this and the preceding Letter-Book as the *Court of the lord the King*. Strictly speaking, the full style of the Court of Aldermen is the "Court of the Mayor and Aldermen in the *Inner Chamber*," to distinguish it from the Court of the Mayor and Aldermen in the *Outer Chamber*, or *Lord Mayor's Court*, the latter being also known as the "Court of the lord the King holden before the Mayor and Aldermen of the City of London."[5]

A curious ordinance is recorded as having been passed by the Mayor and Aldermen in 1485, to the effect that for the

---

[1] At least they do not appear to be recorded in the Letter-Books as they used to be. Only four such commissions are to be found in Letter - Book K, which embraces the long reign of Henry VI., and none in the present Letter - Book, although it records an ordei of the Court of Aldermen in 1471, to the effect that the Sheriffs for the time being should yearly procure a Com-

mission for gaol-delivery of Newgate at their own cost. *Infra*, p. 101.

[2] 4 & 5 William IV., cap. 36.

[3] *Infra*, p. 164.

[4] Cotton MS. Vitellius A xvi., fo. 136 b. Fabyan, p. 666.

[5] Pulling, 'Laws, Customs, &c., of the City,' p. 34. Glyn and Jackson, 'The Jurisdiction and Practice of the Mayor's Court' (ed. 1910), pp. 1, 2.

purpose of avoiding illness, which was daily caused by the Mayor, Aldermen, and Council of the City uncovering their heads when sitting in Court, as well as for saving time and trouble (*ad evitanda......alia tedia et dispendia temporum*),[1] neither the Mayor, Aldermen, nor any of the Council, whilst sitting in the Court of the Inner Chamber (*i.e.*, the Court of Aldermen), should thenceforth uncover their heads, under penalty of losing one penny every time they acted to the contrary, unless it were done for the purpose of showing respect to strangers.[2]

A few months later we find two orders emanating from "my lord Maire" and the Aldermen for the destruction of unlawful nets and sacks of coal deficient in holding capacity. The orders are not dated, but were evidently issued some time between January and April, 1486.[3] The style "the lord the Mayor" or "my lord the Mayor" is frequently met with about this time,[4] but "my lord Mayor" (as in these orders) appears to occur here for the first time. It has long been a moot point as to when and how the Mayor of the City obtained the prefix of "Lord." It was stated in the City's official return to the Royal Commission of 1893 that "the title of the Chief Magistrate of the City of London to be styled 'Lord Mayor' dates back to the Fourth Charter of Edward III. (1354)," but such a statement is manifestly incorrect, for reasons that need not be discussed here.

The true explanation is probably to be found in a misinterpretation of the Latin title *dominus Maior,* which · originally meant nothing more than *Sir* Mayor, as already pointed out in the preceding Calendar.[5] In course of time it came to be translated into "the lord the Mayor," whence it was but a step to "the lord Mayor." In favour of this explanation may be adduced the fact that in 1504 (the year hitherto accepted as furnishing the earliest instance of the kind known in the City's Records) we find recorded both *dominus Maior* and "my lorde

---

[1] This appears to be the only interpretation, unsatisfactory though it be.

[2] *Infra*, p. 228. [3] *Infra*, p. 229.

[4] Journal 7, fos. 144 b, 199 b, 201 b, 236 b.

[5] 'Cal. Letter-Book K,' pp. 243 n., 361.

Mayre."[1]   It was not until 1534 or 1535 that the title "lord Mayor " came to be generally used.

Stow[2] records how William Pole, a yeoman in the Court of King Edward IV., was stricken with leprosy, and how the King granted him a plot of land near Highgate whereon to build a Hospital "for the reliefe and harborow of such leprous persons as were destitute in the kingdome, to the end they should not be offensive to other in their passing to and fro." The same year that the King made this grant, viz., 1472, he caused a writ to be issued to the Mayor and Sheriffs of London and Middlesex ordering the removal to Lazar hospitals of all lepers found on horseback or on foot in the highways of the City and county, as the disease was on the increase, under a heavy penalty of £500 in case of disobedience. The disease was believed at the time to be communicated, not only by the vicious air breathed by the lepers, but even by the sight of them (*eorum oculorum inspeccionem*).[3]   Pursuant to this writ extra precautions were taken to prevent lepers entering the City, and proclamation was made notifying that such lepers as should attempt to enter the City would forfeit their horse if they came on horseback, and their gown or outer garment if they came on foot.[4]

Among the ordinances of the Barbers' Fraternity approved by the Court of Aldermen ten years later (1482), and entered in the Letter-Book, was one enjoining masters to bring their apprentices before the Master and Wardens in order to examine them and judge by their "colour and complexion" whether they were "disposed to be lepur or gowty."[5]

The Letter-Book records returns (usually made *oretenus* by the Recorder for the time being) as to the custom of the City on several points, viz. :—

1. A defendant in the Sheriffs' Court having alleged in bar of a debt an immemorial custom in the City that if an apprentice to a freeman entered into a bond with another freeman in a sum of money, without permission of his master, such bond

[1] Repertory 1, fos. 113 b, 155 b.
Journal 10, fo. 325.
[2] 'Survey' (ed. Kingsford), ii. 146-7.
[3] *Intra*, p. 102.
[4] *Infra*, pp. 102-3.
[5] *Infra*, p. 191.

was void, provided the recipient of the bond was aware of the fact of apprenticeship, and the plaintiff denying the existence of any such custom, the Mayor and Aldermen certified in 1468 that there was no such custom.[1]

That the Court of Aldermen disapproved of apprentices entering into bonds is seen in one of the ordinances of the Barber-Surgeons just mentioned, enjoining freemen of the Guild desirous of taking an apprentice to bring him before the Master and Wardens, in order that he might be examined as to his parentage, and also " if there be on hym any bonde claymed."

2. We have the Recorder's certificate in 1482 as to the custom of foreign attachment in the City.[2] This procedure was for the purpose of compelling the appearance of a debtor in an action at the suit of his creditor, and in default of such appearance gave the creditor power to attach the debtor's property found in the hands of a third party, known as a "garnishee." The procedure was cumbersome and confined to the jurisdiction of the Mayor's Court, but since the decision of the House of Lords in the well-known case *The London Joint Stock Bank* v. *The Mayor of London*, in 1881, the custom has fallen into disuse, although held to be perfectly valid, except where a corporation aggregate is cited to appear as garnishee.

3. Thirdly, we have the Recorder's certificate in the same year (1482) of the City custom which enabled a freeman to devise lands and tenements within the City, in mortmain[4] or otherwise, as well by nuncupative will as by written testament.[5]

4. And lastly the Recorder's return, delivered in 1491, certifying the custom whereby not only freemen, but all inhabitants of

---

[1] *Infra*, pp. 77-8.

[2] *Infra*, pp. 192-3. See also *infra*, pp. 91-2, 147.

[3] House of Lords, 6 App. Cas. 393; Woodthorpe Brandon, ' The Customary Law of Foreign Attachment,' pp. v, vi; Glyn and Jackson, ' The Jurisdiction and Practice of the Mayor's Court,' pp. 7, 8.

[4] By virtue of charter 6 March, 1 Edward III., this privilege did not extend to non-freemen, who occasionally overcame their disability by making over property to freemen, with the object of having it eventually devised in mortmain. See ' Cal. Letter-Book K,' p. 181.

[5] *Infra*, p. 192.

the City had the power to devise lands and tenements in the
City, the question of mortmain not being touched upon.[1]

The leading feature of the Letter-Book, however, is the
large number of ordinances of various Guilds or Companies
submitted to the Mayor and Aldermen for approval and
enrolment. It has already been noted how an endeavour was
made by Parliament in 1437 to restrain the Masters and
Wardens of the various Guilds and Fraternities throughout the
kingdom from making unreasonable ordinances such as they
had no legal power to make, by causing them to bring in their
Charters and Letters Patent before the Justices of the Peace
in the country, and before the municipal authorities in cities and
boroughs.[2] This statute, even if effectively carried out, did
little more in the City of London than strengthen the hands of
the civic authorities in dealing with the City Guilds. In March,
1438, the Wardens of the Mistery of Brewers were questioned
as to their new charter, when they promptly declared their
submission to the Mayor and his Council and readiness to
renounce anything in their charter that was opposed to the
City's liberties.[3] A few weeks later the Wardens of the Cordwainers were ordered to renounce before the Lord Chancellor
all privileges granted by a recently acquired charter, and
after considering the matter for three days submitted.[4] In
1474 the Butchers were fined for making ordinances prejudicial
to the liberties of the City[5]; and the charter granted to the
Bakers in 1486 was only allowed by the Court of Aldermen to
be placed on record on the distinct understanding that the
Bakers would not use it in any way prejudicial to the City.[6]

The statute by this time, however, had proved ineffective,
and it became necessary in 1487 for the Mayor and Aldermen
to pass an ordinance to the effect that thenceforth Wardens of
Misteries should make no ordinances unless the same be
approved by the Mayor and Aldermen for the time being.

[1] *Infra*, p. 280.
[2] See 'Cal. Letter-Book K,' Introd., p. xli.
[3] Journal 3, fo. 11 b.
[4] *Idem*, fo. 16.
[5] *Infra*, p. 128.
[6] *Infra*, p. 241.

Thereupon, we are told, many Wardens brought in their books of ordinances that had not been authorized by the Court, and the folios on which they were recorded were cut out bodily.[1] It would be interesting to learn if there be still extant among the archives of any Livery Company a manuscript of the fifteenth century which bears signs of having experienced this drastic treatment.

Between 1437 and 1487 the number of companies that brought in their *charters* for enrolment scarcely exceeded a dozen, whilst during the same period the companies tha submitted their *ordinances* (not once only, but two or three times) to the Court of Aldermen number over forty. That the order of 1487 had the desired effect is shown by the fact that during the next nine years, viz., between March, 1488 and March, 1497, about the same number of companies are recorded as having brought in ordinances or " articles " for approval and enrolment as in the previous fifty years.

The following are the names of the Guilds recorded in the Letter-Book as having obtained the sanction of the Court of Aldermen for their ordinances, viz. :—

The Bakers (comprising White-bakers and Brown-bakers), the Barber-Surgeons, the Bladesmiths, the Bowyers, the Brewers, the " Brouderers " (embroiderers).

The Carpenters, the Chapemakers (makers of scabbards, &c.), the Cooks, the Coopers, the Cordwainers, the Corsers (horse-dealers), the Curriers, and the Cutlers.

The Dyers.

The Fletchers (arrow-makers), the Founders, the Fruiterers, the Fullers.

The Girdlers, the Glaziers, the Glovers, the Greytawyers (or " Megucers ").

The Hat merchants, the Hurers.

The Innholders.

The Leathersellers, the Loriners.

The Marblers, the Masons.

The Netmakers.

[1] *Infra*, p. 246.

The Painters or Painter-stainers, the Pastelers, the Plumbers, the Pouchmakers, the Pursers, the Pynners.

The Saddlers, the Shermen (shearers of cloth), the Skinners.

The Tailors (afterwards Merchant Tailors), the Tilers, the Turners.

The Upholders (upholsterers).

The Wax-chandlers, the Weavers (British and Foreign), the Woolmen, and the Wyremongers.

It is significant that of the twelve "great Livery Companies" only two have ordinances recorded in the Letter-Book, namely, the Skinners and the Tailors—unless, indeed, we add the Shermen, who afterwards developed into the Company of Clothworkers.

One of the earliest Acts passed in the reign of Edward IV. was that prohibiting the importation of foreign manufactured goods,[1] with the view of encouraging native industries. Yet in spite of this Act, and the numerous restrictions placed on so-called "foreins"[2] (whether non-freemen or aliens) wishing to carry on business in the City, they succeeded in "plucking away" the livelihood from freemen.

A few weeks after the passing of this Act we find the freemen Bladesmiths complaining of "foreyns," from places abroad as well as from the suburbs of the City, selling their inferior wares (or "chaffaire") privately in the City, without bringing it to the public market. They also complained of "foreyns, dwellyng in ferre contrees" of the realm, counterfeiting the trade-marks of freemen, and of the want of skill displayed by so many "unkonnyng" grinders of "sheres" and blades.[3]

In the same year the Fruiterers of the City complained of their business being ruined by "foreins" repairing daily in great numbers to the City and selling their fruit when and

[1] Stat. 3 Edw. IV., cap. 4 [A.D. 1463].

[2] Among other limitations imposed on them was one forbidding them to sell by retail and in the open streets, whilst another forbade them to occupy any house or shop. *Vide infra*, pp. 156, 302.

[3] *Infra*, pp. 25-8.

where they chose, without any restriction or correction, and
prayed that foreigners might be compelled to stand in places
specially appointed for them, and sell fruit on three days of the
week, viz., Monday, Wednesday, and Friday, and no more.[1]
Their petition was granted : but two years later it was found
necessary to allow the foreigners an additional day,[2] and in
1486 the freemen Fruiterers petitioned the Court of Aldermen
that they might be allowed to stand with the foreigners as
freely as they did before the ordinance of 1463.[3]

In 1471 we find a rare instance of the Court of Aldermen
coming to the assistance of the foreigner in the City. By
ancient custom the freemen Bakers, in their Halimotes, made
annual presentments to the Court of Aldermen of what they
found wrong in the conduct of their business. They were
thereby enabled to vent their anger against the intrusive
foreign baker by making false presentments against him,
whilst sparing freemen, and thus to subject him to iniquitous
fines and amercements. In order to remedy this the Court
decreed that two officers should yearly be specially appointed
to assess and limit the penalties so incurred.[4]

Between the freemen bakers and the "foreign" bakers—
bakers from Stratford by Bow and other places in the vicinity
of London—there had always been a continuous struggle. It
was in vain that the civic authorities restricted foreign bakers
to certain hours and certain places for selling their bread ;[5] such
ordinances were either ignored altogether or circumvented.
Thus, when the foreign bakers were told to remove their carts
from their standing by midday,[6] they took to bringing a spare
horse with them, and on these they hawked their bread about
the streets of the City until orders were issued to the contrary.[7]
No wonder the freemen bakers retaliated against the foreigner
in their Halimotes.

---

[1] *Infra*, pp. 31-4.
[2] *Infra*, p. 57.
[3] *Infra*, p. 234.
[4] *Infra*, p. 100.

[5] 'Cal. Letter-Book K,' p. 45.
Cf. *infra*, p. 294.
[6] *Infra*, pp. 295, 301.
[7] *Infra*, pp. 305-6, 308.

A few years later the freemen Glaziers of the City had occasion to complain to the Court of Aldermen of certain " foreyn persones, as well straungers as other, to the number of twenty-eight and more," working secretly at the craft. The City, they said, bore evident tokens of the inefficiency of their work, yet nothing could be done, owing to the Wardens of the Craft having no oversight or correction of non-freemen. They prayed the Court, therefore, to ordain that thenceforth no one should exercise the craft unless he became a freeman of the City and his efficiency was established by the Wardens ; and further, that the Wardens, in conjunction with an officer of the City appointed by the Mayor or Chamberlain, might be authorized to search for bad work, with the view of punishing offenders.[1]

In 1483 the free journeymen of the Fullers prayed the Court that in future no Fullers should employ a foreigner so long as freemen were available for work[2] ; and a similar prohibition was obtained in 1491 by the Painters, provided that freemen could be found as capable as the foreigner, and " as gode chepe."[3]

By that time Parliament itself had again come to the relief of the native craftsman by forbidding any person not born under the King's obeisance to exercise or occupy any handicraft, and ordering all aliens to return to their own country or else to become servants to such of the King's subjects as followed their particular craft.[4] Yet, notwithstanding the restrictions placed upon foreigners by this Act, the Wardens of the Fullers again had occasion to complain to the Court of Aldermen (in 1487) of the low estate to which the Craft had fallen owing to the excessive influx of foreigners, as well as the lax system of apprenticeship and the want of proper supervision of work.[5]

[1] *Infra*, pp. 118-20.
[2] *Infra*, pp. 210-11.
[3] *Infra*, p. 284.
[4] Stat. 1 Ric. III. cap. ix. [A.D. 1484].
[5] *Infra*, p. 242. Similar complaints were made by the Pynners, the Painters, the Skinners, and the Tailors (*infra*, pp. 254, 256-7, 295, 302).

The citizen had other grievances against foreigners, inasmuch as they neither paid scot nor bore lot, as he was obliged to do.[1] They failed, moreover, to sit on inquests in cases involving aliens and denizens, as bound by statute.[2] At one time the fine imposed on defaulters in this respect was no more than 3 pence, but, this amount proving insufficient to compel appearance, new fines were imposed in 1486, extending from 3 pence to 20 shillings, with power of distress.[3]

The activity of aliens in the commerce of the City eventually ruined a number of the lesser trade and craft Guilds and forced them to join hands in self-protection. Thus, in 1476, the Horners and Bottlemakers found themselves too impoverished to meet the demands made upon them by the Crown as well as by the City as separate and independent Guilds. They therefore simultaneously prayed the Court of Aldermen that the members of both crafts might be treated as "Brethren" and jointly bear any burden that might be imposed in future. Their prayer was granted.[4]

Three years later (1479) the Whitetawyers found their numbers so diminished that they experienced difficulty in appointing Wardens of their craft and discharging their civic liabilities. They, too, laid their case before the Court of Aldermen, and prayed that they might henceforth be considered as belonging to the craft of Leathersellers, and that

---

[1] This point was pressed before the Court of Aldermen in 1477 by the Cobblers, and in 1491 by the Painters. *Infra*, pp. 154, 284.

[2] The Stat. 28 Ed. III. cap. xiii. [A.D. 1354] enacted that an inquest, where an alien was a party, should be *de medietate linguæ;* that is to say, that one half of the jurors should be denizens and the other half aliens.

[3] *Infra*, p. 236.

[4] *Infra*, p. 138. There does not appear to be any evidence in the City's records to support statements by the Rev. Dr. Rosedale, chaplain of the Horners' Company, to the effect that the Bottlemakers found it desirable to place themselves under the protection of the Horners' Company in 1362, and so remained until their amalgamation in 1476; or that this grant by the Court of Aldermen gave the Horners *the right to absorb the Bottlemakers!* See 'Short Hist. of the Company,' by H. G. Rosedale, D.D., pp. 16, 23.

all members of the craft of Whitetawyers might be allowed to "change their copies" into the craft of Leathersellers.[1]

A few months later we find a similar complaint made by the Wyredrawers and the Chapemakers, with the result that the Court of Aldermen allowed them to become amalgamated under the name of Wyremongers.[2]

In 1497 the Letter-Book records yet another amalgamation, viz., that of the Pinners and Wyremongers, under the name of Wyresellers. It appears that the Pinners and Wyremongers had so often been at variance with each other, and their numbers had so decreased, that they were unable any longer to "bere scotte lotte nor other charges." They therefore petitioned the Court of Aldermen that they might be made one Fellowship, to be known as "the Crafte and occupacion of Wyresellers, and utterly to dismysse and adnull the namys of Pynners and Wyremongers."[3]

It must not be thought that the presence of the foreign element in the City was an unmixed evil. It was to a certain extent a blessing, inasmuch as the alien frequently introduced new methods, incited competition, and, on occasion, prevented the freeman from unduly enhancing the price of commodities.[4]

The ordinary constitution of a Livery Company embraced a Master, two or more Wardens, a Court of Assistants, a

[1] *Infra*, pp. 164-5; Black, pp. 37-8. In 1484 an order was made by the Mayor and Aldermen that, in order to avoid dissensions likely to arise between the Misteries, no one should in future be translated from one Mistery to another without the consent of the Court of Aldermen. *Infra*, p. 214.

[2] *Infra*, p. 168.

[3] *Infra*, p. 319. In the following year (1498) an amalgamation took place between the Glovers and the Pursers (Letter-Book M, fo. 13), and in 1502 the two Guilds thus united were joined with the Leather-sellers (*id.*, fos. 59 b-60; Journal 10, fos. 255 b [258 b] *et seq.*).

[4] Thus we learn from this Letter-Book that, inasmuch as brewers of the City enhanced the price of beer, the Common Council decreed, in 1478, that foreign brewers might come into the City and freely sell their beer until further orders. *Infra*, pp. 157, 178. On the other hand, the "outrageous price" of imported bow-staves in 1484—the price having been raised from £2 to £8 per hundred —was attributed to the "seditious conspiracy" of Lombards. See Stat. 1 Ric. III. cap. xi.

Livery, and a general body of freemen, including a distinctive class known as Yeomen or Bachelors. The Master was often identical with the Upper or Prime Warden, a title still retained by the Goldsmiths and Fishmongers. During the period covered by the Letter-Book the chief executive officers of the Guilds were the Wardens, the title of Master being comparatively rare. It is remarkable that the Wyresellers are recorded as being ruled by Wardens and a unique officer called an "Umpire."[1]

Occasionally disputes arose as to the right of electing the Wardens. We have seen how, in 1444, the journeymen Weavers claimed the right of election, which they had continued to exercise, as they declared, until within the last six years, when their claim had been disallowed by masters of the mistery who were *householders*. The matter being referred to the Court of Aldermen, and both parties having been heard, that body decreed that in future the masters of the craft[2] or mistery should elect the Wardens, and that journeymen should have no voice in such election.[3]

Similar disputes having arisen in the Butchers' Company in 1466, we find the Court of Aldermen ordaining that thenceforth the election of Wardens should be made by the more influential (*valenciores*) members of the Guild, viz., those of the Livery only.[4]

The ordinances of the Saddlers in 1490 prescribed that on election day all those of the Livery should choose eight persons, and that the outgoing Wardens should select four of them to serve as Wardens for the year ensuing.[5]

It is difficult to say when Courts of Assistants were first called in to take part in the administration of the Livery Companies. It has been stated that the first hint of them occurs in the

---

[1] *Infra*, p. 319.

' Here it is to be noted that a "master of the craft" was one who had risen to that position through apprenticeship, and had proved himself worthy of the title by the produc-tion of a "master piece." He must not be confused with a governor of a Guild known as Master.

[3] 'Cal. Letter-Book K,' p. 290.

[4] *Infra*, p. 67.

[5] *Infra*, p. 276.

Records of the Grocers' Company under the year 1379; and the author of this statement prints what purports to be the very words of the resolution for the appointment in *English* with mediæval spelling.[1] No such resolution under that year appears in the 'Facsimile' of the Company's earliest MS. book, edited by the late Mr. J. A. Kingdon in 1886; and if it had been there, the probability is that it would have been in *French*.

On the other hand, there is a resolution recorded in the Grocers' MS. as having been passed in 1345, and " turnyd in to Englysche be the Avyce of the Fraternite" in 1418.[2] It runs as follows :—

> " *Also at devyse of the Maystres and the feleshyp there beien chosyn vj or x of the compaignie in helpynge and counseylynge of the same Maystres that bien for the yer.*"

The original ordinance is not recorded, but accepting it as a fact, it shows that, at least in the Grocers' Company, the election of Assistants was practically coeval with the establishment of the Guild itself.

In other Guilds the custom of summoning " Assistants " to the Master or Wardens does not appear from the Letter-Book to have become general before the latter half of the fifteenth century. Originally, they were only summoned on special occasions, such as the examination of apprentices on entering their term of service or at its expiration, when they sought to be made freemen ; and those called in to assist on such occasions were usually past Wardens or Bailiffs.[3]

Another special occasion when Assistants were called in to give advice was when a fresh livery or clothing was ordered by the Wardens. This took place every two or three years,

---

[1] Herbert, ' Twelve Livery Companies,' i. 53. He, probably, was only following Baron Heath, who, in order to heighten its verisimilitude, printed the resolution in Gothic characters. Cf. Unwin, ' The Gilds and Companies of London,' p. 218.

[2] Grocers' ' Facsimile,' p. 118.

[3] Unwin, ' The Gilds and Companies of London,' p. 217 ; Sidney Young, ' Annals of the Barber-Surgeons,' p. 243 ; see also ordinances of the Bakers (1476), *infra*, p. 143 ; the Fullers, *infra*, p. 242 ; the Shermen, *infra*, p. 205 ; the Painters, *infra*, p. 257 ; the Weavers, p. 290.

and often proved a hardship to impecunious brethren, unless carried out with discretion.[1]

In 1463 the Mercers appear to have made a considerable advance towards the establishment of a Court of Assistants for general purposes by ordaining that in future twelve sufficient persons should be *yearly* chosen to be Assistants to the Wardens, and that the fellowship would abide by all decisions of a majority of this body.[2] We find a somewhat similar ordinance for governing the Carpenters in 1487, but in their case the Assistants were to be chosen *once a week*.[3] We look in vain in the Letter-Book for any record of a *Standing Court of Assistants* such as exists in most Livery Companies at the present day.

Next to the Master and Wardens and Court of Assistants in order of rank come those entitled to wear the livery or clothing of the Guild, always supposing that such Guild or Fraternity had first been authorized by the Court of Aldermen to have a livery.

The origin of this term "livery" (Lat. *liberatura*) is to be found in the feudal custom of Barons and other great lords "delivering" badges and liveries to their retainers, known as "Livery of Company." This custom grew into such an abuse, and gave rise to so many commotions, that it had to be restrained by a series of statutes extending from the reign of Richard II. to that of Henry VII.[4]

At critical times even the peace of the City itself was menaced by mobs of armed retainers. Hence the ordinance of the Common Council in 1467 (when the all-powerful Earl of Warwick, with his huge retinue, was showing himself obnoxious to the Royal Family), which strictly forbade any

---

[1] See ordinances of the Masons (1481), *infra*, p. 183; the Hurers (1488), *infra*, p. 263; the Saddlers (1490), *infra*, p. 274.

[2] Unwin, *op. cit.*, p. 219, where the writer gives as his authority the "Mercers' records."

[3] *Infra*, p. 241 n.

[4] See 'Cal. Letter-Book H,' pp. 353, 435 n.; 'Cal. Letter-Book I,' p. 119. The statutes were repealed in 1627 by Stat. 3 Car. I. cap. iv. (v.).

freeman or officer of the City to take or use the livery of any lord or magnate, under penalty of disfranchisement and loss of office.[1]

On the other hand, the wearing of liveries by the Mayor and Sheriffs of London and by members of Guilds and Fraternities founded for an honest purpose was expressly permitted by statute.[2] The Mayor, the Aldermen, and the Sheriffs continued, therefore, to wear their respective livery gowns and to grant them to their subordinate officers. In course of time the custom was extended, and livery cloth was granted by the Court of Aldermen to Ministers of State, Officers of the Royal Household, certain Judges of the High Court,[3] and other influential personages whose favour the City desired to obtain.[4]

Liveries of the Mayor, Aldermen, and Sheriffs were renewed every year and varied in colour. This frequent renewal not only led to an accumulation of livery gowns in the hands of the owners,[5] but caused considerable expense to those who had to provide them. The burden became so heavy that in 1389, when the livery-men of the various Companies met in Common Hall to elect a Mayor for the year ensuing, they passed a resolution to the effect that in future the Sheriffs should only give " clothing " to the City's officers and their own serjeants, and that they should no longer ride, but go to Westminster by water or on foot; and, further, that those members of the Guilds who were willing to accompany them should go in their

---

[1] *Infra*, p. 73.

[2] Stat. 13 Henry IV. cap. iii. ; Stat. 8 Henry VI. cap. iv.

[3] In connexion with this custom of giving livery cloth to judicial officers, it may be noted that in 1346 Justices were expressly forbidden by statute to accept fee or gown (*i.e.*, livery cloth) from any party to a suit coming before them. ' Cal. Letter-Book F,' p. 140.

[4] This distribution of livery cloth has continued down to the present day. See Report to the Common Council, 18 December, 1845. The annual cost to the City amounts to £117 10s. 6d.

[5] In 1358 the Mayor, Sheriffs, and Aldermen were expressly forbidden to sell the livery gowns, which they received twice a year for special purposes, within a twelvemonth, under penalty of 100s. ' Cal. Letter-Book G,' p. 93; Introd., pp. xxv, xxvi.

last clothing, and not have new clothing given to them, under penalty of paying a fine of 100 marks into the City's Chamber.[1] In the following year the Court of Aldermen decreed that the expense of providing gowns or liveries on certain prescribed occasions should be defrayed out of dues paid by strangers for brokerage and scavage.[2]

In 1468 the Court of Aldermen passed an ordinance to the effect that thenceforth the Chamberlain for the time being should, on or about Midsummer Day, yearly provide cloth called "Ray"—from its being a striped cloth—for the livery of the Mayor and of the Chamber, and that a sample of the cloth should be submitted to the Mayor and Aldermen.[3] In the same year the Court of Aldermen agreed that Thomas Torald should yearly have a gown of similar cloth and a pension of 6s. 8d. in recognition of his past services to the City;[4] and in 1492 a ray gown at Christmas was granted to Robert Harryson, the City's Attorney in the palatine court of Lancaster, in addition to his salary.[5]

Livery cloth was given twice a year, viz., at Whitsuntide and Christmas, to the Serjeants and Yeomen of the Mayor, Sheriffs, and Chamberlain for the time being; but they got into the habit of having their gowns made of such inordinate length that they were impeded in their duties, and it became necessary for the Common Council to pass an order in 1486 that the gowns should be at least a foot from the ground. Any infringement of this order involved loss of office.[6]

As early as the fourteenth century the City trade and craft Guilds began to assume liveries, with the view, no doubt, of binding their members together in closer association; and having taken this step they firmly believed that "a good time was about to begin."[7] Whether this assumption of a livery was done with the sanction of the Court of Aldermen or not the chronicler does not say. However this may have been, it

---

[1] 'Cal. Letter-Book H,' pp. 347-8.
[2] Id., pp. 350-1.
[3] Infra, p. 81.
[4] Infra, p. 82.
[5] Infra, p. 292.
[6] Infra, p. 230.
[7] Aungier, 'French Chronicle' (Riley's translation), p. 253.

is certain that in later times no such Guild could adopt a livery or clothing without the sanction of the Court, and any attempt to do so was at once put down. Occasionally we find the Yeomen or Bachelors—a class enjoying the freedom of a Guild, but not members of its livery—asserting their independence by forming themselves into a Fraternity and assuming a distinctive livery of their own.[1] This occurred among the Saddlers in 1396[2] and among the Tailors in 1415,[3] but in both cases the Court of Aldermen, being appealed to by the legitimate rulers of each Guild, insisted on the Yeomen accepting their subordinate position.

The livery consisted of two parts, viz., a gown and a hood (*chaperoun*), and in the ordinances of some of the companies we find a distinction drawn between those members who wore the livery and those who only had hoods.[4]

It was changed every two or three years, the cloth being bought for the purpose by the ruling officers of the Guild, to whom those entitled to wear the livery had to apply for sufficient cloth to make a gown, paying for the same a reasonable price. If they disliked the cloth so provided they could take a " scantlon " or " patron " (pattern) of it and get their own gowns on payment of a small fee, but they had to take care that the colour of the cloth they selected matched the colour of the pattern.[5]

It is said that originally all householders of a Guild wore its livery; in course of time, however, a distinction arose between householders who were of the Livery and those who were not of the Livery.[6] Thus in 1431 there were 42 Grocers who

---

[1] It is probable that at the close of the fifteenth century, nearly every Livery Company was supplemented by a yeomanry organization. See Unwin, 'The Gilds of London,' p. 227.

[2] 'Cal. Letter-Book H,' pp. 431-2.

[3] 'Cal. Letter-Book I,' pp. 136-7.

[4] See 'Facsimile of Grocers' MS.' (ed. J. A. Kingdon), i. 156; ii. 195, 196.

[5] See ordinances of the Brewers (*infra*, p. 201); the Saddlers (*infra*, p. 274); the Weavers (*infra*, p. 290).

[6] Unwin, 'The Gilds of London,' p. 226.

were householders and shopholders who were not of the Livery.[1] Similarly, in the ordinances of the Founders recorded in this Letter-Book under the year 1490 we find mention made of householders keeping shop who were not of the clothing.[2] So with the Cutlers we find a distinction drawn between freemen of the clothing and freemen "not beyng of the clothing and occupyng a shoppe "[3]; and so again with the Weavers—those of the livery and householders out of the livery were to dine together on a certain day, those in the clothing paying 12d., and householders out of the clothing 8d.[4]

The fees paid by those "taking up" the Livery varied in different Guilds. With the Saddlers, the customary payment was an ounce of silver or a spoon of silver of the value of 3s. 4d.[5] Any one refusing to obey a "call" to the Livery was liable to a fine, unless his circumstances prevented him undertaking the responsibility and expense of the position.[6]

In elections, whether parliamentary or municipal, the liveryman of the Guilds originally enjoyed no privileges over the citizen who paid his scot and bore his lot. Such elections lay with the *Commonalty* conjointly with the Mayor and Sheriffs for the time being down to 1467, when the election of the Mayor

---

[1] See 'Facsimile of Grocers' MS.,' ii. 198.

[2] *Infra*, p. 272.

[3] *Infra*, p. 256.

[4] *Infra*, p. 291.

[5] *Infra*, p. 274.　　Silver spoons were commonly presented to Guilds on the occasion of a member obtaining the freedom of the City. Cf. ordinance of the English Weavers to the effect that if a Bailiff caused a freeman to be made "of the Chamber" or "of the Charter" for love or favour, he should pay for the said freeman 6s. 8d. to the use of the Craft, and a silver spoon of the value of 4s., according to ancient usage. *Infra*, p. 290-1. In some cases a Guild found itself in possession of so many silver spoons that they had to be sold. See Welch's 'Hist. of the Pewterers' Company,' i. 231, ii. 6 ; Bobart's 'Records of the Basketmakers' Company,' pp. 132, 155.

[6] An ordinance of the Carpenters (1487) forbade the admittance of any member to the "clothing" unless he was worth 20 marks in movable goods or otherwise. Jupp, *op. cit.*, p. 350.

c

and Sheriffs became vested in the Common Council, the Masters of the Guilds *in their livery,* and "other good men specially summoned."[1] It was not, however, until 1703 that an Act of Common Council emphatically declared that the election of Sheriffs belonged to "the Liverymen of the several Companies of the City in Common Hall assembled."[2] After 1404 the City Chamberlain was usually elected on the same day (if not by the same body of electors) as the Sheriffs,[3] and by Act of Common Council of 1695 both the *nomination* (concerning which *vide supra,* p. ix) and the *election* of Chamberlain were vested in the Livery.

At what date the Livery began to usurp the function of the Commonalty in the election of the City's representatives in Parliament is not clear, but there is evidence to show that they had done so long before their claims in this respect were established by the Election Act of 1725 (Stat. 11 George I., cap. 18).[4]

Women were admissible into every trade or craft Guild. There was nothing, moreover, to prevent a single woman being bound apprentice in the City until the year 1407, when a statute was passed forbidding parents to put out a son or daughter as apprentice unless they (the parents) had 20 shillings a year in land or rent.[5] The Act proved abortive in the case of a son or daughter who bound themselves apprentice without consulting their parents,[6] and in 1429 was repealed upon petition of the Mayor, Aldermen, and Commonalty of the City.[7] Widows of freemen were admitted to the Guild of their late husbands, and allowed to carry on the trade or craft exercised by the deceased. Thus it is not an uncommon thing to find women enrolled as members of Guilds where one would

---

[1] *Infra,* p. 73.
[2] Journal 53, fo. 638.
[3] See 'Cal. Letter - Book I,' pp. 33-4.

[4] See Sharpe's 'London and the Kingdom,' iii. 469.
[5] 'Cal. Letter-Book K,' p. 87.
[6] *Id. ibid.*
[7] *Id.,* pp. 104-5.

least expect them, such as the Armourers,[1] the Founders,[2] and the Barber-Surgeons.[3]

Many (if not most) of the Livery Companies had their origin in a religious and social Fraternity, comprising both Brethren and "Sistern," long before they became trade and craft Guilds incorporated by charter. In some cases, however, as, *e.g.*, the Drapers, the Haberdashers, the Dyers, and the Bakers, the right to establish a Fraternity was expressly granted to them by their respective charters of incorporation.[4]

The ordinances of the Masons' Guild are remarkable for the hospitality extended to the wives of members by allowing them to accompany their husbands, " if they will," to the dinner or " recreation " once in every two years, the husband paying 12 pence for himself and 8 pence for his wife on that occasion.[5]

The Guild of Brewers had an exceptionally large number of female members, no less than 39 women being recorded in

---

[1] At Christmas, 36 Henry VIII. [A.D. 1544], Geoffrey Mountford is recorded as having been apprenticed to Rachel Medcalf, "armorer." See 'Register of Freemen,' *temp.* Hen. VIII. and Edw. VI., edited by Chas. Welch, F.S.A., for the London and Middlesex Archæol. Soc., p. 103.

[2] See Stahlschmidt, ' Surrey Bells and London Bell-Founders,' pp. 51, 54.

[3] From the earliest times, we are told, the custom has prevailed of admitting women to the freedom of the Barber-Surgeons' Company; and these freewomen bound their apprentices, both boys and girls, at the Hall. Sidney Young's ' Annals of the Barber-Surgeons,' p. 260.

[4] See the charter of the Drapers (1438), ' Cal. Letter-Book K,' pp. 224-5 ; the charter of the Haberdashers (1450), *id.*, p. 330 ; the charter of the Dyers (1472), *infra*, p. 194 ; the charter of the

Bakers (1486), *infra*, p. 241. On the other hand, the charters granted by Henry VI. to the Fishmongers, the Mercers, and the Grocers make no mention of any Guild or Fraternity, but are directed in each case to the " men of the mistery." ' Cal. Letter-Book K,' pp. 225-6.

[5] *Infra*, pp. 183-4. The Grocers, in the early days of their existence as a Fraternity, were especially generous towards their womankind ; for in 1348 they not only allowed members to bring their wives and a lady companion to their annual dinner, but they declared that thenceforth all wives of members should be esteemed as belonging to the Fraternity, and that widows should continue to attend the dinner after their husbands' decease, on payment of 40 pence (or double the amount paid in their husbands' lifetime), " if they were able." See ' Facsimile of Grocers' MS.,' p. 14.

1417 as wearing the Livery.[1] It has been said that the business of brewing was " almost wholly in the hands of females, and so continued to be till the close of the fifteenth century, if not later."[2] If this be true, it is strange that in the ordinances of the Beerbrewers recorded in this Letter-Book under date 1482[3] women are not once mentioned, whilst in a list of 300 persons recorded as being engaged in the brewing industry in the City in 1420 less than 20 were females.[4]

The ordinances of the various Guilds recorded in the Letter-Book may be divided into three classes, viz. :—

1. Administrative.

2. Religious and charitable.

3. Technical.

1. The first class of ordinances prescribe the manner in which the election of Masters and Wardens was to be made— a ceremony associated with the performance of a solemn Mass, followed by a dinner, "feast," or "recreation"—and the transfer of the money, jewels, and other property of the Fellowship by the outgoing Wardens to the custody of the new Wardens. They also prescribe how often the livery or clothing shall be changed, the number of apprentices a freeman may have in his employ at one time, the settlement of internal disputes without resorting to law, and other particulars of economic interest. Thus they empower the Wardens to search for defective work, and insist upon members attending on all occasions when summoned by the Beadle. They forbid the employment of strangers to do work which could equally well be done by a freeman, and the efficiency of the freemen of any craft was guaranteed by an ordinance which forbade the admission of any one to the freedom until he had been examined by the Wardens and proved "connyng." Quarterage was to be paid by the members, varying in amount according as they were of the Livery or not. This money, as well as half the amount of

---

[1] Unwin, ' Gilds and Companies of London,' p. 191.

[2] 'Liber Albus' (Rolls Series), Introduction, p. lx.

[3] *Infra*, pp. 199-203.

[4] See ' Cal. Letter - Book I,' pp. 233-5.

fines incurred for infringement of the ordinances, went usually into the " Common Box " for the " refreshment " of any brother or sister who had fallen on evil days. Lastly, due respect was ordered to be paid to those in authority, and all " fasyng," " brasyng," and " making of fray " was strictly forbidden.

2. The second class of ordinances relate chiefly to attendance at church and at funerals of deceased members, as well as the distribution of charitable gifts out of the Common Box. Thus, when a Loriner died the members of the Guild were to attend the parish church of the deceased in their " most honest clothyng " for *Dirige* and *Requiem*, and afterwards be present at the interment. Thirty masses were to be sung within eight days for the benefit of the soul of the departed one, at the cost of the Fraternity, provided he or she had kept up their payment of quarterages and other charges during their lifetime. If a member fell into poverty through no fault of his own, he was to receive a weekly sum of 10 pence out of the Common Box if he had served as Warden, and 7 pence if he had not : and on his death his funeral expenses were to be defrayed by the Guild, if his own goods were insufficient.[1]

The Barber-Surgeons submitted a special ordinance to the Court of Aldermen for its approval in 1495, to compel members to attend the funeral of one of their number, under penalty of a fine.[2] Torches, tapers, and other funeral accessories were ready at hand in every Guild to assist in bringing the body of a deceased member " honestly to the earth."[3] The expense was to be defrayed out of the estate of the deceased if practicable, otherwise out of the Common Box.

To this class belong those ordinances which forbade work being carried on by trader or craftsman upon Sundays and certain Festivals and their vigils. Strange as it may appear, it was the Wardens of victualling Guilds like the Butchers and the Bakers who, of their own free will, prayed the Court of Aldermen in 1423 to forbid their members to follow their

---

[1] *Infra*, pp. 265-6.
[2] *Infra*, p. 306.
[3] *Infra*, p. 253. Jupp's ' Hist. of the Carpenters,' p. 348.

business on Sunday, except under certain limitations as to time. In the same year we find the Fletchers, or arrow-makers, asking for an ordinance forbidding them to keep open shop on Sundays and great Festivals,[1] although these were the days on which the citizen and apprentice could best devote themselves to the practice of archery in Finsbury Fields.

At other times the civic authorities took the initiative. Thus in 1444, when Thomas Catworth was Mayor, a proclamation was issued on a certain Sunday in May forbidding any fish-monger, butcher, poulterer, or baker to sell any victual on Sunday unless absolutely necessary. No cook was to bake or roast on a Sunday, and neither cook nor innkeeper was to sell uncooked meat on that day. All marketing was to be finished on Saturday.[2]

In 1484 the Common Council ordered a special clause to be inserted in the Wardmote Commissions to the effect that hucksters of ale or beer in each Ward were to be of the franchise of the City; they were to find surety for good behaviour; they were to shut and bar their doors at a specified time, and allow no one to eat or drink within their houses on Sundays until High Mass was over at their parish churches, but this restriction was not to apply to Innholders and Pastelers, who were allowed to start eating and drinking at home before Mass was over.[3]

Hat merchants were forbidden to expose their wares for sale, not only on Sundays, but on any Festival which the Church prescribed to be preceded by a fasting vigil, as well as on Christmas Day, Easter Sunday, or Whitsunday and the two fol-lowing days. This ordinance emanated from the hat merchants themselves, and was approved by the Court of Aldermen in 1488.[4] In the same year the Fullers desired and obtained the approval of the Court for an ordinance forbidding the setting of cloth upon tenters on Sundays and principal Festivals.[5]

---

[1] 'Cal. Letter-Book K,' p. 10.

[2] *Id.*, p. 293.

[3] *Infra*, pp. 217-18.

[4] *Infra*, p. 255.

[5] *Infra*, p. 262.

In 1495 the Wardens of the Pastelers—who were both piebakers and pastrycooks—prayed the Court of Aldermen that thenceforth they might open two shops on Sunday and no more, viz., one in Bread Street and the other in Bridge Street. They desired this "to thentent that your suppliauntes the gode Folkes of the same Craft may serve Godde the better on the Sonday as trew Cristen men shuld do." Those tending the shops, moreover, were to be changed every Sunday, "and so alwey one to occupie after an other."[1]

3. Some of the ordinances relating to the technical side of the Guilds are of such interest that, when not printed elsewhere, they have been fully set out in this Calendar. This applies to the ordinances of the Bladesmiths, the Fruiterers,[2] the Beerbrewers, the Glasyers, and Upholders. In other cases lengthy abstracts have been given, with occasional extracts *verbatim et literatim* where an ordinance seemed of exceptional importance.

It will be seen that this class of ordinances is more prominent than either of the other two classes; that the religious and social element, so conspicuous in the earlier days of the Guilds, had become largely obscured by the secular and business element. The Carpenters, for instance, when petitioning the Court of Aldermen in 1487 (for the first time, as it appears) that certain ordinances for the better regulation of their Craft might be approved and placed on record, prefaced their petition by reminding the Court that such ordinances were necessary in order to put an end to "such hurtes and deceipts as might be used in suche stuffe as belongeth to the saide Crafte and in divers werkes to be made and wrought by unconnyng persones occupying the same Crafte" within the City and liberties. On the other hand, the earlier ordinances of the Guild, which Mr. Charles Welch, F.S.A., claims to have

---

[1] *Infra*, pp. 311-12.
[2] Whilst the ordinances of this Guild were being put through the press, another copy of them made from the Letter-Book has been printed by Mr. Arthur Gould.

recently discovered at the Public Record Office[1] (and which do not appear to have been ever submitted for approval to the Court of Aldermen), deal almost entirely with the religious and charitable side of the Fraternity.

The ordinances of other Guilds—as, for instance, the Upholders, the Leathersellers, the Fletchers, and the Pursers— are purely technical, their primary object being to ensure good workmanship and protect the public from fraudulence. They had a further object, namely, to protect the free workman, not only from the competition of the foreigner or non-freeman, but also from the rapacity of his fellow-freeman. The latter point is exemplified in an ordinance of the Pastelers, which forbade those employed on the staff of the households of the Mayor or Sheriffs for the time being to provide entertainments for private individuals outside, the professed object being that every man of the Fellowship "may have a competent livyng."[2] A foreigner or stranger undertaking to provide a dinner or supper ran the risk of a fine and imprisonment.[3]

A petition of the good men of the Mistery of Upholders— i.e., Upholsterers—to the Court of Aldermen in 1474, that their Wardens might be authorized to seize all feather beds, mattresses, cushions, and such like household goods found to be deceitfully made, comprising (inter alia) feather beds and bolsters stuffed with feathers and flocks, and pillows stuffed with thistledown and "cattes tailles,"[4] shows an earnest desire

---

[1] Chancery Miscellanea, Bundle 46, No. 465. As a matter of fact, these ordinances were known to the late Miss S. E. Moffat in 1906 (if not, indeed, to the late Mr. J. Toulmin Smith in 1870). Mr. Welch is of opinion that the document formed a return made by the Guild pursuant to the writ issued in 1388 (see ' Cal. Letter-Book H,' p. 336), and here he is probably right. Miss Moffat, on the other hand, in an article printed in the Clare Market Review (May, 1906), distinctly states that the return

of the Carpenters found among the "Guild Certificates" in the Public Record Office was one of the few that were not made pursuant to the writ, but the grounds on which she makes this statement are not given.

[2] Infra, p. 311.

[3] Infra, p. 312.

[4] Not the caudal appendages of the domestic cat, but the flower of a willow, rush, or flag frequently used for seating chairs, making mats, &c. Cf. "catkin," so called from its resemblance to a little cat or kitten.

to promote the common weal, albeit the Mistery itself was to benefit by receiving half of the goods forfeited.[1]

Not only have we the ordinances of the Barber-Surgeons submitted to, and approved by, the Court of Aldermen in 1482 and 1487,[2] but we also have recorded in the Letter-Book the charter granted to the Guild by Edward IV. in 1462.[3] Both the ordinances and the charter are of interest, and are set out in Mr. Sidney Young's ' Annals of the Barber-Surgeons '[4]; but of still greater interest, perhaps, is a petition presented to the Court in February, 1492, by the Wardens and other good folk of the Fellowship of Surgeons enfranchised in the City—" not passyng in noumbre of viij persones "—praying that in consideration of their small number they might continue to be discharged from serving as Constable and from any office necessitating the bearing of armour or weapons, as well as from juries, inquests, &c., as they had been accustomed to be time out of mind. The petition set forth that they had always been treated as Heralds of Arms on battle-fields and elsewhere, and allowed to stand " unharnessed " and " unwepened," seeing that they never "used feates of werre," their sole business being to succour the King's liege subjects in time of need ; but that, nevertheless, at the last election of Constables one of them had been called upon to serve, and would probably be compelled to serve unless the Court favoured their petition, which the Court did.[5]

In 1514 the Wardens, &c., of the Guild of Surgeons, "not passyng in nombre xij persones," petitioned Parliament

---

[1] *Infra*, pp. 120-2. This petition is the more interesting inasmuch as Parliament has recently passed an Act known as the Rag Flock Act, 1911, forbidding the sale of any flock that does not conform to a standard of cleanliness prescribed by the Local Government Board.

[2] *Infra*, pp. 191, 244.

[3] *Infra*, p. 24. This charter was placed on record on the expressed condition that if anything therein should be found contrary to the liberties of the City it should be annulled. *Infra*, p. 23.

[4] Pp. 52-8, 61-2, 63-5.

[5] *Infra*, pp. 286-7. See D'Arcy Power's ' Memorials of the Craft of Surgery,' pp. 79-81, where the date is given as 1491 (correct according to O.S.).

to similar effect, and an Act was passed in conformity with their petition, but extending the privilege also to Barber-Surgeons, so long as the number of twelve was not exceeded.[1]

By an Act of Parliament passed in 1745 (Stat. 18 Geo. II. cap. 15) the Surgeons and the Barber-Surgeons were not only made distinct bodies, but, whereas the former were specially exempted from service as constables, overseers, and other officers, as well as from serving on juries and inquests, the latter body was granted no such privileges.

The exceptional privilege of exemption from serving on assizes, juries, inquests, &c., was also enjoyed by members of the Cooks' Company under their charter of 1482,[2] in consideration of the trouble the members were often put to on occasion of royal entertainments on St. George's Day and other times.

The ordinances of a comparatively unimportant Guild like that of the Tilers are of striking interest. In 1461 we find the Common Council of the City solemnly declaring that in future the Tilers should be reputed as labourers and not be incorporated nor deemed to constitute an Art or Society.[3] In 1468, however, when the manufacture of tiles had become so unsatisfactory that Parliament had to intervene and prescribe the exact manner of preparing the clay for the purpose, the Tilers of the City laid the matter before the Mayor, Aldermen, and *Common Council* (styled "the Court of the lord the King in the Chamber of the Guildhall"!), and prayed that their Fellowship might be restored to the franchises of which they had been deprived, and that they might elect two Wardens who should see that all tiles conformed with the samples in the custody of the City Chamberlain.[4] Their prayer was granted.

A few years later, viz., in 1473, good men of the Mistery of Tilers made an appeal to the *Court of Aldermen*. Experience had taught them that the search for bad tiles and presentation of them to the Chamberlain was more than their

---

[1] Stat. 5 Henry VIII. cap. 6. The Barber-Surgeons were, however, already exempt under their charter.

[2] *Infra*, p. 313.

[3] *Societas* being the Latin term for a company. *Infra*, p. 14.

[4] *Infra*, pp. 76-7.

two Wardens could undertake; they therefore prayed the Court to allow them to appoint three Wardens to carry out the work; and, furthermore, that one half of all tiles presented and forfeited might be applied to the use of the Craft, whilst the rest was to benefit the City's Chamber. This petition was also granted.[1]

The use of tiles for roofing buildings in the City in place of rushes and straw was introduced soon after the fire which committed such havoc within its walls in the year 1212. Among the provisions made for minimizing the risk of fire by what is known as the Second Assize of Buildings, promulgated by Fitz-Alwyne, the City's first Mayor, was one to the effect that roofs were not to be covered with reeds, rushes, straw, or stubble, but only with tiles, shingles, boards, or lead.[2] Nevertheless, there were buildings in the City roofed with straw as late as the beginning of the fourteenth century, for we find Thomas Bat, in 1302, pledging himself to replace by a certain day the straw which covered his houses in the parish of St. Laurence, Candlewick Street, with tiles, or allow the Mayor and Sheriffs to cause the work to be done out of the rents of the same.[3]

In 1362 not only the City, but the greater part of England had been devastated in a different way, namely, by a fierce tempest which razed buildings to the ground or at least stripped them of their roofs. The damage thus done gave occasion to those who had tiles on hand to enhance their price and for tilers to demand higher wages, but a stop was soon put to such proceedings by a peremptory order from the King.[4]

In order to encourage the manufacture of tiles, a curious custom is said to have existed at Reading, in the fifteenth century, of fining barbers who shaved customers in forbidden hours in so many hundred tiles instead of money.[5]

[1] *Infra*, p. 113.
[2] 'Liber Cust.,' i. 87.
[3] 'Cal. Letter-Book C,' pp. 105-6.
[4] 'Cal. Letter-Book G,' p. 138; 'Memorials,' pp. 308-9.

[5] See 'Two Thousand Years of Gild Life,' by Rev. J. Malet Lambert, p. 272.

A somewhat analogous custom is to be found in the Letter-Book, viz., that of recalcitrant members of Guilds being made to pay fines in so many pounds of wax instead of cash.[1]

The Letter-Book records the ending of a long-standing dispute between the Company of the Tailors (not yet entitled "Merchant" Tailors) and that of the Skinners of London touching their claim of precedence on ceremonial occasions.[2] The order of precedence of the Livery Companies varied from time to time and gave rise to no little jealousy. Soon after the accession of Richard III. the question of precedence between the Tailors and the Skinners became so hotly contested that eventually both Companies consented to have the matter submitted to Robert Billesdone, the Mayor, and the Aldermen, and to abide by their judgment. On the 10th April, 1484, the Mayor and Aldermen gave their decision, which is now generally known as the "Billesdone Award." It was to the effect that the Master and Wardens of the Skinners should invite the Master and Wardens of the Tailors to dine with them at their Common Hall every year, on the eve of the Feast of Corpus Christi, if they then made an "oppen dyner," and that the Master and Wardens of the Tailors should similarly invite the Master and Wardens of the Skinners to dine at their Common Hall on the Feast of the Nativity of St. John the Baptist; and further, that the Skinners should take precedence in processions over the Tailors one year, and the Tailors over the Skinners the following year, except that when an Alderman of either Company should happen to be Mayor, his Company should take precedence during his Mayoralty over all other Companies, according to ancient custom.

This award has continued to be observed, with rare exceptions, down to the present day. Once every year the two Companies entertain each other, when the chief toast of the

---

[1] See the ordinances of the Wyremongers (*infra*, p. 185); those of the Hurers (*infra*, p. 263); and those of the Loriners (*infra*, p. 266).

[2] *Infra*, p. 212.

evening (when the dinner takes place at Skinners' Hall) is given as follows :—

" The Master and Wardens of the Worshipful Company of Skinners drink health and prosperity to the Worshipful Company of Merchant Taylors, also to the Worshipful Company of Skinners, Merchant Taylors and Skinners, Skinners and Merchant Taylors, root and branch ; and may they continue and flourish for ever ! "

In responding, the Master of the Merchant Taylors concludes by returning the compliment in a similar toast, with the names of the Companies interchanged.[1]

Some years later the Skinners claimed that the Award was limited to civic processions, and did not affect " general goings and assemblies," but in January, 1521, the Court of Aldermen ruled otherwise.[2]

No attempt was made at the time of Billesdone's Award, nor, indeed, until long afterwards, to settle permanently the order of precedence of the Livery Companies in general. In May, 1512, we find an order of the Common Council to the effect that " all maner of Feloushippes shall kepe the order of goyng in procession and standyng as it was ordeyned in M[ayor] Shaa daies,"[3] but no such ordinance can be found recorded.[4]

Other disputes arose a few years later between the Salters and the Ironmongers and between the Shermen and the Dyers, the cause of the dispute, in both cases, being recorded as " the preeminence of the rowme and place aswell in all their Goynges in all processions as all other goynges Standynges and Rydynges for the busynessys and causes of this Citie."[5]

These disputes led to a settlement of the order of precedence

---

[1] Pridmore, ' Hist. of the Skinners' Company,' pp. 5-6.

[2] Repertory 5, fo. 166 b.

[3] Repertory 2, fo. 133 (134).

[4] Possibly this may refer to a list of the Livery Companies, and the number of liverymen in each Company, recorded as existing at the time John Shaa was Mayor [A.D. 1501-2]. Journal 10, fo. 373 b.

[5] Repertory 3, fos. 64 b-66.

by the Court of Aldermen on the last day of January, 1516, in
the following terms :—[1]

"Here after ensuyth thorder & direccōn taken at this Court
by the Mayr & Aldremen aboveseyd of & for all the Craftes &
Misteres ensuyng   For their Goynges aswell in all processions
as all other goynges Standynges & Rydynges for the busynessys
& causes of this Citie   The seyd Order & direccōn to be from
hensforth fermely observed & kept eny other Rule Order or
direccōn heretofore made to the contrary notwithstanding
Provided alweys that the Felysshippe wherof the Mayre ys for
the yere accordyng to the old custume shall have the preeminence in goyng afore all other Felysshippes in all places
duryng the tyme of Mayralte &c."

This is followed by a list of 48 Guilds in the order prescribed,
the first twelve being :—

  1. Mercers.
  2. Grocers.
  3. Drapers.
  4. Fishmongers.
  5. Goldsmiths.
  6. ⎫ Skinners and Tailors "accordyng to thordnaunce therof
     ⎬ made in the tyme of Mayralte of M[ayor] Byllesdon.
  7. ⎭ L, fo. 196."
  8. Haberdashers.
  9. Salters.
 10. Ironmongers.
 11. Vintners.
 12. Shermen.

This order of precedence of the twelve Great Livery Companies is preserved at the present day.   The Shermen joined
hands with the Fullers in 1528, and the combination became
known as the Clothworkers.

In conclusion may be mentioned two deeds recorded towards
the end of the Letter-Book.   One is dated 4 Dec., 7 Henry VII.
[A.D. 1491], and the other the 21st December of the same year.[2]

---

[1] Rep. 3, fo. 66 b. | [2] *Infra*, pp. 283-4.

By the former licence is given to the Mayor and Commonalty
and their successors by Sir John Fortescue, Knt.,[1] to dig and
break ground in his close, called the "Mewes close" (situate
near Charing Cross), and anywhere else on his property in the
county of Middlesex that may be necessary, for the purpose
of conveying water by conduit-pipes to the City, as well as in
a close called the "Covent Gardyn" held by him on lease under
the Abbot of Westminster. The licence is to hold good for a
term of 180 years and the term of his leasehold interest in the
"Covent Gardyn" without payment of any consideration what-
ever, beyond making such amends to his tenants and occupiers
as "they have used to do or make in tyme past."

By the latter Sir John Fortescue grants to certain Aldermen
and citizens, specifically named, and their executors and assigns
a certain meadow called the "Conducte mede," described as
being situate near the "newe house of the Conducte of
Tybourne," and having on its west side a brook called
"Aybroke," and as abutting on its east side upon a lane called
"Suglane," together with a certain well adjoining the mead;
to hold the same for a term of 180 years from Michaelmas last,
at an annual rental of £4, saving always to the Mayor and
Commonalty their rights of laying pipes on the premises for
conveyance of water to the City.

This being in all probability the last Calendar of the City's
Letter-Books for which the present Editor will be responsible,
he may perhaps be pardoned if he adopts a recommendation
put forward by a reviewer of some recent Calendars of Rolls

---

[1] Known as Sir John Fortescue,
junior, of Punsborne, otherwise
Ponnysbourne, a manor near Hatfield; made a Knight Banneret by
Henry VII., 16 June, 1487, at the
battle of Stoke, near Newark (Shaw's
'Knights of England,' ii. 24); Sheriff
of Hertfordshire and Essex, 1481;
married Alice, youngest daughter of
Sir Geoffrey Boleyn, Mayor of London (1457); appointed Chief Butler
of England by letters patent, 20 Sept.,
1485, one of his predecessors in office
having been John, Earl of Wiltshire,
mentioned *infra*, p. 194. See 'Hist.
of the Family of Fortescue,' by
Thomas (Fortescue), Lord Clermont,
vol. ii. pp. 151, 153, 156, 157, 159.

preserved in the Public Record Office, viz., for " the general reader to select some one or two of the more full and lively of these Calendars for attentive perusal, since he may gather from them in a week's diligent reading a more vivid idea of the England of his forefathers than he will get from the most brilliant pages of the professed historian."

R. R. S.

The Guildhall, London,
    December, 1912.

CALENDAR OF LETTER-BOOKS

OF THE

CITY OF LONDON.

LETTER-BOOK L.

Trade Marks of the following Coopers, 12 Edward IV.— *Fly-leaf.*
18 Henry VII., viz., William Rolff, Richard Cok, John Priour,
Simon Rokesley, John Chamberleyn, John Baker, W. Hunt,
W. Randolf, John Gurney, Robert Sion, Walter Cokk,
W. Cokk, John Rogger, John York, Thomas Elnore, W. Horton,
Geoffrey Farand, Thomas Cusake, Roger Rolf, William
Matrasse, Agnes Asser, John Mynto, Richard Fresshwater,
William Cooke, William Petche, John Turtill, William Baren,
Thomas Cowper, William Trotter, John Aspelyn.

Inspeximus of record of proceedings held before Henry, late *Fly-leaf, dors.*
de facto, but not *de jure*, King of England, to the following *Fo. 1 b.*
effect :—

Pleas held before the King at Westminster, Michaelmas
Term, anno 38 Henry VI. [A.D. 1459]. Precept issued to the
Keeper of the King's prison of Flete or his Lieutenant to bring
up the body of John West, "notary," a prisoner there, together with the reason of his detention, before the King at
Westminster, on Monday next after the Feast of St. Martin
in yeme [11 Nov.], to await a judgment of a jury in a plea of
trespass between the said John West and John Skargyll. Thereupon, on the day appointed, William Venour, Keeper of the said
prison, appeared with the said John West and certified that

B

the said John had been committed to that prison by William
[de Waynflete], Bishop of Winchester and Chancellor, for
divers sums of money which Thomas Baron, John Barly, John
Proufford, and John Warde had recovered against him in the
Court of the lord the King in his Tower of London before
Richard Gower, esquire, the Lieutenant of Henry, Duke of
Exeter, the Constable of the Tower, and John Watkyns, the
Steward of the said Court in pleas of trespass.   Thereupon the
said John West had declared that for none of the above causes
should he have been committed, on the ground that the said
Court in the Tower had always been no more than a Court
Baron, and that the Lieutenant and Steward could only hold
pleas such as appertained to a Court Baron, and that there was
no evidence of the Court in the Tower ever having been a
Court of Record or anything else but a Court Baron, and
this he was ready to prove.   He therefore prayed acquittal.
Cur. ad. vult.   A day given, the prisoner being allowed bail.

On the day appointed, both parties appeared, and the said
Thomas Baron showed the Court that time out of mind a Court
of Piepowder[1] had daily been held before the Lieutenant of the
Constable of the Tower and the Steward for hearing pleas of
debt, trespass, and all kinds of personal actions arising within
the Tower and its precinct, and that in such Court held on the
22nd July, anno 37 Henry VI. [A.D. 1459], he had brought three
several plaints before Richard Gower, then Lieutenant of Henry,
Duke of Exeter, the Constable of the Tower, against the said
John West, as appears on record, and that the said John had
been committed to the Keeper of the King's prison in the
Tower, *quousque, &c.*, and this the said Thomas was ready to

---

[1] The term "piepowder" ("pic-
poudres," "pede pulverósi") was
applied to a court frequented by
merchants hurrying on their way
with dusty feet. "Querelas trans-
euntium per villam qui moram
non poterunt facere qui dicuntur
pepoudrous." : ('Liber Albus,' i. 67.)   It was a court where matters were
speedily determined according to the
law merchant. See paper on 'The
Court of Piepowder,' by the late
Dr. Charles Gross of Harvard University, in *The Quarterly Journal of
Economics*, vol. xx. Feb., 1906.

prove. After several adjournments, the said John West duly appeared before the Court on the day appointed, but the said Thomas Baron made default. The Court thereupon, after consideration of the evidence, and of the fact that the Court in the Tower had always been, and was still, held to be only a Court Baron and not a Court of Record, adjudged that the said John West should be quit and his sureties discharged. In testimony whereof these letters patent of exemplification were made. Witness T[homas] Billyng[1] at Westminster, 20 Oct., 12 Edward [IV.], [A.D. 1472].

Monday, 20 March, 1 Edward IV. [A.D. 1460-1], came William Boylet, John Stone, Thomas Burgeys, and Richard West, tailors, into the Court of the lord the King in the Chamber of the Guildhall, before Richard Lee, the Mayor, and the Aldermen, and entered into bond with Thomas Thorntone, the Chamberlain,[2] in the sum of £90, for payment into the Chamber by the said William Boylet of a like sum to the use of Hugh, Thomas, Richard, and Agnes, children of Richard Rook, late tailor, on their coming of age or the marriage of the said Agnes.

Fo. 2.

Custod' pueror' Ric' Rook.

Friday, 6 Aug., 2 Edward IV. [A.D. 1462], came William Chacombe of co. Northampton, Henry Chacombe, William Burtone, drapers, and John Parisshe, "peautrer," into the Court of the lord the King in the Chamber of the Guildhall,

Custod' pueror' Joh'is Chacombe.

---

[1] Chief Justice of King's Bench; M.P. for the City, 1448; Recorder, 1450-4.

[2] This is the common form of orphan recognizances, although, for brevity's sake, it has not always been fully set out in the Calendar. According to some authorities the Court here mentioned would appear to be the Mayor's Court, over which the Mayor and Aldermen *nominally*, but not judicially, presided, and which exercised an equitable jurisdiction as a Court of Orphans. (Calthrop, 'Ancient Customs, &c., of the City of London,' 1670, p. 100.) On the other hand, however, the Court of Aldermen were by the custom of London guardians of all City orphans. (Bohun, 'Privilegia Londini,' 1723, p. 315. Cf. Calthrop, *op. cit.*, p. 46.) The fact that the Court is styled the "Court of the lord the King" favours the former view, whilst the fact that in later times orphans' recognizances were always recorded in the City's Repertories, or Minute Books of the Court of Aldermen, favours the latter.

before the Mayor and Aldermen, and acknowledged themselves bound . to Thomas "Thorndone," the Chamberlain, in
the sum of 400 marks, for payment, to the Chamberlain for
the time being, of the patrimony due to John, Thomas, William
Leticia, Katherine, Johanna, and Alice, children of John Chacombe, late mercer, on their coming of age, or marriage of
the said daughters.

Fo. 2 b.

Concessio fact'
Tho'e Knolles
de aqua
ducenda ad
prisonas de
Neugate et
Ludgate.

Indenture of grant by Reginald, the Prior of St. Bartholomew in Westsmythfeld, and Convent of the same, to Thomas
Knolles, grocer, allowing him to carry off superfluous water
belonging to the Priory, and conduct it by pipes to the gates of
Neugate and Ludgate, for the relief of poor prisoners there.
Sealed with the seals of the said Prior and Convent, and also
of the said Thomas Knolles, Henry Frowyk being then Mayor,
Robert Cloptone and Thomas Catworth then Sheriffs. Dated
in the Chapter House of the Priory, 20 June, A.D. 1436.

Fo. 3.

Concessio fact'
Thome Knolles
de aqua
ducenda ad
portas de
Neugate et
Ludgate.

Indenture of grant by John Wakeryng, the Master of the
Hospital of St. Bartholomew in Westsmythfeld, and brethren
of the same, to Thomas Knolles, grocer, of their waste water
coming from a cistern near the common fountain and Chapel of
St. Nicholas, to be by him conveyed by leaden pipes to the gates
of "Newgate" and Ludgate, for the relief of poor prisoners
there. Sealed with the common seal of the said Hospital, and
also the seal of the said Thomas Knolles. Dated in the Chapter
House of the said Master and Brethren, 19 May, A.D. 1442.[1]

Fo. 3 b.

3 April, 2 Edward IV. [A.D. 1462], came John Worsoppe,
draper, Thomas Bernewey, draper, John Alburgh, mercer, and
John Broun, mercer, into the Court of the lord the King in the
Chamber of the Guildhall, before Hugh Wyche, the Mayor,
and the Aldermen, and entered into bond with Thomas
"Thorndone," the Chamberlain, in the sum of 250 marks,
for the delivery by the above John Worsoppe, or some
one on his behalf, to the Chamberlain for the time being,
of the patrimony due to Edith and Elizabeth, daughters of

---

[1] This and the preceding grant are noted by Stow ('Survey,' ed. Kings- ford, i. 37, 108), but he omits the dates.

Robert Colby, late draper, when they come of age or marry, together with certain jewels and other goods, comprising (*inter alia*) a standing piece of silver-gilt with the sign of a " Wode-wose "[1] on the top of the cover, silver spoons with " Wode-woses " at the end, silver spoons with " lez unicornes " at the end ; *primaria* (primers ?), and table-cloths (*mensalia*) worked with " Flouris de lice."[2]

Petition to the Duke of Clarence, Steward of England, by Richard Lee, with the common consent of the citizens, by the mouth of the Recorder, that they may be allowed to serve the King at his Coronation, according to custom :—

Fo. 4.
Coronacio
Regis
Edwardi
quarti

" Shewen and besechen unto your goode and gracieux Lord-shipe the Maire and Citeseyns of the Citee of London that Where after the libertees and com'endable custumes of the saide Citee of tyme that no man is mynde is to the contraire Used en-joyed and accustumed the Maire of the same Cite for the tyme beyng by raison of his saide office of Mairalte in his owne persone oweth of right and duetee to serve the King oure allez liege lord in the day of his full noble Coronac'on after mete in such place as it shal please his highnesse to take his spices[3] of Wyne in a cup of gold of our saide liege lord the King and the same cup with the coveryng belongyng thereunto and a layer of gold the said Mair to have and with hym to bere away atte tyme of his departyng for his fee and reward And also that diverse oþ'e Citeseyns þat by the saide Mair and Citee shal þ'to be named and chosen owen of right by the said custume at þe same day to serve in thoffice of Buttlership in helping of the chief buttler of Englond to þe lordes and estates þat shall be at the saide Coronac'on aswell atte table in the halle at mete as at after mete in þe Chambre Beseching your saide lordshipe that Richard Lee nowe Maire and oþ'e Citeseyns of þe Citee forsaide to þe saide office and s'vice nowe chosen whos names in a scedule herunto annexed be specified may be admytted to doo þe saide s'vice as their predecessours Mair

---

[1] Figures of a Satyr or Wild man. See ' Cal. Letter-Book K,' p. 379.

[2] Fleurs-de-lys.

[3] Cf. ' Cal. Letter-Book K,' p. 104.

and Citeseyns of þe saide Cite have in case semblable ben in dayes passed　Also the saide Maire and Citeseyns prayen that they accordyng to þe libertees and Custumes forsaid may sitte in þe day of þe saide Coronac'on at þe table next þe cupbord of þe lifte side of þe hall and that the said Mair may have and enioye his said fee and Rewarde accordyng to his duete."

The above petition being allowed by the said Duke and confirmed by the King's sign manual, the Mayor and citizens ordered the fact to be placed on record to the following effect, viz., that Richard Lee, the Mayor, at the Coronation banquet in the great hall at Westminster, took the first table on the left side of the said hall near the King's cupboard (*cipharium*), and the other citizens with him according to. the liberties and customs anciently used.

Fo. 4 b.　Moreover, the aforesaid Mayor, the boards and tables being removed (*amotis tabulis et mensis subtractis*)[1] in the chamber of the lord the King, serving in his own person, offered wine to the royal mouth in a gold cup, at the same time presenting a golden ewer (*fiolam*) filled with water to temper the wine withal.　Moreover, certain notable men specially appointed thereto, whose names are subscribed, attended the Chief Butler of England both in the hall and chamber according to their privilege. All being over, the said Mayor took and carried away the said gold cup, together with its cover, and also the ewer, as his fee and reward, and so the Mayor, enriched with the royal gift, returned home.

Robert Scrayngham, Thomas Muschamp, Mercers: John Lambe, William Haydok, Grocers; Thomas Eyre, Henry Waver, Drapers; William Chattok, John Bernewell, Fishmongers: Humfrey Hayford, Goldsmith; William Gregory, Skinner: Laurence Wilkynson, Vintner: William Knot, Tailor; William Corbet, Iremonger.

---

[1] " The table being removed and meats withdrawn." ' Report | Coronation Claims, 18 Aug., 1831.' (Printed.)

Record of proceedings which took place at a feast given by
the Serjeants-at-law in their Hall on Monday, 7 Oct., 3 Edward IV. [A.D. 1463],[1] to which Matthew Philip, the Mayor,
and other citizens had been invited, but which they abruptly
left, owing to the Mayor not being allotted the seat of honour
which he had claimed, and which had been given to the Lord
Treasurer. Dinner finished, a deputation, consisting of John
Clay, Knt., John Say, the Speaker, John Denham, and Hugh
Fen, Under-treasurer of England, was dispatched to the Mayor
to assure him that what had taken place did not meet with the
approval of the lords who were present, and to ask him that he
would honour them with his presence the next day at dinner,
when he should be accorded a place suited to his position.
To this the Mayor said he would give an answer the
following day after consulting the Aldermen. When the time
came, and the deputation again appeared in the Inner
Chamber of the Guildhall, answer was made that inasmuch
[ends abruptly].

Fos. 4 b-5.
*Nota de
Convivio
Servientum ad
legem.*

[1] This date is not correct, for
Matthew Philip was not elected
Mayor until 13 Oct., 1463. Stow
records the feast as having taken place
in Michaelmas Term, 4 Edward IV.,
A.D. 1464, and names the Lord
Gray of Ruthin as being Lord
Treasurer at the time ('Survey,' ed.
Kingsford, ii. 36). This appears to
be correct. On the other hand,
William Gregory states that the feast
took place about Midsummer (1464),
and names the Earl of Worcester as
having supplanted the Mayor at a
time when the Earl of Worcester
had ceased to be Treasurer (Gregory's
'Chron.,' p. 222). The Serjeants'
feasts (held on the occasion of new
members to the order) usually took
place at Ely House, Lambeth Palace,
or the Priory of St. John, Clerken-
well. In 1464 the feast took place
at Ely House, within the Liberties
of the City. Hence the Mayor's
insistence upon being granted precedence. (Pulling, 'The Order of
the Coif,' pp. 236-7.) The entry in
the Letter-Book is preceded by a
florid account of the fabulous foundation of the City of London by Brut.
Cf. 'Liber Albus,' i. 497.

[2] This invitation to dine with the
Serjeants on the following day is not
mentioned either by Stow or Gregory.
The latter, however, relates how a
portion of the feast, including divers
"sotelteys" (ornamental devices of
sugar, pastry, &c.), was at once sent to
the Mayor by way of a present, but
when the messengers saw the Mayor
entertaining at his own table with
lavish hospitality, they retired with
shame.

Fo. 5 b.

*Licenc' dat'
Haymanno
Voyet
desponsare
Agnet' filiam
Will'mi
Heydon.*[1]

7 Oct., 2 Edward IV. [A.D. 1462], came Haymann Voyet, physician, and Agnes his wife, daughter of William Heydone, late haberdasher, into the Court of the lord the King in the Chamber of the Guildhall, before Hugh Wyche, the Mayor, and the Aldermen, and acknowledged that he had received his wife's patrimony from Robert Boteler, William Porter, and Richard Wright, goldsmiths.

*Exon'acio
custod' Alic'
Crichefeld fil'
Joh'is
Crichefeld.*

19 Sept., 2 Edward IV. [A.D. 1462], came Johanna Sevenok, Prioress of Haliwell, and Alice, daughter of John Crichefeld, a nun of Haliwell, aged 15½ years, into the Court of the lord the King in the Chamber of the Guildhall, before Hugh Wyche, the Mayor, and the Aldermen, and acknowledged satisfaction for the patrimony of the said Alice.

*Q'd materie
Civitat' pre
omnib'
attendant'
quolibet die
Lune.*

Be it remembered that on the day of SS. Simon and Jude [28 Oct.], 1 Edward IV. [A.D. 1461], on consideration by Richard Lee, the Mayor, Thomas Ursewyk, the Recorder, Hugh Wiche, John Norman, William Marwe, Thomas Scot, William Hulyn, Matthew Philip, John Walden, Ralph Josselyn, William Taillour, Thomas Oulegreve, John Stokker, Richard Flemyng, John Lambert, George Irland, and Robert Basset, Aldermen, it was ordained that on every Monday (except some urgent cause prevents) the City's affairs should be especially attended to, and the consideration of private matters postponed, for the public welfare.

*Officium
garbellag'
speciar'
concess' Joh'i
Stokes.*

Wednesday, 21 Oct., 1 Edward IV. [A.D. 1461], the Office of Garbelage of spices was granted to John Stokes, grocer, at the request of John Fogg, Knt., Treasurer of the King's Household, by Richard Lee, the Mayor, Thomas Ursewyk, the Recorder, John Norman, William Marwe, Thomas Scot, William Hulyn, Matthew "Phelip," John Waldene, Thomas Cook, Thomas Oulegreve, William Taillour, Richard Flemyng, George Irland, and Robert Basset, Aldermen, the said John Stokes paying yearly to the Chamberlain, for the City's use, the sum of 20s.

*Eleccio Vice-
comitum.*

The Feast of St. Matthew, Ap. [21 Sept.], 1 Edward IV. [A.D. 1461], in the presence of Richard Lee, the Mayor, Thomas Ursewyk, the Recorder, John Norman, William Marowe,

---

[1] Here the marginal note does not correspond with the text.

Matthew Philip, John Walden, Thomas Cook, John Feld, Ralph Josselyn, Thomas Oulegreve, William Taillour, Hugh Wyche, John Stokker, George Irland, Richard Flemyng, John Lambert, and Robert Basset, Aldermen, and very many Commoners, summoned to the Guildhall for the election of Sheriffs, John Lok, vintner, was elected one of the Sheriffs of London and Middlesex[1] by the Mayor, and George Irland, grocer, was elected the other Sheriff by the Commonalty.

The same day, Thomas Thorndone, draper, was elected Chamberlain for the ensuing year; Peter Alphold and Peter Calcot were elected Wardens of the City's Bridge; Thomas Oulegreve, William Taillour, Aldermen, William Corbet, Robert Scrayngham, William Hampton, and Nicholas Marchall, Commoners, were elected Auditors of the accounts of the Chamberlain and Wardens in arrear.

Afterwards, viz., on the eve of St. Michael [29 Sept.], the said Sheriffs were sworn at the Guildhall, and on the morrow of the said Feast were presented, admitted, and accepted before the Barons of the Exchequer.

The Feast of the Translation of St. Edward [13 Oct.], 1 Edward IV. [A.D. 1461], in the presence of Richard Lee, the Mayor, Thomas Ursewyk, the Recorder, John Norman, William Marwe, Thomas Scot, William Hulyn, Matthew Philip, Thomas Cook, John Feld, William Taillour, Ralph Josselyn, Thomas Oulegreve, John Stokker, Hugh Wiche, Richard Flemyng, John Walshawe, John Lambert, George Irland, and Robert Basset, Aldermen, and an immense Commonalty, summoned to the Guildhall for the election of a Mayor for the year ensuing, Hugh Wyche, Alderman, was elected.

Afterwards, viz., on the Feast of SS. Simon and Jude [28 Oct.], he was sworn at the Guildhall, and on the morrow was presented, admitted, and accepted before the Barons of the Exchequer.

Fo. 6.
Eleccio Maiori.

---

[1] The custom of recording the election of Sheriffs specifically as Sheriffs of London *and Middlesex* appears to have commenced in 1453. See 'Cal. Letter-Book K,' p. 361.

4 Dec., 1 Edward IV. [A.D. 1461], John Fabyan, draper,
condemned by the Mayor and Aldermen to pay £40 to the
Chamber, for having married Johanna, daughter of Roger
Hasant, late draper, a City orphan, without obtaining permission
from the Mayor and Aldermen.

Afterwards, on the said John making submission and confessing that he had acted through ignorance, half the fine was
remitted.

Warantum
Wardmoti,etc.

12 Dec., 1 Edward IV. [A.D. 1461], Precept to the Aldermen
to hold their Wardmotes.[1]

Fo. 6 b.

Jud'm pillorii
Simo'is
Ludbroke pro
quadam
obligac'oe
fraud ter per
ipsum facta.

27 Oct. [1 Edward IV.], Simon Ludbroke summoned before
the Mayor and Aldermen for practising a fraud upon Johanna,
late wife of John Martyn, and at the time married
to Thomas Pynde, taverner, by a certain bond made
between the said Johanna and Robert Snell, " brasyer,"
whereby she became bound to the said Robert in the sum of
£40, and the said Robert became similarly bound to the said
Johanna in a like sum, that they would abide by the judgment
of the said Simon and a certain Thomas Pilche as arbitrators
between them. There was, however, fraud in the matter, inasmuch as Robert Snell's bond was conditioned, whereas the
other bond was without condition, and had been forged by the
said Simon. On appearing before the Mayor and Aldermen,
the said Simon confessed that the bond had been fabricated for
the purpose of frightening the said Johanna into a marriage
with the said Robert Snell, who thought her to be a widow.
Thereupon the said Simon was committed to prison until the
matter should be fully considered.

Afterwards, viz., on the 13th December, the said Simon, at
the suggestion of Thomas Pynde, stood on the pillory for half
an hour, the said Thomas being warned to take no action on
account of the deception practised on his wife. Nevertheless,
the said Thomas, whilst the said Simon was on the pillory,
took away the ladder, and caused rotten eggs to be thrown at
him, and for want of the ladder, the said Simon had to stand

[1] In similar terms to the Precept set out in ' Cal. Letter-Book K,' p. 215.

on the pillory a whole hour contrary to the decree of the Mayor. For so doing, the said Thomas was summoned before the Mayor and Aldermen, and confessing his guilt was committed to prison, for, says Seneca, *vindicta vindictam requirit.*[1] After two days, he made submission, and it was then agreed that he should pay a fine of £20 as an example for others not to slight the commands of superiors. On the 16th Dec. the fine was reduced to £10.

Proclamation ordering every sufficient freeman to hang out at his window or door a lantern, with a candle light therein of 12 to the pound at least, at the hour of " vii of the bell " at night, and forbidding the casting of dung or rubbish into the open streets or lanes.

Proclamacio pro vicis Civit' mundand' et candelis in vicos palam illuminand'.

Thursday, 5 Nov., 1 Edward IV. [A.D. 1461], ordinance by the Common Council to the effect that John Hornecastell, Serjeant of the channel (*canell'*)[2] for the time being, shall go round the City with constables of each Ward to cleanse the streets and lanes of the City, and, wherever they find mud or other unclean thing, to distrain those whose duty it is to remove it, and not to surrender the distress until a fine of 4 pence be paid to the Chamber. If an attempt be made at rescue, the offenders to be committed to prison at the discretion of the Mayor and Aldermen.

Fo. 7.

Ordinacio facta pro mundac'oe Civitat'.

---

[1] The entries in this Letter-Book recording matters of fact are frequently introduced by a preamble of an affected and pedantic character. Cicero, for instance, is quoted touching the importance of bestowing special care upon children, in a matter relating to City orphans (*supra*, fo. 5). This affectation was introduced by John Carpenter (see 'Memorials,' p. 580), and was continued by William Dunthorn, who had succeeded to the office of Town Clerk in October, 1461 ('Journal' 6, fo. 7 b). The 'Liber Dunthorn,' preserved among the City's archives,

was compiled by him chiefly from the Letter-Books, and he was the first Town Clerk who habitually signed public documents with his surname only, a mode of signature occasionally resorted to by John Carpenter (see 'Cal. Letter-Book I,' p. 197), and Roger Tonge *alias* Spicer ('Cal. Letter-Book K,' p. 397, note), and one which it eventually became customary for Town Clerks to follow, as at the present day.

[2] Kennel or gutter. As regards the nature of his duties, see the terms of his oath of office, set out in 'Calendar Letter-Book D,' p. 201.

Precept for an armed watch to be kept by night in every Ward, between 9 P.M. and 4 A.M., and for lanterns to be hung out. [No date.]

A schedule of the number of men to be provided by each Ward to keep the watch.   Total, 285 men.

Q'd Tegulat-
ores Laborarii
reputentur.

Friday, 2 Oct., 1 Edward IV. [A.D. 1461], ordinance by the Common Council, there being present Richard Lee, the Mayor, Thomas Ursewyk, the Recorder, John Norman, William Marwe, Thomas Scot, William Hulyn, John Walden, John Feld, John Stokker, Thomas Oulegreve, John Walsshawe, William Taillour, Ralph Josselyn, Richard Flemyng, John Lambert, Hugh Wyche, and Robert Basset, Aldermen, and an immense Commonalty, that tilers of the City shall thenceforth be reputed as labourers, and shall not be incorporated nor be deemed to constitute an Art or Society.[1]

Q'd
Amerciamenta
Cur' Maioris
int' Camer'
et Vic' London'
equaliter
dividantur.

Monday, 9 Nov., 1 Edward IV. [A.D. 1461], it was agreed by Hugh Wiche, the Mayor, Thomas Scot, Richard Lee, Matthew Philip, Thomas Cook, John Feld, William Taillour. Thomas Oulegreve, John Stokker, William Marwe, John Middelton, George Irland, and Robert Basset, Aldermen, that amercements in the Mayor's Court should be equally divided between the Sheriffs and the Chamber.

Q'd querele
coram Vic' cap-
iend' per eor'
clericos debile
intrentur, etc.

Thursday, 13 Nov., the same year, it was ordained by Hugh Wyche, the Mayor, and the Aldermen, that all plaints thenceforth to be taken by clerks of the Sheriffs should be by them taken and enrolled in the Compters, or in full Sheriffs' Court in the Guildhall, and not elsewhere, under penalty of losing their office.

4 Feb., 2 Edward IV. [A.D. 1462-3], ordinance by Thomas Cook, the Mayor, and the Aldermen, that Margaret Clarenceux, widow of Roger Clarenceux, King of Arms, shall have a house assigned to her by the Chamberlain of the yearly value of 6s. 8d.

---

[1] Notwithstanding this ordinance, the Tilers were restored to their franchises as a Fellowship in 1468. *Vide infra*, fos. 56-56 b.

At a Common Council held on Friday the 25th Sept., 1 Edward IV. [A.D. 1461], there being present Richard Lee, the Mayor, Thomas Ursewyk, the Recorder, John Norman, John Walden, John Feld, Ralph Josselyn, William Taillour, Thomas Oulegreve, Hugh Wyche, John Stokker, John Walsshawe, Robert Basset, Richard Flemyng, and John Lambert, Aldermen, and an immense Commonalty, Richard Bowherst was appointed collector of all issues and amercements of vendors of ale within the liberty of the City, making a return of the same to the Chamberlain for the time being.

Fo. 7 b.

Eleccio Ric'i Bowherst ad colligend' am'ciamenta.

The same day, permission was granted to the recently elected Sheriffs, viz., George Irland and John Lok, to have as many Serjeants as they may deem necessary, the ordinance of the 8th July, 30 Henry VI. [A.D. 1452], notwithstanding.[1]

Licenc' dat' Vicecomitibus ad h'end' tot s'vient' q't eis videbitur exped'.

20 March, 2 Edward IV. [A.D. 1461-2], Philip, son of John Bulwyk, late grocer, a City orphan of full age, acknowledged satisfaction for all jewels and utensils bequeathed to him by his parents.

Exon'ac io custod' Ph'i Bulwyk.

Record of a dispute having arisen between the citizens of London and merchants of Almaine touching the repair and custody of Bishopesgate, the latter claiming under an ancient " composition " the repair and custody of one part above the gate,[2] whilst the custody of the two parts below appertained to the citizens. By virtue of which composition the said merchants claim a mansion over the gate, and the right to demise it at will for a term of years, and also claim, in time of war, to guard two parts above the middle of the gate, viz., one where " le portcolys " is situate, and another part over the battlement, whilst the citizens guard the parts below ; but the said merchants claim to be bound to undertake the burden provided only they receive the emoluments of the gate. The deed of " composition " being thereupon examined by the Mayor and Aldermen, it was found that the said merchants had no right to

Qualiter Maior sumpsit seisinam porte de Bisshopes- gate eo q'd m'catores de Hansa Ale- man' etc.

---

[1] See 'Cal. Letter-Book K,' p. 345. When the number of Serjeants was limited to eight.

[2] See 'Liber Albus,' i. 485-8 ; ' Cal. Letter-Book C,' p. 41.

the mansion over the gate, but in return for certain privileges they enjoyed in the City, they were bound to undertake the aforesaid duties. It was further found that they were not bound in time of war to defend the middle part, viz., where the "Portcoles" was situate, but had to defend the portion above the battlement, the part near the "Portcoles" being too perilous in war time to commit to the custody of foreigners.

On the 5th March, 1 Edward IV.[1] [A.D. 1460-1], the said merchants appeared on summons before the Mayor and Aldermen in the Inner Chamber, and were asked, as they had often been asked before, to deliver up the keys, so that the gate, which had fallen into decay, might be repaired. This they refused to do. Thereupon it was agreed by Hugh Wiche, the Mayor, John Norman, William Marowe, Geoffrey Boleyn, William Hulyn, Richard Lee, Matthew Philip, John Walden, Ralph Verney, John Stokker, Ralph Josselyn, William Taylour, Thomas Coke, John Lambard, John Walsha, Richard Flemmyng, Robert Basset, and George Irland, Aldermen, that the Mayor should personally go and take seisin of the gate in the City's name. Notice being sent to the merchants to attend at the gate, they were asked to deliver up the keys, and on their refusal, the Mayor ordered new keys to be made, took seisin of the gate, and expelled the merchants of Almaine.

Fo. 8.

*Concessio fact'
Will'mo
Calbeck
mansionis in
porta de
Bisshopesgate.*

7 April, 2 Edward IV. [A.D. 1462], ordinance by Hugh Wiche, the Mayor, John Norman, Thomas Scot, William Hulyn, Richard Lee, Ralph Verney, William Tailour, Matthew Philippe, Richard Flemmyng, Robert Basset, Thomas Oulegreve, George Irland, and John Stokdon, Aldermen, that, inasmuch as the merchants of Almaine residing in the City refused to repair the gate of Bishopesgate, contrary to the terms of the " composition " made between them and the City, William Calbeck, one of the Serjeants-at-Mace, to whom the mansion over the said gate had been granted by the Mayor and Aldermen, should lay out money on the repair of the said gate under the supervision of the Chamberlain, by whom he should be reimbursed.

[1] Probably clerical error for 2 Edw. IV.

5 Feb., 1 Edward IV. [A.D. 1461-2], ordinance by Hugh *De liberacione Record'.*
Wiche, the Mayor, John Norman, Geoffrey Boleyn, Richard Lee,
Matthew Philippe, Ralph Verney, Thomas Oulegreve, Thomas
Coke, John Stokker, Richard Flemmyng, John Walshaw,
George Irland, Robert Basset, and John Stokdon, Aldermen,
that no record affecting the liberty of the City be delivered to
any one before it has been openly shown to the Mayor and
Aldermen in full court, under penalty of loss of office ; and,
further, that no clerk in the Mayor's Court deliver any record
out of the rolls or books, but the Common Clerk or his deputy
shall deliver such records.

The same day, it was ordained by the said Mayor and *De Clericis Cur' Maioris.*
Aldermen that all clerks of the Mayor's Court should be
removable at the will of the Common Clerk, and others
appointed in their place (but further consideration was taken
by the Mayor and Aldermen for the said clerks, as appears in
the oath of the said Common Clerk[1]).

The same day Richard Norman, "draper," was presented *Custod' de Blakwelhall concess' Ric'o Norman.*
to the Mayor and Aldermen by the Wardens of the Mistery of
Drapers (*pannar'*) to execute the office of Keeper of Black-
wellhall,[2] he paying a yearly ferm of 40 marks to the Chamberlain. Should the profits of the office be less than 40 marks,
a portion of the said ferm to be remitted. Also there was

---

[1] The words in parenthesis added
by a later hand. It is not improb-
able that these ordinances were passed
at the instigation of William Dunthorn
himself, who was *ex officio* Registrar
of the Mayor's Court. The oath
recorded in the City's 'Book of
Oaths' (compiled *temp.* Eliz., see
'Repertory' 21, fo. 77) contains
the following clause : — "Also
ye shall kepe no Clerk under
you but such as shalbe abled and
admitted by the Maior and Aldermen
of the said Citty for the tyme being
and sworne before the said Maior and
Aldermen, nor any such Clerke remove without the assent of the said
Maior and Aldermen." By an earlier
oath, recorded in the 'Liber Albus'
(i. 311-12), the Common Clerk bound
himself to be responsible for his
clerks, whom he (apparently) appointed, but who had to be sworn
before the Mayor and Aldermen.

[2] More properly "Bakewell hall,"
the tenement deriving its name from
the family of Bauquell (N.B. not
Banquell) or Backwell. It was used
at this time as a market to which
foreigners were bound to bring their
woollen cloth before being put to sale.
See 'Cal. Letter-Book H,' p. 449.
Stow's 'Survey' (ed. Kingsford),
ii. 336-7.

granted to the said Richard the office of aulnage[1] (*ulnagii*)
within the liberty of the City, he paying yearly to the Chamberlain the sum of £4.

*Ordinacio
concern'
Piscenar'.*

1 March, 1 Edward IV. [A.D. 1461-2], ordinance by Hugh
Wyche, the Mayor, John Norman, William Marowe, William
Hulyn, Richard Lee, William Taillour, John Walden, Matthew
Philippe, Ralph Verney, Ralph Josselyn, John Lambard,
Robert Basset, and John Stokdon, Aldermen, that the Fish-
mongers, who had made certain ordinances on their own
account, should show them to the Court, and that in future they
should use no ordinances until they had been confirmed by the
Court.[2]

Fo. 8 b.

*Exon'acio
Joh'is Whitby
ab assis', etc.*

16 Aug., 2 Edward IV. [A.D. 1462], writ received by Hugh
Wyche, the Mayor, George Irlond and John Lok, the Sheriffs,
to discharge John Whitby, " wexchaundeler," from assizes, &c.,
if he be found to be over 70 years of age.   Discharged accordingly.

*Exon' Ric'i
Frome ab
assis', etc.*

20 Aug., the same year, Richard Frome, skinner, discharged
by Hugh Wyche, the Mayor, and the Aldermen, from serving
on juries, &c., owing to his infirmities.

*Exon' Rob'ti
Russell ab
assis', etc.*

The same day Robert Russell, goldsmith, similarly discharged for like cause.

*Exon' Will'i
Haddon ab
assis'.*

15 Oct., 2 Edward IV. [A.D. 1462], William Haddon, draper,
similarly discharged for like cause.

*Exon'acio
custod'
Walteri
Haydon.*

17 March, 2 Edward IV. [A.D. 1461-2], came Walter, son of
William Haydon, an orphan of full age, into the Court of the
lord the King in the Chamber of the Guildhall, before Hugh
Wyche, the Mayor, and the Aldermen, and acknowledged
satisfaction for his patrimony.

---

[1] The assize of cloth measured by
the aulne or ell.

[2] By Statute 15 Henry VI. cap. 6
[A.D. 1437] no ordinances of Guilds
were to be carried into effect before
being thus authorized.   See 'Cal.
Letter-Book K,' Introd. p. xli.   In

1382 the Fishmongers had shown
such great reluctance to lay their
charters before the Court of Aldermen, that a peremptory order had
to be made for bringing them in by a
certain day.—'Cal. Letter-Book H,'
p. 193.

3 April, 2 Edward IV. [A.D. 1462], ordinance by the Mayor and Aldermen that inasmuch as certain woollen cloths, of the manufacture of "Northcuntre," had been claimed by Richard Styherst as his property, when they were not his property, but belonged to Antony Centurion, a foreign merchant, and had been sold to George Folkeryn, a merchant of Venice, through the medium of Leonell Centuryon and Astelyn de Caneto, the said cloth should be forfeited to the use of the Sheriffs. But because the aforesaid George did not know that the cloth belonged to some foreigner, and was not the property of the said Richard Styherst, as he asserted, it was adjudged that the said cloth should be returned to the said George, who should pay a fine of £10 for the same.

Finis pro barganeo fact' int'for insecum et forins.c'.

7 May, 2 Edward IV. [A.D. 1462], ordinance by the Mayor and Aldermen that all Rolls and Records in the custody of the Chamberlain or Under Chamberlain should be delivered by indenture to the Common Clerk, and remain in the custody of the same in the upper Chamber, so that in future he shall be responsible for them, and not deliver any Record without his undertaking to be responsible for it; and that other books and Records shall be delivered to him by indenture, as is ordained on his election.[1]

Fo. 9.
De custod' libror' et Rotulor'.

21 May, 2 Edward IV. [A.D. 1462], came William, son of William Thornell, late mercer, into the Court of the lord the King in the Chamber of the Guildhall, before the Mayor and Aldermen, and acknowledged satisfaction for his patrimony. Wherefore Robert Strother and William Denton and their sureties are quit.

Exon'acio custod' Will'mi Thornell.

16 July, 2 Edward IV. [A.D. 1462], licence granted to Laurence Test, draper, to marry Johanna, daughter of Thomas Style, late mercer, a City orphan.

Licenc'concess' Laur' Test ad desponsand Johannam Style.

---

[1] This ordinance (like the one touching the appointment and removal of the clerks of the Mayor's Court, *supra*, p. 15) was probably passed at Dunthorn's suggestion.

Con cess' fact'
Johi' Goode
subcos ervatori
aque Thamis'
de R'end' duos
servientes, etc.

6 Aug., 2 Edward IV. [A.D. 1462], it was adjudged by the Mayor and Aldermen that John Goode, Bailiff of the water of the Thames, should have 10 marks yearly for himself and his two servants (serjeants?), and a yearly reward of 5 marks during the pleasure of the Court. And, further, that Yon Machyn, his servant (serjeant?), should be discharged, and that he should elect two others, who should have a livery.

Exon'acio
custod'
Philippi
Bulwyk.

4 Sept., the same year, came Philip, son of Henry Bulwyk, late grocer, into the Court of the lord the King in the Chamber of the Guildhall, being a City orphan of full age, and acknowledged satisfaction for his patrimony.

L'ra de privato
sigillo pro
m'cat' de
Hanza Alem'.

Letter of Privy Seal reciting a grant made by the King to the merchants of Almaine that they may enjoy all their former privileges until Christmas A.D. 1462, and bidding [the Mayor, &c.] not to molest them. Dated at the King's manor of Grenewiche, 26 Dec., 1 Edward IV. [A.D. 1461].[1]

Fo. 9 b.

Custod'
pueror'
Will'mi
Wellys.

19 Jan., 2 Edward IV. [A.D. 1462-3], came John Saverey, "irmonger," John Aleyn, goldsmith, Robert Cambleyn, "peautrer," William Spencer, grocer, and Robert Studley, scrivener, into the Court of the lord the King in the Chamber of the Guildhall before Thomas Cook, the Mayor, and the Aldermen, and acknowledged themselves bound to Thomas Thorndone, the Chamberlain, in the sum of £106 13s. 4d., for the payment of certain sums to Alice, Margaret, and Isabella, daughters of William Wallis, as soon as they come of age or marry.[2]

Licenc' dat'
Joh'i Asshwell
ad desponsand'
etc.

24 Jan., 2 Edward IV. [A.D. 1462-3], licence granted to John Asshwell, late apprentice to John Worshop, draper, to marry Yda, daughter of Robert Colby, draper, a City orphan.

---

[1] Issued, apparently, in consequence of the Hanseatic merchants having been ejected from Bishopsgate for failing to keep the gate in repair. *Supra*, pp. 13-14.

[2] Marginal note to the effect that the above recognizance is void touching the said Margaret, inasmuch as she had entered the convent of St. Mary de Pratis, near the town of St. Albans; and further, that on the 20th February, 18 Edward IV. [A.D. 1478-9], came John Smale, who had married the above Alice, and acknowledged satisfaction.

1 Feb., the same year, a similar licence granted to Thomas Kelet, grocer, to marry Petronilla, daughter of Robert Stokker, draper.

Licenc' dat' Tho'e Kelet ad despouss'.

The same day, it was ordained that no freeman should be discharged from serving on juries, &c., except with the consent of the Mayor and Aldermen or the greater part of them.

Ordinac' de exon' ab assis' et enquest'.

28 April, 2 Edward IV. [A.D. 1462], judgment given by Hugh Wyche, the Mayor, the greater part of the Aldermen, and the City Council, acting as arbitrators in a dispute between Geoffrey Boleyn, Alderman and mercer, and William Redknappe, mercer, touching a wall and chimney (*caminus*) which the said William had pulled down in the parish of St. Mary de Alder-marie Chirche in Cordewanerstrete.[1]

Fo. 10.

Arbitrium redditum int' Galfr'm Boleyn Aldr'm et Will'm Redknappe.

19 Oct., 1 Edward IV. [A.D. 1461], appointment of John Stokes, grocer, to the office of Garbeller.[2]

Officium garbellag' concess' Joh'i Stokes.

6 April, 2 Edward IV. [A.D. 1462], Richard Grene, gent., admitted Attorney in the Court of the lord the King in the City[3] by Thomas Cook, the Mayor, and the Aldermen.

Ric'us Grene admiss' in Attorn' in Cur' Vic'.

Letter under the Mayoralty seal to the Dean and Chapter of St. Paul's, presenting William Asshille for admission to the second of the three chantries founded in the said church by Sir John Pulteney, Knt., vacant by the resignation of Sir Thomas Polton, chaplain. Dated 22 April, A.D. 1463.

Fo. 10 b.

Presentacio ad cant' Joh'is Pulteney.

Letter under the Mayoralty seal to Thomas [Kempe], Bishop of London, presenting John Burbage, Rector of the church of St. Faith *in criptis*, for admission to the chantry founded by Roger Beyvyn in the chapel over the charnel-house in St. Paul's churchyard[4] in exchange with Sir John Couper, perpetual chaplain of the said chantry. Dated 11 May, A.D. 1463.

Presentacio ad Cantariam sup' ossamenta mortuor' in Cimiterio sc'i Pauli.

---

[1] Cf. *infra*, fo. 29.
[2] Marginal note *vacat quia antea.* *Vide sup.*, p. 8.
[3] Generally known as the Mayor's Court; but here, apparently, it means the Sheriffs' Court.
[4] Cf. 'Cal. Letter-Book I,' p. 91 ; 'Cal. of Wills Court of Husting,' i. 29.

Carta domini Reg' concess' tenent ville de Walshale.

Writ to all Sheriffs, Mayors, Bailiffs, &c., not to exact toll from men of the manor of Walshale [Walsall], that manor being of the ancient demesne of the Crown, and therefore free of toll. Witness the King at Westminster, 12 Jan., 2 [Edward IV., A.D. 1462-3].

The above was allowed by Thomas Cook, the Mayor, and the Aldermen whose names appear in the Journal for the 9th May, 3 Edward IV. [A.D. 1463],[1] and ordered to be carried into execution within the City.

Fo. 11.

Eleccio Vicecomitum.

Tuesday the Feast of St. Matthew [21 Sept.], 2 Edward IV. [A.D. 1462], in the presence of Hugh Wyche, the Mayor, John Norman, William Marowe, Thomas Scot, William Hulyn, Richard Lee, Matthew Philip, John Waldeyn, Thomas Cook, Thomas Oulegreve, John Stokker, Richard Flemyng, John Lambard, John Walshawe, John Stoktone, and George Irlond, Aldermen, and very many Commoners summoned to the Guildhall for the election of Sheriffs for the year ensuing, Bartholomew James, draper, was elected one of the Sheriffs by the Mayor, and William Hamptone, the other Sheriff, by the Commonalty.

The same day, Thomas Thorndone, draper, was elected Chamberlain; Peter Alfold and Peter Calcot, Wardens of London Bridge; Thomas Oulegreve and John Stokker, Aldermen, and William Redknap, mercer, Thomas Danyel, dyer, William Corbet, and Robert Scranynham, Commoners, elected Auditors of the account of the Chamberlain and Wardens.

Afterwards, viz., on the eve of St. Michael [29 Sept.], the said Sheriffs were sworn at the Guildhall, and on the morrow of the Feast were presented and admitted, &c., before the Barons of the Exchequer.

Eleccio Maioris.

Thursday, the Feast of Translation of St. Edward [13 Oct.], 2 Edward IV. [A.D. 1462], in the presence of Hugh Wyche, the Mayor, John Norman, William Marowe, Thomas Scot, William Hulyn, Richard Lee, Matthew Philip, Thomas Cook, Ralph Josselyn, Thomas Oulegreve, William Taillour, John Stokker, Richard Flemmyng, George Irlond, Robert Basset,

[1] Journal 7, fo. 27.

John Walsawe, John Stokton, and William Hamptone, Aldermen, Bartholomew James, one of the Sheriffs, and an immense Commonalty summoned to the Guildhall for the election of a Mayor for the year ensuing, Thomas Cook was elected.

Afterwards, viz., on the Feast of SS. Simon and Jude [28 Oct.], he was sworn at the Guildhall, and on the morrow was presented, admitted, and accepted, &c., before the Barons of the Exchequer.

23 Nov., 2 Edward IV. [A.D. 1462], ordinance by the Mayor and Aldermen that the Assessors of the Ward of Bassyngshawe pay 28s., the amount at which the seld of Blakwelhall was assessed by them for the last loan of 2,000 marks to the King, inasmuch as they unjustly assessed the said seld and Richard Norman, the City's tenant. *Nota de Assess' selde de Blakwelhalle.*

Writ to the Sheriffs notifying that Parliament would meet at Leicester on the 7th March next, instead of at York on the 5th of February, as directed by a former writ. Witness the King at Westminster, 10 Jan., 2 Edward IV. [A.D. 1462-3]. *Br'e pro parliamento.*

Another writ to the Sheriffs for the election of four citizens to attend a Parliament to be held at Westminster on the 29th April next.[1] No Sheriff to be returned. Witness the King at Westminster, 20 Feb., 2 Edward IV. [A.D. 1462-3]. *Fo. 11 b.*
Br'e pro parliamento.

Pursuant to the above writ there were elected William Marowe, Alderman, Thomas Ursewyk, the Recorder, Thomas Wynselowe, draper, John Bromer, fishmonger. *Cives pro parliam'.*

At a Common Council held on Saturday, 11 March, 3 Edward IV. [A.D. 1462-3], there being present Thomas Cook, the Mayor, John Norman, William Marowe, William Hulyn, Hugh Wyche, John Walden, Richard Flemmyng, John Walshae, Robert Basset, Matthew Philippe, Ralph Josselyn, [George] Irland, John Stokdone, William Hamptone, Aldermen, and an immense Commonalty, it was ordained :—

That all latrines over the ditch of Walbroke should be abolished. *De latrinis sup' fossat' de Walbroke.*

---

[1] This Parliament sat, by virtue of several prorogations, at Westminster and York until 1465 (' Rot. Parl.,' v. 496-570).

Nota de mundaco'e et reparaco'e fossat' de Walbroke.

Also that the owner of land on each side of the said ditch shall clean his portion of the same, and pave and vault it up to its middle line. If the owner should refuse to carry out this order, his land should go to any one who was willing to do so, to hold the same to him and his heirs.

Imprisona-ment' Rob'ti Bifeld.

4 March, 2[1] Edward IV. [A.D. 1462-3], it was agreed by Thomas Cook, the Mayor, and the Aldermen that Robert Bifeld, girdler, should be committed to Neugate for saying that the Mayor was an unjust judge, and that Hugh Wyche, Alderman, was the same, in a dispute between the said Robert and John Lokesdeen, his late servant.

Ordinac' fact' de les lighters in Thamisia.

At a Common Council held on Monday, the 2nd May, 3 Edward IV. [A.D. 1463], there being present Thomas Cook, the Mayor, Thomas Scot, William Hulyn, Hugh Wyche, Matthew Philippe, William Taillour, Thomas Oulegreve, John Stokker, John Lambard, " John "[2] Irlond, William Hamptone, John Stokdone, and Ralph Verney, Aldermen, it was ordained that no one should receive on his wharf the cargo of any ship unless discharged by batels and " lighters " of freemen of the City, or of others resident in the same and in lot and scot, under penalty of 20*s.*

Fo. 12.

Ordinac'o fact' pro les lighterssmen.

A schedule of charges to be made by " lightermen " for carriage of merchandise from various places on the river to the City, *per* " tonne tighte "[3] and " laste."[4]

At a Common Council held on Friday, 6 May, 3 Edward IV. [A.D. 1463], in the presence of Thomas Cook, the Mayor,

---

[1] Clerical error for 3.

[2] Clerical error for George.

[3] Probably meaning casks tightly packed. The term appears to have been synonymous with *tun-weight*. By a statute of 1472 (St. 12 Edward IV. cap. II.) merchant strangers trading with England were ordered to import four bow-staves for every tun weight (*pois de toneaue*) of other merchandise ; whilst a petition to Parliament on the same subject, and about the same time, uses the term " tuntight " (' Rot. Parl.,' vi. 156). In a table of fees taken by packers and waterside porters of the City for shipping and landing merchandise of strangers appended to the charter to the City dated 5 September, 16 Charles I. [A.D. 1640], we find charges made for brimstone *the ton loose,* and for 100 reams of paper *loose.*

[4] A last is a measure used for fish, hides, &c. A last of herring nominally = 10,000 fish, but is actually more.

Thomas Scot, William Hulyn, Hugh Wyche, William Taillour, Richard Flemmyng, George Irland, John Stokdon, Thomas Oulegreve, John Stokker, John Walsawe, Robert Basset, John Locke, and William Hamptone, Aldermen, and an immense Commonalty, it was agreed :—

That strangers bringing wool or other merchandise into the City or without the gates shall pay the custom of old due ; and if such merchandise be coloured (*colorentur*) by the " Wolpakkers " or others, a fine shall be imposed at the discretion of the Mayor and Aldermen.

De custuma m'cand' extraneor' intrant' et exeunt' per portas etc.

That no one living within the liberty of the City shall buy sand or gravel of any denizen or foreigner except sand and gravel from the ditches of the City, and bought on the spot, paying the same as they would to others, under penalty of 20 pence for every cartload bought otherwise ; and that the penalty should be applied for the benefit of the ditches.

De gravello et zabulo que fodiuntur in fossat' Civit'.

That the letters patent granted by the King to the Barbers of the City using the faculty of Surgery and shown to this Court be entered of record ; provided that if anything in future be found therein contrary to the liberties of the City the same shall be annulled.

Alloc' carte Barbitons'.

Also that Mary Okam of Calais shall have a lease of her dwelling-house in that town for a term of 50 years, at an annual rent of 5 marks 6 shillings and 8 pence ; for which grant the said Mary gave 12 cushions (*pulvinaria*) for the decoration of the inner Chamber of the Guildhall.

Concess' fact' Marie Okam de vill' Calis'.

Also that the ordinances of the Hurers entered in Letter-Book H, fo. xlix [b], and in Letter-Book K, fo. clxxii, touching the fulling of hats and caps,[1] shall thenceforth be strictly observed.

Inspeximus Charter of Edward IV. to the town of " Maudone " [Maldon, co. Essex]. Dated at Westminster, 13 May, 3 Edward IV. [A.D. 1463].[2]

Fo. 12 b. Carta Burgens' de Maudon'

---

[1] To be fulled by hand and foot, and not sent to mills. 'Cal. Letter-Book K,' p. 220.

[2] Cf. 'Cal. Letter-Book K,' pp. 362-3.

Be it remembered that the above charter was allowed by Thomas Cooke, the Mayor, and the Aldermen, the 20th May, the same year.

Fo. 13.
Carta
Barbitons'.

Charter of incorporation of the Barbers of London using the faculty of Surgery granted by Edward IV., 24 Feb., in the first year of his reign [A.D. 1461-2].[1]

The charter is subscribed as being granted under Privy Seal, with the authority of Parliament, and for £10 paid into the hanaper.

Fo. 13 b.
De lege non
vadianda.

Be it remembered that on the 24th May, 3 Edward IV. [A.D. 1463], it was declared by Thomas Cook, the Mayor, John Norman, William Hulyn, Richard Lee, Thomas Scot, Hugh Wych, William Taillour, Richard Flemmyng, Robert Basset, Ralph Verney, William Hamptone, and George Irland, Aldermen, assembled for business in the Court of the lord the King in the inner Chamber of the Guildhall,[2] that according to ancient custom of the City a debtor is barred from waging his law in any City Court by the plaintiff producing a written acknowledgment by the defendant of the debt.

Fo. 14.

Ordinacio de
tractu pontis
London'.

Proclamation for keeping the Midsummer watch.   Dated 12 June, 3 Edward IV. [A.D. 1463].

Be it remembered that on the 6th June, 3 Edward IV. [A.D. 1463], it was agreed by Thomas Cook, the Mayor, and the Aldermen that the drawbridge of London Bridge should be raised for all ships wanting to pass through, as was agreed in the Common Council held on the 5th May last past;[3] and that the Bridge-masters shall take for every draw (*tractu*)

---

[1] The charter, with the Great Seal attached, is preserved among the archives of the Company of Barber-Surgeons, and is endorsed as having been enrolled in this Letter-Book. A transcript of the charter in the possession of the Company, together with translation, will be found printed in Sidney Young's 'Annals of the Barber-Surgeons,' pp. 52-8.

[2] This must undoubtedly be the Court of Aldermen, notwithstanding it being styled "the Court of the lord the King.'' Cf. 'Cal. Letter-Book K,' pp. 228-9, where the editor expressed a different opinion.

[3] Recorded *supra*, fo. 12, but marked in the margin, *vacat quia postea.* The date of the Common Council is there given as Friday the 6th (not the 5th) May.

6 pence and no more; and if the Bridge-masters refuse to
draw the bridge for 6 pence when desired, they shall forfeit
3s. 4d. of their own goods to the use of the Chamber.

Letters patent appointing the Keepers of the peace within
the City and Sheriffs of the same to be Commissioners for levying the subsidy imposed on foreigners by the last Parliament
held at Redyng.[1] Witness the King at Westminster, 8 March,
3 Edward IV. [A.D. 1462-3].

Com'issio pro pecuniis de Alienigen' levand'.

30 July, 3 Edward IV. [A.D. 1463], came the Wardens and
many others of the Mistery of Bladesmythes into the Court
of the lord the King in the Chamber of the Guildhall,
and presented a petition to the Mayor and Aldermen as
follows :—

Fos. 14 b-15 b.

Ordinacio de Bladesmythes.

" Mekely besechen' the Wardeins and Felisship of the Crafte
of Bladesmythes of the seide Citee That where as divers
Foreyns Bladesmythes aswele of foreyn townes as of places
nygh the suharbes of the seide Citee comyng and repayryng to
the seide Citee usen to selle in Innes and other privat and
unlefull places theire chaffaire that they bryng to the Citee
to sell and not to places therto assigned by the ordinance
of the seid Citee, and for to eschue suche untrew and disseyvable chaffare so brought and solde to the hurt of the comon'
people Please it youre goode lordeship and wise discrec'ons
to graunt and ordeign that al suche foreyns that from
hensforward comen and usen the seide Citee shall bryng
theire almanere Chaffare to Ledenhall there to be solde
opynly on merkate dayes there accustumed and in non'
other places upon payne of forfaiture of all suche chaffare
so solde in eny other place within the Fraunchese of the
seide Citee And that all other actees and ordinances a
fore this tyme graunted by youre noble p'decessours for the
wele of the seide Crafte entred in the Chambre of the Yeldehall
of London[2] be goode and effectuell accordyng to the seide
grauntes.

---

[1] In March, 1453. See ' Cal.
Letter-Book K,' p. 368.

[2] Cf. ordinances of 1408. Riley's
' Memorials,' pp. 569-70.

" And over that forasmoche as divers Foreyns dwellyng in ferre contrees of this Reaume counterfeten the markes of Bladesmythes of this Citee and sellen theire blades to divers persones of this Citee and by the same persones aren solde ayen for London blades to grete disclaunder of the seide Craft and disceyte of the Kynges people It like unto youre full wise discrecions to ordeign and graunte that all suche blades so retailled and solde from hensforward in whos handes thei been founde of the seide Citee bi due serche therof made by the Wardeins of the seide Craft of Bladesmythes for the tyme beyng to gider w^t an officer of youres may be utterly forfette.

" Also forasmoche as oftentymes by divers unkonnyng Grynders of the seide Citee many good blades and sufficient aren' sore appeired[1] to grete disclaunder of the London blades That it please unto your full wise discrecions to ordeign and graunte that from henssforward no maner foreyn take upon him to use the occupacion of Gryndyng of Blades within the seide Citee and fraunchise therof on lesse than that persone so sette a werke be fraunchesed and proved within the seide Citee upon payn of paying at every tyme founden' defectif xii$d$.

" Also forasmoche as divers persons enfraunchesed in the seide Crafte have custumably used to goo sende and offre untreu and disseyvable Chaffare to sell in divers Covert and privy places for light chepe to the grete disceyte of the Com'on people Please it youre right sadde and wise discrec'ons to graunte and ordeign that no personne enfraunchesed of the seide Crafte in the same Citee by him self nor by noon other persone in no wise shall bere no manere chaffare of the seide Craft out of his house to offre to eny persone to sell unto suche tyme that the saide Chaffare be duely serched by the Wardeins of the same Crafte for the tyme beyng and founde by the seide Wardeins able upon payn of forfeiture of the same and to make fyne at every tyme that he therof be founde defectyf and duely convicte upon the same vj$s$. viij$d$. Whereof that oon'

---

[1] Impaired. *Apeire* answers to a | *peius*, worse (Skeat), Old Fr. *am-*
Low Lat. form *adpriorare*, from | *peirer, empeirer*.

halff to the seide yeldehall and that other halff to the Comon' Boxe of the seide Crafte.

"Also fcrasmoche as often tymes divers unkonnyng Grynders of sheres and blades of the seide Citee goyng a boute in the same Cite and desiren to have the gryndyng of mennes sheres and blades for right litle value For the covetisenes of the which men taken them there sheres and blades to grynde and thanne they been evill grounde and some tyme in stede of gryndyng but whette by the which the comon people been gretely disceyved and withoute remedy Wherefore please it youre saide discrecions to ordeyn and graunte that noo persone enfraunchesed in the seide Crafte take upon him to grynde eny mennes sheres except Shermensherys that is to say clothesheris or blades[1] withoute he do it sufficiently and werkmanly And if any manne be founde defectif in that poynt by complaynt made of any persone that thanne the party so hurte to be restored to his hurtes by the discrecion of the Wardeins of the same Crafte for the tyme beyng and to make fyn to the Comon' Boxe of the seide Craft accordyng to the seide defence [sic] nor that no personne enfraunchesed in the seide Crafte shall not goo oute of his house to praye desire nor fecche eny ware or Chaffare to make or grynde nor that noo personne of the seide Crafte shall not bere nor send his marke to eny foreyn to be sette upon eny werke by the foreyn to be made w'oute that there be noo man enfraunchesed of the seide Crafte of sufficient konnyng to make the same upon paynne to pay at every tyme that eny of the personnes enfraunchesed of the seide Crafte be founde defectif in eny of the poyntes aforeseid xxd. wherof that oone halff to the yeldehall aforeseid and that other halff to the comon' boxe of the seide Crafte.

"And where as the co'ialtee of the seide Crafte to the honure of God and of oure blissed lady his moder of long tyme

---

[1] In 1423, when two or three individuals at the most appear to have enjoyed the monopoly of grinding shears for shermen, for which they were in the habit of making excessive charges, an ordinance was passed by the Mayor and Aldermen restricting their independence. See 'Cal. Letter-Book K,' pp. 22-4.

passed have founde used and kept certeyn lyghtes bernyng
bifore the ymages of oure lady as well in the Cathedrall
Chirche of Seynt Poule, as in the Chirche of the Freres
Menours, dyvers persones of the seide Crafte been obstynat
and woll not bere there parte to the sustinance of the seide
lightes nor obey the somons of there Wardeins for suche
Correccions and necessaries as long to the seide Crafte to the
grete trouble and hurte of the same Craft   Please it therfore
youre lordship' and wise discrecions to graunte and ordeign
that every persone of the seid Craft disobeyng to pay his parte
duly sette upon him to the sustinaunce of the seide lightes or that
disobeyeth eny somons made unto him by the Wardeins of the
seide Crafte for the tyme beyng make fyne of iiij*d.* or ellys to
losse at every tyme a pownde a [*sic*] wexe Whereof that oone
halff to the yeldehall aforeseid and that other halff to the
Comon' Boxe of the seide Crafte.

Fo. 15 b.
" Also that no man enfraunchesed in the seide Crafte of Bladesmythes shall take upon him forhensforward to make no manere
of ware aperteynyng to the same Crafte unto suche tyme that
he have chosen him a merk and it shewed unto the Wardeins
of the seide Crafte for the tyme beyng and to iiij of the same
Craft suche as the same Wardeyns woll calle unto them[1] and
by theym admitted and enrolled in the yeldehall of London in
avoidance of the prejudice that might therby growe to eny
other persone of the same crafte so as every mannys werk
therby may be knowen upon payn to pay at every tyme that he
is founde defectif in this articule xiij*s.* iiij*d.* that oone half to the
Yeldehall of London and that other half to the comon' Boxe of
the seid Crafte."

Their petition granted.

Fos. 15 b-16 b.
Letters patent appointing Richard Raulyns, John Brown,
merchant, Robert Drope, draper, John Ades, goldsmith, John

Comissio
direct'
Collectorib'
pro auxilio
levando.
Maresshall, mercer, William Overay, fishmonger, William
Redeknap, mercer, Nicholas Marchall, " irmonger," Peter
Draper, " irmonger," William Porter, goldsmith, and John

---

[1] An embryo Court of Assistants.

Forster, skinner, to be Commissioners for levying the City's portion of the sum of £31,000—part of an aid of £37,000 granted by Parliament for the defence of the realm, the balance of £6,000 being devoted to the relief of impoverished towns[1]—in accordance with the terms of an indenture made between the said Commissioners on the one part, and Richard Lee, Hugh Wiche, Ralph Verney, and William "Taillard" (Taillour), Aldermen, William Edward, grocer, and John Steward,[2] chandler, on the other part. Witness the King at Westminster, 1 July, 3 Edward IV. [A.D. 1463].

Letters patent appointing the above Richard Lee, Hugh Wych, Ralph Verney, and William "Taillard," Aldermen, William Edward, and John Steward to apportion the relief allowed the inhabitants of the City in levying the above aid. Witness the King at Westminster, 1 July, 3 Edward IV. [A.D. 1463].

Comissio pro parte auxilii vocat' deducciones assidend'.

Precept to the Aldermen in respect of a moiety of the above, and to cause the amount to be levied for which their several Wards were liable, on all persons having lands, tenements, or rents of the yearly value of 10s. or goods and chattels of the value of 5 marks. Dated 27 July, 3 Edward IV. [A.D. 1463].

Fo. 17.

Warantum pro auxilio levand'.

1 July, 3 Edward IV. [A.D. 1463], came John Asshewell, draper, and Edith his wife, into the Court of the lord the King in the Chamber of the Guildhall, before Thomas Cook, the Mayor, and the Aldermen, and acknowledged they had received from John Worshop, draper, a sum of money and jewels bequeathed to the said Edith by Robert Colby her father.

Exon'acio custod' Edithe Asshewell.

15 Dec., 2 Edward IV. [A.D. 1462], licence given by John Norman, Thomas Scot, William Hulyn, William Taillour, John Oulegreve, Ralph Verney, John Stokker, Ralph Josselyn, John

Exoneracio Will'i York piscinar' ab omnib' officiis.

---

[1] 'Rot. Parl.,' v. 497-8. The amount of relief accorded to the City of London was £115 3s. 3d.

[2] A great benefactor to the Tallow-chandlers' Company. See his will enrolled in the Court of Husting in 1473, where he describes himself as John "Stuward," and as being Master of the Tallow-chandlers' Company at the time of making his will, viz., Dec., 1472 ('Cal. of Wills,' ii. 569).

Lambard, Richard Flemmyng, George Irlond, Robert Basset, and William Hamptone, Aldermen, to Thomas Cook, the Mayor, to discharge William York, fishmonger, from serving any office, on his paying a sum of money, at the discretion of the said Mayor, for the repair of the City's ditches. On the following 19th March the said William York was accordingly discharged on payment of 100 marks.

Afterwards, viz., on the 20th Sept., 3 Edward IV. [A.D. 1463], it was agreed by Thomas Cook, the Mayor, William Marowe, Hugh Wyche, John Walden, John Stokker, William Taillour, Thomas Oulegreve, Richard Flemmyng, John Stokdon, Robert Basset, John Walsawe, William Hamptone, William Constantyn, and John Tate, Aldermen, that the above discharge should hold good.

A deed under the Mayoralty seal discharging the above William York as recorded. Dated 19 March, 3 Edward IV. [A.D. 1462-3].

Fo. 17 b.

Exon'acio Joh'is Burton ab assisis etc.

4 Oct., 3 Edward IV. [A.D. 1463], John Burton, tailor, discharged by Thomas Cook, the Mayor, and the Aldermen from serving on juries, &c., owing to his infirmities.

Custod' pueror' Edwardi Benet.

30 August, 3 Edward IV. [A.D. 1463], came Thomas Brewes and John Stone, tailors, and William Redknape, mercer, into the Court of the lord the King in the Chamber of the Guildhall, before Thomas Cook, the Mayor, and the Aldermen, and entered into bond with Thomas Thorndone, the Chamberlain, in the sum of 200 marks for the payment of 100 marks to John and Thomas, sons of Edward Benet, late tailor, respectively on their reaching the age of 24 years.

Admissio Thome Acton in officium attorn' in Cur' Vic'.

21 Oct., 3 Edward IV. [A.D. 1463], Thomas Acton, junior, " gentilman," admitted and sworn an attorney in the Court of the lord the King in the City.[1]

Fo. 18.

Ordinacio de Fruterers.

20 Oct., 3 Edward IV. [A.D. 1463], came into the Court of the lord the King in the Chamber of the Guildhall, before Thomas Cook, the Mayor, and the Aldermen, the Wardens,

[1] See note [3] *supra*, p. 19.

and many other men of the mistery of Fruiterers, and presented
a petition in the following terms :—

" Full mekely shewen alle the persones enfranchesed in the
Mistiere and occupacion of Fruterers of the saide Citee   Howe
that they of tyme oute of mynde at their grete cost charge
and aventure have used and yet daily usen aswel to the grete
pleasir of the King the Lordes and other gentils and straungiers
resortyng unto this Citee as of the governours and other enhabi-
tantes bothe riche and poore of the same to provide and ordeyn
for al maner dentee frutes and other aswel of the growing
of straunge contrees as of this land after that the saisons of the
yeer requiren to the grete honour and wele of all this saide
Citee as wele is knowen   And howe also your saide besechers
at all tymes have bene like as they yet ben as redy and
welwilled after their simple powers to be contributorie to the
charges of this saide Citee for the seurte saufgard and honour
therof as any other Conciteseyns of like haveour or power
within the same and so entend with goddis mercy and your
goode supportacions and favours to contynue   Yet nowe is
it so what for the inordinate behaving and demeanyng of
Foreins in grete nombre daily repairyng unto this Citee with
their frutes which comonly and namely nowe of late be suffred
to uttre and sille almanere suche frutes as they bryng at all
seasons and tymes of the wike and in alle places of this Citee
at their owne willes and pleasirs keping neither the comon
market dayes nor places therto ordeyned and assigned contrary
to alle goode and politiq' reules of this Citee in that behalf
of tyme oute of mynde used and accustumed And no correcion
theruppon doone but rather by their hostes and other of this
Citee favoured supported and coloured to the comon deceipt
and hurt of the saide Citee and to the disclaundre hinderaunce
and empoverissyng of youre saide besechers in sundry wises
Please it therfore your grete wisdoms of youre blessed disposi-
cions in tender considerac'on of the premisses and howe also newe
ordenaunce or reules in certeyn concernyng the seid mistier
or occupacion of Fruterers as yet ben establisshed made and
entred of Record in the Chambre of the Guihald of the Citee

forseid (?)   For lacke whereof diverse and many defaultes
bene oftentymes fonde among youre saide besechers not duely
corrected to ordeyn enact and establissh for the Comon Wele
of this Citee and for the goode reule of the saide Crafte thise
ordenaunces folowing fro this tyme forward to be observed and
putte in due execucion in the saide crafte and to be auctorised
of Recorde perpetuely in the seide Chambre   And youre saide
besechers shall ever devoutely pray to god for you.

" First that every persone enfraunchesed in the saide mistier
and occupying the same within the Franchise therof shall be
redy at all manere resonable somons and warnyng of the
Wardeins of the same occupacion for the tyme beyng that is to
sey for matiers touching or in any maner wise concernyng the
goode reules and guydyng of the saide occupacion for the
honeur of this Citee And if any persone so enfranchesed absent
him after any suche somons withoute cause resonable and
therof be duly convict Pay to þᵉ Chambre of this Citee vjs. viijd.
half therof to the same Chambre and that other half to the
comon boxe of the said mystier.

"Also that no persone enfranchesed in the saide occupac'on
from hensforth take into his service any stranger or foreyn for
less terme then a yeere ne that any suche personne enfranchised
in any wise procure any mannys servaunt oute of his service
nor take any servaunt that hath been or is in service with
a nother fruterer enfranchised before he knou wel that the
same servaunt hath complete his covenauntes and is aggreed
with his former maister upon peyne of forfaiture and lesyng at
every tyme that he is founde defectif in eny of thise poyntes
vjs. viijd. that one moite therof to the said Chambre and that
oþer moite to the comon boxe aforesaide.

Fo. 18 b.   "Also for asmyche as divers foreins of the Cuntrey that
bringen frute into this Citee to be solde usen to leve their best
frutes in their ynnes where they be loigged bothe within þis
Citee and the Suburbes therof and there prively sille them in
grete to the forein fruterers and hulsters [huksters ?] of this
Citee at theire owne prices and with the werst frute therof

gone hokkyng[1] a boute from strete to strete and from place to
place within the said Cite at al tymes of the wike And nether
kepen the seasoun nor place of the market of the same to
te [*sic*] grete disceit and hurt of the comons therof wich as it is
conceved and it were duely kept as it oweth to be and like as
of olde tyme it hath been shulde cause them to sille unto the
comons better penyworthes then they nowe doon   It is
ordeyned that all maner foreyns of the Cuntrey that bringen
frute by lond to this Citee to be solde stande and sille their
frute in the comon and opyn market place of this Citee therto
ordeyned and assigned that is to sey on the pament [*sic*] of
Westchepe from þe standard there toward the grete conduyt
at Greschirch and at the Fryers Meynours and in no nother
place within the frauncheis of the seid Citee   And that the seide
foreyns from hensforth bryngyng frute be londe to the Citee to
be solde as is a foresaid stande in the seide places to selle their
frutes iij dayes in the wike oonely[2] that is to say Monday
Wendisday and Friday unto the oure of xij of the clocke a fore
noon from the fest of Alhalowen until Whitsontyde upon peyne
of forfaiture of all suche frutes solde and founde in any other
tyme or place within the saide Citee to be solde   And that this
Article extende also and be executorie to and upon all suche
foreyn Fruterers as have served within this Citee   And nowe
to thentent as it is demed that they woll not be enfranchesed
nor be under correccion ne reule neither cotributorie to the
charges of this Cite dwellen in the Suburbes therof   And
ageyns all ordre and goode reules of the same by long tyme
have used like as they daily usen to com unto the same Citee
with theire frutes and with them in all places within þe
Fraunchise therof when and as often as them liketh standen and
goon to sille them more liberaly then any freman of the same.

"And over this that all persones enfraunchised in that occupacion by them self and their servantes stande and walke with
their frutes to sille them in all places of this Citee and the

---

[1] Hawking.   [2] Amended in 1465. *Vide infra,*
                                 fo. 35.

D

Franchise þ'of when and wheresom ever it shall like them except it shall not be lefull to ony suche fruterer to stond emongys the saide foreyns nor in any wise medle with foreyn fruterers in beyng or silling at the saide place and tyme of market upon peyne of forfaiture aswel of all suche frute of their owne as is founde beyng emonges suche foreyn Fruterers to be solde as of all other frute duely proved bought or solde ageyns this ordenaunce   And over that to lese at every tyme vj_s._ viij_d._ halff therof to the use of the saide Chambre and that oþer half to the comon boxe of the seide mistier of Fruterers."[1]

Their petition granted.

Custodia Rob'ti Man- felde filii Joh'is Manfelde.

9 Sept., 3 Edward IV. [A.D. 1463], came William Ware, "sporiour," living in St. John's Street, and John Forster of Sevenok, co. Kent, "husbondman," into the Court of the lord the King, before Thomas Cooke, the Mayor, and the Aldermen, and acknowledged themselves bound to Thomas Thorndone, the Chamberlain, in the sum of 100_s._

The above recognizance to be void on condition the said John Forster maintain and clothe Robert, son of John Manfelde, until he come of age, and then deliver to him two mazers, a set of prayer-beads[2] of silver, and a gold ring of the value of 33_s._ 4_d._

Fo. 19.
Eleccio Vicecomit'.

Wednesday the Feast of St. Matthew [21 Sept.], 3 Edward IV. [A.D. 1463], in the presence of Thomas Cook, the Mayor, John Norman, William Marowe, William Hulyn, Richard Lee, Hugh Wyche, John Walden, William Taillour, Thomas Oulegreve, Richard Flemmyng, John Walshaw, George Irlond, John Stokdon, William Costantyn, John Tate, William Hamptone, Aldermen, and very many Commoners summoned to the Guildhall for the election of Sheriffs, Thomas Muschamp

---

[1] Another set of Ordinances of the Fruiterers were approved in 1486. *Infra*, fo. 220.

[2] *Unum par precum.* Cf. *une peire paternosters* (Letter-Book G, fo. 153 b ; 'Memorials,' pp. 327, 455).

"Of smal coral aboute hir arm she bar
A peire of bedes."
         Chaucer, Prol. 159.
A "pair" (Lat. *par*) is often used of a set of things of equal size, *e.g.*, "a pair of stairs" for a flight of stairs.

was elected one of the Sheriffs of London and Middlesex by the Mayor, and Robert Basset was elected the other Sheriff by the Commonalty.

The same day, Robert Colwych,[1] tailor, was elected Chamberlain for the year ensuing; Peter Alfold and Peter Calcot were elected Wardens of London Bridge; John Stokker and Richard Flemmyng, Aldermen, and William Redknap, mercer, Thomas Danyell, dyer, John Stone, tailor, and Richard Frome, skinner, Commoners, were elected Wardens of the accounts of the Chamberlain and Wardens in arrear.

Afterwards, viz., on the eve of St. Michael [29 Sept.], the said Sheriffs were sworn at the Guildhall, and on the morrow of the said Feast were presented, admitted, and accepted before the Barons of the Exchequer.

22 Sept., 3 Edward IV. [A.D. 1463], came John Mortymer, Thomas Peersson, John Ulffe, and John Scowe, fishmongers, and William Neelle, vintner, into the Court of the lord the King, before Thomas Cook, the Mayor, and the Aldermen, and entered into bond with Thomas Thorndone, the Chamberlain,[2] in the sum of £50 for payment into the Chamber, by the said John Mortymer, of the patrimony respectively due to Thomas, Alice, and Rose, children of Adam Thurkyld, late fishmonger, on their coming of age or marrying.

Custodia pueror' Ade Thurkyld.

At a Common Council held on Monday, the 26th Sept., 3 Edward IV. [A.D. 1463], in the presence of Thomas Cook, the Mayor, Thomas Ursewyck, the Recorder, William Marowe, William Hulyn, Richard Lee, Hugh Wiche, John Walden, William Taillour, Thomas Oulegreve, John Stokker, John Walshawe, Richard Flemmyng, John Lambard, George Irlond, John Stokdon, Robert Basset, William Costantyn, John Tate, William Hamptone, Aldermen, and an immense Commonalty, Thomas Burgoyne and John "Rigkeby," gentlemen, were

Fo. 19 b.

Eleccio Thome Burgoyne et Joh' Rygby subvic'.

---

[1] Alderman of Farringdon Without, 1474-6; of Coleman Street Ward, 1476-80; Sheriff, 1475-6.

[2] Notwithstanding Robert Colwych having been elected Chamberlain the previous day.

elected and admitted to the office of Under-sheriffs of the City for the year ensuing.[1]

Eleccio Joh'nis Stokker in co'em venatorem.

The same day, John Stokker, gentleman, was admitted by the said Mayor and Aldermen, with the assent of the Commonalty, to the office of Common Hunt[2] of the City *loco* William Sudbury, he receiving yearly his livery and £10 for fee and rewards during good behaviour.

Eleccio Joh'is Baldwyn in co'em servient' ad legem.

The same day, John Baldewyn was elected Serjeant-at-law *loco* Thomas Bryan.

Q'd plumbum clavi et Worstede hospitentur et vendant' apud Ledenhall.

The same day, it was ordained by the Mayor and Aldermen, with the assent of the Commonalty, that lead, nails, and cloth called "worstedes," which hitherto had been housed in "Bosomysyn"[3] and there privately sold as well to freemen as to foreigners, contrary to the liberty of the City, should thenceforth be housed and sold at the "Ledenhall,"[4] and nowhere else, under penalty of forfeiture, the owner of lead so housed paying to the Chamberlain one penny per piece until sold.

Consi'lis billa miss' fuit cuilibet Aldr'o.

"We charge and com'aunde you that a noon' after the sight of this ye do due serche to be made w'in your Warde of all maner suspecte persones logged and harboured w'in youre saide Warde And of al other of whom the cause of their beyng

---

[1] At the present day Sheriffs appoint their own Under-sheriffs for their year of office. In 1441 it had been decreed by the Common Council that thenceforth Under-sheriffs should remain in office during good behaviour, their frequent removal having caused much inconvenience and expense. See 'Cal. Letter-Book K,' p. 257.

[2] As to this office, see 'Cal. Letter-Book H,' pp. 122n., 132, 133.

[3] Or more correctly "Blossoms" Inn in St. Laurence Lane, so called from the family of Blosme. See 'Cal. Letter-Book F,' p. 136n. In 1456 it appears as "Bosum is Inne" ('Cal. of Wills, Court of Husting,' ii. 540). The name survives in Blossom Inn Yard.

[4] Stow ('Survey,' ed. Kingsford, i. 155-6) recites a petition of the Commonalty to the Common Council in 1503, praying that foreigners bringing lead, nails, ironwork, and "wolsteds," &c., to the City for sale may be compelled to bring the same to the open market of the Leadenhall, and not elsewhere, "like as of old time it hath beene used," under penalty of forfeiture. This petition does not appear to be recorded either in the City's Journal or Letter-Book of the day.

there is unknowen And that ye in al goodely hast have afore us the names of al theym So that we maye have knoulege of their rule and demeanyng And to make provision for the goode guydyng of theym in kepyng of the peas within youre saide Ward. Wreten &c." [No date.]

At a Common Council held on Wednesday, the 12th Oct., 3 Edward IV. [A.D. 1463], in the presence of Thomas Cook, the Mayor, Thomas Ursewyk, the Recorder, John Norman, William Marowe, William Hulyn, Richard Lee, Hugh Wyche, Matthew Philip, Ralph Josselyn, William Taillour, John Lambard, Richard Flemmyng, John Irlond, John Stokdon, William Costantyn, John Tate, Nicholas Marchall, Robert Basset, Aldermen, and an immense Commonalty, it was ordained that all latrines near " lez gitties " at Bridewell be destroyed before the Feast of All Saints [1 Nov.] next ensuing, under penalty of 100s.; and that those who had been charged with throwing filth into the Fleet ditch shall cleanse that part of the ditch adjacent to their premises before Christmas next, under penalty of £10.

Fo. 20.

Q'd latrine apud Brydes- well des- truantur.

The same day, it was ordained that the Basketmakers, Goldewiredrawers, and many other foreigners holding open shops in divers parts of the City, contrary to the liberty of the same, shall thenceforth cease to hold such shops within the liberty of the City, but live at Blancheappilton[1] so long as there are tenements enough there ; provided always that if a foreign [shopholder] shall then be inhabiting a house of the yearly value of 40s. or more, he shall reside at Blancheappilton before Easter next, if he wishes to remain in the City, and if the house be of lesser value, before Christmas next [if he wish to hold a shop and to remain in the City].[2]

Q'd lez Basket- makers et alii forincici [sic] tenentes shopas com'orent' apud Blanche- appelton'.

---

[1] In 1582 a tenement is recorded as situate in " Blanchapelton vel Marck- lane." Hust. Roll, 265 (73). It was a manor near Mark Lane, in part belonging to the family of Ros of Hamelake, and partly to the Bohuns, Earls of Hereford. See Stow's 'Survey' (ed. Kingsford), i. 149-50 ; ii. 294.

[2] In the ordinance as recorded in Journal 7, fo. 43, the Latin equiva- lent for the words here placed in brackets are omitted.

Eleccio Maioris.

The Feast of the Translation of St. Edward [13 Oct.], 3 Edward IV. [A.D. 1463], in the presence of Thomas Cook, the Mayor, the Prior of Christechurch, John Norman, William Marowe, William Hulyn, Richard Lee, Hugh Wiche, Matthew Philip, Ralph Josselyn, Thomas Oulegreve, William Taillour, Ralph Verney, John Stokker, Richard Flemmyng, John Lambard, John Walshae, George Irlond, John Stokton, William Costantyn, John Tate, William Hamptone, Nicholas Marchall, Robert Basset, Aldermen, Thomas Muschamp, one of the Sheriffs, and an immense Commonalty, summoned to the Guildhall for the election of a Mayor for the year ensuing—Matthew Philip was elected.

Afterwards, viz., on the Feast of SS. Simon and Jude [28 Oct.], he was sworn at the Guildhall, and on the morrow was presented, admitted, and accepted, &c., before the Barons of the Exchequer.

Nota de Amerciament' Cur' Maioris.

Friday, 14 Oct., 3 Edward IV. [A.D. 1463], ordinance made by Thomas Cook, the Mayor, and the Aldermen, that amercements of the Mayor's Court shall thenceforth be duly and faithfully levied, so that the Mayor for the time being shall receive yearly of the same the sum of 10 marks, in compensation for the money each Mayor had been accustomed to receive from foreign brokers practising in the City ;[1] and that the rest shall go to the Chamber to satisfy the [Aldermen in such things (*de rebus suis*) as they were accustomed yearly to receive from the Mayor. It was further ordained that the Common Clerk[2] for the time being shall deliver to the Serjeant [of the Chamber ?] extracts of such amercements, and shall receive the issues of the same, rendering account thereof to the Mayor and Auditors of the Chamber for the time being.

At a Common Council held on the 15th Oct., 3 Edward IV. [A.D. 1463], it was ordained by Thomas Cook, the Mayor, and the Aldermen, with the assent of the Commonalty, inasmuch as

---

[1] See 'Cal. Letter-Book H,' p. 350.

[2] It has already been noted (*supra*, p. 15n.) that the Town Clerk for the time being was *ex officio* Registrar of the Mayor's Court, and so continued down to 1801, when the office of Registrar was made an independent one.

many actions heretofore had been commenced in the Mayor's Court, some of them long pending and some not prosecuted to the end, with the intention that the prosecutor in such cases should take the opportunity of the absence of a defendant to recover judgment, that thenceforth any one commencing an action in the said Court, and not prosecuting his bill within a quarter of a year, should be amerced.

22 Oct., 3 Edward IV. [A.D. 1463], came John Alburgh, Robert Twygge, John Broun, Richard Syffe, mercers, into the Court of the lord the King in the Chamber of the Guildhall, before Thomas Cook, the Mayor, and the Aldermen, and entered into bond with Robert Colwych, the Chamberlain, in the sum of £308 for the delivery of a certain sum of money and jewels to the Chamberlain for the time being, to the use of William, son of John Lock, the same having been bequeathed to the said William by his father or accrued to him by the death of John his brother.

Fo. 20 b.

Custod' Will'i pueri Joh'is Lok.

25 Oct., 3 Edward IV. [A.D. 1463], came Elizabeth, widow of John Locke, late mercer, William Redknap, John Alburgh, and William Alburgh, mercers, into the Court of the lord the King, before Thomas Cook, the Mayor, and the Aldermen, and entered into bond with Robert Colwych, the Chamberlain, in the sum of £349 6s. 8d. for the delivery by the said Elizabeth of a certain sum of money and jewels to the Chamberlain for the time being, to the use of Rose and Anne, daughters of John Lock, on their marriage, the same having been bequeathed to them by their father, or accrued to them by the death of John their brother.[1]

Custod' Rose e Anne pueror' Joh'is Lok.

26 Oct., 3 Edward IV. [A.D. 1463], came John Alburgh, John Shelley, John Sturmyn, mercers, and Henry Toller, grocer, into the Court of the lord the King, before Thomas Cook, the Mayor, and the Aldermen, and entered into bond with Robert Colwych, the Chamberlain, in the sum of £382 13s. 4d. for the

Fo. 21.

Custod' Steph'i et Elizabethe pueror' Johannis Lok.

[1] Margin : a note to the effect that the above recognizance became void 4 Sept., 16 Edward IV. [A.D. 1476], inasmuch as ...... Cokkyn, gentleman, who married the above Elizabeth, received the money, &c., due to his wife by the hands of John Shelley, mercer.

delivery of a certain sum of money and jewels to the Chamberlain for the time being, to the use of Stephen and Elizabeth, children of John Lock, the same having been bequeathed to them by their father, or accrued to them by the death of John their brother.

16 Nov., 3 Edward IV. [A.D. 1463], Thomas Ludford, of Westminster, "scryvanere," condemned to stand on the pillory for forging a bond, whereby Robert Fenn, "clotheman," was falsely bound to John Broun, as well as other bonds.

At a Common Council held on Saturday, 15 Oct., 3 Edward IV. [A.D. 1463], it was ordained by Thomas Cook, the Mayor, John Norman, William Hulyn, Richard Lee, Hugh Wyche, Ralph Josselyne, William Taillour, Thomas Oulegreve, Richard Flemmyng, John Stokdone, William Costantyn, John Tate, Robert Basset, and Nicholas Marchall, Aldermen, with the consent of the Commonalty, that in future no one, denizen or foreign, shall act as broker in any contract or bargain within the City or liberty thereof under penalty of 100s.

16 Nov., 3 Edward IV. [A.D. 1463], came Thomas Bledlow, John Warde, John Clerk, grocers, William Rednapp, mercer, and Thomas Herward, draper, and entered into bond with Robert Colwych, the Chamberlain, in the sum of £324 3s. 11¾d., for the payment by the said Thomas Bledlow of a similar sum to the Chamberlain for the time being, to the use of Rose and Agnes, daughters of John Broun, when they come of age or marry, the same being their patrimony.

"Be it remembred that by Mathewe Philipp Maire Aldremen and Co'es of the Citee of London in theire Comune Consell holdene in the Yeldehall of the saide Citee the xxx day of Decembre the yeere of the reign of Kyng Edwarde the iiijth after the conquest the iij^{de} At the request praier and desire of the weldisposed blessed and devote woman Dame Agnes 'Foster '¹ for the ease and comfort and releef of al the powre

---

¹ Wife of Stephen "Forster," fishmonger, M.P. for the City, 1435 ; Alderman of Bread Street Ward, 1444-58 ; Sheriff, 1444-5 ; Mayor, 1454-5. Here is another instance of the title "Dame" being applied to one whose husband never received the honour of knighthood. For other instances see 'Cal. Letter-Book K,' p. 273n.

prysoners beyng in the Gaoles and countours of the saide Citee certeyn Articles[1] here after folowing concernyng the saide prisoners were made stablisshed enacted and ordeigned.

"First for asmoche as the custodye governaunce and kepyng of Neugate Ludgate and al other Gates and posternes of this Citee be longen to the Maire Aldremen and Comons of the saide Citee. Therfore by thauctorite aforesaid it is ordeigned that the Newark[2] now late edified by the saide Dame Agnes for for thenlargyng of the Prysone of Ludgate aforesaid frome hensfourth be hadde, repute, and takene as a parte and parcell of the saide prysone of Ludgate so that bothe the olde and the newe werke of Ludgate aforesaide be oone Prysone Gaole kepyng and charge for evermore.[3]

"Item it is ordeigned that all the ordenauncys made in the tymes of the Mairalties of William Staundone and Robert Chicheley late Mairys of the saide Citee entred in the Boke called K the lxxxx leef[4] concernyng the kepyng of the saide Gaole of Neugate and sillyng of vitaille in the same Gaole as brede, Flessh, Fyssh, Woode, Cooles, Candell, Ale, lampes and all other thinges to the saide prysoners necessarye or belongyng occupyng of beddis if the prysoners have couches puttyng in Irons of prysoners and fyndyng of Seurtees aswell for the performyng of þᵉ saide Ordenaunce as thise Articles folowing shall

[1] Articles, much to the same effect, were promulgated in 1488. *Vide infra*, fos. 245 b-247.

[2] New work.

[3] This passage is quoted by Stow ('Survey,' ed. Kingsford, i. 39) almost *verbatim*. He adds particulars of the new work here mentioned in the following terms :—"The said quadrant strongly builded of stone, by the before named Stephen Forster and Agnes his wife, containeth a large walking place by ground of 38 foot & halfe in length, besides the thicknesse of the walles, which are at the least sixe foote, makes all togither 44 foote and a halfe, the bredth within the walles is 29 foote and a half, so that the thicknesse of the walles maketh it 35 foote and a halfe in bredth. The like roome it hath over it for lodgings, and over it againe faire Leades to walke upon well imbattailed, all for fresh ayre, and ease of prisoners, to the ende they should have lodging and water free of charge."

[4] See 'Cal. Letter-Book K,' pp. 124-7. The ordinances, however, here referred to were made during the Mayoralty of Nicholas Wotton (1430-1) ; whereas Staundone was Mayor in 1392-3 and 1407-8 ; and Chichele in 1411-12 and 1421-2.

hereafter aswell extende to the kepyng, fees, sillyng of all suche maner of vitaille and other thinges to the saide prisoners behoofull beddis, Couches and puttyng in yrons of prysoners and fyndyng of Seurtees in, of, and for bothe the Countours and Ludgate as the saide Gaole of Neugate.

"Item it is ordayned that no Freman nor Frewoman[1] of this Citee nor any other honest persone committed unto Ludgate as prisoner paye no rent, tribute nor hire for his loggyng there but suche fees as been conteyned in the saide ordenaunces entred in the saide boke of K.

"Item it is ordeyned that no maner of Keper of any of the saide Gaole of Neugate, Ludgate nor eny of the Countours of the saide Citee take any more of any Gentilman, Freman or Frewoman of this Citee for their borde and bedde to be hadde of the saide Keper for a woke then iijs. nor of any persone beyng of thastate of a yoman for bedde and borde a woke thanne ijs. and if any suche Gentilman, Freman or Frewoman or eny of thastate of a yoman be inprisoned in any of the saide prisones by lasse space than a woke and havyng bedde and borde w^t the Keper of any of the saide prysones thanne the saide Gentilman, Freman or Frewoman shall pay after the rate of iijs. a woke and the persone of thastate of a yoman after the rate of ijs. a woke.

"Item it is ordeigned by the auctorite a foresaide that if any Keper of the saide Gaole Ludgate or Countours anythyng attempte, labour or doo contrary to the saide Ordenaunces and articles or any parcell of theym and thereof be duely convycte and atteynte by feithfull reporte of the iiij visitours to the Maire and Aldremen therof made that he at the first tyme pay unto the saide visitours for the tyme beyng xxs. at the seconde tyme xls. and at the thirdde tyme be discharged of the kepyng of all maner Gaoles and prisons within the saide Citee for þe space of v yeere thanne next immediately folowyng.

---

[1] Ludgate was specially provided as a prison for men and women who enjoyed the freedom of the City, and hence was known as *le Franche-prison*. See 'Cal. Letter-Book H,' p. 97n.

" Item it is ordeigned that every yeere in the Fest of Seint Mathew thappostel be chosen ij Curatys and ij Co'iers of the saide Citee to here the compleyntes of the prysoners in the saide Gaole and prisones and to knowe and understande howe the saide Articles and ordenaunces been observed and kepte, the almes and silver of the boxes of the saide Gaole and prysones been dispensed, for what cause every prisoner is there in-prisoned And to dispose the waters of the conduytes of the saide Gaoles of Neugate and prisone of Ludgate aforesaide And that it shalbe leefull at every tyme whanne it shall please the said Curattes and ij Co'iers to entere in to the saide Gaole and prysones for the causes a fore rehersed   Whereuppon by vertue of this ordinaunce been chosen Maister Thomas Ebrall,[1] Maister Edward Story,[2] Curattes, John Maldone and Thomas Dorchestre, Co'ers, for the yeere next ensuyng, &c."[3]

15 Jan., 3 Edward IV. [A.D. 1463-4]. came Elizabeth, widow of Richard Payne, late draper, and Richard Langton, draper, into the Court of the lord the King in the Chamber of the Guildhall, before Matthew Philipp, the Mayor, and the Alder-men, and acknowledged themselves bound to Robert Colwych, the Chamberlain, in the sum of £1,400 in place of the said Richard Payne, who had become surety for patrimony due to the children of Thomas Hawkyn (whose widow Margaret had married George Irland), as recorded in Book K, fo. 289.[4]

Fo. 23.

Securitas pro bonis legat' pueris Thome Hawkyn.

1ſ Jan., 3 Edward IV. [A.D. 1463-4], came Thomas Peersson, fishmonger, John Paryssh, " peautrer," Henry Chacombe, draper, and Richard Phippes, " stokfyshmonger," &c., and similarly entered into bond in the sum of £158, for the pay-ment of that sum into the Chamber, to the use of Thomas and

Custod' pueror' Edwardi Warmyngton.

---

[1] Rector of All Hallows, Honey Lane.
[2] Rector of All Hallows the Great. Fellow of Pembroke Hall, Camb., and Chancellor of the University ; Bishop of Carlisle, 1468 ; translated to Chichester, 1478; died 29 Jan., 1503 (Hennessy, 'Novum Reper-torium,' p. lix).

[3] In 1521, the yearly appointment of curates and commoners for the purpose here set out having been neglected for " a great seasoun," the Common Council decreed that thence-forth it should be duly carried out. Journal 12, fo. 147.
[4] See ' Cal. Letter - Book K,' pp. 378-9.

John, sons of Edward Warmyngton, late grocer, on their coming of age.

Fo. 23 b.

Custod' Rogeri Holbeche filii Rog' Holbeche Orphani Civitat'.

24 Jan., 3 Edward IV. [A.D. 1463-4], came Robert Mildenale, "gentilman," Thomas Humfray, "taillour," William Glademan, mercer, and Peter Bisshop, "peautrer," &c., and similarly entered into bond in the sum of £100, for the payment into the Chamber of the patrimony due to Roger, son of Roger Holbeche, late tailor, on his coming of age.

Fo. 24.

Concessio fact' Joh'i Walden Ald'ro.

3 Feb., 3 Edward IV. [A.D. 1463-4], grant by the Mayor and Aldermen to the venerable Alderman, John Walden, to continue to hold his mansion house (formerly the mansion house of John Reynwell)[1] for the term of his life at an annual rent of £20, with reversion, on his death, to his heirs and assigns for a term of two years.[2] No alienation to be made of the house without the consent of the Mayor and Aldermen. The Chamberlain for the time being to make all reasonable repairs both inside and outside the house, when requested by the tenant or his deputy.

Exon'acio custod' Beatricis filie Bertrandi "Saunx."

17 Feb., 3 Edward IV. [A.D. 1463-4], came John Beste, "taillour," and Beatrix his wife, daughter of Bartrand "Saunz," into the Court of the lord the King in the inner Chamber of the Guildhall, before Matthew Philipp, the Mayor, and the Aldermen, and acknowledged satisfaction for the sum of £20 bequeathed to the said Beatrix by her father. The said Mayor, Aldermen, and Chamberlain, as well as the sureties, viz., John Silvester, Richard Lokwood, John Cornysshe, John Abell, and John Bourton, saddlers, are therefore quit.

---

[1] Possibly the great house described by Stow as being situate in Dowgate Ward, and as sometime pertaining to John Reynwell, Fishmonger and Alderman, who made it over to the Mayor and Commonalty for pious uses. In 1475 the tenement was granted by the Mayor, &c., to the Hanse merchants, and was known as the Stalhof or Steelyard, and, sometimes, as *Gildehalda Teutonicorum.*

Stow's 'Survey' (ed. Kingsford), i. 234; ii. 319. Cf. *infra*, fo. 108 b.

[2] Walden dying shortly after the date of this grant, his widow and executrix Margaret, in the following September, surrendered her interest in the tenement to the Mayor and Aldermen, and received in return a lease of the same for a term of four years at the same rent as before. *Infra*, fo. 32.

10 Feb., 3 Edward IV. [A.D. 1463-]4, Alan Johnson, tailor, discharged by Matthew Philipp, the Mayor, and the Aldermen from serving on juries, &c., owing to increasing old age.

Exon'acio Alani Johnson ab assisis.

21 Jan., 3 Edward IV. [A.D. 1463-4], William Bulwyk, grocer, similarly discharged for like cause.

Exon'acio Will'i Bulwyk ab assisis.

" Be it remembred that for the renuyng and new exercisyng of the market to be hadde at Quenehithe convenietly as it hath ben in dayes passed for the wele and ease of the substaunce of the Comons of the Citee of London   The which market be inconvenienticis that hath fallen by the Brigge and otherwise hath ben withdrawen to the grete hurt of moche people in manyfold wise   It was ordeigned enacted and establisshed by Mathew Philipp Maire, John Norman, William Marowe, William Hulyn, Richard Lee, Thomas Cook, John Walden, William Taillour, Thomas Oulegreve, John Stokker, Rauff Verney, Richard Flemmyng, George Irland, John Stokdon, William Costantyn, John Tate, Nicholas Marchall, Aldremen of the Citee of London, with thassent of þe comons in their Comon Counsell in the Chambre of the Yeldehall the xth day of the moneth of Februar' the iij^{de} yeere of the reign of Kyng Edward the iiijth [A.D. 1463-4] holden assembled   That Almaner Shippes Bottes and other vesselles grete and smale resortyng to the Citee of London with vitaille to be solde to retaile shalbe demeaned in puttyng to sale of the same by thadvise and commaundement of the Maire of the saide Citee for the tyme beyng in maner and fourme that foloweth perpetuely to endure, that is to say, that if ther come or resorte to the said Citee but oone Shipp, bote, or other vessell at a tyme w^t any vitaill or vitailles þ^t is to say Salt, Whete, Rye or other Corn that com from beyonde the See, or other Graynes, Garlik, Oynouns, Heryng, Sprottes, Elys, Whityng, Places, Coddes, pagan'¹ Makarell, Pigell',² Heryng, or any other vitaill or w^t ij or iij soortes

Fo. 24 b.

Ordinacio fac't pro novo mercat' k'end' apud Quenehith.

---

¹ Stow (' Survey,' ed. Kingsford, ii. 9-10), who gives a brief abstract of these regulations, made, doubtless, from the Letter-Book, omits this word ; possibly on account of its having presented the same difficulty of interpretation to him as it does to the present editor.

² Possibly meaning Pig, or pig-nosed eel.

of any of the saide vitail to be put to sale and retailled in þe water, the same Shipp, bote or vessell shall goo to Quenehith, and ther make the sale of þᵗ vitail or vitailles soo beyng in that Shipp or oþer Bote or Vessell. And if ther come ij Shippes, botes or oþ' ij vessell wᵗ oone manere of any of the saide vitaille, that oon therof shal resorte to Billyngesgate and that other to Quenehith. And if þer come iij Shippes, bote or other iij vessell wᵗ oone maner of any of the saide vitaille ij of them to Quenehith and the iijᵈᵉ to Billyngesgate And if ther come iiij shippes, botes or oþ' iiij vessell wᵗ oon manere of any of the saide vitaille ij of them to Billyngesgate and ij to Quenehith And if ther come v Shippes, botes or vessell of oone manere of any of the saide vitaille iij of them to Quenehith and ij of them to Billyngesgate And if ther come vj Shippes, botes, or other vessell wᵗ oon manere of the said vitaille iij of them to Billyngesgate and iij of them to Quenehith and so upward after the Rate of the noumber of Shippes, botes or oþ' vessell of oon manere vitaille that so shal come or resorte in to Thamise to be departed to the saide Billyngesgate and Quenehith as is afore-saide Forseen alwey that if ther come eny grete Shippes with Salt or any other vitaille in to Thamise fro the Baye[1] or any other place that may not come to any of the saide Keys for his discharge or sale therof That thanne the marchaunt or mar-chauntes, owner or owners of suche maner Shipp and salt or any other manere vitaill that dischargith by lighter bote or any other vessell shalbe demeaned in puttyng to sale by the wey of Retaill therof in their lighters or other vessell at the saide Keys in manere and fourme as is afore declared in other Shippes botes or other vessell that may in them selff resorte to the saide Keys And that the owners of suche Shippes or vitaille so comyng or Resortyng to the saide Citee shal make and drawe theire lottes by the oversight of the Maire for the tyme beyng among them self which of them shall passe through the Brigge to Quenehith, and which shal abide at Billyngesgate or þᵗ any price be sette to the sale upon any of the saide vitaille by the Maire for the tyme beyng at any of the saide Keys.

---

[1] Bay of Biscay.

" Forthermore that whanne and as ofte as the Ele Shippes resorten to the saide Citee that the half of the noumbre of the said Shippes or suche parte of them as after the Rate and fourme abovesaid is expressed shal passe through the Brigge of the saide Citee and be at Roode[1] oon the West side of the Brigge afore Merlowes Keye[2] or ellswhere oon the same side and the residue to remayne and abide on the Esteside of the saide Brigge and the owners of the saide Shippes so beyng oon the West side of the saide Brigge afore Merlowes Key or elles where shall daily towe their same Shippes to þe same Key and there to make their weying and sale of their Elis and to resorte nyghtly in to þe streme ageyn if they lust Or ell' if the owners woll not towe theire saide Shippes to the saide Key they them selff shall fynde Botes at theire owne costes to convey the people to theire saide Shippes and fro the same to bye theire saide Elys and in like wise to be ordeyned for the Shippes remaynyng oon the Estside of the saide Brigge And that there be oone Weyer ordeyned and assigned for the saide Shippes remaynyng oone the Estside of the saide Brigge and a nother for the Shippes ridyng oone the West side of the saide Brigge And that the water bailly for the tyme beyng shal in his owne personne make due serche in every of the saide Shippes every day before the tyme of weying for and as many of Elis called Kempes or rede Elis as they can fynde of them and cast them in to Thamise upon a payne to þe rered upon him by the discrecion of the Maire as ofte as any other manne can fynde the contrary And that ther be taken more diligent oversight of the sortes of them so that they be of suche gretenes and lenght as of olde tyme hath bene accustumed and as it is enrolled in the Chamber of the Yeldehall.

Fo. 25.

" Also that the owners of all the Risshe Botes that from hensforth shall resorte to this Citee shal have utterance and sale of theire Risshes in the places hereafter folowing that is

---

[1] Be at anchor or ride.
[2] Named after Richard Marlow, ironmonger, a native of Great Marlow, co. Bucks, and benefactor to the Ward of Queenhithe. ' Cal. of Wills.' ii. 428-9 ; Stow, ' Survey' (ed. Kingsford), ii. 5.

to sey atte Watergate, at Towre, at Botulphes Warff, Dougate, Pouleswarff, Baynardes castell, Fletebrigge and Tempelbrigge[1] and in noon other place. Provided alweys that the owners of the saide Risshe botes pay unto the Chamberleyn of London for the tyme beyng as it hath been accustumed in tymes passed at Quenehith and at oþ' places where Risshes have been solde to pay And that the grete Poste standyng at Quenehith aforesaide lettyng Shippes be drawen up And that the Chamb'leyn and other possessours of the Groundes and live-lodes a bowte the same Quenehith in hasty tyme every personne after his rate do to be clensed the saide hithe of all filth, bi the which the vessels thider resortyng may have their easy comyng yn And that þᵉ Carters and porters be compelled to serve the people in their Cariages and Portages from hensfourth as it is enacted in the Chambre of the Yeldehall."

Ordinauns of Foreyn "Husters." By the same Common Council it was ordained that no foreign huckster of beer or ale should sell by retail after the Feast of the Annunciation [25 March].

Custod pueror Thome Bristall. 28 Feb., 3 Edward IV. [A.D. 1463-4], came Margery, widow of Thomas Bristall, fishmonger, Robert Tooke, "irmonger," Stephen Wolff [and] William Bristall, fishmongers, into the Court of the lord the King in the Chamber of the Guildhall, before Matthew Philipp, the Mayor, and the Aldermen, and entered into bond with Robert Colwych, the Chamberlain, in the sum of £20 for the delivery into the Chamber of certain money and household goods to the use of Johanna and Margaret, daughters of the said Thomas Bristall, on their coming of age or marrying.

Fo. 25 b.

Custoa'jueror Joh'is Broun. 16 March, 4 Edward IV. [A.D. 1463-4], came Thomas Bledlow, grocer, John Maldone, grocer, William Redknappe, Stephen Stychemerssh, Robert Talbot, mercers, [and] Hugh

---

[1] Temple Bridge or Temple Stairs, a landing-place built on piles extending well into the Thames. Old writers not infrequently wrote of Lambeth Bridge at a time when there was no bridge, but only landing stairs to the ferry. Thus Archbishop Parker writes in 1568 of Queen Elizabeth "coming by Lambeth bridge into the fields, and I according to duty meeting her on the bridge." 'Correspondence of Matthew Parker, D.D., 1535-1575' (Cambr. Univ. Press, 1853), p. 311.

Brice, goldsmith, and similarly entered into bond in the sum of £383 6s. 8d. for payment into the Chamber of a like sum, to the use of Rose and Agnes, daughters of John Broun, pursuant to the will of Stephen Broun, their grandfather.[1] Mention made of another daughter of the said John named Katherine, then deceased.

The same day came William Haydok, grocer, John Brampton, fishmonger, John Fabian, draper, and Richard Awbrey, haberdasher, and entered into bond in the sum of £83 6s. 8d., which sum, together with the sum of £383 6s. 8d. in the hands of the above Thomas Bledlow, had been committed to him by the Mayor and Aldermen in trust for Rose, Agnes, and Katherine (then deceased), daughters of the above John Broun.

Fo. 26.

Custod' bonor' Rose et Agnetis filiar' Joh'is Broun.

27 March, 4 Edward IV. [A.D. 1464], William Heyman, merchant of the Hanse of Almaine, condemned by Matthew Philipp, the Mayor, and the Aldermen to forfeit five lasts of herring which he had deceitfully packed, mixing old with new, to the use of the prisoners in Neugate and Ludgate, and, further, to pay a fine of £20.

Fo. 26 b.

Finis pro fals' paccione allec'.

16 April, 4 Edward IV. [A.D. 1464], came John Ferley, Thomas Bernewey, William Stokker, John Pake, junior, drapers, and entered into bond in the sum of £100 for payment into the Chamber of the sum of £80, to be equally divided between Almeric, Thomas, Robert, and Margaret, children of Thomas Colby, late draper, when they come of age or marry.

Custod' pueror' Thome Colby pannarii.

24 April, 4 Edward IV. [A.D. 1464], came Richard Phippes, Thomas Pierson, Edmund Newman, fishmongers, and John Pareys, "peautrer," and entered into bond in the sum of £70 for the delivery into the Chamber of certain money and chattels to the use of William, Agnes, Margery, Elizabeth, and Alice, children of the late William Luke, at times specified.

Fo. 27.

Custod' pueror' Will'mi Luke pandoxatoris.

---

[1] See the will of Stephen Broun, grocer, dated 28 April, 1462, but not proved and enrolled in the Husting until February, 1466. 'Cal. of Wills,' ii. 553-4.

E

Fo. 27 b.

Custod'
pueror' Will'i
Luke civis
et Pandoxa-
toris London'.

26 April, 4 Edward IV. [A.D. 1464], came Edward Luke, "bruer," William Wake, waxchandler, Thomas Tymeo, "taillour," John Frankelyn, "bruer," and William Pynde, draper, and entered into bond in the sum of 50 marks for payment into the Chamber of 40 marks, to the use of Elizabeth and Alice, daughters of William Luke, late brewer, at times specified.

Fo. 28.

Custod'
pueror' Thome
Plomer civis
et scriptor'
London'.

4 May, 4 Edward IV. [A.D. 1464], came Alice, late wife of Thomas Plomer, scrivener, John Edward, salter, Thomas Bevill, haberdasher, and John Stapleton, grocer, and entered into bond in the sum of 100 marks for the payment into the Chamber of the sum of 80 marks, to be equally divided among Agnes, Margaret, and Thomas, children of the said Thomas Plomer, when they arrive at a certain age or marry.

Fo. 28 b.

Custod'
pueror' Thome
Carter civis et
coriour
London'.

9 May, 4 Edward IV. [A.D. 1464], came Johanna, late wife of Thomas Carter, "coriour," John Stoundon, Nicholas Hyne, "coriours," and John Arnold, "lethersiller," and entered into bond in the sum of 100 marks for the payment of 10 marks respectively and the delivery of divers chattels to Johanna, Margery, and Clemence, daughters of the said Thomas Carter, when they come of age or marry. The chattels comprise silver spoons, a flat piece (*peciam planam*) of silver of "Parys," a primer with silver clasps,[1] a "bolle pece," and a piece of silver "chased."

Fo. 29.

Custod'
pueror' Thome
Ernest civis
et aur'
London'.

14 May, 4 Edward IV. [A.D. 1464], came Walter Mettyngham, "gentilman," who married Alice, widow of Thomas Ernest, goldsmith, Robert Clebery, vintner, and William Philipp, goldsmith, and entered into bond in the sum of £30 for the payment into the Chamber of a like sum when Matthew, son of the said Thomas Ernest, shall have come of age.

Exon'acio
Walt'i
"Brens" ab
assisis.

28 April, 4 Edward IV. [A.D. 1464], Walter "Bren," "irmonger," discharged by Matthew Philipp, the Mayor, and the Aldermen, from serving on juries, &c., owing to increasing old age.

Exon'acio
Ric'i Selwod
bassis'.

7 May, 4 Edward IV. [A.D. 1464], Richard Selwod, skinner, similarly discharged for like cause.

---

[1] *Unum primarium cum clapsis de argento.* Cf. *supra*, p. 5.

2 June, 4 Edward IV. [A.D. 1464], John Miles, "sporiour," similarly discharged on account of infirmities.

Exon'acio Joh'is Miles ab assis'.

15 May, 4 Edward IV. [A.D. 1464], decree by Matthew Philipp, the Mayor, William Marowe, William Hulyn, Richard Lee, Thomas Cook, Hugh Wiche, William Taillour, Ralph Verney, Thomas Oulegreve, William Hamptone, Robert Basset, Nicholas Marchall, and John Tate, Aldermen, with the assent of Dame[1] Anne, widow of Geoffrey Boleyn, Alderman,[2] and of Ralph Verney, one of the executors of the said Geoffrey, that a certain bond entered into by William Redknappe, mercer, on the 14th April, anno 2 Edward IV. [A.D. 1462], in a controversy with the said Geoffrey Boleyn touching the abatement of a chimney,[3] should be cancelled.

Exon'acio Will'i Redknappe de quadam recogn'.

15 May, 4 Edward IV. [A.D. 1464], ordinance by Matthew Philipp, the Mayor, the Recorder, William Marowe, William Hulyn, Richard Lee, Hugh Wiche, Thomas Cook, William Taillour, Ralph Verney, Thomas Oulegreve, William Hamptone, Robert Basset, Nicholas Marchall, and John Tate, Aldermen, in their whole Court in the inner Chamber of the Guildhall, that the composition made between the Cordewaners and Cobelers anno 12 Henry IV., and recorded in Letter-Book I, fo. 106,[4] be carried into execution under penalty, and that the Chamberlain should levy the fines on those "Cobillers" who had broken the composition by "makyng of crochettes and lappys of new lether and in medelyng of new lether with olde otherwise than it is in the saide composicioun conteyned."

Fo. 29 b.

Judicium redditum int' Cordewaners et Cobillers.

23 May, 4 Edward IV. [A.D. 1464], came Elena, widow of Edmund Donybat, late fruiterer, William Cardemaker, grocer, and Thomas Rumbald, mercer, and entered into bond in the sum of 50 marks for the payment into the Chamber of

Custod' Alicie Donybat filie Edmundi Donybat orph' Civitat'.

---

[1] Another instance of the assumption of the title "Dame" by one who had strictly no legal right to it.

[2] Of Castle Baynard Ward 1452-1457; of Bassishaw from 1457 until his death in 1463; Sheriff 1446-7; Mayor 1457-8. His grandson, Sir Thomas Boleyn, was father of Anne Boleyn, sometime wife of King Henry VIII.

[3] Cf. *supra*, p. 19.

[4] 'Cal. Letter-Book I,' p. 96.

40 marks to the use of Alice, daughter of the said Edmund
Donybat, when she comes of age or marries.

28 May, 4 Edward IV. [A.D. 1464], came good men, exercising
the mistery of Berebruers, into the Court of the lord the King
in the Chamber of the Guildhall, before Matthew Philipp, the
Mayor, William Marowe, Richard Lee, John Waldene, William
Taillour, Ralph Verney, Thomas Oulegreve, Robert Basset,
William Hamptone, John Stoktone, John Tate, Nicholas Marchall, Aldermen, and presented the following petition :—

"To the full honorable lord the Maire and Worshipfull
soveraignes the Aldermen of the Citee of London

"Shewen mekely unto youre goode Lordshipp and maistershippes the goode folke of this famous Citee the which usen
Berebruyng within the same that where all Mistiers and Craftys
of the saide Citee have rules and ordenaunces by youre grete
auctoritees for the comon wele of this honorable Citee made
and profite of the same Craftys So that every Craft shulde be
demeaned as trouth and goode conscience requiren in eschuyng
of all falsehode and untrouth   But as for bruers of Bere as yet
beene none Ordenaunces nor Rules by youre auctorites made
for the comon wele of the saide Citee for the demeanyng of the
same Mistiere of Berebruers For lacke of which ordenaunces
and rules the people of this Citee myght be gretely disceyved
as in mesure of Barelles Kilderkyns and Firkyns and in hoppes
and in other Greynes the whiche to the saide Mistiere apper-
teynen   Forasmoche as they have not ordenaunces ne Rules
set amongis theym like as other occupacions have It is surmysed
upon theym that often tymes they make theire Bere of unseasonable malt the which is of litle prise and unholsome for
mannes body for theire singuler availe Forasmoche as the
comon people for lacke of experience can not knowe the perfit-
nesse of Bere aswele as of the Ale   Please it therfore youre
saide lordshipp and Maistershippes the premisses tenderly
considered to enact and establisshe that from hensforth no man
of what degre or condicion he be take upon hym to sill any
Bere within the Citee of London by Barelles Kilderkyns or
Firkyns but if the barell and other vessell conteigne after the

assise accordyng to an Acte late made by the Auctorite of a Comon Councell entred of Recorde in the Cambre [sic] of the Yeldehall that is for to say the Barell xxxvi galons, the Kilderkyn xviii galons and the Firkyn ix galons[1] upon payne of forfature of þe same vessell and for to lose vjs. viijd. as ofte as hee so dothe that oone half to the Chambre of London and that other half to theym that shall presente it   And also that no manne nether Freman nor foreyn take upon hym to brewe any Bere or sill any Bere wtin the Citee aforesaide or brew Bere out of this Citee and sil it unto any personne of the saide Citee to be dronke wtin the same but if it be made of sesonable malt hoppes and other greynes the which to the saide Mistier apperteignen and holsome for mannes body upon payne of forfature of the same Bere made contrary to this ordenaunce in whos handys it shalbe founde and to lose xiijs. iiijd. to be devided as the saide vjs. viijd. as ofte as he so is takyn in defaut   And furthermore that yerly from hensfourth of the feleashippe of Berebruers wtin the Citee of London and to the Citee servyng ij sufficiaunt and able persones occupying the saide Mistere of Berebruers by the Maire and Aldermen for the tyme beyng be chosen and sworn duly and treuly wt the Chamberleyn for the tyme beyng or ell' wt an officer by the Maier to theym assigned to serche and present all the defautes[2] to the Chambirleyn and the names of all that dothe contrary to this ordenaunce."

The above articles approved and ordered to be placed on record.

Letter from Matthew Philipp, the Mayor, and Robert Colwich, the Chamberlain, to Thomas [Kempe], Bishop of London, presenting Master Thomas Bame, chaplain, for admission to one of the five chantries founded in the Chapel of the B. Mary near the Guildhall by Adam Fraunceys and Henry Frowyk, vacant by the death of Sir Walter Cheseman. Dated 13 June, A.D. 1464.

Fo. 30 b.

Presentacio Tho'e Bame ad quamdam Cantar' quinq' Cantariar' in capella b'te Mie juxta Guihald'.

---

[1] In 1420 the Coopers, who were sworn to examine the measures used by brewers, were charged not to place their marks upon any barrel containing less than 30 gallons, or any kilderkin of less than 15 gallons. 'Cal. Letter-Book I,' p. 237.

[2] Officers known down to the present day as Ale-conners. Cf. 'Cal. Letter-Book H,' p. 71.

[Fos. 30 b, 31, two orphans' recognizances recorded, but annulled, because again recorded later on.]

Fo. 31 b.

Custod' Alicie filie Galfridi Boleyn orph' Civitatis.

24 July, 4 Edward IV. [A.D. 1464], came William Wellys, William Redknappe, John Shelley, Robert Gregory, and John Broun, mercers, and entered into bond in the sum of £696 13s. 4d. for the delivery into the Chamber of a like sum and certain jewels of the value of £30 to the use of Alice, daughter of Geoffrey Boleyn, late Alderman, when she arrives at the age of 25 years or marries.

Br'e d'ni Reg' pro Moneta.

Writ to the Sheriffs to make proclamation to the effect that those bringing silver in "bolion," plate, or otherwise, to the King's Mint at the Tower, should thenceforth receive 33s. sterling for every pound weight of silver, instead of 29s. as heretofore. Witness the King at "Stampford," 13 Aug., 4 Edward IV. [A.D. 1464].[1]

Fo. 32.

Concess' fact' Margarete Walden de quadam domo.

7 Sept., 4 Edward IV. [A.D. 1464], came Margaret, widow and executrix of John Walden, late Alderman, and surrendered her estate and interest in the tenement granted to her late husband in the preceding February. Thereupon the Mayor and Aldermen granted her a lease of the same tenement for a term of 4 years at the same rent as formerly.[2]

Custod' Rob'ti filii Joh'is Kynton orphani Civitat'.

27 Aug., 4 Edward IV. [A.D. 1464], came William Mannyng and John Mannyng, haberdashers, John Potteman, "taillour," and James Rome, "marbuler," and entered into bond in the sum of £20 for payment into the Chamber of a like sum to the use of Robert, son of John Kynton, late "wyirdrawer," on his coming of age.

Fo. 32 b.

Exon'acio Will'i Bretoun ab assis'.

26 Oct., 4 Edward IV. [A.D. 1464], William Bretoun, grocer, discharged from serving on juries, &c., owing to increasing old age.

Exon'acio Thome Bret aur' ab assis'.

26 Oct., the same year, Thomas Bret, goldsmith, similarly discharged for like cause.

Fo. 33.

Custod' Ric'i Claver filii Ric'i Claver orph' Civitat'.

31 Aug., 4 Edward IV. [A.D. 1464], came Alice, widow of Richard Claver, late mercer, John Norlong, William Pratte, and Ralph Kempe, mercers, and entered into bond in the sum

---

[1] Cf. Ruding, 'Annals of the Coinage,' ii. 32.

[2] Cf. *supra*, p. 44.

of 200 marks for the payment into the Chamber of a like sum to the use of Richard, son of the said Richard Claver, on his coming of age.

19 Sept., 4 Edward IV. [A.D. 1464], decree by the Mayor and Aldermen that the Vicar of Gillyngham, co. Kent, shall receive yearly from the Chamberlain the sum of 5 marks for the exhibition of a priest, provided he find a suitable one, to celebrate for the soul of John Philpot, Knt., in accordance with the terms of his will;[1] and further, that the said vicar shall be paid 5 marks which were in arrear.

Concess' fact' Vicar' de Gillyngham quinque marc'.

The Feast of St. Matthew [21 Sept.], 4 Edward IV. [A.D. 1464], in the presence of Matthew Philipp, the Mayor, Thomas Ursewyk, the Recorder, John Norman, William Marowe, William Hulyn, Hugh Wiche, Thomas Oulegreve, William Taillour, John Yong, George Irlond, John Stoktone, William Hamptone, Nicholas Marchal, Humphrey Hayford, Robert Basset, Aldermen, Thomas Muschamp, Sheriff of the City, and very many Commoners summoned to the Guildhall for the election of Sheriffs—John Tate was elected one of the Sheriffs of London and Middlesex by the Mayor, and John Stone, tailor, was elected the other Sheriff by the Commonalty.

Fo. 33 b.

Eleccio Vicecomit'.

The same day, Robert Colwich, tailor, was elected Chamberlain for the year ensuing ; Peter Alfold and Peter Calcot were elected Wardens of London Bridge; Ralph Josselyn, Ralph Verney, Aldermen, John Aleyn, goldsmith, William Persone, "taillour," John Stone, "taillour," and Richard Frome, skinner, Commoners, were elected Auditors of the accounts of the Chamber and of the Wardens of London Bridge in arrear.

Afterwards, viz., on the eve of St. Michael [29 Sept.], the said Sheriffs were sworn at the Guildhall, and on the morrow of the said Feast were presented and admitted before the Barons of the Exchequer.

[1] See his will, dated Nov., 1381, and proved and enrolled in the Court of Husting in July, 1382. 'Cal. of Wills,' ii. 275.

Ordinacio de servientib' et clericis. Vicec'.

At a Common Council held on Tuesday, the 25th Sept., 4 Edward IV. [A.D. 1464], it was decreed that the ordinance made *temp.* William Gregory, Mayor, touching Sheriffs, their Clerks and Serjeants,[1] should be thenceforth duly observed ; and further, that the said ordinance be yearly read at the Common Council next held after the Feast of St. Matthew [21 Sept.], so that it may be known whether the outgoing Sheriffs had observed it or not.

Custod' pueror' Will'i Knot Cissoris orphan' Civitatis.

9 Oct., 4 Edward IV. [A.D. 1464], came William Parker, " taillour,'' William Persone, " taillour,'' Thomas George, saddler, and John Lewes, dyer, and entered into bond in the sum of 140 marks for the payment into the Chamber of 20 marks respectively to the use of Richard, John, Edward, and Thomas, sons of William Knot, senior, late tailor, on their coming of age ; and a similar sum, together with divers chattels, to Mary and Alianora, daughters of the said William Knot, on their coming of age or marriage.

Fo. 34.

Eleccio Maioris.

The Feast of the Translation of St. Edward [13 Oct.], 4 Edward IV. [A.D. 1464], in the presence of Matthew Philipp, the Mayor, the Prior of Christchurch, John Norman, William Hulyn, Richard Lee, Thomas Cook, Thomas Oulegreve, Ralph Verney, William Taillour, John Yong, John Lambart, George Irlond, John Walsha, William Hamptone, Robert Basset, John Stokdone, William Costantyn, John Tate, Nicholas Marchall, Humphrey Hayford, and William Edward, Aldermen, John Stone, Sheriff, and an immense Commonalty, summoned to the Guildhall for the election of a Mayor for the year ensuing— Ralph Josselyn was elected Mayor.

Afterwards, viz., on the Feast of SS. Simon and Jude [28 Oct.], he was sworn at the Guildhall, and on the morrow was presented, admitted, and accepted before the Barons of the Exchequer.

Custod' pueror' Mathei Hall au' orphan' Civitat'.

24 Oct., 4 Edward IV. [A.D. 1464], came John Aleyn, Thomas Stirelond, Richard Messenger, and John Savery, goldsmiths, and entered into bond in the sum of 200 marks for the payment

---

[1] See 'Cal. Letter-Book K,' pp. 345-7. Also cf. *supra*, p. 13 ; *infra*, fo. 221 b.

into the Chamber of the sum of 100 marks, to the use respectively of Katherine and Johanna, daughters of Matthew Hall, late goldsmith, on their coming of age or marriage.

A general proclamation touching the assise of measures, forestalling of victuals and merchandise, the assignment of market-places for poulterers, the obstruction of streets with rubbish, and other matters. No date.

Fos. 34 b-35.
*Proclamacio
Magna.*

17 Dec., 5 Edward IV. [A.D. 1465], ordinance by the Mayor and Aldermen that foreign fruiterers shall sell their fruit in the places assigned, on Monday, Wednesday, Friday, and Saturday, notwithstanding the ordinance made *temp.* Thomas Coke, Mayor, on the 20th Oct., 3 Edward IV. [A.D. 1463].[1]

Fo. 35.
*Ordinacio
q'd Fruterers
forinseci ven-
dant fructus
suos per iiijᵒʳ
dies in sep-
timanar.*

19 Feb., 4 Edward IV. [A.D. 1464-5], Nicholas Boile, draper, discharged by Ralph Josselyn, the Mayor, and the Aldermen, from serving on juries, &c., owing to increasing old age.

Fo. 35 b.
*Exon'acio
Nich'i Boile
ab assis'.*

20 Dec., 4 Edward IV. [A.D. 1464], came John Ferley, Thomas Bernewey, John Pake, and William Stokker, drapers, and entered into bond in the sum of £20 for payment into the Chamber of a like sum, to the use of Thomas and Robert, sons of Thomas Colby, on their coming of age, the said money being their patrimony, their sister Elizabeth being deceased.

*Custod' pue-
ror' Thome
Colby orph'
Civitatis.*

10 Jan., 4 Edward IV. [A.D. 1464-5], came Robert Wilkynson, Robert Toke, John Saverey, "irmongers," and William Baldewyn, "sherman," and entered into bond in the sum of £20 for payment into the Chamber of a like sum, to the use of Richard, son of Richard Holbeche, on his coming of age.

Fo. 36.
*Custod' Ric'i
Holbeche filii
Ric'i Holbeche
orph' Civitatis.*

12 Feb., 4 Edward IV. [A.D. 1464-5], came Thomas Herward, Thomas Tymcot, drapers, Thomas Bledlow, grocer, and Robert Broun, "irmonger," and entered into bond in the sum of £200 for the payment of a like sum into the Chamber, to the use of Thomas, son of Thomas Eyre, deceased, on his arriving at the age of 24 years.

*Custod' Thome
Eyre fil'
Thome Eyre
orph' Civitat'.*

16 Feb., 4 Edward IV. [A.D. 1464-5], came Robert Miller, Henry Parnesse, drapers, Thomas Brice, mercer, and William Birde, "sadiller," and entered into bond in the sum of £100 for the payment into the Chamber of a like sum to the use of

Fo. 36 b.
*Custod' Thome
Eyre filii
Thome Eyre
orphani Civit'.*

[1] *Vide supra*, p. 33.

Thomas, son of Thomas Eyre, on his arriving at the age of 24 years.

Exon'acio cus-
tod' honor' Rose
et Agnet' filiar'
Joh'is Broun.

5 March, 5 Edward IV. [A.D. 1464-5], came Peter Pekham and Agnes his wife, administrators of the goods of Rose and Agnes, daughters of John Broun, into the Court of the lord the King in the Chamber of the Guildhall, before Ralph Josselyn, the Mayor, and the Aldermen, and acknowledged satisfaction for the sum of £324 3s. 11¾d., being a third part of the goods and chattels of the said John Broun, and appertaining to the said Rose and Agnes when alive, according to the custom of the City. Thereupon Thomas Bledlowe, John Warde, John Clerk, William Redknappe, and Thomas Herward are made quit.

Fo. 37.

Custod' Mar-
geric filie Joh'is
Strete auri-
fabri orphane
Civitatis.

8 March, 5 Edward IV. [A.D. 1464-5], came John Lynne, " wolman," Averey Corneborowe, " irmonger," John Aleyn and Roger Spenser, goldsmiths, and entered into bond in the sum of 100 marks for the payment into the Chamber of a like sum, to the use of Margery, daughter of John Strete, late goldsmith, on her coming of age or marriage.

Custod' pue-
ror' Ric'i Birde
orph'. Civitat'.

14 March, the same year, came Thomas Dalstone, glover, William Hynkersell, grocer, and William Pewall, " barbour," and acknowledged themselves bound in the sum of £20 for the payment into the Chamber of the sum of £3 6s. 8d. to the use of Stephen and John, sons of Richard Birde, late "talugh-chaundeler," respectively, on their coming of age, and a like sum to the use of Johanna, daughter of the said Richard, on her coming of age or marriage.

Fo. 37 b.

Exon'acio
Clement' Rus-
sell ab assis'.

15 March, the same year, Clement Russell, cordwainer, discharged from serving on juries, &c., owing to increasing old age.

"By the Kyng to oure Right trusty and welbeloved the Maire of oure Citee of London.

Litt'a sub pri-
vato sigillo pro
Coronac' Eliza-
beth' Regine.

"Right trusty and welbeloved We grete you wele. And Forasmoche as we have certainly appoynted and concluded the Coronacion of our moost dere and moost entierly beloved wiff

the Quene[1] to be at our palois at Westm' upon the Sonday
before Witsonday next comyng we woll and pray you that at
the saide day and place ye for that cause yeve your personell
attendaunce theire in suche apparell as is according to youre
astate and honour. And that ye leve not this in any wise.
Yevene under oure pryve seal at oure Manoir of Shene the
xiij day of Aprill."

16 May, 5 Edward IV. [A.D. 1465], came Isabella, widow of
John Riche, mercer, John Reynkyn, John Marchall, and Thomas
Riche, mercers, and entered into bond in the sum of 500 marks
for the payment into the Chamber of a like sum, to the use of
Thomas, son of the said John Riche, on his coming of age.

Fo. 38.

Custod' Thome Riche filii Joh'is Riche orphani Civitat'.

The same day, the said Isabella and the rest entered into
bond in the sum of 1,000 marks for the payment into the
Chamber of a like sum, to the use of John, son of John Malvern,
late haberdasher, on his coming of age.

Custod' Joh'is Malvern filii Joh'is Malvern orphani Civitatis.

25 June, 5 Edward IV. [A.D. 1465], came William Maryner,
William Horn, John Edward, and Thomas Houghton, salters,
and entered into bond in the sum of £26 for delivery into the
Chamber of 10 marks and divers chattels, to the use of George,
John, and Margaret, children of John Grene, respectively.

Fo. 38 b.

Custod' pueror' Joh'is Grene orph' Civitatis.

18 July, 5 Edward IV. [A.D. 1465], grant by Ralph Josselyn,
the Mayor, and the Aldermen that John Stokker, the Common
Hunt, shall receive yearly 5 marks besides his fee on account
of his services. The grant not to be drawn into precedent.

Fo. 39.

Concessio fact' Joh'i Stokker co'i venatori.

22 Aug., 5 Edward IV. [A.D. 1465], agreed by the same that,
for the sum of £20 paid into the Chamber, no action shall be
taken against William York, fishmonger, for using a different
mistery from that in which he was admitted to the freedom
of the City.

Concessio fact' Will'o York piscenar'.

---

[1] Elizabeth Woodville. Her coronation took place on the 26th May,
1465, and was made the occasion of
conferring Knighthood of the Bath
upon Ralph Josselyn, the Mayor, and
three Aldermen, viz., Thomas Cook,
Hugh Wyche, and John Plomer, together with Henry Waver, who afterwards became an Alderman. Gregory, p. 228; Beaven's 'Aldermen,'
p. 256.

Fo. 39 b.

*Custod' pue-
ror' Reymundi
Vawe al' dict'
Munnyng
orph' Civitatis.*

9 Sept., 5 Edward IV. [A.D. 1465], came William Nele, "vynter," John Mortymer, fishmonger, William Laurence, grocer, and John Holman, "hurer," and entered into bond in the sum of £60 for the payment into the Chamber of the sum of £30, to the use respectively of Agnes and "Alionora," daughters of Reymund Vawe *alias* Munnyng, late vintner, when they shall come of age or marry.

*Custod' Alicie
fil' Reymundi
Vawe al' dict'
Munnyng
orph' Civitatis.*

11 Sept., 5 Edward IV. [A.D. 1465], came Robert Russell, "talughchaundeler," Everard Fryer, "armurer," William White, "talughchaundeler," and Thomas Aleyn, skinner, and entered into bond in the sum of £30 for the payment into the Chamber of a like sum, to the use of Alice, daughter of the above Reymund, on her coming of age or marriage.

Fo. 40.

*Eleccio Vice-
comitum.*

The Feast of St. Matthew [21 Sept.], 5 Edward IV. [A.D. 1465], in the presence of Ralph Josselyn, the Mayor, John Norman, William Hulyn, Richard Lee, Hugh Wiche, Thomas Cook, William Taillour, John Oulegreve, George Irland, John Yong, Robert Basset, William Hamptone, Humphrey Hayford, William Edward, Bartholomew James, John Bromer, and John Tate, Aldermen, John Stone, Sheriff, and very many Commoners summoned to the Guildhall for the election of Sheriffs—Henry Waver was elected one of the Sheriffs of London and Middlesex by the Mayor, and William Costantyn, skinner, was elected the other Sheriff by the Commonalty.

The same day, Robert Colwich, tailor, was elected Chamberlain; Peter Alfodd and Peter Calcot were elected Wardens of London Bridge; and John Yong and Robert Basset, Aldermen, Thomas Gay, junior, tailor, William Haryot, "sherman," John Aleyn, goldsmith, and William Person, "hurer," Commoners, were elected Auditors of the accounts of the Chamber and Wardens of the Bridge in arrear.

Afterwards, viz., on the eve of St. Michael [29 Sept.], the said Sheriffs were sworn at the Guildhall, and on the morrow of the said Feast were presented, admitted, &c., before the Barons of the Exchequer.

3 Oct., 5 Edward IV. [A.D. 1465], George Mountford, gentle- *Admissio* man, on letters of the King and Queen [*sic*], admitted and *Georgii Mount-* *ford in officium* sworn an Attorney in the Court of the lord the King in the *Attorn' in Cur'* City, by Ralph Josselyn, the Mayor, and the Aldermen. *Vic' etc.*

The Feast of the Translation of St. Edward [13 Oct.], *Fo. 40 b.* 5 Edward IV. [A.D. 1465], in the presence of Ralph Josselyn, *Eleccio* the Mayor, the Prior of Christchurch, John Norman, William *Maioris.* Hulyn, Richard Lee, Thomas Cook, Matthew Philipp, Ralph Verney, William Taillour, John Yong, Thomas Oulegreve, John Lambert, Robert Basset, George Irlond, John Stoktone, William Hamptone, John Tate, William Costantyn, Humphrey Hayford, William Edward, Bartholomew James, and John Bromer, Aldermen, Henry Waver, Sheriff, and an immense Commonalty summoned to the Guildhall for the election of a Mayor for the year ensuing—Ralph Verney was elected.

Afterwards, viz., on the Feast of SS. Simon and Jude [28 Oct.], the said Mayor was sworn at the Guildhall, and on the morrow was presented, admitted, &c., before the Barons of the Exchequer.

9 Nov., 5 Edward IV. [A.D. 1465], writ to the Sheriffs to *Ereccio Fur-* cause proclamation to be made as follows :— *car' juxta* *Turrim.*

"For asmuch as the vij[th] day of this present moneth of Novembre Galowes waren erecte and sette up beside oure Towre of London within the libertees and fraunchises of oure Citee of London in derogacion and prejudice of the libertees and fraunchises of the seide Citee The Kyng oure sov'aigne lord woll it be certeinly understande that the ereccion and settyng up of the seide Galowes was not doone by his com- maundement Wherfore the Kyng oure saide sov'aigne lord woll that the ereccion and settyng up of the seide Galowes be not president nor ensample therby hereafter to be taken in hurte prejudice or derogacion of the Fraunchises libertees and privi- leges of the seide Citee Which he at al tymes hath hadde and hath in his benivolence tender favour and goode grace."

31 Jan., 5 Edward IV. [A.D. 1465-6], ordinance by Ralph *Q'd ficus et* Verney, the Mayor, Thomas Ursewik, the Recorder, John *Rasemi sunt* *victual'.* Norman, William Hulyn, Richard Lee, Thomas Cook, Matthew

Philipp, William Taillour, Thomas Oulegreve, William Hamptone, John Lambart, George Irlond, John Stoktone, William Costantyn, Robert Basset, John Bromer, William Edward, Bartholomew James, and Hugh Wiche, Aldermen, that figs and raisins should thenceforth rank as victuals, and, as such, be sold at a price fixed at the discretion of the Mayor.

Custod' Joh'is Akers filii Joh'is Akers orph'i Civit'.

15 Feb., 5 Edward IV. [A.D. 1465-6], came John Lane, junior, and Robert Wilkynson, "irmongers," Stephen Clampard, "blaksmyth," John Nele, John Pecok, and John Burell, grocers, and entered into bond in the sum of £100 for payment into the Chamber of a like sum, to the use of John, son of John Akers, late grocer, on his coming of age.

Fo. 41.

Custod' Joh'is Akers filii Joh'is Akers orph'i Civit'.

The same day came John Lane, junior, "irmonger," Stephen Clampard, "blaksmyth," and Robert Wilkynson, "irmonger," and entered into bond in the sum of £23 16s. 6½d. for the delivery into the Chamber of divers pieces of silver plate, to the use of the above orphan on his coming of age.

Exon'acio Will'i Boilet de quadam recogn'.

13 May, 6 Edward IV. [A.D. 1466], came Hugh, son of Richard Rook, late tailor, and acknowledged satisfaction for the sum of £40, due to him as patrimony, for payment of which William Boilet, John Stone, Thomas Burgeys, and Richard West, tailors, stood bound. They are therefore now quit.

Fo. 41 b.

Custod' Will'i Boleyn filii Galfr'i Boleyn orph'i Civit'.

5 April, 6 Edward IV. [A.D. 1466], came Hugh Joye, John Marchall, Robert Bifeld, and John Alburgh, mercers, and entered into bond in the sum of £236 for the delivery into the Chamber of the sum of £200 and certain jewels valued at £36, to the use of William, son of Geoffrey Boleyn, late Alderman, on his arriving at the age of 25 years or marrying.

Custod' Johanne filie Thome Elys orphane Civitatis.

7 May, 6 Edward IV. [A.D. 1466], came Robert Hardwyk, draper, Richard Everley, mercer, Richard Massynger, goldsmith, and Roger Scrippe, barber, and entered into bond in the sum of 100 marks for the payment into the Chamber of a like sum, to the use of Johanna, daughter of Thomas Elys, late draper, on her coming of age or marriage.

10 May, 6 Edward IV. [A.D. 1466], came William Purches, mercer, Thomas Bledlowe, John Warde, John Stokes, grocers, and entered into bond in the sum of £236 for the delivery into the Chamber of the sum of £200 and certain jewels of the value of £36, to the use of Thomas, son of Geoffrey Boleyn, late Alderman, on his arriving at the age of 25 years or marrying.

12 May, 6 Edward IV. [A.D. 1466], came Dame[1] Katherine Marowe, widow, John Reynkyn, John Marchall, Thomas Riche, mercers, and Philip Hardbeen, grocer, and entered into bond in the sum of £1,860 for the delivery into the Chamber of divers sums of money and jewels, to the use of William, Thomas, Johanna, and Katherine, children of William Marowe, late Alderman, the same being bequeathed to them by their said father, and accruing to them by the decease of Agnes, their sister.[2]

13 May, 6 Edward IV. [A.D. 1466], came Thomas Vandernak, William Rotheley, John Aleyn, and Richard Wright, goldsmiths, and entered into bond in the sum of £200 for the payment into the Chamber of a like sum, to the use of Thomas, son of Thomas Eyre, late draper, on his coming of age, the said money having been bequeathed to the said orphan by Simon Eyre, his grandfather.[3]

16 May, the same year, came Ralph Kempe, John Baker, Henry Bumstede, and William Sewster (?), mercers, and entered into bond in the sum of £100 for the payment into the Chamber by the said Ralph of a like sum, to the use of John, Robert, and Thomas, sons of the said Ralph Kempe, on

---

[1] Another instance of an unwarranted assumption of the title by the widow of a man who never received the honour of knighthood. Cf. *supra*, pp. 40, 51.

[2] A marginal note to the effect that on the 28th April, 19 Edward IV. [A.D. 1479], Robert Frogmarton, who married the above Katherine, daughter of William Marowe, came into Court, before Richard Gardyner, the Mayor, and the Aldermen, and ac-

knowledged satisfaction for his wife's property.

[3] A marginal note declares the above recognizance to be void, inasmuch as the above Thomas Eyre (the orphan) was dead, and the said Thomas Vandernak, on the 26th April, 9 Edward IV. [A.D. 1469], had delivered to Thomas Herward, draper and executor of Simon Eyre, the said sum of £200, in the presence of William Taillour, the Mayor.

their coming of age, the said money having been bequeathed
to them by John Burton, their uncle.

Fos. 43-4.

*Ordinacio
Pictorum.*

9 June, 6 Edward IV. [A.D. 1466], came good men of the
Mistery of Painters into the Court of the lord the King in the
Chamber of the Guildhall, before Ralph Verney, the Mayor,
William Hulyn, Richard Lee, Hugh Wyche, Thomas Cook,
Matthew Philip, Ralph Josselyn, William "Thaillour," Henry
Waver, Bartholomew James, John Stokdone, William Costan-
tyne, William Edward, and Humphrey Hayford, Aldermen,
and prayed that certain ordinances might be approved.[1]

Fo. 44.

*Ordinacio de
Chapemakers.*

The same day came good men of the Mistery of Chapemakers before the said Mayor and Aldermen, and prayed (*inter
alia*) that they might elect yearly two Wardens of the Craft, to
be presented and sworn at the Guildhall, who should " make
trewe and dewe serche as ofte as nede requireth...of almaner
ware and chaffar belongyng to the saide Crafte and theym to
presente to the Chamberleyn for the tyme beyng, that is to saye
Chapes,[2] Cheynes of laton and iron that is made of wire, gratys
for gynger and for brede, Shoobokeles, Claspys for gownes, botes
and shone, anlettes[3] tailed and rounde, sovels,[4] almaner Candel-
stikkys made of plate, Spones of tynne, broches of tynne and
dripyngpannes of plate blak and white, And that almaner such
ware or Chaffar by theym at any tyme founde defectyf or
unlefully made be forfaite and the makers and sellers of such
ware soo founde defectyf to paye at every such tyme iijs. iiijd.
that oone halff therof to the Chamber of the Yeldehall of the
saide Citee and the other halff to the use of the co'ialte of the
saide Crafte."

Their petition granted.

---

[1] The petition and ordinances are
set out in the return made by the
Painters to the Livery Companies'
Commission of 1884 (iii. 613-14).
The transcriber, however, has misread
"common servant" as *common hunt*,
and "called" as *oiled*. Here again
it is to be noted that the Wardens
were to be assisted in their duties
of search, &c., by eight or six honest
freemen of the craft, who were to be
presented, admitted, and sworn in the
Mayor's Court.

[2] The metal work of scabbards.

[3] Tags or pieces of metal attached
to the ends of laces or points.

[4] Shovels.

3 July, 6 Edward IV. [A.D. 1466], came Roger, son of Roger Holbeche, late tailor, and acknowledged satisfaction for his patrimony, and granted acquittance to Robert Mildenale, gentleman, and Thomas Humfray, tailor, his father's executors.

Fo. 44 b.
Exon'acio
Thome
Humfray de
quadam
recogn'.

23 May, 6 Edward IV. [A.D. 1466], came Thomas Hillard, John Hungerford, John Pake, junior, and John Becham, drapers, and entered into bond in the sum of 100 marks for the payment into Court of a like sum, to the use of Margery, daughter of John Gregory, late goldsmith, on her coming of age or marrying.[1]

Letters patent appointing Ralph Josselyn, Knight and Alderman, to be Justice to determine pleas among the merchants of Almaine, according to the law merchant.[2] Witness the King at Westminster, 16 March, 6 Edward IV. [A.D. 1465-6].

Fo. 45.
L're patent'
pro Rad'o
Josselyn
essend' Alder-
man' Then
tonic' apud le
Stileyerde.

27 June, 6 Edward IV. [A.D. 1466], came William Philippe, Robert Butler, goldsmiths, and John Savery, salter, and entered into bond in the sum of £150 for the payment into the Chamber of the sum of £50, to the use of Katherine, Alice, and Elizabeth respectively, daughters of John Deverse, late goldsmith, on their coming of age or marrying.

22 July, 6 Edward IV. [A.D. 1466], came Katherine Blakman, widow, Thomas Herward, draper, William Chamberleyn, "Foundour," and Richard Chaloner, fishmonger, and entered into bond in the sum of £52 2s. 11½d. for the delivery into the

---

[1] A marginal note declares the above recognizance to be void, inasmuch as Katherine, the wife of Thomas Elys, had received from the above John Hungerford the above sum of 100 marks bequeathed to the said Margery, since deceased, pursuant to the will of the said John Gregory.

[2] By the terms of the "composition" of 1282 the Hanse merchants were allowed to have *their* Alderman (*i.e.*, one of their own choosing), as hitherto, provided he was a freeman of the City, and presented to the Mayor and Aldermen, to be by them sworn to maintain justice.—'Liber Albus,' i. 487. Thus in 1320 we find John le Long, an *Easterling*, Alderman of the Hanse. — 'Cal. Letter-Book E,' pp. 119, 120. In course of time, however, the office appears to have been usually held by an Alderman of the City of London, appointed by the King.—Cf. 'Cal. Letter-Book K,' p. 401.

Chamber of the sum of 20 marks and divers chattels (comprising a standing silver piece, parcel gilt, and cover with a flower on the top called a " columbyne "), to the use respectively of Thomas and Johanna, children of William Blakman, late tailor, on their coming of age or marrying.[1]

Fo. 46.

Custodia pueror' Joh'is Colet.

17 Aug., 6 Edward IV. [A.D. 1466], came Thomas Chaterley, William Shore, William Redknappe, and Robert Gregory, mercers, and entered into bond in the sum of £600 for the payment into the Chamber of the sum of £100, to the use respectively of Robert, John, Geoffrey, Alice, Agnes, and Johanna, children of John Colet, late mercer.[2]

Fo. 46 b.

Eleccio Vicecomitum.

The Feast of St. Matthew [21 Sept.], 6 Edward IV. [A.D. 1466], in the presence of Ralph Verney, the Mayor, John Norman, William Hulyn, Richard Lee, Hugh Wiche, Matthew Philippe, Thomas Ursewyk the Recorder,[3] William Taillour, Thomas Oulegreve, George Irland, Robert Basset, John Tate, John Stokton, William Hamptone, Humphrey Hayford, William Edward, Bartholomew James, Henry Waver, and William Costantyne, Aldermen, and very many Commoners, summoned to the Guildhall for the election of Sheriffs—John Bromer was elected one of the Sheriffs of London and Middlesex by the Mayor, and Henry Brice, fuller, was elected the other Sheriff by the Commonalty.

---

[1] A marginal note to the effect that on the 27th July, 9 Edward IV. [A.D. 1469], the above Thomas Blakman acknowledged satisfaction for his property.

[2] A marginal note to the effect that the above Robert and John Colet, being of full age, and William Whit, mercer, who married the above Alice, came on the 14th Feb., 14 Edward IV. [A.D. 1474–5], and acknowledged satisfaction, and likewise Richard Blisset, who married the above Agnes ; and that on the 24th July, 1 Richard III. [A.D. 1483], the above Geoffrey also acknowledged satisfaction.

[3] This appears to be the first occasion of the Recorder being placed, in order of precedence, after the Aldermen who had served as Mayor, and before the junior Aldermen—the place that the Recorder occupies at the present day. It will be seen, however, in the following pages, that he soon regained his former position. *Vide infra*, fos. 108, 109, &c.

The same day, Robert Colwich, tailor, was elected Chamberlain; Peter Alfold and Peter Calcot were elected Wardens of London Bridge; John Bromer and Robert Basset, Aldermen, Thomas Gay, junior, William Hariot, sherman, Simon Smyth, grocer, and John Brampton, fishmonger, Commoners, were elected Auditors of the accounts of the Chamber and of the Wardens of London in arrear.

Afterwards, viz., on the eve of St. Michael [29 Sept.], the said Sheriffs were sworn at the Guildhall, and on the morrow of the said Feast were presented and admitted before the Barons of the Exchequer.

29 Aug., 6 Edward IV. [A.D. 1466], ordinance by Ralph Verney, the Mayor, and the Aldermen, that thenceforth the inhabitants of the Ward of Castelbaynard shall have the toll issuing from the boats of William Stephyns, capper, bringing rushes for sale to Quenehithe, or of some other boat, towards the cleansing of the common " lystoft "[1] of the Ward.

Habitantes Warde Castilbaynard h'eant unam batell' pro mundac' etc.

3 Sept., 6 Edward IV. [A.D. 1466], precept by Ralph Verney, the Mayor, and the Aldermen, to Henry Astell, fishmonger, that he with all speed set up (*erigere*) his house, which diverges towards the soil appertaining to the Mistery of Saddlers, and prevents the Wardens of the said Mistery from building on it; the said Wardens having promised to assist the said Henry in putting the matter right, with a contribution of 40s.

Judicium pro Cellariis.

5 Sept., 6 Edward IV. [A.D. 1466], disputes having arisen over the election of the Wardens of the Butchers, the Mayor and Aldermen decree that thenceforth the election should be made by those of the Livery only.

Fo. 47.
Ordinacio Carnific' pro eleccione Gardian'.

27 March, 6 Edward IV. [A.D. 1466], petition to the Mayor and Aldermen by John Lovegold that he may have the business of clearing all privies within the City and liberties for a term of 10 years, at 2s. 6d. per ton; the business having been hitherto imperfectly performed by others at an exorbitant

Concessio fact' Joh's Lovegold pro mundaco'e cloac'.

---

[1] A laystall or midden.   See ' N.E.D.,' *s.v.* Laistoff.

charge. After due consideration it was agreed on the 3rd October next following that the petitioner should undertake the work, taking no more than 2s. 2d. a ton.

Fo. 47 b.
Exon'acio Ric'i Wasket ab assis' etc.

28 Oct., 6 Edward IV. [A.D. 1466], Richard Wasket, "foundour," discharged by Ralph Verney, the Mayor, and the Aldermen, from serving on juries, &c., owing to increasing old age.

Eleccio Maioris.

Monday the Feast of Translation of St. Edward [13 Oct.], 6 Edward IV. [A.D. 1466], in the presence of Ralph Verney, the Mayor, the Prior of Christchurch, John Norman, William Hulyn, Richard Lee, Thomas Cook, Matthew Philippe, Ralph Josselyn, Thomas Ursewyk the Recorder, William Taillour, Thomas Oulegreve, John Lambard, George Irlande, Robert Basset, John Stoktone, William Hamptone, John Tate, William Edwarde, William Costantyne, Humphrey Hayford, Bartholomew James, John Bromer, Aldermen, Henry Brice, Sheriff, and an immense Commonalty, summoned to the Guildhall for the election of a Mayor for the year ensuing—John Yong was elected.

Afterwards, viz., on the Feast of SS. Simon and Jude [28 Oct.], he was sworn at the Guildhall, and on the morrow was presented, admitted, &c., before the Barons of the Exchequer.

Concessio fact' Joh'i Morley.

13 Oct., 6 Edward IV. [A.D. 1466], grant by the Mayor and Aldermen to John Morley, the Mayor's Swordbearer, of a house over the entrance gate of the Guildhall, lately occupied by Richard Power,[1] late the City's Swordbearer.

Judicium Pillorie.

William Barett, of the parish of St. Sepulchre, "couper," who had been convicted of bribing jurors in order to obtain favourable verdicts, condemned to be carried through the City on a horse without saddle, and to stand on the pillory in Cornhill, with a paper on his head proclaiming his offence; and further, to be discharged of all manner of "offices of worship" in the City. [No date.]

[1] In 1446 he was granted a yearly allowance of 20s. until a suitable house was provided for him.—'Cal. Letter-Book K,' p. 315.

A general Proclamation of divers ordinances, so that strangers coming to the City might not plead ignorance of them. They chiefly provide for keeping clean the streets of the City and the river Thames; they forbid forestalling and regulate the trade of poulterers, fishmongers, &c.

Fos. 47 b-48 b.
Proclamatio magna.

29 Nov., 6 Edward IV. [A.D. 1466], came John Brokford, John Hungerford, John Beauchamp, drapers, and Richard Messynger, goldsmith, and entered into bond in the sum of £100 for the payment into the Chamber of a like sum, to the use of Elizabeth, daughter of William Styfford, late scrivener, on her coming of age or marriage.

Fo. 48 b.
Custodia Elizabeth' filie Will'i Styfford orphane Civitatis.

2 Dec., 6 Edward IV. [A.D. 1466], came Thomas Risby, "brasier," John Shugbourgh, William Burtone, and William Holme, drapers, and entered into a similar bond for like purpose.

Fo. 49.
Custod' Elizabeth' filie Will'i Styfford orphane Civitatis.

28 Nov., 6 Edward IV. [A.D. 1466], came Thomas Gresham, senior, Thomas Gresham, junior, hatters, John Bradsha, haberdasher, and Robert Lewgor, "wexchaundeler," before the Mayor and Aldermen, and entered into bond in the sum of £24 for the payment into the Chamber of a like sum, to the use of William, Richard, Alice, and Elizabeth, children of John Snowdon, late tailor, when they come of age or marry.

Custodia pueror' Joh'is Snowdon.

2 Aug., 6 Edward IV. [A.D. 1466], came John Worshoppe, Robert Valaunce, George Kneseworth, William Kendall, drapers, and entered into bond in the sum of 40 marks for the payment into the Chamber of a like sum, to the use of William, son of Thomas Gosse, late mercer, on his coming of age.

Fo. 49 b.
Custod' Will'i Gosse filii Thome Gosse orphani Civitat'.

12 Dec., 6 Edward IV. [A.D. 1466], came Laurence Teste, John Fabyan, Stephen Fabian, and Thomas Kippyng, drapers, and entered into bond in the sum of 400 marks, 54 shillings, for the payment into the Chamber on the Feast of All Souls [2 Nov.], 1474, of a like sum, to the use of John, son of John Crowtone, on account of patrimony and jewels bequeathed to the said orphan.

Fo. 50.
Custod' Joh'is Crowtone filii Joh'is Crowtone orphani Civitatis.

Custod' pueror'
Joh'is Ran-
dolff' orphan'
Civitat'.

25 Jan., 6 Edward IV. [A.D. 1466-7], came John Randolffe, John Sturmyn, William Purches, and Walter Patsille, mercers, and entered into bond in the sum of 80 marks for the payment into the Chamber of a like sum, to the use of John, Anne, Isabella, and Alice, orphans of the City [*sic*], and children of the said John Randolffe[1]—the same having been bequeathed to them by John Norlong, late mercer—when they come of age or marry.

Fo. 50 b.
Judicium
Pillorie pro
recepc'oe
pecunie pro
veredc'o.

25 Feb., 6 Edward IV. [A.D. 1466-7], ordinance by John Yong, the Mayor, William Hulyn, Richard Lee, Thomas Cook, Matthew Philippe, Ralph Josselyne, Thomas Ursewyk the Recorder, William Taillour, Thomas Oulegreve, John Lambart, George Irland, John Stokdone, William Costantyne, John Tate, John Plomer, Henry Waver, William Edward, Bartholomew James, and John Bromer, Aldermen, that William Perchemyner, William Pake, and John Flete should be taken on horseback, without saddle, and placed on the pillory in Cornhill for taking money from Henry Astell, a fishmonger, for the purpose of bribing a jury in a cause between the said Henry and Johanna Cotton, widow, and that proclamation be made in form prescribed.

Concessio
fact' Joh'i
West porte de
Algate.

6 March, 7 Edward IV. [A.D. 1466-7], grant by the Mayor and Aldermen to John West, the Mayor's Serjeant-at-mace, to have the mansion over the gate of Algate on the same terms as it was lately held by John Houghtone.

Fo. 51.
Custod Thome
Eyre filii
Thome Eyre
orphani
Civitatis.

9 March, 7 Edward IV. [A.D. 1466-7], came Richard Hale, Bartholomew Horwod, and Martin Harlewes, grocers, and entered into bond in the sum of £100 for payment into the Chamber of a like sum, to the use of Thomas, son of Thomas Eyre, on his coming of age, the money having been bequeathed to the said orphan by Simon Eyre, his grandfather.[2]

---

[1] In 1394 the daughters of John Tiddesbury were treated as City orphans, although both of their parents were alive.—'Cal. Letter-Book H,' p. 410.

[2] A marginal note to the effect that the recognizance was void inasmuch as the orphan had died, and on the 15th April, 9 Edward IV. [A.D. 1469], the above Richard Hale had paid the money to Thomas Herward, draper, executor of Simon Eyre.

Letter from John Yong, the Mayor, under the Mayoralty Seal, to the Dean and Chapter of St. Paul's, presenting Sir William Denyshill, chaplain in the diocese of Oxford, for admission to the second of the three chantries founded in the said church for the souls of Sir John Pulteney, Knt., and of Sir William Milford, and Sir John Plesseys, late Archdeacons of Colchester, vacant by the resignation of Sir John Carlile. Dated 26 March, A.D. 1467.

Presentacio Will'i Denys-hill capell'i ad secundam Canter' etc. in eccl'ia sc'i Pauli.

A similar letter to Thomas [Kempe], Bishop of London, presenting Thomas Mason, chaplain, for admission to a perpetual chantry founded in the Chapel of St. Mary near the Guildhall for the soul of Roger de Depeham. Dated 26 March, 7 Edward IV. [A.D. 1467].

Presentacio Thome Mason' ad Canteriam in Capell' b'te Marie juxta Guihald' etc.

Tuesday, 16 June, 7 Edward IV. [A.D. 1467], ordinance of the Common Council forbidding the use of measures for buying and selling wine, salmon, herring, &c., within the City, unless they contain prescribed quantities, and are sealed with the City's seal by an officer of the Chamber of the Guildhall.

Fo. 51 b.

Ordinacio pro sigillaco'e mensur'.

9 July, 7 Edward IV. [A.D. 1467], John Hall, " chesemonger," discharged by the Mayor and Aldermen from serving on juries, &c., owing to his infirmities.

Exon'acio Joh'is Hall ab assis'.

Saturday, 20 June, 7 Edward IV. [A.D. 1467], in the presence of John Yong, the Mayor, William Hulyn, Ralph Josselyn, Ralph Verney, Hugh Wyche, Thomas Urssewyk the Recorder, William Taillour, Thomas Oulegreve, George Irland, John Lambart, Robert Basset, John Stokton, William Edward, and John Bromer, Sheriff, Aldermen, and very many Commoners, assembled in the Guildhall at 2.0 P.M.—John Stokton, Alderman and Mercer, was elected Sheriff *loco* Henry Brice, who had died the preceding night, to remain in office until the following Michaelmas, and never again to be re-elected ; for which privilege he paid to the Chamberlain the sum of £100 for the repair of the Conduit.

Fo. 52.

*Eleccio Joh'is Stokton in unum Vice'
Civitatis London loco Henr' Bryce qui obiit.*

On the following Monday he was presented before the Barons of the Exchequer.

Custod' Thome   18 July, 7 Edward IV. [A.D. 1467], came Elizabeth Pounde,
Pounde filii
Rob'ti Pounde   widow, John and Robert Pounde, grocers, and entered into
orph' Civitatis. bond in the sum of 50 marks for the payment into the Chamber
of a like sum, to the use of Thomas, son of Robert Pounde,
late grocer, on his coming of age.[1]

Fo. 52 b.   7 Sept., 7 Edward IV. [A.D. 1467], came Hugh Joye, John
Custod' Will'i Sturmyn, Richard Syffe, mercers, and Thomas Ostriche, haber-
Boleyn filii
Galfr'i Boleyn dasher, and entered into bond in the sum of £236 for the
orph'i Civitat'. delivery into the Chamber of the sum of £200 and certain
jewels, to the use of William, son of Geoffrey Boleyn, late
Alderman, on his reaching the age of 25 years.[2]

Eleccio   Monday the Feast of St. Matthew [21 Sept.], 7 Edward IV.
Vicecomit'.   [A.D. 1467], in the presence of John Yong, the Mayor, the Prior
of Christchurch, John Norman, Richard Lee, Hugh Wiche,
Thomas Cook, Ralph Josselyn, William Taillour, Thomas
Oulegreve, George Irland, Robert Basset, John Tate, William
Costantyne, William Edward, Bartholomew James, John Stok-
tone, Humphrey Hayford, and John Bromer, Aldermen, and
very many Commoners, summoned to the Guildhall for the
election of Sheriffs—Thomas Stalbroke was elected one of the
Sheriffs of London and Middlesex by the Mayor, and Humphrey
Hayfford, goldsmith, was elected the other Sheriff by the
Commonalty.

The same day, Robert Colwich, tailor, was elected Chamberlain; Peter Calcot and Richard Frome were elected Wardens
of London Bridge; John Lambar and William Edward, Aldermen, Simon Smyth, grocer, John Bramptone, fishmonger,
Robert Sympson and John Crosseby, grocers, Commoners,
were elected Auditors of the accounts of the Chamberlain and
Wardens of London Bridge in arrear.

Afterwards, viz., on the eve of the Feast of St. Michael
[29 Sept.], the said Sheriffs were sworn at the Guildhall, and

---

[1] A marginal note to the effect
that the orphan acknowledged satisfaction 17th Sept., 16 Edward IV.
[A.D. 1476].

[2] A marginal note states that the
recognizance is void as appears in the
Journal, 9th March, 13 Edward IV.
[A.D. 1472–3]. Journal 8, fo. 43b.

on the morrow of the said Feast were presented, admitted, &c., before the Barons of the Exchequer.

Wednesday, 23 Sept., 7 Edward IV. [A.D. 1467], ordinance by John Yong, the Mayor, John Norman, Richard Lee, Hugh Wiche, Thomas Cook, Ralph Josselyn, Thomas Urssewyk, the Recorder, William Taillour, Thomas Oulegreve, George Irland, Robert Basset, William Costantyn, John Tate, Humphrey Hayford, William Edward, John Stoktone, Batholomew James, and John Bromer, Aldermen, and the Commonalty of the City— that no freeman or Officer of the City shall take or use the livery of any lord or other magnate under penalty of losing his freedom and office for ever.[1]

Fo. 53.

Ordinacio q'd Officiarii non utantur liberatur' magnat'.

In the same Common Council it was ordained that thenceforth the election of Mayor and Sheriffs should be made only by the Common Council, the Masters and Wardens of each Mistery of the City, coming in their livery, and by other good men specially summoned for the purpose.

Ordinacio pro eleccione Maioris et Vicec'.

In the same Common Council it was agreed that no Officer or other person enjoying the freedom of the City by virtue of his office alone, should continue to enjoy the freedom after the termination of his office.

Ordinacio pro admittend' in lib'tatem ex officio.

Tuesday the Feast of Translation of St. Edward [13 Oct.], 7 Edward IV. [A.D. 1467], in the presence of John Yong, the Mayor, the Prior of Christchurch, John Norman, William Hulyn, Richard Lee, Hugh Wyche, Thomas Cook, Matthew Philippe, Ralph Josselyn, William Taillour, John Lambert, Thomas Oulegreve, George Irland, Robert Basset, John Tate, John Stoktone, William Hamptone, William Costantyne, Bartholomew James, John Bromer, Henry Waver, William Edward, and Humphrey Hayford, Aldermen, Thomas Stalbroke, Sheriff, and an immense Commonalty, summoned to the Guildhall for the election of a Mayor for the year ensuing—Thomas Oulegreve was elected.

Eleccio Maioris.

---

[1] This ordinance was necessitated by the attitude taken up by the Earl of Warwick towards the King and his wife's family, the Woodvilles. In the summer of the following year Parliament again forbade " liveries of company," as it had frequently done before. ('Rot. Parl.,' v. 632.)

Afterwards, viz., on the Feast of SS. Simon and Jude [28 Oct.], he was sworn at the Guildhall, and on the morrow was presented, admitted, &c., before the Barons of the Exchequer.

Custod' Joh'is Nicholson filii Joh'is Nichol-son orph' Civitatis.

17 Nov., 7 Edward IV. [A.D. 1467], came Henry Derby, "talughchaundiller," Peter Bisshope, "peautrer," Robert Parker, draper, and John Dey, and entered into bond in the sum of £80 for the payment into the Chamber of £73, to the use of John, son of John Nicholson, late "stacioner," on his coming of age.

Fo. 53 b.

Judicium Pillorie pro fabricacione unius false l're.

" Forasmoche as Gilbert ' Ridder ' that here standith as a man not dredyng god nor shame of the worlde falsely and subtelly feyned and forged in the name of oone James Degyn' a false lr'e writene by John Baron' that here standith beryng date at Maydestone the tuesday after Seint Andrewes day [30 Nov.] where as in dede it was writene and made in this Citee in Paternoster rowe by the saide John Baron' which lr'e was directed unto the Worshipfull persone Richerd Lee Alderman desiryng by the same to have hadde delyv'ed of the saide Ric' Lee xxs. in money and ij yerdes of blewe medley cloth and that by certayne tokyns conteynede in the seide lr'e Where as in dede the same James Degyn' never was prive nor knowyng any suche lr'e like as the saide Gilbert ' Rider ' hath openly confessed afore the Maire and Aldermen Therfore it is considred by the saide Maier and Aldermen that the saide Gilbert shulde stonde here on this pillory by the space of a quarter of an howre in example to all other disposed to offende in any suche wise and the saide John Baron' for his wrytyng to stand on a stole under this Pillory by the same tyme &c."

Fos. 53 b-55.

Ordinacio de Lethersillers.

14 Dec., 7 Edward IV. [A.D. 1467], came good men of the Mistery of " Lethersillers " into the Court of the lord the King in the Chamber of the Guildhall, before Thomas Oulegreve, the Mayor, William Hulyn, Richard Lee, Thomas Cook, Ralph Verney, John Yong, Robert Basset, George Irland, William Costantyne, Humphrey Hayford, Bartholomew James, William Taillour, and William Edward, Aldermen, and showed how in

former days the exercise of their craft was confined to the City of London, and that points and laces, originally made of leather wrought of sheep-fells, lambs-fells, and calves-fells, in course of time came to be made of the fells of "wildware," viz., of hart, hind, buck, doe, roe, goat, and kid, as being stronger, and how on that account the members of the craft had obtained from the Court of Aldermen, during the Mayoralties of Sir Richard Whityngton and Robert Large, an ordinance forbidding the use of sheep-leather, calves-leather, and lambs-leather. Of late, however, it had been found impossible to observe that ordinance, owing to the lack of "wildware" coming from Norway, Spain, Guienne, and Scotland, and the Wardens, apprentices, and others became guilty of perjury. They prayed therefore that the above ordinance might be annulled, and that certain other ordinances for governing the Mistery might be approved.[1]

Their petition granted.

18 Dec., 7 Edward IV. [A.D. 1467], came Henry Folyat, grocer, Richard Carter, " curriour," Robert Colyns, "skynner," and Edmund Graveley, carpenter, and entered into bond in the sum of £20 to the effect that the said Henry Folyat, or some one on his behalf, will acquire certain lands and tenements which, after the decease of Johanna, widow of Thomas Pert, remain to Elena,[2] daughter of John Amady.

Fo. 55 b.

Custod' Elene Amady filie joh'is Amady.

18 Dec., 7 Edward IV. [A.D. 1467], came Gilbert Vyncent, " sergeant," William Bromeseld, cutler, William Birde, fuller, Robert Orcherd, "gentilman," Edmund Graveley, carpenter, and entered into bond in the sum of £20 for the payment into the Chamber by the said Gilbert of a like sum, to the use of Thomas, son of John Hopkyns, late goldsmith, on his coming of age.

Custod' Thome Hopkyns filii Joh'is Hop kyns orph' Civitatis

---

[1] The ordinances are set out in Black's 'Hist., &c. of the Leather-sellers' Company,' pp. 32-5.

[2] Margin : 22 April, 16 Henry VII. [A.D. 1501], came Henry Newton, "girdeler," who married the above Elena, and acknowledged, &c.

Fo. 56.

Presentacio Joh'is Gregory ad quandam Canteriam quinq' Cantariar' in Capella b'te Marie juxta Guihald' London'.

Letter from the Mayor and Chamberlain to Thomas [Kempe], Bishop of London, presenting John Gregory, chaplain, for admission to one of the five chantries founded in the Guildhall Chapel by Adam Fraunceys and Henry Frowyk. Dated under the seals of the said Mayor and Chamberlain 2 Feb., A.D. 1467[-8].

Ordinacio fact' pro mensuratorib' salis.

11 Feb., 7 Edward IV. [A.D. 1467-8], a controversy having arisen between Thomas Oulegreve, the Mayor, and the Wardens of the Mistery of Salters touching the appointment to the office of Measurer of Salt, it was ordained by the said Mayor and William Hulyn, Hugh Wiche, Thomas Cook,[1] Ralph Josselyn, Ralph Verney, John Yong, John Lambert, Robert Basset, John Stoktone, William Costantyne, Henry Waver, John Bromer, William Edward, John Tate, and Bartholomew James, Aldermen, assembled in the inner Chamber of the Guildhall, after consulting ancient precedents, that thenceforth the Wardens of the said Mistery should, as of old accustomed, present to the Mayor and Aldermen a Measurer of Salt, to be by them admitted and sworn to that office, unless there be reasonable cause to the contrary.

Ordinacio de Tegulatorib'.

18 Feb., 7 Edward IV. [A.D. 1467-8], came good men of the Mistery of Tilers into the Court of the lord the King in the Chamber of the Guildhall, before Thomas Oulegreve, the Mayor, William Hulyn, Richard Lee, Hugh Wyche, Thomas Cook, Ralph Josselyn, Ralph Verney, Thomas Ursewyk the Recorder,[2] John Stoktone, William Hamptone, John

---

[1] It is recorded that "Sir Thomas Cook, Knyght and Alderman ".(he having received the honour of Knighthood with three other Aldermen in 1465), was this year arrested for treason ; that he was brought to trial at the Guildhall and acquitted, but was afterwards committed to the King's Bench, whence he only obtained his release on payment of a fine of £8,000 to the King. Cotton MS. Vitellius A xvi, fo. 127 (Kingsford's 'Chronicles of London,' p. 179). In November of the same year he was discharged (*exoneratur*) from his Aldermanry (Broad Street Ward) by the King's orders.—Journal 7, fo. 182. He afterwards became Alderman of Bread Street Ward ; but was displaced in 1471. See Beaven's 'Aldermen of London,' pp. 47, 72, 256. He appears, however, again as an Alderman in 1472. *Infra*, p. 94.

[2] See note *supra*, p. 66.

Plomer, Bartholomew James, Humphrey Hayford, and William Taillour, Aldermen, and presented a petition to the said Mayor and Aldermen and Common Council complaining that tiles were then so insufficiently wrought that instead of enduring for 40 or 50 years as they used to do, they lasted no more than 3 or 4 years. They explained to the Court that tiles should be made " with batter temperd cley that is to saye the cley therof shulde be diged and caste at Mighelmasse and soo lye open to Cristmas thanne next folowing, and thanne to be turned and caste ayen wherby the marle and the chalke shulde breke out like as chalkestones and cloddis liyng in the Frost ar woned to doo And thanne in the March thanne next ensuyng therof shulde be made tyles goode and profitable like as it have been of olde tyme, but it is soo in theis daies the Tiles been made soo hastely not havyng the wether and processe of tyme as it is aforerehersed."[1]

They pray therefore that the Fellowship of the Craft of Tilers may be restored to its franchises, notwithstanding any Act of the Common Council to the contrary ;[2] that it may elect two Wardens, to be sworn before the Mayor and Aldermen, to present falsely made tiles, and that all tiles should conform to the samples in the custody of the City Chamberlain, &c.

Their petition granted.

In a plea of debt on demand of 10 marks levied in the Court of the lord the King, before Thomas Stalbroke, one of the Sheriffs, between Thomas Houghton, plaintiff, and George Warre, defendant, by reason of a recognizance made by the

Fo. 56 b.

Consuetudo concern' apprentic.

---

[1] Cf. "An Act for making of Tile" (Stat, 17 Edw. IV. cap. iv. A.D. 1477), which prescribed (*inter alia*) that the earth for making tiles "shall be digged and cast up before the first day of November next before that they shall be made, and that the same earth be stirred and turned before the first day of February then next following the same digging and casting up, and not wrought before the first day of March next following ; and that the same earth before it be put to making of Tile be truly wrought and tried from stones, and also that the veins called Malin or Marle and Chalk..... shall be lawfully and truly severed and cast from the earth whereof any such Tile shall be made."

[2] See ordinance of 1461, *supra*, p. 12.

said George in favour of the said Thomas, the said defendant, in bar of the debt, alleged an immemorial custom in the City, to the effect that if any apprentice of a freeman made a bond in any sum of money to another freeman, without permission of his master, the freeman to whom the bond was delivered knowing the fact of apprenticeship, such a bond was void.

Fo. 57.

The plaintiff denied the existence of such a custom, and on the 22nd March, 8 Edward IV. [A.D. 1467–8], the Mayor and Aldermen certified that such a custom did not exist.

Custod' pueror' Jo'his Gugge peautrer orph' Civitat'.

14 April, 8 Edward IV. [A.D. 1468], came Everard Newkyrk, Peter Bisshop, Thomas Godelok, "peautrers," and John Martyn, "taillour," and entered into bond in the sum of £40 for the delivery into the Chamber of the sum of 10 marks and divers jewels and silver plate, to the use of Elena, Isabella, Margaret, and Johanna, daughters of John Gugge, late "peautrer," when they severally come of age or marry, the aforesaid Everard having been appointed guardian of the said orphans.

Fo. 57 b.

Nota quendam arrest' per Thomam Wyngfeld Cust' Marisc' infra lib'tatem et iterum rest' etc.

Be it remembered that on the 28th April, 8 Edward IV. [A.D. 1468], in the presence of Thomas Oulegreve, the Mayor, and the Aldermen, in the inner Chamber of the Guildhall, Thomas Wyngfeld, Keeper of the King's Marshalsea—by whose order John Doys, "berebruer," had been arrested within the liberty of the City, viz., between St. Katherine's Hospital and the bridge there, and carried to the Marshalsea, and there imprisoned contrary to the liberty of the City—promised to release the said John Doys and restore him to the same place where he had been arrested ; and that was done immediately after midday of the same day, in the presence of the Prior of Christchurch, Thomas Stalbroke, one of the Sheriffs, the Chamberlain, and the Common Clerk, who had been appointed by the Court to receive the said John Doys at that spot.

Custodia Joh'is Horn filii Roberti Horn orph'i Civitat'.

20 May, 8 Edward IV. [A.D. 1468], came Philip Hardben and Bartholomew Horewoode, grocers, William Heryot, sherman, and Thomas Ostriche, haberdasher, and entered into bond in the sum of £300 for the payment into the Chamber of the sum of £275 10s. 4½d., to the use of John, the youngest son (*filius ac*

postumus) of Robert Horne, deceased, on his coming of age or marriage, which sum, in addition to £11 17s. ½d. due from Nicholas Sharpe to the said orphan, formed a third part of the goods left by the said Robert to be distributed among Johanna, Anna, Robert, and the aforesaid John, his children.

24 May, 8 Edward IV. [A.D. 1468], came the above Philip, Bartholomew, William, and Thomas, and entered into a bond in the sum of £300 for the payment into the Chamber of a like sum to the use of Robert, son of Robert Horne, late Alderman,[1] on his arriving at the age of twenty-four years, by the above Philip, who had been appointed guardian to the said orphan.

Fo. 58.

Custodia Roberti Horn filii Roberti Horne orphani Civitatis.

15 May, 8 Edward IV. [A.D. 1468], Hugh Broun, grocer, discharged by the Mayor and Aldermen from serving on juries, &c., owing to deafness.

Exoneracio Hug' Broun groc'i ab assisis etc.

30 July,[2] 8 Edward IV. [A.D. 1468], Stephen Fabyan, draper, presented by the inhabitants of Bridge Ward, together with others [not named],[3] according to custom, in order that one of them might be elected Alderman of that Ward, and thereupon the said Stephen was so elected by Thomas Oulegreve, the Mayor, Richard Lee, Ralph Josselyn, Thomas Urssewyk the Recorder, William Taillour, George Irland, Robert Basset, John Stoktone, William Hamptone, John Tate, William Costantyn, Bartholomew James, William Edwarde, John Bromer, and John Warde, Aldermen; and because the said Stephen refused to undertake the burden and to take the oath, he was committed by the said Mayor and Aldermen to Newgate until favour should be shown him.

Fo. 58 b.

Imprisona-mentum Ste-phani Fabyan q' recusavit recipere officium Al-dermannat'.

Afterwards, viz., on the 31st July, the said Stephen was released, inasmuch as it was found on examination by the said Mayor and Aldermen that he had not sufficient estate to maintain the dignity of the office of Mayor and Sheriff.[4]

---

[1] Of Bridge Ward, 1444-56.
[2] Elsewhere the date given is 23 July. Journal 7, fo. 175 b.
[3] Their names are recorded in the Journal referred to in preceding note as John Brampton, fishmonger, and Simon Smyth and Richard Rawlyns, grocers.
[4] In the following year he was elected Alderman of Bishopsgate Ward, but was again discharged on similar grounds. *Infra*, fo. 6 4b.

Eleccio Vicecomit'.

Wednesday the Feast of St. Matthew [21 Sept.], 8 Edward IV. [A.D. 1468], in the presence of Thomas Oulegreve, the Mayor, William Hulyn, Richard Lee, Matthew Philippe, Ralph Josselyn, John Yong, William Taillour, George Irland, John Stokdone, William Costantyn, John Tate, John Bromer, Bartholomew James, Humphrey Heyfford, William Hampton, William Edward, Henry Waver, and John Warde, Aldermen, and very many Commoners summoned to the Guildhall for the election of Sheriffs—Simon Smyth was elected one of the Sheriffs of London and Middlesex by the Mayor, and William Heryot, sherman, was elected the other Sheriff by the Commonalty.

The same day Robert Colwich, tailor, was elected Chamberlain; Peter Calcot and Peter Alfold were elected Wardens of London Bridge; and William Edwarde and William Hamptone, Aldermen, Robert Sympson, draper, John Crosseby, grocer, Roger Tygoo, " taillour," and William Cardemaker, grocer, Commoners, were elected Auditors of the accounts of the Chamber and of the Wardens of London Bridge in arrear.

Afterwards, viz., on the eve of St. Michael [29 Sept.], the said Sheriffs were sworn at the Guildhall, and on the morrow of the said Feast were presented, admitted, &c., before the Barons of the Exchequer.

Eleccio Maioris.

Thursday the Feast of Translation of St. Edward [13 Oct.], 8 Edward IV. [A.D. 1468], in the presence of Thomas Oulegreve, the Mayor, the Prior of Christchurch, William Hulyn, Richard Lee, Matthew Philippe, Ralph Josselyn, John Yong, Thomas Urssewyk the Recorder, William Taillour, John Lambart, Robert Basset, George Irland, John Stoktone, john Tate, Humphrey Hayfford, William Hamptone, William Edwarde, William Costantyn, Bartholomew James, John Bromer, John Warde, and Thomas Stalbroke, Aldermen, Simon Smythe and William Heryot, the Sheriffs, and an immense Commonalty summoned to the Guildhall for the election of a Mayor for the year ensuing—William Taillour was elected.

Afterwards, viz., on the Feast of SS. Simon and Jude [28 Oct.], the said Mayor was sworn at the Guildhall, and on the morrow was presented, admitted, &c., before the Barons of the Exchequer.

28 Oct., 8 Edward IV. [A.D. 1468], ordinance by William Taillour the Mayor, William Hulyn, Richard Lee, Matthew Philippe, Ralph Josselyn, John Yonge, Ralph Verney, Thomas Urssewyk the Recorder, George Irland, Robert Basset, John Stokdone, William Hamptone, John Tate, John Bromer, William Edwarde, Humphrey Hayfford, Bartholomew James, John Warde, and Thomas Stalbroke, Aldermen, that thenceforth every year the Chamberlain for the time being, about the Feast of the Nativity of St. John Bapt. [24 June], shall provide cloth called "Ray" for the Feast of the Nativity of our Lord next ensuing for the livery of the Mayor and of the Chamber, and that the said Chamberlain shall submit a sample thereof to the Mayor and Aldermen.

De liberatura Maioris et Cam'e.

22 Nov., 8 Edward IV. [A.D. 1468], ordinance by the Mayor and Aldermen that thenceforth there shall be elected yearly by the Mayor and Aldermen a Sub-escheator, who shall in no wise be changed by the Mayor, and pursuant to this ordinance Robert Corffe, "gentilman," was elected and sworn to that office.

Fo. 59.
De eleccione Subeschaetoris.

9 Dec., 8 Edward IV. [A.D. 1468], came John Shelley, John Alburgh, Ralph Kempe, and William Sewster, mercers, and entered into bond in the sum of £17.

Recogn' pro pu'is Thome [sic] Hill.

The condition of the above recognizance appears in the Journal of that date.[1]

9 Dec., 8 Edward IV. [A.D. 1468], came Richard Wellys, grocer, John Thomson, brewer (*pandoxator*), Robert Turnour and Henry Prune, tailors, and entered into bond in the sum of £20 for payment into the Chamber by the said Richard

Custodia Thome Hill filii Ric'i Hill orphan' Civitatis.

---

[1] Journal 7, fo. 184, where it is recorded that the recognizance is to be void on condition the above John Shelley pays into the Chamber a like sum to the use of Richard, son of *Richard* Hill, late haberdasher, on his coming of age, that sum being part of a sum of £80 bequeathed by Richard Hill, the father, to John, Thomas, Richard, and Henry, his sons.

Wellys of a like sum to the use of Thomas, son of Richard Hille, late haberdasher, on his coming of age.

Fo. 59 b.

Custodia pueror' Joh'is Devers orph' Civitatis.

17 Dec., 8 Edward IV. [A.D. 1468], came Humfrey Gentilez, merchant of "Luca," Amaneus[1] Bartet and William Clement, drapers, and Thomas Hertwell, saddler, and entered into bond in the sum of £50 for the payment into the Chamber by the said Humfrey of a like sum to the use of Thomas and Raphael, sons of John Devers, the same being patrimony bequeathed to them and Elizabeth their sister, since deceased.

Feod' concess' Thome Torald.

20 Jan., 8 Edward IV. [A.D. 1468-9], grant by William Taillour, the Mayor, William Hulyn, Richard Lee, Matthew Philippe, Ralph Josselyn, Thomas Oulegreve, Thomas Urssewyk the Recorder, George Irland, John Bromer, Thomas Stalbroke, Robert Drope, John Crosseby, Ralph Verney, John Stoktone, and John Warde, Aldermen, to Thomas Torald, "gentilman," of a gown of ray and a sum of 6s. 8d., to be delivered yearly out of the Chamber for life, on account of his services to the City.

Custod' Ric'i Holbeche fil' Ric'i Holbeche orph' Civitatis.

8 Feb., 8 Edward IV. [A.D. 1468-9], came William Kerver, fishmonger, Henry Neville, "iremonger," and Ralph Bere, and entered into bond in the sum of 100 marks for the delivery into the Chamber by the said William Kerver of the sum of 40 marks and certain jewels to the use of Richard, son of Richard Holbeche, deceased, on his coming of age.

Judicium redditum sup' uno Vicecomit' pro strict' custod'.

9 Feb., 8 Edward IV. [A.D. 1468-9], whereas Simon Smythe, one of the Sheriffs of the City, had been convicted of having imprisoned John "Wetherley," draper, in the Poultry Compter, in a dark room, and had put him in irons and bound his arms behind him with iron manacles; and, further, had bound his neck with an iron fastening to his feet, which were in stocks, so that his neck was bent and his whole body hung in the stocks,

---

[1] A Latin form of the French "Amanieu," a common Christian name in Guienne. See *Notes and Queries*, 3 Sept., 1910, p. 197. That being so, the name recorded in 'Calendar Letter-Book A,' p. 127, "Amanin" de Terriz, as that of a burgess of St. Emilion, should have been read "Amaniu," although it is also recorded in the Latin form "Amanicinus," or "Amanicius."

away from the ground and without other support, so that through excessive pain he despaired of his life, and so continued for almost an hour, until the said Simon, moved by his outcry, released him from his torture, leaving him, however, still in irons on the ground; and whereas the said Simon had taken divers goods and jewels from the prisoner, it was ordained by William Taillour, the Mayor, and the Aldermen that the said Simon should restore the said goods and jewels to the said John Wetherley, and pay him the sum of £100 for the ill-treatment inflicted, and further should himself be committed to Ludgate prison, there to remain until, &c., as a warning to others.

8 March, 9 Edward IV. [A.D. 1468-9], came William Enfeld, Thomas Enfeld, and Thomas Bonde, fishmongers, and Thomas Randys, girdler, and entered into bond in the sum of 50 marks for the payment into the Chamber of the sum of 20 marks by the said William Enfeld to the use of William, son of John Bolton, late cordwainer; and a sum of 10 marks to the use of John, the youngest son (*postumus filius*) of the same, on their coming of age; and a further sum of 20 marks bequeathed to Mark, another son of the same, since deceased.

Fo. 60 b.
*Custod'
pueror' Joh'is
Bolton orph'
Civitatis.*

The same day came William Hole, William Pembrige, and Thomas Cole, skinners, and Nicholas Plumme, " hurer," and entered into bond in the sum of 500 marks for payment into the Chamber by the said William Hole of a like sum to the use of Robert, son of Robert Horne, on his attaining the age of 24 years.

*Custod'
Roberti Horn
filii Roberti
Horn orph'
Civitat'.*

26 March, 9 Edward IV. [A.D. 1469], whereas John " Witherley " had publicly declared that he had been cruelly treated by Simon Smythe, one of the Sheriffs, in his Compter, for which he had received £100 by way of compensation, when he had not been treated in such a manner, the charge against the Sheriff being due to his imagination, to the great scandal of a Sheriff of the City, it was adjudged by William Taillour, the Mayor, William Hulyn, Ralph Josselyn, Ralph Verney, Thomas Oulegreve, Thomas Urssewyk the Recorder, George Irland, Robert Basset, John Stoktone, William Hampton, Bartholomew James, Thomas Stalbroke, Henry

Fo. 61.
*Judicium
reddit' pro
scandal' super
uno Vice-
comit'.*

G 2

Waver, John Warde, and Richard Gardyner, Aldermen, that, in accordance with the custom of the City in such cases, the said John "Witherley" should pay the Sheriff the sum of 50 marks by way of damages. This having been done, the Sheriff acknowledged himself satisfied.

Fos. 61 b-62.

Proclamacio contra Provisores Regis.

Royal proclamation warning the King's subjects against demands made by Purveyors for the royal household unless they showed their authority under the Great or the Privy Seal, and confirming the ordinances touching purveyance made by Statute 23 Hen. VI. cap. i., by which statute the Serjeant of the Catery (*Sergeaunt de lacaterie*)[1] was bound to satisfy all damages, debts, and executions recovered against any purveyor under him who was unable himself to satisfy the same. [No date.][2]

Fos. 62-63 b.

L're paten' Regis de prostracione unius Gurgitis in Thamis'.

Inspeximus of letters patent granted to William [Herbert], Earl of Pembroke, authorizing him to make a weir across the Thames called "Overthwartwere" from the Middlesex shore to the Surrey shore in the place of an old weir called "Holgyllys were," and cancelling the same as being prejudicial to the franchise of the City. Witness the King at Westminster, 28 April, 9 Edward IV. [A.D. 1469].[3]

Fo. 63 b.

Ordinacio de pulsacione campane de Bowcherche.

Saturday, 22 April, 9 Edward IV. [A.D. 1469], an ordinance of the Common Council to the effect that, whereas it had been of old accustomed, for the peace of the City and keeping due time at night, for the great bells, and especially the great bell called "Bowbell," and the bells in the churches of All Hallows Berkyng, St. Giles without Crepilgate, and St. Bride in Fletestrete, to be struck at the accustomed hours, viz., at the ninth hour on festivals and holidays (*ferialibus*)......[ends abruptly].

Ordinacio de paviment' et caminis ligneis.

12 June, 9 Edward IV. [A.D. 1469], ordinance by the Common Council that defective pavement shall be kept in repair by the occupiers of the tenements facing the pavement, under penalty

---

[1] In 1362 (Stat. 36 Edward III. cap. ii.) the name of *Purveyor* (which had become hateful) had been changed into *Acatour* or *Catour* (*i.e.* Buyer).

[2] For previous statutes and ordinances touching Purveyors, see 'Cal. Letter-Book I,' pp. 288-98.

[3] An inspeximus of this revocation is preserved at the Guildhall. Cf. 'Cal. Patent Rolls' (1467 - 77), p. 111.

of distress being levied for the repair of the same ; and forbidding the use of wooden (" treen ") chimneys, under penalty of a fine.

4 July, 9 Edward IV. [A.D. 1469], came William Heryot, sherman, John White, John Catell, and Simon Rudby, " vynters," and entered into bond in the sum of £50 18s. 5d. for the delivery into the Chamber by the said William Heryot of the sum of £40 and certain jewels to the use of Johanna, daughter of John Swift, late vintner, on her attaining the age of fifteen years or marriage.

Fo. 64.
*Custod'
Johanne
Swifte fil'
Joh'is Swifte
orph' Civitat'.*

12 July, 9 Edward IV. [A.D. 1469], came Robert Colman, Nicholas Hynde, and John Bakon, "coriours," and Robert Ewell, "lethersiller," and entered into bond in the sum of 5 marks for the delivery into the Chamber by the said Robert Colman of the sum of 20s. and divers chattels to the use of Nicholas, son of Robert Clerk, late " bruer," on his coming of age.

Fo. 64 b.
*Custodia
Nich'i Clerk
fil' Rob'ti
Clerk orph'
Civitat'.*

18 July, 9 Edward IV. [A.D. 1469], ordinance by the Mayor and Aldermen that Stephen Fabyan should be committed to Neugate for refusing to undertake the office of Alderman of the Ward of Bisshopesgate,[1] there to remain until he either undertakes the office or pays £100 to the use of the Commonalty for his contempt.[2]

*Imprisonament' Steph'i
Fabian.*

29 July, 9 Edward IV. [A.D. 1469], ordinance by William Taillour, the Mayor, Richard Lee, Ralph Josselyn, Ralph Verney, John Lamberd, George Irland, John Stoktone, John Tate, Bartholomew James, William Edward, John Bromer, Henry Waver, John Warde, Thomas Stalbroke, and Richard Gardyner, Aldermen, that no one in future should be admitted Alderman of any Ward unless his goods, chattels, and hopeful debts amounted to £1,000, and any one so elected should be

---

[1] The date of his election is not recorded. The last Alderman removed to Walbrook on the 7th June (Beaven).

[2] He had been elected Alderman of Bridge Ward a year before, and had been committed to prison for refusing to undertake the office, but had been released the following day, on the ground that it had been proved that he had insufficient means to bear the burdens of Mayoralty and Shrievalty. *Supra*, p. 79.

discharged on his swearing that his property did not reach that sum.

By virtue of the above ordinance the above Stephen Fabyan received his discharge.

Fo. 65.

Eleccio Vicc'.

Thursday the Feast of St. Matthew [21 Sept.], in the presence of William Taillour, the Mayor, William Hulyn, Matthew Philippe, Thomas Oulegreve, George Irland, Robert Basset, John Tate, Bartholomew James, William Edward, Thomas Stalbroke, John Bromer, John Crosseby, John Warde, Robert Drope, Richard Gardyner, Aldermen, Simon Smythe and William Heriot, the Sheriffs, and very many Commoners summoned to the Guildhall for the election of Sheriffs— Richard Gardynèr, mercer, was elected one of the Sheriffs of London and Middlesex by the Mayor, and Robert Drope, draper, was elected the other Sheriff by the Commonalty.

The same day Robert Colwich was elected Chamberlain for the year ensuing; Edward Stone, "irmonger," and John Jurdan, tailor, were elected Wardens of London Bridge; and William Hampton and John Tate, Aldermen, Roger Tygoo, William Cardemaker, William Philippe, and William Hole, Commoners, were elected Auditors of the accounts of the Chamber and of the Wardens of the Bridge in arrear.

Afterwards, viz., on the eve of St. Michael [29 Sept.], the said Sheriffs were sworn at the Guildhall, and on the morrow of the said Feast were admitted, &c., before the Barons of the Exchequer.

Custodia Joh'is Benet filii Rogeri Benet orph' Civitatis.

2 Oct., 9 Edward IV. [A.D. 1469], came Thomas Sewrangh, James Symond, William Ball, " taillours," and John at Well, " bruer," and entered into bond in the sum of £40 for the delivery into the Chamber of 6 marks and certain chattels, and for collecting certain rents of tenements belonging to Johanna, widow of Roger Benet, to the use of John, son of the said Roger Benet, on his coming of age.

Fo. 65 b.

Eleccio Maioris.

Friday the Feast of Translation of St. Edward [13 Oct.], 9 Edward IV. [A.D. 1469], in the presence of William Taillour, the Mayor, the Prior of Christchurch, William Hulyn, Richard Lee, Matthew Philippe, Ralph Josselyn, Ralph Verney, John

Yong, Thomas Oulegreve, Thomas Urssewyk the Recorder, George Irland, Robert Basset, William Hamptone, John Tate, William Edward, John Bromer, Henry Waver, John Warde, John Crosseby, and Robert Drope, Aldermen, Richard Gardyner, one of the Sheriffs, and an immense Commonalty summoned to the Guildhall for the election of a Mayor—Richard Lee was elected.

Afterwards, viz., on the Feast of SS. Simon and Jude [28 Oct.], he was sworn at the Guildhall, and on the morrow was presented, &c., before the Barons of the Exchequer.

20 Oct., 9 Edward IV. [A.D. 1469], ordinance by the Mayor and Aldermen that neither William Baldry, Bailiff of Billynges-gate, nor any future Bailiff, shall take any money or custom from corn-meters, as the said William had been accustomed to do, viz., a farthing for every two quarters of grain.[1]

7 Nov., 9 Edward IV. [A.D. 1469], came John Dunne, senior, William Redknappe, Ralph Kempe, and William Hynde, mercers, and entered into bond in the sum of £220 for the delivery into the Chamber by the said John Dunne of the sum of £180, together with a standing cup of silver gilt and a primer, to the use of John, son of Robert Gregory, late mercer, on his coming of age.

Custod' Joh'is Gregory fil' Rob'ti Gregory orph' Civitat'.

13 Nov., 9 Edward IV. [A.D. 1469], came Thomas Corbrande, Henry Bumstede, William Purches, and John Cowper, mercers, and entered into bond in the sum of £120 for the delivery into the Chamber by the said Thomas Corbrande of the sum of £195, and of a silver-gilt "coblet" and cover, to the use of Emma, daughter of Robert Gregory, late mercer, on her coming of age or marriage.

Fo. 66.

Custodia Emme fil' Rob'ti Gregory orphane Civitatis.

21 Nov., 9 Edward IV. [A.D. 1469], John Lambe, "browderer," discharged by Richard Lee, the Mayor, and the Aldermen from serving on juries, &c., owing to increasing old age.

Fo. 66 b.

Exon'acio Joh'is Lambe ab assis'.

22 Nov., 9 Edward IV. [A.D. 1469], Henry Derby, "talugh-chaundiller," similarly discharged on account of his being continually engaged on the public affairs of the City.

Exon'acio Henr' Derby ab assis'.

---

[1] Annulled 19 Jan., 11 Edward IV. [A.D. 1471-2]. *Infra*, p. 95.

Imprisona-
mentum
Roberti Colyns
et finis quia
recessit in
quadam
Jurata.

27 Dec., 9 Edward IV. [A.D. 1469], Robert Colyns committed to Newgate by the Mayor and Aldermen, and fined 40s., for refusing to give a verdict when impanelled on a jury and contemptuously quitting the Court.

Custodia
Margarete fil'
Joh'is Hum-
berstone.

17 Jan., 9 Edward IV. [A.D. 1469-70], came John Trewynard, " sherman," William Boilet and Richard West, " taillours," and Henry Logan, mercer, before the Mayor and Aldermen, and entered into bond in the sum of £10 for payment into the Chamber by the said John Trewynard of a like sum to the use of Margaret, daughter of John Humberstone, late vintner, on her coming of age or marriage.

Fo. 67.
Custodia
Elizabeth'
Gregory filie
Roberti
Gregory.

27 Jan., 9 Edward IV. [A.D. 1469-70], came Thomas Corbrond, William Purches, Henry Newman,[1] and Richard Heynes, mercers, and entered into bond in the sum of £105 for the delivery into the Chamber of a sum of £85 and six silver " gobelettes " and a silver covercle parcel-gilt by the said Thomas Corbrond, to the use of Elizabeth, daughter of Robert Gregory, late mercer, on her coming of age or marriage.

Fo. 67 b.
Custodia
pueror' Will'i
Wodehous
orph' Civi-
tatis.

30 Jan., 9 Edward IV. [A.D. 1469-70], came William Waldyngfeld, John Hungerford, John Beauchamp, and William Bracebrigge, drapers, and entered into bond in the sum of 100 marks for payment into the Chamber by the said William Waldyngfeld of a like sum to the use of John, Percivall, Nicholas, Margaret, and Elizabeth, children of William Wodehous, late draper, on their coming of age or marriage.

Fo. 68.
Custod'
pueror' Thome
Crofte orph'
Civitatis.

The same day came Thomas Walcot, " taillour," John Lewes, dyer, John Lewes, " taillour," Richard Harkyn, " bowier," and William Person, " taillour," and entered into bond in the sum of £100 for payment into the Chamber of £80 by the said Thomas Walcot to the use of Robert, Stephen, Margery, and [*blank*], the youngest (*postumus*) child, children of Thomas Crofte, late tailor, on their coming of age or marriage.

---

[1] Thomas Crispe, mercer, is recorded by interlineation as having taken the place of Henry Newman, who had quitted the City.

6 Feb., 9 Edward IV. [A.D. 1469-70], William Parotte, tailor, discharged by the Mayor and Aldermen from serving on juries, &c., owing to infirmity of mind and body.

Fo. 68 b.
*Exon'acio
Will'i Parotte
ab assis'.*

8 March, 10 Edward IV. [A.D. 1469-70], William Felde, brewer (*pandoxator*), similarly discharged on account of increasing old age.

*Exon'acio
Will'i Felde
ab assis'.*

17 Sept., 10 Edward IV. [A.D. 1470], John Koyfote, skinner, similarly discharged for like cause.

*Exon'acio
Joh'is Koyfote
ab assis'.*

18 Feb., 9 Edward IV. [A.D. 1469-70], came John Thomson, "bruer," Robert Turner, "taillour," John Birte, fuller, and Robert Smyth, "bruer," and entered into bond in the sum of £20 for payment into the Chamber by the said John Thomson of a like sum to the use of Thomas, son of Richard Hille, late haberdasher, on his coming of age.

*Custodia
Thome fil'
Ric'i Hill
orph' Civi-
tatis.*

Writ of *certiorari* to the Mayor and Aldermen touching proceedings taken against Peter Pekham in the Chamber of the Guildhall. Witness the King at Westminster, 26 Oct., 9 Edward IV. [A.D. 1469].

Fo. 69.
*Judicium
Petri Pekham
prop' inobe-
dienciam fact'
Aldr'o.*

Return made to the above by William Taillour, the Mayor, and the Aldermen, to the effect that on the 7th October last Peter Pekham, a freeman of the City, had used opprobrious words to John Tate, Alderman of Tower Ward, thereby breaking the oath of obedience taken by him on admission to the freedom of the City; that being several times summoned to appear in the Court of the lord the King in the inner Chamber of the Guildhall, before the Mayor and Aldermen,[1] he refused to appear, in contempt of the said lord the King and of his said Court; that further, the said Peter had torn up his certificate of freedom in the presence of the Mayor, and wished to surrender it, but this the Mayor would not permit as subversive of the government of the City. For these reasons proceedings had been taken against the said Peter in the Chamber of the Guildhall.[2]

---

[1] This undoubtedly means the Court of Aldermen, although that Court was not usually styled the "Court of the lord the King."

[2] Referring, probably, to the Mayor's Court, which (except for a brief period, as appears in 'Cal. Letter-Book I,' p. 80) sat in the "principal" or "outer" Chamber of the Guildhall, and was known as the "Court of the lord the King" in the City.

Thereupon, on the 31st Oct., the King issued his writ to the Mayor and Aldermen to proceed in the matter according to the law and custom of the City.

Afterwards, viz., on the 10th Nov., it was adjudged by Richard Lee, the Mayor, William Hulyn, Matthew Philip, Ralph Josselyn, John Yong, Thomas Oulegreve, William Taillour, George Irland, Robert Basset, John Stoktone, William Hamptone, Henry Waver, John Tate, Bartholomew James, John Crosseby, John Warde, Robert Drope, Richard Gardyner, and William Edward, Aldermen, that for his offence the said Peter should be committed to Newgate until further orders, and should pay a fine of 100 marks. The fine was reduced by the mediation of the Chancellor of England to £20, and this amount being paid three days later, the said Peter was released.

Fos. 69b–70b.
Carta Zonari-
orum.

Inspeximus Charter incorporating the Girdlers of London. Dated 6 Aug., 27 Henry VI. [A.D. 1449].[1]

Fo. 70 b.
Exon'acio
Joh'is Tyson
ab assis'.

17 June, 10 Edward IV. [A.D. 1470], John Tyson, "taillour," discharged by the Mayor and Aldermen from serving on juries, &c., owing to deafness and other infirmities.

Exon'acio
Will'i
Nyghtyngale
ab assis'.

3 July, 10 Edward IV. [A.D. 1470], William Nyghtyngale, glover, similarly discharged owing to increasing old age.

Exon'acio
Will'i Setone
ab assisis.

23 July, 10 Edward IV. [A.D. 1470], William Setone, cutler, similarly discharged owing to deafness and other infirmities.

Custodia
Thome Knyf
filii Joh'is
Knyf orph'
Civitatis.

27 July, 10 Edward IV. [A.D. 1470], came Matilda Knyf, widow, Stephen Clampard, "blaksmyth," John Quenesone, "vynter," and Richard Bristall, "taillour," into the Court of the lord the King in the Chamber of the Guildhall, before Richard Lee, the Mayor, and the Aldermen, and entered into bond with Robert Colwiche, the Chamberlain, in the sum of £40 for the delivery to the Chamberlain by the said Matilda of

---

[1] The original charter appears to be in the possession of the Company. See 'Historical Account' by W. Dumville Smythe, Clerk to the Com- | pany, pp. 46–7. The date of the charter, however, is there wrongly given as 1448.

divers goods and chattels to the use of Thomas, son of John Knyf, late "corser," on his coming of age.

29 Aug., 10 Edward IV. [A.D. 1470], came Richard Langton, Robert Fitz Herbert, Robert Godewyn, and Henry Skelton, drapers, and entered into bond in the sum of £200 for payment into the Chamber by the said Richard Langton of certain sums of money to the use of Thomas, son of Richard Payne, late draper, on his coming of age, and of Margaret, daughter of the said Richard, on her coming of age or marriage.

Fo. 71.

Custod' pu'or Ric'i Payne orph' Civitat'.

Friday the Feast of St. Matthew [21 Sept.], 10 Edward IV. [A.D. 1470], in the presence of Richard Lee, the Mayor, Matthew Philippe, Ralph Josselyn, Ralph Verney, John Yong, William Taillour, George Irlond, Robert Basset, John Stoktone, Bartholomew James, John Tate, John Bromer, John Crosseby, John Warde, William Heriot, John Croke, and William Stokker, Aldermen, Robert Drope and Richard Gardyner, the Sheriffs, and very many Commoners summoned to the Guildhall for the election of Sheriffs—John Crosseby, grocer, was elected one of the Sheriffs for London and Middlesex by the Mayor, and John Warde, mercer, was elected the other Sheriff by the Commonalty.

Fo. 71 b.

Eleccio Vicec'.

The same day Robert Colwich, tailor, was elected Chamberlain; Edward Stone, "irmonger," and Peter Calcot, draper, were elected Wardens of London Bridge; and Robert Basset and John Tate, Aldermen, and William Philip, goldsmith, William Hole, skinner, Philip Harpedene, grocer, and John Stokker, draper, Commoners, were elected Auditors of the accounts of the Chamber and of the Wardens of London Bridge in arrear.

Afterwards, viz., on the eve of St. Michael [29 Sept.], the said Sheriffs were sworn at the Guildhall, and on the morrow of the said Feast were presented, admitted, &c., before the Barons of the Exchequer.

21 Sept., 10 Edward IV. [A.D. 1470], a declaration made by the Mayor and Aldermen, sitting in the Court of the lord the King in the inner Chamber of the Guildhall, for transacting the

De lege non vadiand' sup' attachiamento.

business of the City,[1] that, by the ancient custom of the City, when any one prosecutes an action for debt against another in any Court of the lord the King within the City, and the defendant be attached by money in the hands of another, and that other person appears and defends his law in bar of execution of the money so attached, and the plaintiff produces evidence in writing under the hand of him in whose hands the money is attached that the money was a debt, the defendant shall be barred from waging his law, &c.

Saturday the Feast of Translation of St. Edward [13 Oct.], 10 Edward IV. [A.D. 1470],[2] in the presence of Richard Lee, the Mayor, the Prior of Christchurch, Matthew Philippe, Ralph Josselyn, Ralph Verney, John Yong, William Taillour, George Irland, Robert Basset, William Hamptone, John Stoktone, John Tate, William Edward, Bartholomew James, John Croke, William Heriot, William Stokker, John Crosseby, John Warde, Robert Drope, Richard Gardyner, John Broun, John Bromer, and Thomas Stalbroke, Aldermen, and an immense Commonalty summoned to the Guildhall for the election of a Mayor—John Stoktone was elected Mayor for the ensuing year.

Afterwards, viz., on the Feast of SS. Simon and Jude [28 Oct.], he was sworn at the Guildhall, and on the morrow

---

[1] Here again (cf. *supra*, p. 89) the Court of Aldermen appears as the "Court of the lord the King." Attention has already been drawn (*supra*, p. 24 n.) to the fact that in a similar declaration of the custom prevailing in actions for debt recorded in 1439 (see 'Cal. Letter-Book K,' pp. 228–9), a doubt was expressed in the Calendar as to the Court referred to being the Court of Aldermen; but inasmuch as the Mayor and Aldermen are recorded on both occasions as sitting for the purpose of transacting the business of the City, and in the *inner*, and not the outer Chamber of the

Guildhall, they were clearly sitting as a Court of Aldermen.

[2] The Letter-Book ignores the fact that Henry VI. had been restored to the throne and that Edward was a fugitive. His flight had been proclaimed in the City on the 1st October, and the record of what subsequently took place in the City must be looked for in the City's Journal of that time (Journal 7, fos. 223 b–225). See also Sharpe's 'London and the Kingdom,' i. 311-12. The Journal, moreover, recognizes the regnal year 49 Henry VI. (fos. 227 b, 228 b–229, 230-2 b).

was presented, admitted, &c., before the Barons of the Exchequer.

28 Oct., 10 Edward IV. [A.D. 1470], came Thomas Creket, John Whitebrede, Richard Marchall, fishmongers, and John Thomson, " bruer," before John Stoktone, the Mayor, and the Aldermen, and entered into bond in the sum of £20 for the payment into the Chamber by the said Thomas Creket of a like sum to the use of Johanna, daughter of John Reymund, late "netmaker," on her coming of age or marriage.

Custodia Johanne filie Joh'is Reymund orph' Civitat'.

15 Nov., 10 Edward IV. [A.D. 1470], came Margaret Barkby, widow, John Dagvile, " surgion," John Barkby, "gentilman," and William Stephyns, baker, and entered into bond in the sum of 100 marks for the delivery into the Chamber by the said Margaret of the sum of £10 and certain chattels to the use of Alice, daughter of John Barkby, late baker, on her coming of age or marriage.

Fo. 72 b.

Custod' Alicie filie Joh'is Barkby orphan' Civitat'.

17 Dec., 10 Edward IV. [A.D. 1470], came John Sturmyn, Richard Syffe, William Fyncham, and John Castell, and entered into bond in the sum of 100 marks for the payment into the Chamber by the said John Sturmyn of a like sum to the use of John, son of John Polyll, late haberdasher, on his coming of age.

Fo. 73.

Custod' Joh'is filii Joh'is Polyll orph' Civitatis.

30 May, 10 [*sic*] Edward IV. [A.D. 1471], came Agnes Codnam, widow, John Dey,.... John Bremonger, draper, and John Martyn, " wodemonger," and entered into bond in the sum of 40 marks for the payment into the Chamber by the said Agnes of a like sum to the use of William, Isabella, Alice, and Johanna, children of William Codnam, late tallow-chandler, on their coming of age or marriage.

Custod' pueror' Will'i Codnam orphan' Civitatis.

15 June, 11 Edward IV. [A.D. 1471], came Agnes Heyward, widow, Robert Billesdon, haberdasher, William Alburgh, mercer, and John Benyngton, grocer, and entered into bond in the sum of £250 for the payment into the Chamber by the said Agnes of £125 to the use of Elizabeth and Thomas, children of John Heyward, when they come of age or marry.

Fo. 73 b.

Custod' pueror' Joh'is Heyward orphan' Civitatis.

Fo. 74.
Custod' Will'i filii Will'i Codnam orphan' Civitatis.

5 July, 11 Edward IV. [A.D. 1471], came Henry Vaveser, "brasier," Nicholas Vaveser, "brasier," John Seint John, "sadiller," and William Remyngton, baker, and entered into bond in the sum of 20 marks for the payment into the Chamber by the above Henry of the sum of 10 marks to the use of William and Isabella, children of William Codnam, late "talughchaundiller," when they come of age or marry.

Fo. 74 b.
Custod' Alicie filie Will'i Codnam orph' Civitatis.

5 July, 11 Edward IV. [A.D. 1471], came Robert Lully, William Corbet, Thomas Crull, and William Milne, "irmongers," and entered into bond in the sum of 10 marks for the payment into the Chamber by the above Robert of a like sum to the use of Alice, daughter of William Codnam, late tallow-chandler, on her coming of age or marriage.

Custod' Johanne filie Will'i Codnam orphan' Civitatis.

3 July, 11 Edward IV. [A.D. 1471], came John Hole, "gentilman," John Norrys, "skynner," James Symond and Robert Gilmyn, "taillours," and entered into bond in the sum of 10 marks for the payment into the Chamber by the above John Hole of a like sum to the use of Johanna, another daughter of the above William Codnam, on her coming of age or marriage.

Custod' pueror' Thome Baker orphan' Civitatis.

12 July, 11 Edward IV. [A.D. 1471], came William Persone, junior, William Persone, senior, Thomas Walcotte and Thomas Brounflete, "taillours," and entered into bond in the sum of 25 marks for payment into the Chamber by the above William Persone, junior, of the sum of £10 to the use of Thomas, son of Thomas Baker, and 10 marks to the use of Agnes, daughter of the same, when they come of age or marry.

Fo. 75.
Custod' pueror' Thome Burgeys orphan' Civitatis.

The same day came William Gall, John Stodard, John Philip, "taillours," and Thomas Sutton, "talughchaundiller," and entered into bond in the sum of £100 for payment into the Chamber by the above William of a like sum to the use of John, Johanna, Hugh, Alice, and Elizabeth, children of Thomas Burgeys, late tailor, when they come of age or marry.

Fo. 75 b.
Ordinacio pro mensuratorib' blador'.

19 January, 11 Edward IV. [A.D. 1471-2], ordinance by John Stoktone, the Mayor, Thomas Cooke,[1] Matthew Philip, Ralph Josselyn, John Yong, Ralph Verney, William Taillour, George Irland, Robert Basset, William Hamptone, Bartholomew James,

---

[1] See note *supra*, p. 76.

William Edward, William Stokker, William Heriot, John Ward, John Broun, John Crosseby, Richard Gardyner, and John Bromer, Aldermen, that corn-meters within the liberty of the City shall pay the Bailiff of Billingesgate, according to ancient custom and the ordinance recorded in Letter-Book G, fo. lxxxviii [b], for every two quarters of corn measured one farthing; and that the Bailiff of Billingesgate shall pay the measurers for measuring 10 pence in 20s. This ordinance to apply to the measuring of corn belonging both to natives and foreigners.

13 July, 11 Edward IV. [A.D. 1471], came John Ganne *alias* Bourne, Robert Slewrith, William More, Henry Wright, "sadillers," and John Wade, "taillour," before the Mayor and Aldermen, and entered into bond in the sum of £6 for the payment into the Chamber by the said John Ganne of a like sum to the use of Thomas, Margaret, and Agnes, children of Odowin a Meredeth, late "sadiller," when they come of age or marry.

Custod' pueror' Odowyny a Meredeth orphan' Civitatis.

30 Aug., 11 Edward IV. [A.D. 1471], came Thomas Champeney, Thomas Sewall, "talughchaundillers," and John Catell, "vynter," before the Mayor and Aldermen, and entered into bond in the sum of 100 marks for the payment into the Chamber by the said Thomas Champeney of a like sum to the use of John, son of Roger Champeney, when he attains the age of 26 years.

Fo. 76.

Custod' Joh'is Champney filii Rog'i Champney.

4 Sept., 11 Edward IV. [A.D. 1471], came Juliana Caster, widow, John Bele and Henry Sewall, "gentilmen," and Thomas Aleyn, skinner, before the Mayor and Aldermen, and entered into bond in the sum of 40 marks for the delivery into the Chamber by the said Juliana of the sum of £20 19s. ¼d., or certain goods and chattels valued at that sum, to the use of William, son of John Jenkyn *alias* Warrewyk, on his coming of age.

Custod' Will'i fil' Joh'is Jenken al' Warrewyk.

4 Oct., 11 Edward IV. [A.D. 1471], came Edmund Newman, William Overey, Thomas Pierson, and John Doo, "stokfisshmongers," before the Mayor and Aldermen, and entered into bond in the sum of £400 for the delivery into the Chamber by the said Edmund of the sum of £300, and certain goods and chattels, to the use of Margaret, Alice, and Johanna, daughters

Custod' pueror' Ric'i Phippes orphan' Civitatis.

of Richard Phippes, late fishmonger, when they arrive at the age of 20 years or marry.

Fo. 76 b.
Custod' Joh'is
filii Joh'is
Lambe orph'
Civitatis.

30 Nov., 11 Edward IV. [A.D. 1471], came Emma Lambe, widow, William Cardemaker, grocer, Thomas Unton, draper, and Richard Hadlegh, grocer, before the Mayor and Aldermen, and entered into bond in the sum of £80 for the payment by the said Emma into the Chamber of a like sum to the use of John, son of John Lambe, late grocer, on his coming of age.

Fo. 77.
Custod' Joh'is
filii Joh'is
Treguran
orphan' Civi-
tatis.

25 Oct., 11 Edward IV. [A.D. 1471], came Johanna Treguran, widow, John Dunne, senior, mercer, Thomas Gay, junior, " taillour," and John Ryvers, " skynner," and entered into bond in the sum of £80 for the payment into the Chamber by the said Johanna of a like sum to the use of John, son of John Treguran, late vintner, on his coming of age.

Fo. 77 b.
Custodia
pueror' Joh'is
Beaufrer.

8 Nov., 11 Edward IV. [A.D. 1471], came Richard Adlyngton, Richard Wright, fishmongers, John Taillour, glover, and Thomas Stacy, fuller, and entered into bond in the sum of £20 for payment into the Chamber by the above Richard Adlyngton of a like sum to the use of Alionora and Alice, daughters of John Beaufrer, when they come of age or marry.

Eleccio Vice-
comitum.

Saturday the Feast of St. Matthew [21 Sept.], 11 Edward IV. [A.D. 1471], in the presence of John Stokton, the Mayor, Richard Lee, Matthew Philippe, John Yong, William Taillour, George Irland, Robert Basset, William Hamptone, William Edward, Bartholomew James, William Stokker, William Haryot, John Tate, Richard Gardyner, Robert Drope, Thomas Stalbroke, John Broun, Robert Billesdon, John Bromer, John Crosseby, and John Warde, Aldermen,[1] and very many Commoners summoned to the Guildhall for the election of Sheriffs—John Shelley, mercer, was elected one of the Sheriffs of London and Middlesex by the Mayor, and John Aleyn, goldsmith, was elected the other Sheriff by the Commonalty.

---

[1] The scribe has written *Vice-comitum*, a title applicable only to the last two named, viz., Crosseby and Warde, who were Sheriffs as well as Aldermen.

The same day Robert Colwiche, tailor, was elected Fo. 78
Chamberlain for the year ensuing; Peter Calcot, draper, and
Edward Stone, "irmonger," were elected Wardens of London
Bridge; Robert Basset and Humphrey "Haifford," Aldermen,
Philip Harpdene, grocer, John Stokker, draper, Thomas
Warner, "sadiller," and William Galle, "tailour," Commoners,
were elected Auditors of the accounts of the Chamber and of
the Wardens of London Bridge in arrear.

Afterwards, viz., on the eve of the Feast of St. Michael
[29 Sept.], the said Sheriffs were sworn at the Guildhall, and
on the morrow of the said Feast were presented, admitted, &c.,
before the Barons of the Exchequer.

Letter from Thomas Faucomberge,[1] captain and leader of *L'ra directa*
King Henry's people in Kent, to the Commonalty of the City, *Co'itati per*
Thomam Fau-
desiring to be allowed to pass with his force through the City *comberge Capi-*
in order to seek out and oppose the usurper of the throne. *tan' Kanc'.*
He assures the citizens that they had been misinformed as to
his purpose to despoil the City, and notifies them that he had
desired the Mayor and Aldermen to let him have an answer
at Blackheath by 9 o'clock on Friday. Dated at Sittingbourn
[Wednesday], 8 May [A.D. 1471].[2]

Reply of the Mayor, Aldermen, Sheriffs, Common Council, Fos. 78-78 b.
Masters, Wardens of Crafts, and Constables of the City to the *Responsio*
above letter, acknowledging its receipt, and setting forth that *ejusdem l're.*
King Edward, their sovereign lord, on leaving the City after
his victory at Barnet on Easter Day last [14 April], had
charged them to keep the City on his behalf and to suffer no
disturbance therein. On that account they dared not admit
him, for experience had taught them that his followers would
soon get beyond control. As for a statement he had caused
to be published, that he had been appointed Captain of the

---

[1] Generally known as the "bastard" Falconbridge, being a natural
son of William Nevill, first Lord
Falconbridge (or Fauconberg) and
Earl of Kent, the earldom becoming
extinct on his decease in 1463.

[2] This letter, together with the
reply of the Mayor and Aldermen, is
set out in full in Sharpe's 'London
and the Kingdom' (iii. 387-91).

H

Navy of England, &c., by the late King Henry, at the recommendation of the Earl of Warwick, whom he evidently supposed to be still alive, they assured him that the Earl was dead, and that his corpse, as well as that of his brother the Marquis Montagu, had been exposed to view for two days in St. Paul's. The writers proceed to give him the names of divers nobles and others who had fallen in battle at Tewkesbury on Saturday, the 4th May, and other particulars which they had learnt from letters under the King's own hand as well as from eyewitnesses who had been specially dispatched for the purpose of reporting on the state of the field to the civic authorities. In conclusion, they exhort him to do as they had done, and to acknowledge Edward IV. as the rightful king. If he would do this, they would stand by him, and would even plead for royal favour on his behalf; but as to letting him and his host pass through the City, that was out of the question. Dated at the Guildhall, 9 May [A.D. 1471].

Fo. 79.

De insultu Kanc' apud Algate et Bisshopesgate.

Be it remembered that the Mayor and Aldermen, with the assent of the Common Council, fortified the bank of the water of the Thames between Castle Baynard and the Tower against a large fleet which had appeared near the Tower; and further, that on Sunday, the 12th May, an attack was made upon London Bridge and the new gate there by Kentish seamen and other rebels, who had set fire to divers houses called " berehouses " near the Hospital of St. Katherine; that the attack on London Bridge was renewed on the following Tuesday, when thirteen tenements were fired, and that a force of rebels, 5,000 strong, assailed the gates of Aldgate and Bishopsgate, but were repelled at great loss, and many of them drowned whilst attempting to get on board their boats at Blackwall; and lastly, that on the eve of the Ascension (16 May) King Edward came to the City with a large force and conferred the honour of Knighthood upon John Stokton, the Mayor, Richard Lee, Matthew Philip, Ralph Verney, John Yong, William Taillour, George Irland, William Hampton, Bartholomew

James, Thomas Stalbroke, and William Stokker, Aldermen, as well as upon Thomas Ursewyk the Recorder.[1]

Sunday the Feast of the Translation of St. Edward [13 Oct.], 11 Edward IV. [A.D. 1471], in the presence of John Stokton, the Mayor, the Prior of Christchurch, Richard Lee, Matthew Philip, Ralph Josselyn, John Yong, William Taillour, Robert Basset, George Irland, William Hampton, John Tate, William Edward, Humphrey Hayfford, Bartholomew James, John Bromer, John Crosseby, John Warde, Richard Gardyner, Robert Drope, John Broun, William Stokker, Robert Billesdon, Aldermen, John Shelley and John Aleyn, Sheriffs, and an immense Commonalty summoned to the Guildhall for the election of a Mayor for the year ensuing—William Edward was elected.

Eleccio Maioris.

Afterwards, viz., on the Feast of SS. Simon and Jude [28 Oct.], he was sworn at the Guildhall, and on the morrow was presented, admitted, &c., before the Barons of the Exchequer.

8 Nov., 11 Edward IV. [A.D. 1471], came William Bakon, haberdasher, Simon Turnour...John a Massam, salter, and Michael Harrys, draper, before the Mayor and Aldermen, and entered into bond in the sum of 40 marks for the delivery into the Chamber of a like sum and three silver bowls to the use of John, Thomas, and Robert, sons of William Alhede, late draper, when they come of age or marry.

Custodia pueror' Will'i Alhede draper orphan' Civitatis.

12 Nov., 11 Edward IV. [A.D. 1471], came Henry Bumstede, Ralph Kempe, William Pratte, and Thomas Fabian, mercers, before the Mayor and Aldermen, and entered into bond in the sum of £75 for the delivery into the Chamber by the said Henry Bumstede of a like sum to the use of John, Anne, and Katherine, children of Simon Dawdeley, late mercer, when they come of age or marry.

Fo. 79 b.

Custod' pueror' Simonis Dawdeley orphan' Civitatis.

22 Nov., 11 Edward IV. [A.D. 1471], came Nicholas Muston, "taillour," John Alburgh, Richard Shiffe, and William Purchace, mercers, and entered into bond in the sum of 40 marks

Fo. 80.

Custod' pueror' Edmundi Donabat orph' Civil'.

---

[1] A translation of the record of these proceedings by the Kentish rebels is set out in 'London and the Kingdom' (iii. 391-2).

H 2

for the payment into the Chamber of a like sum by the said Nicholas to the use of Alice, daughter of Edmund Donabate, late fruiterer, on her coming of age or marriage.

Custod' Ric'i Drope fil' Walter' Drope orphan' Civitatis.

22 Nov., 11 Edward IV. [A.D. 1471], came John Eryk, "upholder," Thomas Lewte, "gentilman," William Hulot, "bocher," and Thomas Goldeherst, "skynner," and entered into bond in the sum of £40 for the delivery into the Chamber of divers sums of money and chattels by the above John to the use of Richard, son of Walter Drope, late butcher, on his coming of age.

Fo. 80 b.

Judicium Roberti Richard' pro quadam falsitate.

Writ of *certiorari* to the Mayor and Sheriffs touching the imprisonment of Robert Richardes, late mercer. Dated at Westminster, 28 Jan., 11 Edward IV. [A.D. 1471-2].

Return made to the above writ by William Edward, the Mayor, and John Aleyn and John Shelley, the Sheriffs, to the effect that the above Robert had been committed to prison for having forcibly and fraudulently extorted 70 old gold nobles from Alice Kyng and Elena Ryder of Suthwerk.

Fo. 81.

De Halimoto Pistorum.

14 Dec., 11 Edward IV. [A.D. 1471], ordinance by the Mayor and Aldermen that the Halimote of the Bakers should thenceforth be observed, according to ancient custom, and the articles recorded in the ' Liber Albus,'[1] and that—inasmuch as bakers of London sworn in the said Halimote make presentments yearly, as it seems, to the Mayor and Aldermen, from envy and malevolence of foreign bakers, and make no presentments touching bakers residing within the liberty of the City—there shall be thenceforth elected yearly by the Mayor and Aldermen two affeerers (*afferatores*) to assess and limit, according to their discretion, the amercements arising out of such presentments to the use of the Sheriffs.

---

[1] See ' Liber Albus' (Rolls Series), i. 356-8; ' Liber Cust.,' i. 104-5. Four principal Halimotes were held in the course of a twelvemonth, which all bakers were bound to attend, under penalty of a fine of 21 pence, viz., the first before Michaelmas, the second after Christmas, the third at the close of Easter, and the fourth after the Nativity of St. John the Baptist.

14 Dec. [A.D. 1471], ordinance by the Mayor and Aldermen that the Sheriffs of the City for the time being shall yearly, at their own cost, procure a commission for gaol-delivery of Newgate.

De Commissione pro Gaola de Neugate delib'ana'.

19 Feb., 11 Edward IV. [A.D. 1471-2], came Alice Rawlyns, widow, John Parys, "peautrer," Richard Awbrey, haberdasher, and John Fabian, draper, before the Mayor and Aldermen, and entered into bond in the sum of £533 6s. 8d. for the delivery into the Chamber by the said Alice of the sum of £400 and certain jewels to the use of Katherine and Agnes, daughters of Richard Rawlyns, late grocer, when they come of age or marry.

Custod' pueror' Ric'i Rawlyns orph' Civitatis.

Charter of incorporation of the Tallow Chandlers of London. Witness the King at Westminster, 8 March, 2 Edward IV. [A.D. 1461-2].[1]

Fo. 81 b.

Carta de Talughchaun-delers.

16 March, 12 Edward IV. [A.D. 1471-2], came Katherine Stokker, widow, William Corbet, "irmonger," Richard Syffe and John Baron, mercers, before the Mayor and Aldermen, and entered into bond in the sum of £200 for the payment into the Chamber by the said Katherine of a like sum to the use of William, son of John Stokker, late Alderman, on his coming of age.

Fo. 82.

Custodia Will'i Stokker filii Joh'is Stokker orph' Civitatis.

21 March, 12 Edward IV. [A.D. 1471-2], ordinance by the Mayor and Aldermen that John le Motener, a Frenchman, living under the safe conduct of the lord the King, be discharged from a suit brought against him by Bartholomew Deux on a contract made prior to the issue of the safe conduct.

Fo. 82 b.

Exon'acio cujusdam a quadam accione quia fuit sub salvo conductu d'ni Regis.

" Be it Remembred that where John Goldman taillour levied certeyne accions of trespasses aswel the xiij day of Marche the xij[th] yeere of the Reigne of Kyng Edward the iiij[th] [A.D. 1471-2] as the xiiij day of the same moneth before John Shelley one of the Shereffes of London ayenst Stace Whopser maryner Cornel de Ostende otherweise called Cornel Calun maryner Cristian Tewes maryner and Andrewe Scot maryner

Exon'acio defend' ab accione quia querens confessus fuit transgr' fact' fuisse extra Civitatem.

[1] Printed in 'Records of the Company of Tallow Chandlers,' edited by M. F. Monier-Williams (1897), pp. 38-40.

and forasmoche as the cause of the saide accions before William Edward Maire and thaldermen of the saide Citee the xxj day of Marche the xijth yeere of the reigne of Kyng Edward the iiijth was by the confession of the saide Goldman unto theym clerely understond that it was not determynable within the saide Citee by the course of the lawe of the same Forasmoche as the trespasses surmytted in the same accions were done upon the see without the fraunchise of the saide Citee It was jugged and demed by the same Maire and Aldermen that the [said] Stace Cornel Cristian and Andrewe and theire seuertes in the saide accions of the same accions shulde clerely be dismyssed and discharged."

Br'e pro leprosis ammovend'.

Writ to the Mayor and Sheriffs of London and Middlesex ordering the removal of all lepers found in the highways of the City and county, on horseback or on foot, to the hospitals and sequestered places prepared specially for them, inasmuch as leprosy was on the increase, the disease being infectious from the air the lepers breathe and the sight of their eyes (*eorum occulorum inspeccionem*). This order to be carried out, under a penalty of £500. Witness the King at Westminster, 25 April, 12 Edward IV. [A.D. 1472].[1]

Fo. 83.

28 April, 12 Edward IV. [A.D. 1472], ordinance by William Edwarde, the Mayor, and the Aldermen, that Keepers of the gates of the City should be sworn to prevent lepers entering the City, and that all Constables and Beadles should be thenceforth sworn on Monday after the Feast of the Epiphany[2] in each year, and that proclamation should be made to the effect that " no lepour nor any persone enfecte with the same sikenesse of lepour entre or come w^tin the libertee of this Citee of London upon payne of lesyng of his horse if he come ridyng

---

[1] According to Stow ('Survey,' ed. Kingsford, ii. 146-7), the King himself was brought into close touch with leprosy about this time, inasmuch as William Pole, a Yeoman of the Crown, was stricken with the disease, and Edward made him a grant of a small plot of ground to the north of London to assist him in erecting a hospital for lepers.

[2] Otherwise known as Plow Monday, on which day a General Court of Wardmote is held for receiving Ward presentments, swearing in of constables, &c.

on horse bake and of his gown or upper garment of his body accordyng to the lawes and usages of this Citee."

Judgment by the Mayor and Aldermen that John Jordan, who had been convicted of a criminal assault upon Margery Scovile, who was under 14 years of age, should pay the said Margery the sum of £40 for his offence, the money to remain in the hands of the Chamberlain until the said Margery shall have arrived at full age or marry; and further that the said John, after his discharge from prison, should leave the City within 20 days, under penalty of £200 and further imprisonment, and be deprived of the freedom of the City and be treated as a stranger.

Judicium propt' rapt' cujusdam muliercule.

22 Nov. [A.D. 1471], certain barrels and pots of treacle seized and brought to the Guildhall by order of William Edward, the Mayor, as being unwholesome, the same having been brought to London in galleys by Galleymen, whose names are subscribed.

Fo. 83 b.

Judicium super les Galymen pro falsa triaci.

Afterwards, viz., on the 14th April, 12 Edward IV. [A.D. 1472], the Mayor summoned to the inner Chamber of the Guildhall the following persons, viz., Master Roger Marchall and Master Wolford Cook, Doctors in Medicine, John Clerk, John Matsale, John Colvyle, Richard Hale, Thomas Walker, Thomas How, William Godfrey, Robert Wrightbolt, John Huntley, Martin Harlewes, John Broun, William Spencer, John Berell, junior, Laurence Bere, Robert Marchaunt, John Harrys, and Thomas Hert, apothecaries, who declared on oath the said treacle to be unwholesome.

Thereupon proclamation made for the same to be burnt at the Standard in Chepe, at "the hill in Cornhill," and in Tower Street, as a warning to others.

Proclamacio fact' pro combustione false triaci.

4 June, 12 Edward IV. [A.D. 1472], came Richard Awbrey, haberdasher, Nicholas Okerford, William "A thowe," vintners, and Richard Roger Barker [*sic*], before the Mayor and Aldermen, and entered into bond in the sum of 20 marks for the payment into the Chamber by the said Richard Awbrey of a like sum to the use of Elizabeth, daughter of John Crosse, on her coming of age or marriage.

Fo. 84.

Custod' Elizabeth' Crosse filie Joh'is Crosse orph' Civitat'.

Custod'
Margarete
filie Rob'ti
Fitz John
orph' Civitatis.

11 June, 12 Edward IV. [A.D. 1472], came William Baynard, "taillour," Henry Cheseman, "skynner," William Aunsell, "couper," and John Clerk, horner, and entered into bond in the sum of £20 for the payment into the Chamber by Thomas Fitz John, of Waltham Cross, of a sum of £16 to the use of Margaret, daughter of Robert Fitz John, late draper, on her coming of age or marriage.

Fo. 84 b.
Custod'
pueror' Will'i
Hayes orph'
Civitatis.

20 June, 12 Edward IV. [A.D. 1472], came John Clerk, John Stokes, Thomas Norlong, grocers, and Richard Golofer, mercer, before the Mayor and Aldermen, and entered into bond in the sum of £60 for the payment into the Chamber by the said John Clerk of a like sum to the use of Paul, Juliana, and Agnes, children of William Hayes, late fishmonger, on their coming of age or marriage.

Fo. 85.
Statutum ne
visceral'
bestiar' pro-
jiciantur in
aquam
Thamisie.

Petition presented by the Commonalty of the City to the Parliament held at Winchester in the octave of Hillary, anno 16 Richard II. [A.D. 1392-3], against an ordinance passed in the previous Parliament forbidding the slaughtering of beasts by butchers within the City and certain limits of the same, whereby the price of meat had been unduly enhanced, and praying that the Mayor and Aldermen might be allowed to prescribe certain places within their franchise where beasts might be slaughtered.

Thereupon answer was given to the effect that the King willed that a house for the use of butchers should be erected on the side of the Thames near the tenement of Robert de Parys, and that all dunghills and rubbish between the Palace of Westminster and the Tower of London on either side of the river should be removed by the Feast of Pentecost next ensuing.[1]

Fo. 85 b.
Br'e ne quis
projiciat
aliquod sordi-
dum in aquam
Thamisie sub-
pena xl^{li}.

Writ to the Mayor and Sheriffs of London and Middlesex to enforce the observance of the above ordinance, and keep the river free from filth, &c., under penalty. Witness the King at Westminster, 4 July, 12 Edward IV. [A.D. 1472].

[1] 'Rot. Parl.,' iii. 306.

5 June, 12 Edward IV. [A.D. 1472], Richard West, "taillour," ......Wotton, William White, John Jakys, and Nicholas Mille fined various amounts for false cloth.

21 July [A.D. 1472], ordinance of the Common Council "that no wollen cloth nor clothes from thensfourth be shorn except cancellyng[1] but if it be fully wette upon payne of forfaiture of the same cloth in whose handis straung' or other so ever it shalbe founde and the Sherer therof shal lose his sherys and pay xxs. for every pece cloth to the use of the Co'ialtee as ofte as he shall shere any cloth or clothes not before fully wette Also that no man' put or do to be put any wollen cloth after it be shorn upon the teyntour to be sette or drawen oute in length and brede[2] upon payne of forfaiture of the same cloth or clothes and he that shall so sette it shal pay for his grete falsehode for every pece xls. to the use aforsaide," &c.

18 Aug., 12 Edward IV. [A.D. 1472], came Thomas Belle, "wexchaundiller," Nicholas Boile, draper, Thomas Cape, stockfishmonger, and Mark Huchon, "wexchaundiller," and entered into bond in the sum of £46 13s. 4d. for the payment into the Chamber of the patrimony (£40) due to Peter, Margery, and Johanna, children of John Crosse, and a further sum of 20 marks accruing to them by the death of William Crosse their brother, on their coming of age or marriage.[3]

28 Aug., 12 Edward IV. [A.D. 1472], came Richard Elryngton, "bruer," John Cossale, "bocher," Nicholas Barowe, "sadiller," and William Galle, "taillour," before the Mayor and Aldermen, and entered into bond in the sum of £56 6s. 10d.

[1] Cf. Stat. 1 Ric. III. cap. viii. "No Shearman nor other person ......shall shear nor cancel any cloths......except such cloth be before fully watered." This clause is cited in the 'New English Dict.' (s.v. 'Cancel'), but without any satisfactory explanation of the term in connexion with cloth manufacture. The term may possibly mean the cutting out of badly or imperfectly woven pieces.

[2] The reason given is that cloth that had been fully wetted and shorn and then put on the tenter to be "set and drawn" shrinks when exposed again to any wet, to the prejudice of the buyer. Cf. *infra*, fo. 179.

[3] Marginal note. 6 March, 12 Henry VII. [A.D. 1496-7], came William Dixson, draper, who married the above Margery, and William Drefett, wax-chandler, who married the above Johanna, and acknowledged satisfaction for their wives' property.

for the delivery into the Chamber by the above Richard Elryngtone of the sum of £40 and certain goods and chattels to the use of Ralph and John, sons of Robert Michell, late " bruer," when they come of age or marry.

29 Aug., 12 Edward IV. [A.D. 1472], came James Cawode, " gentilman," John Blakborne, " sherman," William Willoughby and Nicholas Walker, " peautrers," and entered into bond in the sum of £40 for the payment into the Chamber by the above James of a like sum to the use of John and Agnes, children of John Rokley, late brewer, when they come of age or marry.[1]

1 Sept., 12 Edward IV. [A.D. 1472], came Alice Cadman, widow, John Draper, William Shosmyth, and John Snothe, skinners, and entered into bond in the sum of £3 for the payment into the Chamber by the said Alice of a like sum to the use of Robert, son of John Cadman, late " wyer-drawer," on his coming of age.[2]

The same day came Margaret Braybroke, widow, William Stede, " vynter," Thomas Babham, grocer, and James Smyth, fishmonger, and entered into bond in the sum of £40 for the payment into the Chamber by the said Margaret of a like sum to the use of Margaret and John, children of John Smyth, late draper, when they come of age or marry.[3]

11 Sept., 12 Edward IV. [A.D. 1472], came Katherine Martyn, widow, John Martyn, mercer, Thomas Kippyng and George Kneseworth, drapers, and entered into bond in the sum of £80 for the payment into the Chamber by the said Katherine of a like sum to the use of Elizabeth, daughter of the said John Martyn, on her coming of age or marriage.[4]

---

[1] Margin. 15 May, 13 Henry VII. [A.D. 1498], the above John, son of John Rokley, acknowledges satisfaction.

[2] Margin. 17 Jan., 8 Henry VII. [A.D. 1492-3], came the above Robert and acknowledged satisfaction.

[3] Margin. 22 Feb., 6 Henry VII. [A.D. 1490-1], came Robert Asteley, who married the above Margaret, and acknowledged satisfaction for his wife's patrimony. The same day the portion of the above John, who had died under age, was delivered to Margaret Braybroke, his mother.

[4] Margin. 29 May, 19 Edward IV. [A.D. 1479], came John Gaynesford, who married the above Elizabeth, and acknowledged satisfaction for his wife's patrimony.

11 Sept., 12 Edward IV. [A.D. 1472], William White, "talughchaundiller," discharged by William Edward, the Mayor, and the Aldermen from serving on juries, &c., owing to infirmity.

Fo. 89.
Exon'acio Will'i White ab assisis.

Sunday the Feast of St. Matthew [21 Sept.], 12 Edward IV. [A.D. 1472], in the presence of William Edward, the Mayor, Matthew Philip, William Taillour, George Irlond, Robert Basset, William Hampton, John Tate, John Bromer, William Heryot, Bartholomew James, Thomas Stalbroke, John Warde, John Crosseby, Richard Gardyner, John Broun, Robert Drope, Robert Billesdone, and William Stokker, Aldermen, and very many Commoners summoned to the Guildhall for the election of Sheriffs for the year ensuing—Thomas Bledlowe, grocer, was elected one of the Sheriffs of the City of London and Middlesex by the Mayor, and John Broun, mercer, was elected the other Sheriff by the Commonalty.

Fo. 89 b.
Eleccio Vicec'.

The same day Robert Colwich, tailor, was elected Chamberlain; Edward Stone and Peter Calcot were elected Wardens of London Bridge; Humphrey Hayfford and John Warde, Aldermen, Thomas Warner, "irmonger," William Galle, "taillour," John Worsop, draper, and William Parker, "taillour," Commoners, were elected Auditors of the accounts of the Chamber and Wardens of the Bridge in arrear.

Afterwards, viz., on the eve of St. Michael [29 Sept.], the said Sheriffs were sworn at the Guildhall, and on the morrow of the said Feast were presented, admitted, &c., before the Barons of the Exchequer.

25 Sept., 12 Edward IV. [A.D. 1472], came Thomas Basse, John Stokker, John Pake, junior, and William Gibson, drapers, and entered into bond in the sum of £34 6s. 6d. for the delivery into the Chamber of the sum of £27 10s. 9d. and divers goods and chattels to the use of William, son of John Hynde, late stockfishmonger, on his coming of age.

Custod' Will'i filii Joh'is Hynde.

Monday the Feast of Translation of St. Edward [13 Oct.], 12 Edward IV. [A.D. 1472], in the presence of William Edward, the Mayor, the Prior of Christchurch, Matthew Philip, Knt., Ralph Josselyn, Knt., John Yong, Knt., William Taillour, Knt.,

Fo. 90.
Eleccio Maioris.

John Stokton, Knt., Robert Basset, William Hampton, Knt., John Tate, John Bromer, John Crosseby, Knt., Humphrey Hayfford, Richard Gardyner, Bartholomew James, Knt., William Heriot, Thomas Stalbroke, Knt., Robert Drope, William Stokker, Knt., Robert Billesdone, John Broun, and Thomas Bledlowe, Aldermen, and an immense Commonalty summoned to the Guildhall for the election of a Mayor—William Hamptone was elected.

Afterwards, viz., on the Feast of SS. Simon and Jude [28 Oct.], he was sworn at the Guildhall, and on the morrow was presented, admitted, &c., before the Barons of the Exchequer.

Custod'
pueror' Thome
Godyn orph'
Civitatis.

14 Oct., 12 Edward IV. [A.D. 1472], came Richard Syffe, John Sturmyn, and William Alburgh, mercers, and entered into bond in the sum of £51 for the payment into the Chamber by the above Richard of a like sum to the use of Elizabeth, Alice, and Margaret, daughters of Thomas Godyn, late mercer, on their coming of age or marriage.[1]

Fo. 90 b.

Custod' Eliza-
beth' filie
Joh'is Gwey-
mere orphan'
Civitatis.

1 Dec., 12 Edward IV. [A.D. 1472], came Agnes Gweymere, widow, Peter Johnson, draper, William Smalwod, "peautrer," and Robert Colsale, hurer, before the Mayor and Aldermen, and entered into bond in the sum of £37 for the delivery into the Chamber by the said Agnes of a sum of £20 and divers goods and chattels to the use of Elizabeth, daughter of John Gweymere, late "sadiller," on her coming of age or marriage.[2]

Fo. 91.

The same day came Thomas Bougham, "sherman," William Houghton, William Kendall, drapers, and John Wareyn, fuller, and entered into bond in the sum of £16 19s. 4d. for the delivery into the Chamber by the said Thomas of specific sums of money and divers pieces of silver plate to the use of

---

[1] Margin. 1 June, 21 Edward IV. [A.D. 1481], came Henry Cantlowe and Philip Ball (?), who had married the above Elizabeth and Alice, and acknowledged satisfaction, the above Margaret being dead.

[2] Margin. Satisfaction acknowledged 16 June, 22 Edward IV. [A.D. 1482], by John Hill and the above Elizabeth his wife.

Richard, John, and Elena, children of Hugh Judde, late "sherman," when they respectively come of age or marry.[1]

4 Dec., 12 Edward IV. [A.D. 1472], ordinance of the Common Council for the enforcement, after due notice, of an ordinance made anno 41 Edward III., to the effect that a sack of coals shall fully contain 8 bushels, under penalty of the defaulter being placed on the pillory and his sacks burnt under him.[2]

Fo. 91 b.

Ordinacio fact' pro falsis saccis carbonum.

12 Nov., 12 Edward IV. [A.D. 1472], came John Stokker, "gentilman," William Purches, Roger Bonyfaunt, mercer, and Robert Cartleage, "gentilman," before the Mayor and Aldermen, and entered into bond in the sum of 200 marks for payment into the Chamber by the aforesaid John of a like sum to the use of William, Alice, Elizabeth, and Cecilia, children of Thomas Cartleage, late goldsmith, when they come of age or marry.[3]

Custodia pueror' Thome Cartleage orph' Civitatis.

Fo. 92.

12 Jan., 12 Edward IV. [A.D. 1472-3], came William Clerk, grocer, and Alice his wife, daughter of William Wodehous, late draper, and acknowledged satisfaction for his wife's patrimony. Therefore William Waldyngfeld, John Hungerford, John Beauchamp, and William Bracebrigge, drapers, are quit.

Exon'acio custod' Alicie filie Will'i Wodehous.

8 Feb., 12 Edward IV. [A.D. 1472-3], came William Pembrige, William Shosmyth, Thomas Dalham, skinners, and Henry Dodde, "taillour," before the Mayor and Aldermen, and entered into bond in the sum of £10 for the payment into the Chamber by the said William Pembrige of a like sum to the use of John, son of Thomas Pembrige, on his coming of age.

Fo. 92 b.

Custod' Joh'is Pembrige filii Thome Pembrige orphan' Civitatis.

---

[1] Margin. The above orphans, John and Elena, acknowledged satisfaction 18 March, 8 Henry VII. [A.D. 1492-3]; and the above Thomas Bougham notified the Mayor and Aldermen that Richard Judde, the other orphan, had died at the age of 30, having previously received his property.

[2] 'Cal. Letter-Book G,' p. 220; 'Memorials,' pp. 335-6. Cf. 'Cal. Letter-Book I,' p. 214.

[3] Margin. 23 March, 4 Henry VII. [A.D. 1488-9], came Thomas Brokton, "taillour," who married the said Elizabeth, and acknowledged satisfaction, his wife's sister Alice being dead; also 1 Oct., 8 Henry VII. [A.D. 1492], came William Fowler, "dier," who married the above Cecilia, and did likewise; and on 23 Oct., 10 Henry VII. [A.D. 1494], came the above William and did likewise.

Custod' Joh'is
Polhill' filii
Joh'is Polhill'.

Fo. 93.

The same day[1] came Stephen Gibson, John Gowlard or Cowlarde, Thomas Corbronde, and Henry Newman, mercers, and entered into bond in the sum of £23 11s. 7d. for the payment into the Chamber by the said Stephen of a like sum to the use of John, son of John Polhille, on his coming of age.

Custodia
pueror' Will'i
Brynknell or-
phan' Civi-
tatis.

12 Feb., 12 Edward IV. [A.D. 1472-3], came Felix Brynknell, widow, William Alburgh, mercer, John Dey, cutler, and William Cruse, haberdasher, and entered into bond in the sum of 50 marks for the payment into the Chamber by the said Felix of the sum of 20 marks to the use of Thomas, son of William Brynknell, on his coming of age, and a sum of £20 to the use of Margaret, Elizabeth, and Matilda, daughters of the said William, on their coming of age or marriage.

Fo. 93 b.
Exon'acio
custod' Agne-
tis et Alianore
filiar' Rey-
mundi Vawe
al' Monnyng.

9 Feb., 12 Edward IV. [A.D. 1472-3], came John Swan and Thomas Bromfeld, Wardens of the Fraternity of St. Mary and St. Dunstan in the church of St. Dunstan in le West, and acknowledged the receipt of a sum of £30 from William Laurence, grocer, and John Mortymer, fishmonger, the money having accrued to the said Wardens by the decease of Agnes and Alianora, daughters of Reymund Vaw, otherwise Monnyng (or Munnyng), pursuant to the last will of the said Reymund.

Fo. 94.
Exon'acio
custod' Alicie
fil' Ric'i
Phippes.

19 Feb., 12 Edward IV. [A.D. 1472-3], came John Crowche, fishmonger, and Alice his wife, daughter of Richard Phippes, late fishmonger, and acknowledged satisfaction for his wife's patrimony (£100) and divers jewels.

Exon'acio
custod' Will'i
Boleyn filii
Galf'i Boleyn.

9 March, 13 Edward IV. [A.D. 1472-3], came William, son of Geoffrey Boleyn, late Alderman, and acknowledged satisfaction for his patrimony.

Exon'acio
custod' Alicie
filie Galfridi
Boleyn.

The same day came John " Fortscu," esquire, and acknowledged satisfaction for the patrimony of Alice his wife, daughter of Geoffrey Boleyn, late Alderman.

Custod' pueror'
Joh'is Bolton
orphan'.

28 May, 13 Edward IV. [A.D. 1473], came John Stephynson, Thomas Goldhirst, skinners, Nicholas Kirkeby, " hostiller," and John Sethesby, " bower," and entered into bond in the

---

[1] A similar bond is recorded *infra*, fo. 93 b, as having been made on the 16th Feb., but void on account of its having been already recorded here.

sum of 50 marks for the payment into the Chamber by the said John Stephynson of a like sum to the use of William and John, sons of John Bolton, late cordwainer, when they come of age or marry.[1]

27 July, 13 Edward IV. [A.D. 1473], came Johanna Wetton, widow, Thomas Walker, grocer, Giles Kyng, wax-chandler, and Richard Sabyn, tailor, and entered into bond in the sum of 50 marks for the payment into the Chamber by the said Johanna of a like sum to the use of Ralph, Emma, and Marion, children of William Wetton, late grocer, when they come of age or marry.

Fo. 94 b.
Custodia pueror' Will'i Wetton orph' Civitatis.

Tuesday the Feast of St. Matthew [21 Sept.], 13 Edward IV. [A.D. 1473], in the presence of William Hamptone, the Mayor, the Prior of Christchurch, Matthew Philip, Knt., Ralph Verney, Knt., John Yong, Knt., William Edward, William Taillour, Knt., Robert Basset, George Irland, Knt., John Tate, John Bromer, John Crosseby, Knt., Humphrey Hayfford, Richard Gardyner, Bartholomew James, Knt., William Heryot, Thomas Stalbroke, Knt., Robert Drope, William Stokker, Knt., Robert Billesdone, John Broun, and Thomas Bledlowe, Aldermen, and very many Commoners summoned to the Guildhall for the election of Sheriffs—William Stokker, draper, was elected one of the Sheriffs of London and Middlesex by the Mayor, and Robert Billesdone, haberdasher, was elected the other Sheriff by the Commonalty.

Fo. 95.
Eleccio Vice-comit'.

The same day Robert Colwiche, tailor, was elected Chamberlain of the City; Edward Stone and Henry Bumstede were elected Wardens of London Bridge; William Heryot, John Warde, Aldermen, and Robert Hardyng, goldsmith, Thomas Hille, grocer, John Worsoppe, draper, and William Parker, tailor, Commoners, were elected Auditors of the account of the Chamberlain and Wardens in arrear.

---

[1] A marginal note records that on the 13th Dec., 2 Ric. III. [A.D. 1484], John Broun, mercer, became one of the sureties *loco* Nicholas Kirkeby, deceased; and that on the 12th Sept., 1 Henry VII. [A.D. 1485], and 11 June, 2 Henry VII. [A.D. 1487], the Prior of St. Bartholomew and William, son of John Bolton, acknowledged satisfaction for the said William's patrimony, his brother John being deceased.

Afterwards, viz., on the eve of St. Michael [29 Sept.], the said Sheriffs were sworn at the Guildhall, and on the morrow of the said Feast were presented, admitted, &c., before the Barons of the Exchequer.

24 Sept., 13 Edward IV. [A.D. 1473], grant by the Mayor and Aldermen of the custody of Bishopsgate to Henry Snowe, to hold in the same manner as lately held by William Caldebek.

Fo. 95 b.

Eleccio Maioris.

Wednesday the Feast of Translation of St. Edward [13 Oct.], 13 Edward IV. [A.D. 1473], in the presence of William Hamptone, the Mayor, the Prior of Christchurch, Ralph Verney, Knt., William Taillour, Knt., William Edward, Robert Basset, John Tate, Robert Drope, Bartholomew James, Knt., Thomas Stalbroke, Knt., John Warde, Richard Gardyner, William Stokker, Knt., Robert Billesdone, Edmund Shawe, John Broun, and Humphrey Haifford, Aldermen, and an immense Commonalty summoned to the Guildhall for the election of a Mayor for the year ensuing—John Tate was elected.

Afterwards, viz., on the Feast of SS. Simon and Jude [28 Oct.], he was sworn at the Guildhall, and on the morrow was presented, admitted, &c., before the Barons of the Exchequer.

Ordinacio Hostillar'.

The Feast of SS. Simon and Jude [28 Oct.], 13 Edward IV. [A.D. 1473], came the Wardens and good men of the mistery of Hostelers before the Mayor and Aldermen, and prayed that it might be ordained that all those of the said craft and mistery who were freemen of the City and kept inns within the City and its liberty should thenceforth be called "Inholders," and not "Hostillers," and their apprentices enrolled and made free of the City by the same name of "Inholders" for evermore.

Thereupon it was ordained by the Mayor and Aldermen that the above petition should be placed on record, in consideration of the sum of 10 marks paid by the said Wardens to the use and repair of the City Conduit.

Custod' pueror' Joh'is Thorpe orph' Civitatis.

19 Dec., 13 Edward IV. [A.D. 1473], came Robert Hunt, John Hunt, grocers, John Lewes, "taillour," and Richard Wiscard, draper, before the Mayor and Aldermen, and

entered into bond in the sum of £30 for the payment into the Chamber by the said Robert of a like sum to the use of John, William, and Elizabeth, children of John Thorpe, late grocer, when they come of age or marry.[1]

23 Nov., 13 Edward IV. [A.D. 1473], came Marion Stathum, widow, Thomas Kneseworth, fishmonger, William White, mercer, and Thomas Cornysshe, "sadeler," and entered into bond in the sum of £40 for the payment into the Chamber by the said Marion of a like sum to the use of Anne, daughter of Nicholas Stathum, on her coming of age or marriage.

Fo. 96.
Custod' Anne filie Nich'i Stathum.

24 Nov., 13 Edward IV. [A.D. 1473], ordinance by the Mayor and Aldermen that citizens of Coventry should be quit of toll, &c., in the City of London.[2]

Fo. 96 b.
Exon'acio Civium Civi-tat' Coventr' de theolonio etc.

3 Dec., 13 Edward IV. [A.D. 1473], came good men of the mistery of Tylers into the Court of the lord the King, before John Tate, the Mayor, and the Aldermen, and prayed that they might be allowed to elect three Wardens (instead of two, as hitherto) to be overseers, and to make search in the said occupation ; and, further, that one half of all "tile" presented and forfeited might be applied to the use of the craft, the other half going to the use of the Chamber.

Ordinacio Tegulat'.

Their petition granted.

16 Dec., 13 Edward IV. [A.D. 1473], came John Berell, senior, Thomas Oo, Robert Racheford, and John Clerk, grocers, and entered into bond in the sum of £200 for the payment into the Chamber by the said John Berell of a like sum to the use of Beatrix and Margaret, daughters of Richard Hale, late grocer, when they come of age or marry.

Fo. 97.
Custod' pueror' Ric'i Hale orphan' Civitatis.

---

[1] Margin. 12 March, 8 Henry VII. [A.D. 1492–3], came the above William, son of John Thorpe, and acknowledged satisfaction for his patrimony, and that of John and Elizabeth, his brother and sister, who had died.

[2] The late Dr. Charles Gross has pointed out the relationship of Coventry with the City of London through the City of Lincoln. See ' The Gild Merchant,' i. 246, 249.

I

Fo. 97 b.
Exon'ac'
Maioris Al-
dror' ac
Cam'ar' pro
c^{ti} legat' Ag-
neti fil' Joh'is
Mildenale de-
funct' per
Thomam
" *Oulegrave.*"

16 Dec., 13 Edward IV. [A.D. 1473], came William Mendame, who married Agnes, daughter of John Mildenale, deceased, and received from Robert Colwiche, the Chamberlain, the sum of £100, bequeathed to the said Agnes by Thomas "Oulegreve," late Mayor of the City.

Custod' Eliza-
beth' Person
filie Will'i
Person orph'
Civitatis.

14 Jan., 13 Edward IV. [A.D. 1473-4], came Johanna Person, widow, John Lewes, Martin Petewyn, "taillours," and Alexander Wilson, "bruer," and entered into bond in the sum of £40 for the payment into the Chamber by the said Johanna of a like sum to the use of Elizabeth, daughter of William Person, late tailor, on her coming of age or marriage.

Fo. 98.

Custod'
pueror' Joh'is
Selley orph'
Civital'.

14 Jan., 13 Edward IV. [A.D. 1473-4], came Margaret Selley, widow, John Parker, scrivener, William Whitewey, mercer, and Thomas Cotton, "sergeaunt," and entered into bond in the sum of £16 2s. for the payment into the Chamber by the said Margaret of a like sum to the use of William, Ralph, James, and John, sons of John Selley, late tailor, when they come of age.

Fo. 98 b.
Custodia Petri
Walcote filii
Thome Wal-
cote orph'
Civit'.

19 Jan., 13 Edward IV. [A.D. 1473-4], came Alexander Basyngthwayte, William Galle, "taillours," Alexander Wilson and Richard Elthryngton, "brewers," and entered into bond in the sum of 51 marks 5s. for the payment into the Chamber by the said Alexander of a like sum to the use of Peter, son of Thomas Walcote, late tailor, on his coming of age.

Ordinacio
Allutar'.

14 Jan., 13 Edward IV. [A.D. 1473-4], came good men of the mistery of Cordwainers and presented a petition to the Mayor and Aldermen, to the effect that whereas it had been ordained by the Common Council, on the 24th day of September, 13 Edward IV. [A.D. 1473], that "cobelers" should observe the ordinances made anno 12 Henry IV.,[1] the said "cobelers" had failed to observe them, whereby the petitioners had been put to great expense in making their search. They therefore

---

[1] See 'Cal. Letter-Book I,' p. 96; 'Cal. Letter-Book K,' p. 182.

prayed to be allowed to take for their own use a portion of every fine levied on the " cobelers " for their default.

1 Feb., 13 Edward IV. [A.D. 1473-4], came Thomas Acton, "gentilman," Henry Wiche, "iremonger," William Bolley, haberdasher, and Robert Brook, baker, before the Mayor and Aldermen, and entered into bond in the sum of 50 marks for the payment into the Chamber by the above Thomas Acton of a like sum to the use of Katherine, "Truda," Agnes, Cecilia, Alice, John, and William, children of the said Thomas Acton, when they come of age or marry.

Fo. 99.

Custodia pueror' Thome Acton.

1 March, 13 Edward IV. [A.D. 1473-4], came John Langrige, Henry Eburton, John Chittok, and John Brugys, drapers, and entered into bond in the sum of £145 5s. 6d. for the delivery into the Chamber by the said John Langrige of the sum of £120 and certain goods and chattels to the use of Margery, Richard, and William, children of Walter Langrige, late draper, when they come of age or marry.[1]

Fo. 99 b.

Custod' pueror' Walt'i Langrige or- phan' Civitat'.

9 March, 14 Edward IV. [A.D. 1473-4], came Simon Smyth, John Smert, Robert Ryvell, and John Benyngton, grocers, and entered into bond in the sum of £306 18s. 9d. for the delivery into the Chamber by the said Simon of the sum of £241 11s. 2d. and certain jewels and plate to the use of Thomas, son of John "Heyward," late haberdasher, on his coming of age.

Fo. 100.

Custod' Thome Hay- ward filii Joh'is Hay- ward orph' etc.

15 March, 14 Edward IV. [A.D. 1473-4], came Thomas Wymark, "bruer," Alan Johnson, "copersmyth," Robert Altofte, goldsmith, and Thomas White, "bruer," and entered into bond in the sum of £12 6s. 8d. for the delivery into the Chamber by the said Thomas Wymark of the sum of £10 and a mazer cup (*murra*), harnessed with silver and gilt, to the use of Anne, daughter of John Hucchon, when she comes of age or marries.

Custod' Anne fil' Joh'is Hucchon orph' Civitatis.

---

[1] Margin. On the 9th May, 1 Henry VII. [A.D. 1486], came Laurence Ailmer, draper, who mar- ried the above Margery, and the said William Langrige the son, also John Langrige, draper and executor of the above Richard Langrige, who, being of full age, made his will and died, and acknowledged satisfaction for the property of the said Margery, William, and Richard.

I 2

Fo. 100 *b.*

Custod'
pueror' Roberti
Payfote orph'
Civitatis.

30 March, 14 Edward IV. [A.D. 1474], came Thomas Thomson, "taillour," Thomas Hertwell, "sadiller," Robert Walthowe and Martin Petewyn, "taillours," and entered into bond in the sum of 20 marks for the payment into the Chamber by the said Thomas Thomson of a like sum to the use of Thomas, John, Johanna, and Margaret, children of Robert Payfote, when they come of age or marry.

Fo. 101.

Custod'
pueror' Henr'
Picas orph'
Civitatis.

21 April, 14 Edward IV. [A.D. 1474], came Johanna Picas, widow, John Draper, William Payne, and Oliver Danyell, skinners, and entered into bond in the sum of £20 for the payment into the Chamber of a like sum by the said Johanna to the use of Agnes, Marcia, Thomas, and John, children of Henry Picas, late skinner, when they come of age or marry.

Fo. 101 *b.*

Custod' Steph'i
Lane fil' Joh'is
Lane orph'
Civitat'.

14 June, 14 Edward IV. [A.D. 1474], came Peter Draper, John Saverey, John Gloys, "irmongers," and John Draper, "skynner," and entered into bond in the sum of 400 marks for the payment into the Chamber by the said Peter of a like sum to the use of Stephen, son of John Lane, late "irmonger," on his coming of age.[1]

Fo. 102.

Custod' Anne
Davy fil'
Oliveri Davy
orph' Civi-
tatis.

21 June, 14 Edward IV. [A.D. 1474], came Michael Harrys, William Bulstrode, drapers, John Parys, "peauterer," and Thomas Undernak, goldsmith, and entered into bond in the sum of £300 for the payment into the Chamber by the said Michael of a like sum to the use of Anne, daughter of Oliver Davy, late goldsmith, when she comes of age or marries.

Custod'
Percivall
Wodehous
fil' Will'
Wodehous
orph' etc.

4 July, 14 Edward IV. [A.D. 1474], came John Hille, John Pake, junior, Thomas Sampton, and John Wolchirche, drapers, and entered into bond in the sum of 20 marks for the payment into the Chamber by the said John Hille of a like sum to the use of Percivall, son of William Wodehous, late draper, on his coming of age.

---

[1] Margin. 14 Feb., 8 Henry VII. [A.D. 1492-3], came the above | Stephen and acknowledged satisfaction for his patrimony.

"Be it remembred that this is the Dutie belonging to the Pakker of London[1] ordeigned accordyng to the old Custume the iij^{de} day of Novembre the xiiijth yeer of the Reign of Kyng Edward the iiijth [A.D. 1474] by John Tate, Maire of the Citee of London, Humfrey Starky, Recordour, Mathew Philippe, William Taillour, William Edward, William Hampton, Humfrey Hayford, Bartilmew James, Robert Drope, Thomas Stalbroke, John Warde, Thomas Bledlowe, William Stokker, Robert Billesdon, and Thomas Hill, Aldremen of the same Citee :—

Fo. 102 b.

De officio Co'is Pacca-toris.

" First of a cloth cont' xxiiij yerdes, ij*d*.

" Item iij peces of karsey,[2] ij*d*.

" Item iiij pec' of streits,[3] ij*d*.

" Item iij pec' of worstedes, ij*d*.

" Item iiij Oxe hydes, ij*d*.

" Item c Calve Felles, iiij*d*.

" Item c Shepe Felles, vj*d*.

" Item c Morkyn',[4] and lamb Felles, iiij*d*.

" Item c Paslarges,[5] vj*d*.

" Item c goodes of Coton cloth and Frise, vj*d*.

" (The Pakker finding Rope for the above.)

" Item for cariage of a Fother lede, xij*d*.

" Item for sealyng of a barrell vessel of vj^c, iiij*d*.

" Item for sealyng of a litill barrell, ij*d*.

[1] Cf. " A table of fees taken by the Packers and Waterside Porters for shipping and landing the goods or merchandise of Strangers " is appended to the City's charter, 16 Charles I. [A.D. 1640], already referred to *supra*, p. 22, note 3. Package and Scavage dues had been granted to the City by charter dated 26 August, anno 1 Edward IV. [A.D. 1461], and still preserved at the Guildhall.

[2] A coarse kind of cloth, possibly so called from its manufacture having originated at the village of Kersey, co. Suff.

[3] Narrow cloth. Cf. Stat. 18 Henry VI. cap. xvi., where it is distinguished from broad cloth (*lact drap*).

[4] " Morkins " appears as a skin in the Schedule of Scavage dues appended to the charter, 5 Sept., 16 Charles I. [A.D. 1640], preserved among the City's archives. The term is supposed to apply to the skin of an animal that has died of disease or by an accident (Halliwell, ' Archaic Dict.').

[5] Meaning doubtful.

"Item for sealyng of a litill Fanget[1] of cloth, ij*d*.

"Item for a wey of Talugh, j*d*.

"Item for a wey of Chese, j*d*.

"Item for c Cony Felles, ob'.

"Item for sealyng of every barrell pipe chest and Fardell pakked by the Pakker or not pakked by hym, iiij*d*.

"Item for ladyng of a cart to Hampton or to Sandwiche, vj*d*.

"Item for unladyng of a Cart fro Hampton or fro Sandwiche, vj*d*.

"Also for cariage and Portage of all wolle Felles Tynne all maner bales and all oþere m'chaundises in London fro the water of Theamys unto þe houses of Straungers and fro the same houses unto the water aforesaid shuld be caried or of any oþere m'chaundises in any hous for the tyme beyng which ought to be caried and the Pakker to take for his labour xij*d*. of a lode and it be housed at the Waterside inward vj*d*. of a lode   Except a Galey liyng at the key the Patron thereof to have lib'tie for the goodes of his galey to ley them a londe w^t his servauntes and no ship elles shall ley a londe there ne in none oþere place no maner m'chaundises but by the Pakker Also the Patrone ne no manne elles shall cart no maner m'chaundises from the keys but by the pakker."

Fo. 103.

Judicium Collistrigii pro fals' depo- sico'e fact' coram Maiore et Aldr'is.

John Rawlyn and Thomas Gryffyn condemned to stand on the pillory for falsely swearing that they were present when John Chittok, draper, made a certain covenant with Thomas Loy, thereby preventing the said John Chittok from waging his law in an action between him and the said Thomas Loy. [No date.]

Ordinaco'es de Glasyers.

27 July, 14 Edward IV. [A.D. 1474], came good men of the Mistery of Glasyers, and presented to the Mayor and Aldermen the following petition :—

"To the right honourable lord the Mair and thaldremen of the Citee of London Mekely besechen your good lordshipe and Maistershippes your pouere Oratours the Wardeyns and

---

[1] Ital. *fangotto*=*fagotto*, a bundle. Cf. "a faggot of steel"; mentioned | in schedule attached to charter, 16 Charles I.

other goode Folkes enfraunchesed of and in the Craft or
mystere of Glasiers of the said Citee   Where in tyme passed
when Fremen oonely of the same Citee exercised and used the
same craft or mystery w^{t}in the same Citee and the lib'tie þereof
by the ov'sight serche and correccion of the Wardeyns of the
same craft and mistere for the tyme beyng all man' of werk'
concernyng the said Craft and Mistere were truely and profit-
ably made and wrought w^{t}oute sleight fraude or deceite to the
pleasur' of Almyghty god and þe comon profet of the people
of þe Citee aforesaid as by the old werkes of the said Craft
and Mistere of old tyme made it may appere more at large
unto nowe of late daies certein Foreyn persones as well
straungers as other to þe noumbre of xxviij^t and more in secrete
corners as Chaumbres and oþere private places of the said Citee
and nye thereunto adjoynyng some of theym of grete untrueth
and subtilte and some for lak of kunnyng have used and daily
use to werk and exercise deceivably and unkunnyngly the said
craft and Mistere as it may full evedently appere by divers of
their werkes nowe of late by sundry of theym so made and set
up in divers places of the said Citee of whom nor of whose
werk the Wardeyns of the said Craft and Mistere for the tyme
beyng in no wise can or may for the causes aforesaid have
any oversight serche or correccion   That it wold like your
said goode lordship and Maistershippes the premisses considred to do ordeigne enacte and establissh for evermore that
no maner of persone hereafter straunger nor other in any wise
take uppon theym to excercise nor use the said Craft or   Fo. 103 b.
Mistere w^{t}in the said Citee nor the lib'tie thereof except that
thei be Fremen of the said Citee and therunto enhabled and
approved connyng men in the same Craft or mystere by the
Wardeins and ij oþere of the said Craft and mystere moste
expert and hable in the same by the said Wardeins for þe tyme
beyng to theym to that entent to be named and chosen   And
that þe Wardeins of the said Craft and Mistere for the time
being w^t an Officer of the saide Citee by the Mair or Chamb'-
leyn of the same for the tyme being to theim appoynted and
assigned shall mowe at all tymes hereafter make due serche of

almaner of werk concernyng the said Craft or Mistere to be made wrought or used w'in the said Citee or þe lib'tie þerof And that thei shall mowe at all tymes hereafter take and brynge afore the Maire or Chamb'lein of the said Citee for the tyme being all maner of werk concernyng the saide Crafte or Mistere by theym so taken and not sufficiently made and wrought and the maker þereof The same maker þerefore to be punysshed and make fyne after the discrec'ons of the said Mair and Chamberleyn or oon of theym for the tyme being According to their or his dem'ites or dem'ite in that behalf and the lawes and Custumes of þe said Citee in suche cases of old tymes used w'in the Citee aforesaid The oon half þ'eof to be applied to thuse of the Co'ialtie of the same Citee and the oþ'e half þ'eof to thuse of the Co'ialtie and pore people of the said Craft and Mistery And all suche werke or werkes so as is aforesaid by the said Wardeyns and Officer to be taken deceivably and not sufficiently made and wrought thei to be adiugged and det'myned after the discrecions or discrecion lawes and Custumes aforesaid And your said pou'e Oratours shall specially pray to almyghtey God for your noble estates their lives lastyng."

Their petition granted.

Ordinac'oes de Upholders. The same day came good men of the Mistery of Upholders[1] and presented to the Mayor and Aldermen the following petition :—

"To the right honorable lord the Maire and his right worshipful brethren the Aldremen of the Citee of London Shewen unto your goode lordshippe and Maistershippes the Wardeins and the goode Folkes of the Craft of Upholders of the said Citee That where as divers enfraunchesed in the said Citee daily usen to utter and sell divers and many wares

---

[1] Or Upholsterers ; dealers, for the most part, in second-hand furniture. Literally, an *up-holder*=an *under-taker*—the one undertaking to *furnish* your house when alive, and the other your funeral when dead. Riley, 'Memorials,' p. 282n. An upholder is also said to have acted as auctioneer, a business not infrequently associated with that of an undertaker at the present day. See Skeat's Glossary to 'Piers the Plowman,' p. 456.

and m'chaundises belongyng to þe said Craft as Federbeddes pylowes matrasses Quysshens Quyltes and suche oþ'e which the Bier seeth w^toute and knoweth not the stuf w^tin Whereof the bier is gretely and many tymes deceived as it hath bene in tymes passed sufficiently proved before the said Wardeins and also many persones daily bene deceived of thassise of beddes as in Celers[1] Curteins Sparvers[2] and oþ'e and also of Cov'lettes of Englissh makyng which been thynne drevyn and in sondry weyes deceivably made which is not oonely to the grete hurt of the Bier þ'eof but also to the Rebuke of the said Craft and grete diswirship of the said Citee And in tyme commyng to the utter distruccion of the said Craft w^toute a Resonable and a convenient Remedie the rather by your goode lordshippe and Maistershippes be provided in that behalff And for asmoche as Fetherbeddes and bolsters stuffed w^t Fedders and Flokkes Pelewes of down stuffed w^t thistill downe and Cattes Tailles Materas stuffed w^t here[3] and Flokkes and sold for Flokkes[4] Materasse of netis here and hors here which is called Tanners here Jakkes made with Roten Cloth and paynted clothes of old wollen cloth Quysshens stuffed w^t here and sold for Flokkes which been deceivably made to the hurt of the Kynges liege people Pleas it therefore your said lordshippe and Maister-shippes to graunte and enacte that from hensforth the Wardeins of the said Craft for the tyme being may have power and auctorite w^t a Sergeaunt assigned unto theym by your said lordshippe and Maistershippes to over see and serche w^tin the said Citee all suche wares and m'chaundises as been perteynyng to the said Craft and as been abovereshersed and shewed and offerd to be sold and all suche wares and m'chaundises as been in their said serche found not sufficiently nor truely made nor wrought to take and sease and theym to the Chamb'leyn of the said Citee for the tyme being to present

Fo. 104.

---

[1] Canopies or testers for beds.

[2] The framework of a bed, to which were attached the curtains, valences, &c. The term was thus applied to the bed itself, "a sparver bed" (Halliwell).

[3] Hair.

[4] It may be worth noting that in in 1912 a "Rag Flock Bill" is before the House of Commons for the purpose of preventing similar frauds.

and bryng accordyng to their Othes yeerly made before your said lordshippe and Maistershippes   That oone halff of all suche forfeites to be applied to the use of the Chambre of this Citee and that oþere halff to the said Crafte   And this for the love of God and in wey of Charitee."

Their petition granted.

Custod' pueror'
Henrici Stone
orph' Civitatis.

23 Sept., 14 Edward IV. [A.D. 1474], came John Quykesley, " chesemonger," John Laurence, " taillour," John Audley, " girdiller," and Nicholas Crosse, " cordewaner," and entered into bond in the sum of £13 17s. 1d. for the delivery into the Chamber by the said John Quykesley of divers chattels, comprising a standing piece of silver with cover parcel-gilt and surmounted by three lions and a " columbyne "[1]; another piece, silver-gilt, with three lions and a crown on " le knop "; a low piece (*bassam peciam*) of " Parys " silver, " enameled in the bothom " with red (*blodio*) and green ; and a similar piece, " enameled cremysyn," to the use of John, William, Johanna, and Agnes, children of Henry Stone, late stockfishmonger, when they come of age or marry.

Fo. 104 b.

Eleccio Vic'.

The Feast of St. Matthew [21 Sept.], 14 Edward IV. [A.D. 1474], in the presence of John Tate, the Mayor, Matthew Philip, Ralph Verney, John Yonge, William Taillour, William Edward, William Hamptone, Robert Basset, Bartholomew James, Humphrey Hayford, Thomas Stalbroke, Robert Drope, Richard Gardyner, John Warde, John Broun, William Heriot, Thomas Bledlowe, Edmund Shawe, Thomas Hille, William Stokker, Robert Billesdone, and Robert Colwiche,[2] Aldermen,

---

[1] Cf. " unam peciam parcell' deaurat' stantem et coopert' cum uno flore in summitate cooperculi ejusdam pecii [*sic*] vocat' a columbyne." *Supra*, p. 66.

[2] Recently elected Alderman of Farringdon Ward Without. He appears to have ceased to be elected City Chamberlain on that account, although many Aldermen had previously filled the office of Chamberlain. From his day, however, down to 1765 (when Stephen Theodore Janssen, Alderman of Bread Street Ward, was elected Chamberlain) no Alderman was Chamberlain, except Peter Rich, who became Chamberlain on the King's nomination in 1684 and 1688. From 1765 down to the present day Aldermen have invariably been elected Chamberlain (with the exception of Benjamin Scott, 1858-92), but all of them (except John Wilkes, 1779-97) resigned their Aldermanic gowns on their election as Chamberlain.

and very many Commoners summoned to the Guildhall for the election of Sheriffs—Thomas Hille, grocer, was elected one of the Sheriffs for London and Middlesex by the Mayor, and Edmund Shaa, goldsmith, was elected the other Sheriff by the Commonalty.

The same day William Philip, goldsmith, was elected Chamberlain of the City ; Peter Calcot and William Galle were elected Wardens of London 'Bridge ; and William Heriot and Richard Gardyner, Aldermen, Thomas Hille, grocer, Robert Hardyng, goldsmith, William Hole, skinner, and Gilbert Keyes, tailor, Commoners, were elected Auditors of the account of the Chamberlain and Wardens in arrear.

Afterwards, viz., on the eve of St. Michael [29 Sept.], the said Sheriffs were sworn at the Guildhall, and on the morrow of the said Feast were presented, admitted, &c., before the Barons of the Exchequer.

1 Oct., 14 Edward IV. [A.D. 1474], came John Cowlard, mercer, Nicholas Augur, mercer, Henry Davers, mercer, and Thomas Clarell, grocer, and entered into bond in the sum of 250 marks for the payment into the Chamber by the said John Cowlard of the sum of £100 and 100 marks to the use respectively of Simon and Agnes, children of Thomas Mason, late grocer, when they come of age or marry.

Fo. 105.

Custod pueror' Thome Mason orph' Civitat'.

At a Common Council held 5 Oct., 14 Edward IV. [A.D. 1474], proclamation was ordered to be made by John Tate, the Mayor, Humphrey "Sterky" the Recorder, Matthew Philip, John Yonge, William Taillour, William Hampton, William Edward, Robert Basset, Humphrey Hayford, Bartholomew James, Thomas Stalbroke, John Warde, Robert Drope, William Heriot, William Stokker, John Broun, Robert Billesdon, Thomas Bledlowe, Edmund Shaa, and Thomas Hille, Aldermen, as follows :—

Fo. 105 b.

Ordinac'o conc'nen' Candelar' et Carnifices.

"FORASMOCHE as Candill' is sold daily w'in the Citee of London at more excessive price than in daies passed it hath been accustumed to the grete hurte of the Kynges liege people and importable Charge of the poore folk of the Citee of London The which excessive price as it is certeinly understond groweth

by the inordinate covitice and by Covyne made betwene the
Bochers of the saide Citee whiche havyng no Respecte to the
common wele of the same ingrose the Talugh and bryng it into
fewe handes and afterward sell it oute of the same Citee the
saide Citee being unserved ; and also melt the same talough to
thentent to kepe it from Corrupcion unto suche tyme as thei
may sell it at suche price as it may pleas theym and divers
also of the saide bochers do melt their talough and thereof do
make Candell' and utter and sell the said talough and Candill
oute of the Citee aforesaid ; Whereof of verrey necessite must
ensue scarsty of Talough and consequently excessive price of
Candell within the Citee aforesaid ; Therefore to eschewe the
hurtes and Inconvenientes aforerehersed   In the Common
Counsell holden the vth day of Octobre the xiiij^e yeere of the
Reign of Kyng Edward the iiij^{th}   It is ordeigned and enacted
that no bocher ne none other for hym ne none other havyng
Talough to sell w^tin the Citee of London or otherwise from
hensfurth shall sell nor put to saille any talough w^tin the Citee
of London or to be caried sold or delivered oute of the Citee
of London unto suche tyme as it be understond by the Mair and
Aldremen of þe said Citee for the tyme being what quantite of
Talough is w^tin the same Citee and that there be sufficiaunt
and ynough talough for makyng of Candell and to serve the
same Citee and the same Talough sell to makers of Candell'
of the said Citee at suche price as the said Mair and Aldremen
shall assigne and none otherwise uppon payne of Forfaitoure
of the same Talough sold unto the contrarye in whos handes it
may be founde or the value thereof the said payne alwey to
renne uppon the Seller.

  " Also that no Bocher w^tin the said Citee of London sell any
Talough to any persone to make Candell' w^tin the same Citee
unto suche tyme that the saide Maire and Aldremen for þe
tyme being have sett a convenient price after their discrecions
of the same talough uppon payne abovereherced.

  "Also that no Bocher w^tin the Citee aforesaid sell nor bye
of any bocher of the same Citee ne of none oþere persone of
þe same any maner talough uppon payne abovesaide.

"Also that no Bocher of the same Citee from hensfurth shall melt nor do to be moltone any maner of Talough nor sell nor make nor do to be made any maner Candell' w'in the said Citee or w'oute by eny maner of fraude excepte for his necessary expense w'in his owne houshold uppon the payne above-reherced.

"Furthemore it is ordeigned and enacted that no Talough-chaundler nor noone other persone occupiyng makyng of Candell' w'in the saide Citee hereafter shall bye no Talough of any bocher nor of any oþere person within the saide Citee unto suche tyme as the Mair and Aldremen for the tyme being have sett a convenient price uppon the same Talough and the same Candell to be made of clene Talough and Cotton uppon payne of Imprisonment and to make fyne after the discrecion of the Maire and Aldremen for the tyme being.

"Also it is ordeigned and enacted that the price of the Talough yet being in the bochers handes and after this to be delivered by covenaunt unto the Chaundlers shall be modered by the discrecion of the Maire and Aldremen Soo that the saide Chaundelers shall mowe sell for jd. $\frac{1}{4}d$. the lb."

Thursday the Feast of Translation of St. Edward [13 Oct.], 14 Edward IV. [A.D. 1474], in the presence of John Tate, the Mayor, the Prior of Christchurch, Matthew Philippe, Knt., Ralph Josselyn, Knt., John Yonge, Knt., William Taillour, Knt., William Edward, William Hamptone, Knt., Robert Basset, Humphrey Hayford, Bartholomew James, Knt., John Warde, Thomas Stalbroke, Knt., Robert Drope, William Heriot, Richard Gardyner, John Broune, Thomas Bledlowe, Robert Billesdone, and Edmund Shaa, Aldermen, and an immense Commonalty summoned to the Guildhall for the election of a Mayor—Robert Drope was elected.

Fo. 106.

Eleccio Maioris.

Afterwards, viz., on the Feast of SS. Simon and Jude [28 Oct.], he was sworn at the Guildhall, and on the morrow was admitted, accepted, &c., before the Barons of the Exchequer.

Writ to the Mayor and Sheriffs to bring up the body of John Denys, "barbour," a prisoner, together with cause of detention,

&c. Witness T[homas] Billyng[1] at Westminster, 22 Oct., 14 Edward IV. [A.D. 1474].

Fo. 106 b.

Br'e et Return' ubi dicitur q'd quidam fuit co'is pronuba.

Return made to the above by John Tate, Mayor, Edmund Shaa and Thomas Hille, Sheriffs of the City, to the effect that the cause of the detention of the above John Denys was his being a common bawd, and also a plaint of debt pending against him and Matilda his wife, at the suit of John Wayneshede, " bocher."

Custod' pueror' Joh'is Lok orph' Civitatis.

4 Nov., 14 Edward IV. [A.D. 1474], came John Kyng, " taillour," John Garard, " skynner," Thomas Bovy, " fleccher," and Thomas Hewet, " upholder," before the Mayor and Aldermen, and entered into bond in the sum of £14 13s. 4d. for the delivery into the Chamber by the said John Kyng of the sum of £6 13s. 4d. to the use of Nicholas, son of John Lok, late " wexchaundler," and £4 to the use of Alice and Agnes respectively, daughters of the same, when they come of age or marry.[2]

Fo. 107.

Custod' pueror' Joh'is Bacon orph' Civitatis.

10 Dec., 14 Edward IV. [A.D. 1474], came Margaret Bacon, widow, Philip Barker, " irmonger," William Harrys, " upholder," and John Barker, goldsmith, before the Mayor and Aldermen, and entered into bond in the sum of £36 for the delivery into the Chamber by the said Margaret of a sum of £30 and certain silver cups and spoons to the use of Robert, John, and Johanna, children of John Bacon, late " curriour," when they come of age or marry.

Fo. 107 b.

Custod' pueror' Nich' Hynde Curriour orph' Civitat'.

13 Dec., 14 Edward IV. [A.D. 1474], came Thomas Shelley, Ralph Kempe, Robert Yarum, mercers, and John Materdale, tailor, and entered into bond in the sum of £140 for the payment into the Chamber by the said Thomas Shelley of divers sums of money to the use of Thomas, John, Johanna, and Isabella, children of Nicholas Hynde, late " curriour," when they come of age or marry.

Fo. 108.

Saturday, 9 Jan., 14 Edward IV. [A.D. 1474-5], Nicholas Rawlet, chaplain, taken suspiciously with the wife of John

---

[1] Chief Justice of the King's Bench; Recorder of London, 1450-4.

[2] Margin. 10 Feb., 2 Henry VII. [A.D. 1486-7], came Robert Sharpe, " joyner," who married the above Alice, and acknowledged satisfaction for his wife's patrimony, as well as for money accruing to her by the death of Nicholas her brother and Agnes her sister.

Jacobe, the woman not consenting to any unlawful act. Proclamation thereupon made according to custom, &c., and the said Nicholas delivered to the Ordinary, &c.[1]

At a Common Council held on Saturday, 11 Feb., 14 Edward IV. [A.D. 1474-5], there being present Robert Drope, the Mayor, Humphrey Starky the Recorder, Ralph Josselyn, Knt., William Taillour, Knt., Robert Basset, John Crosby, Knt., Richard Gardyner, Thomas Stalbroke, William Stokker, Knt., John Broun, Robert Billesdone, Robert Colwiche, Edmund Shaa, and Thomas Hille, Aldermen, it was agreed that "le Styleyerd," the property of the City, inhabited by merchants of the Hanse of Almaine and of the yearly net value of £70 3s. 4d., should be surrendered to the King, the said King, with the authority of Parliament, granting to the Mayor and Commonalty the above sum out of the fee ferm paid by the Sheriffs.[2] It was further agreed that a tenement belonging to the Prior of "Elsyngspitill" near "le Styleyerd," held by the Mayor and Commonalty on lease for a term of 32 years, should be exchanged with the King for an annual sum of £13 16s. 8d. out of the same fee ferm.

Concessio f'a m'cator' Hanse Aleman' de le Styleyerd etc.

At a Common Council held on Thursday, 16 Feb., 14 Edward IV. [A.D. 1474-5], there being present Robert Drope, the Mayor, Humphrey Starky the Recorder, John Yonge, Knt., William Taillour, Knt., William Edward, William Hamptone, Knt., Robert Basset, John Crosby, Knt., Thomas Stalbroke, Knt., Richard Gardyner, John Browne, Thomas Bledlowe, Edmund Shaa, and Thomas Hille, Aldermen, it was agreed that a conveyance should be made of the "Styleyerd" to the merchants of the Hanse in perpetuity, at an annual rent of £70 3s. 4d.; and further, that the tenement appertaining to the

Fo. 108 b.

Concessio f'a m'cat' Hans' Aleman' de le Styleyerd.

---

[1] As to the practice of dealing with criminous priests in the City, see 'Cal. Letter-Book I,' Introd., pp. xliii-xliv.

[2] Stow records letters patent of 15 Edward IV. whereby the King and Parliament granted the Steelyard to the said merchants, the above sum being paid yearly to the Mayor and Commonalty as rent. ('Survey,' ed. Kingsford, i. 234.)

Prior of "Elsyngspitell" should be demised to the same for a term of 32 years, at an annual rent of £13 16s. 8d.

Custod'
pueror' Will'i
Wodehous
orphan' Civit'.

The last day of February, 14 Edward IV. [A.D. 1474-5], came John Lokton, John Briges, drapers, Henry Massy, goldsmith, and John Blackbourne, "sherman," before the Mayor and Aldermen, and entered into bond in the sum of £40 for the payment into the Chamber by the said John Lokton of a like sum to the use of Elizabeth, Margaret, and Nicholas, children of William Wodehous, late draper, when they come of age or marry.[1]

Fo. 109.

Nota q'd Cives
London' con-
senser' obedire
Bulle Nich'i
Pape super ob-
lac'oibus etc.

At a Common Council held Friday, 3 March, 14 Edward IV. [A.D. 1474-5], there being present Robert Drope, the Mayor, Humphrey Starky the Recorder, Ralph Josselyn, Knt., William Edward, John Tate, Robert Basset, Humphrey Hayford, John Crosby, Knt., Richard Gardyner, John Broun, Thomas Bledlowe, William Heriot, Edmund Shaa, Thomas Hille, and Robert Colwiche, Aldermen, it was agreed that thenceforth the citizens and inhabitants of the City should obey the Bull of Pope Nicholas [V.] touching oblations to be made to City curates,[2] provided the said Bull be exemplified by the seals of the Archbishop of Canterbury and the Bishop of London.

Finis xl li
quia Carni-
fices fecer' Or-
dinac'oes ex
auctoritate
propria.

5 May, 15 Edward IV. [A.D. 1475], one half of a fine of £40, lately imposed on certain butchers for having made ordinances contrary to the liberty of the City, remitted by Robert Drope, the Mayor, Humphrey Starky the Recorder, Ralph Josselyn, Knt., William Taillour, Knt., William Edward, William Hamptone, Knt., John Tate, Robert Basset, Humphrey Hayford, Thomas Stalbroke, Knt., Bartholomew James, Knt., William Heriot, William Stokker, Knt., and John Broun, Aldermen. The rest of the fine paid to the Chamberlain.

[1] Margin. On the penultimate day of March, 10 Henry VII. [A.D. 1495], came Thomas Hyet, draper, who married the above Margaret, and acknowledged satisfaction for his wife's patrimony, as well as for money accruing to her by the death of Elizabeth her sister.

[2] See 'Cal. Letter-Book K,' p. 360n.

9 May, 15 Edward IV. [A.D. 1475], came John Middeltone, senior, Thomas Hosier, Robert Elys, and Richard Haymond before the Mayor and Aldermen, and entered into bond in the sum of 40s. for the payment into the Chamber by the said John of a like sum to the use of John Middeltone his son on his coming of age.

Fo. 109 b.

Custod' Johannis Middeltone filii Joh'is Middeltone sen'.

At a Common Council held 12 May, 15 Edward IV. [A.D. 1475], there being present Robert Drope, the Mayor, Humphrey Starky the Recorder, Matthew Philip, Knt., Ralph Josselyn, Knt., John Yonge, Knt., William Taillour, Knt., William Edward, William Hampton, Knt., John Tate, Robert Basset, Humphrey Hayford, Bartholomew James, Knt., William Heriot, John Warde, John Broune, William Stokker, Knt., Thomas Bledlowe, Robert Billesdone, Robert Colwiche, Edmund Shaa, and Thomas Hille, Aldermen, it was agreed that merchants of the Hanse of Almaine should have all their liberties confirmed under the Common Seal.

Concessio facta m'cat' Aleman'.

26 April, 15 Edward IV. [A.D. 1475], petition of good men of the Mistery of Cooks that certain ordinances might be approved to the following effect (*inter alia*) :—

Fos. 109 b—110 b.

Ordinaciones Cocorum.

That " for asmoche as divers persones of the saide Craft w[t] their handes embrowed and fowled be accustumed to drawe and pluk other Folk as well gentilmen as other comon people by their slyves and clothes to bye of their vitailles whereby many debates and strives often tymes happen ayenst the peas " —such conduct should be forbidden, under penalty.

That no one of the Craft sell fish and flesh together on Wednesdays.

That no one of the Craft " bake rost nor seeth Flessh nor Fisshe ij tymes to sell," under penalty.

That no one " sell any vitailles to any huxter that is to say Elys Tartes nor Flawnes[1] nor any suche bake metes sauf onely to fre persones of the said Citee nor no mold ware be made by hande nor by mold to sell in their Shoppes nor to any huxter

---

[1] A light cake not unlike a pancake. Cf. Roger le Flauner, ' Cal. Letter-Book B,' p. 5. Riley's ' Memorials,' Introd., p. xxi.

K

to retaill nor to any other but if it be bespoken fore to the Feests," under penalty.

That no one of the Craft "colour nor mayntene any foreyn persone nor sett him awerk as long as theer is any freman to set awerk that can werk."

That no one of the Craft "sende any maner Roost vitaille to any place but it be paied fore in money to the value of the vitaille withoute plegge or it go oute of their dores or be cutte of their broches[1] ...... Provided alwey . that if any of the saide feolasshipe sell any vitaille Rawe or unseasonable that than he satisfye the Bier of his hurtes and make fyne of vj*s.* viij*d.*"

The ordinances to be shown to the whole of the Fellowship twice a year at a convenient place, under penalty.

The ordinances approved.

Fo. 110 b.
De pipis aque
a Ludgate
usque Newgate
etc.

15 June, 15 Edward IV. [A.D. 1475], ordinance by Robert Drope, the Mayor, Humphrey Starky the Recorder, John Yonge, Knt., William Taillour, Knt., William Edward, William Hamptone, Knt., Robert Basset, Humphrey Hayford, Thomas Stalbroke, Knt., John Warde, William Heriot, Thomas Bledlowe, John Broune, Robert Colwiche, Edmund Shaa, and Thomas Hille, Aldermen, that the new pipes for the Conduit from Ludgate to Newgate should thenceforth be repaired, if necessary, by the City, and that a flow of water through the same should not be stayed so long as sufficient water for the service of the City be brought by the Great Conduit.

Fo. 111.
Jud'm Pillor'
pro vendico'e
de Saunders
false mixt' etc.

John Davy condemned to the pillory and to imprisonment for fabricating a powder which he called "Saunders."[2] [No date.]

Q'd canes non
circumvagent
in vicis.

23 June, 15 Edward IV. [A.D. 1475], ordinance by the Common Council "that no persone hold nor have a dogge or dogges nor sawte Biche[3] usyng to go at large oute of his Cloise

---

[1] Spits.

[2] "Saunders, white or red," occurs in the Scavage Table of Rates appended to the charter of 16 Charles I.

The powder appears to have been derived from sandalwood.

[3] A bitch on heat, "sawte" being = assault.

or kepyng by day nor by nyght w^in the Fraunchese of this Citee except gentil[1] houndes and Bochers dogges being no sawte Biche to the which it shall be lefull to go at large by day and not by nyght uppon payne to pay xl*d.* to thuse of the Chambre of every dogge or sawte biche goyng at large contrary to this Acte And if any persone praye for any persone doing the contrary [he] shall pay xl*d.* to the Chambre for his praier for every persone that he praith fore."

1 July, 15 Edward IV. [A.D. 1475], came William Stokker, Knt., and William Heriot, Aldermen, John Stokker and John Pake, drapers, before the Mayor and Aldermen, and entered into bond in the sum of £400 for payment into the Chamber by the said William Stokker of a like sum to the use of John, Katherine, Johanna, and Anne, children of Thomas Riche, late mercer, when they come of age or marry,[2] the said money having been bequeathed to them by John Fenne, late stock-fishmonger.

Custod' pueror' Thome Riche mercer orphan' Civitat'.

4 Aug., 15 Edward IV. [A.D. 1475], came Thomas Hoy, "joynour," Peter Bisshop, "peauterer," John Lawrence, "taillour," and John Hanson, "glasier," before the Mayor and Aldermen, and entered into bond in the sum of £20 for payment into the Chamber by the said Thomas Hoy of a like sum to the use of Mark and John, sons of Nicholas de Corone, on their coming of age.

Fo. 111 b.

Custod' pueror' Nich'i de Corone.

Robert Parys and Thomas Martyn condemned to the pillory for having falsely sealed a bill unto John Nicholl, grocer, for certain wares bought by them of the said John Nicholl, under the fictitious names of John Parys and John Waytes. [No date.]

Fo. 112.

Jud'm Collistrig' pro falsasigillaco'e cujusdam bille.

1 Sept., 15 Edward IV. [A.D. 1475], came Henry Nevell, William Fuller, William Milne, "irmongers," and John Smart, grocer, and entered into bond in the sum of £100 for the pay-

Custod' Will'i filii Joh'is Fctplace Pannar'.

---

[1] Cf. 'Cal. Letter-Book H,' p. 311.

[2] Margin. 22 Aug., 3 Henry VII. [A.D. 1487], came Richard Thornell, mercer, who married the above Anne, and acknowledged satisfaction for the sum of £100 due to his wife ; also, on the 13th June, 18 Henry VII. [A.D. 1503], came William Welbek, Alderman, who married the above Katherine, and acknowledged satisfaction for his wife's portion.

ment into the Chamber by the said Henry of a like sum to the use of William, son of John Fetplace, late draper, on his coming of age.

Fo. 112 b.

Custod' Margarete filie Joh'is Fetplace Pannar'.

The same day the above entered into another bond in the sum of £16 for the payment into the Chamber of a like sum to the use of Margaret, daughter of the above John Fetplace, on her coming of age or marriage.

Presentacio Will'i Drope ad quandam Cantariam quinque Cantariar' in Capella b'te Marie jux'' Guyhald' London'.

Letter from Robert Drope, the Mayor, and William Philip the Chamberlain, to Thomas [Kempe], Bishop of London, presenting William Drope, chaplain, for admission to one of the chantries founded in the Guildhall Chapel by Adam Fraunceys and Henry Frowyk, vacant by the death of John Thornkyn. Dated 7 Sept., A.D. 1475.

Fo. 113.

Q'd duo Aldr'i unius Mister' non simul no'ientur in elecco'e Maioris.

At a Common Council held 13 Sept., 15 Edward IV. [A.D. 1475], there being present Robert Drope, the Mayor, Humphrey Starky the Recorder, Matthew Philip, Knt., Ralph Verney, Knt., John Yonge, Knt., William Taillour, Knt., William Hamptone, Knt., John Tate, Robert Basset, Bartholomew James, Knt., Thomas Stalbroke, Knt., John Broun, Robert Billesdone, Thomas Bledlowe, William Stokker, Knt., Edmund Shaa, Thomas Hille, and Robert Colwiche, Aldermen, it was agreed that thenceforth two Aldermen of the same Craft or Mistery should not be nominated together by the Commoners of the City for one of them to be elected Mayor.[1]

Qualit' Gardian'Misterar' debent venire ad elecco'em Maioris et Vicecom'.

At the same Common Council it was agreed that the Masters and Wardens of the Misteries, together with good men of the same assembled in their halls or other convenient places, shall proceed together to the Guildhall, clothed in their last livery for the election of a Mayor, and clothed in their previous livery for the election of Sheriffs. Also that no others except good men of the Common Council shall be present at such elections.

---

[1] This ordinance does not appear to have attracted the notice of writers on the subject, and, indeed, it is difficult to understand its real object. Nearly a century before (viz., in 1384) an ordinance had been passed forbidding more than 8 members of the same Guild being returned to the Common Council. — 'Cal. Letter-Book H,' pp. 227-8. Journal 8, fo. 108 b.

At the same Common Council it was agreed that no Alderman should bring into the Guildhall at such elections more than one servant to carry his gown (*armulausam*).

De jamul' Aldr̄or' venien' ad elecco'em Maioris et Vic'.

The Feast of St. Matthew [21 Sept.], 15 Edward IV. [A.D. 1475], in the presence of Robert Drope, the Mayor, Humphrey Starky the Recorder, Matthew Philip, Knt., Ralph Verney, Knt., John Yonge, Knt., William Taillour, Knt., William Edward, William Hampton, Knt., John Tate, Robert Basset, Humphrey Hayford, Bartholomew James, Knt., Thomas Stalbroke, Knt., Richard Gardyner, William Heriot, William Stokker, Knt., John Broun, Robert Billesdon, Thomas Bledlowe, Robert Colwiche, Edmund Shaa, and Thomas Hill, Aldermen, and very many Commoners summoned to the Guildhall for the election of Sheriffs—Hugh Brice, goldsmith, was elected one of the Sheriffs of the City of London and Middlesex by the Mayor, and Robert Colwiche, tailor, was elected the other Sheriff by the Commonalty.

Eleccio Vice-comitum.

The same day William Philippe, goldsmith, was elected Chamberlain of the City; William Galle and Edward Stone were elected Wardens of the City Bridge; Richard Gardyner and John Broun, Aldermen, William Hole, pepperer, Gilbert Kays, tailor, Robert Hille, goldsmith, and John Warde, grocer, Commoners, were elected Auditors of the account of the Chamberlain and Wardens in arrear.

Afterwards, viz., on the eve of St. Michael [29 Sept.], the said Sheriffs were sworn at the Guildhall, and on the morrow of the said Feast were presented, admitted, &c., before the Barons of the Exchequer.

3 Oct., 15 Edward IV. [A.D. 1475], William Pounde, butcher, discharged by Robert Drope, the Mayor, and the Aldermen from serving on juries, &c., owing to infirmities of age.

Exon'acio Will'i Pounde ab Assisis.

Friday the Feast of Translation of St. Edward [13 Oct.], 15 Edward IV. [A.D. 1475], in the presence of Robert Drope, Mayor, the Prior of Christchurch, Matthew Philippe, Knt., Ralph Verney, Knt., John Yonge, Knt., William Taillour, Knt., William Edward, William Hamptone, Knt., John Tate,

Fo. 113 b.

Eleccio Maioris.

Robert Basset, Humphrey Hayford, Bartholomew James, Knt., Thomas Stalbroke, Knt., Richard Gardyner, William Heriot, William Stokker, Knt., Robert Billesdone, John Broune, Thomas Bledlowe, Edmund Shaa, Thomas Hille, and Robert Colwiche, Aldermen, and an immense Commonalty summoned to the Guildhall for the election of a Mayor—Robert Basset was elected Mayor for the year ensuing.

Afterwards, viz., on the Feast of SS. Simon and Jude [28 Oct.], the said Mayor was sworn at the Guildhall, and on the morrow was presented, admitted, &c., before the Barons of the Exchequer.

Exon'ac'
Jacobi Watson
ab assis'.

20 Oct., 15 Edward IV. [A.D. 1475], James Watson, cord-wainer, discharged by Robert Drope, the Mayor, and the Aldermen from serving on juries, &c., owing to infirmity.

Exon'ac'
Nich'i Violet
ab assisis.

25 Oct., same year, Nicholas Violet similarly discharged for like cause.

Qualit' Maior
debet attrahere
mat'rias et que-
rel' [?] coram
se in exami-
nac'oe.

7 Nov., 15 Edward IV. [A.D. 1475], ordinance by Robert Basset, the Mayor, Humphrey Starky the Recorder, Ralph Josselyn, Knt., William Taillour, Knt., William Edward, John Tate, Thomas Stalbroke, Knt., William Heriot, Richard Gardyner, John Broun, Thomas Bledlowe, Edmund Shaa, Thomas Hille, and Robert Colwiche, Aldermen, as follows :—

" First where the defendaunt causeth his mater' to be take up' by writte into any Courte that þe Kyng hath and afterward it hapneth to be remitted unto the lawe of this Citee For asmoche as the same Defendaunt hath ones Refused the Juges of this Citee and the same matier' hath be examyned by þe higher Juges—his said matier' shuld never be take up' in Examynacon.

Fo. 114.

" Item where nowe of late it hath been used sumtyme at thinstaunce of þe pleyntif and otherwhile at thinstaunce of the Defendaunt the Maire to permitte the parties to kepe in his handes matiers and accions commensed in the Courtes of this Citee till a certeyn day or ell' til thei have been by yonde the See or other plac' til thei have doone theire besynesses and Returned ayeyn unto this Citee. It is thought that the Maire shuld in nowise take up any matier' in that man'e forme but that the same Pleintif or Defendaunt make Attorney or sum other persone for to shewe the matier' of Conscience in the said matier' or ell' the same matier' to be Remitted to the lawe.

" Item it is thought that the Maire shuld take no matier' into his handes but if it appere to hym that it is a matier' of Conscience And that than' he prefixe the partie a day at þe Yeldhall to shewe his matier and that þe same Sergeaunt that taketh it up' shall warne that oþere partie to be at the Yeldhall the same day and the same Sergeaunt to make Reaport at the Yeldhall the same day wheþere he hath warned þe said partie or nay and than the Maire to procede to examinacion & to geve Jugement or ell' brynge the parties to compromise if the parties will consente or ell' Remitte the matier to the lawe.

" Item it is thought that the Maire shuld take no matier' into his hand' until suche tyme as the partie be greved and hath no Remedy by the Cours of the Common lawe, for if any matier be at an Issue or triall of xij men or may come to an Issue or triall of xij men the partie is not hurt ne greved til he knowe wheþere xij men will passe ayenst hym or not.

" Item it is thought that the Maire shuld take up' no matier into his hand' unto the tyme that the partie hath founde sufficiaunt suertie that he shuld sue no delay oute of this Citee or ell' Jugement to be geven uppon condicion if he sue any delay that than' the Jugement to stande, for it were a Rebuke unto the Maire hangyng the matier' before hym that it shuld be hadde oute of his hand' by writte to the delay of that other partie."

17 Nov., 15 Edward IV. [A.D. 1475], ordinance by Robert Basset, the Mayor, Humphrey Starky the Recorder, Matthew Philippe, Knt., Ralph Josselyn, Knt., John Yonge, Knt., William Taillour, Knt., William Hamptone, Knt., John Tate, Robert Drope, Thomas Stalbroke, Knt., William Heryot, Thomas Bledlowe, and Robert Colwiche, Aldermen, that in future " galymen " should not wander about the city for the purpose of selling their wares, under penalty of forfeiture, but should sell glass and similar wares brought from abroad in their shops

Q'd les galy- men non cir- cumvagent in Civitate cum rebus suis vendendis.

and not elsewhere, and should not sell any kind of cloth or other goods by retail, under similar penalty.

*Q'd custodes
Estivar' non
hospitent viros
nec mulieres
per noctem.*

24 Nov., the same year, ordinance by the above Mayor and Recorder, and Matthew Philipp, Knt., John Yonge, Knt., William Taillour, Knt., Bartholomew James, Knt., William Heriot, Thomas Stalbroke, Knt., John Broun, John Tate, William Edward, Humphrey Hayford, Richard Gardyner, Edmund Shaa, and Thomas Hille, Aldermen, that Keepers of Stews should not harbour men or women at night, under penalty prescribed, and that they should find surety for their good conduct.

Fo. 114 b.

*Custod'
pueror' Joh'is
Fenne orphan'
Civitatis.*

6 Dec., 15 Edward IV. [A.D. 1475], came Richard Quatermayns, Richard Fowler, fishmongers, Thomas Harward and Thomas Unton, drapers, before the Mayor and Aldermen, and entered into bond in the sum of £758 19s. $\frac{1}{2}d.$ for the payment into the Chamber by the said Richard Quatermayns of a like sum to the use of Hugh and Margaret, children of John Fenne, late stockfishmonger, when they come of age or marry.

Fo. 115.

*Custod'
pueror' Joh'is
Fenne orph'
Civit'.*

The same day came Robert Derlyngton, fishmonger, Henry Davers, mercer, Laurence Fyncham, fishmonger, and William Fyncham, mercer, before the Mayor and Aldermen, and entered into bond in the sum of £758 19s. $\frac{1}{2}d.$ for the payment into the Chamber by the said Robert of a like sum to the use of John and Elizabeth, children of the above John Fenne, when they come of age or marry.[1]

Fo. 115 b.
*Proclamac'o
cont^a mendicos
et vagabundos.*

Proclamation made 22 Nov., 15 Edward IV. [A.D. 1475], by " My lord the Maire," on the King's behalf, for vagabonds and masterless people to leave the City, under penalty of the stocks.

*De locis ubi
naves et batall'
ducent' victual'
apud Quene-
hith debent
jacere.*

12 Dec., 15 Edward IV. [A.D. 1475], ordinance by Robert Basset, the Mayor, Humphrey Starky the Recorder, John Yonge, Knt., William Taillour, Knt., Humphrey Hayford, Bartholomew James, Knt., Thomas Stalbroke, Knt., Richard

---

[1] Margin. 26 Aug., 19 Edward IV. [A.D. 1479], came Nicholas Mattok, fishmonger, who married the above Elizabeth, and acknowledged satisfaction for his wife's property ; also on 31 Aug., 22 Edward IV. [A.D. 1482], came the above John Fenne, the son, and acknowledged satisfaction.

Gardyner, William Heriot, Thomas Bledlowe, William Stokker, Knt., John Broun, Edmund Shaa, and Thomas Hill, Aldermen, that ships and boats bringing oysters and mussels and other victual to the City for sale, which vessels and boats used to lie at Quenehithe near the soil of the Fishmongers (*Solum Piscenar'*), should thenceforth lie on the other side of Quenehithe, near the soil appertaining to the City; the said ordinance to take effect from Christmas next.

16 Dec., 15 Edward IV. [A.D. 1475], ordinance by Robert Basset, the Mayor, and the Aldermen that thenceforth Sessions at Newgate should be held at least five times a year, four times by the Sheriffs and once by the Mayor, or twice if necessary, provided that the Sheriffs hold the first four Sessions and the Mayor the fifth and sixth if need be; and that on the day when Sessions shall be held neither the Mayor nor Sheriffs should thenceforth invite more to dinner than the King's Justices and two Aldermen who had already served as Mayor, and two other Aldermen who had not been Mayor, the Recorder, the Common Serjeant and Clerks of the Court, and twelve jurymen or more, if more there be; and that the Mayor and Sheriffs at each Session held by them should give to the jurors of Middlesex 20s., or 26s. 8d. if need be, at their discretion, for their refreshment (*pro jantaculo*).

De Session' apud Newgate quinquies in aº tenend'.

Letter from Robert Basset, the Mayor, and Humphrey Starky the Recorder, to Thomas [Kempe], Bishop of London, presenting Richard Spillesbury, chaplain, for admission to the chantry founded in the chapel of V. Mary, near the Guildhall, for the soul of Roger de Depeham. Dated 31 Jan., 15 Edward IV. [A.D. 1475-6].

Fo. 116. Presentacio Ricardi Spillesbury ad Cantariam in Capella B'te Marie juxta Guyhald'.

16 Feb., 15 Edward IV. [A.D. 1475-6], ordinance by Robert Basset, the Mayor, and the Aldermen that all freemen of the City living within 20 miles outside shall come in with their families by Michaelmas next, and if living beyond 20 miles by Christmas next, or forfeit their freedom.

Q'd lib'i ho'ies manen' ex° Civitat' di-vertant se infra certum tempus ad candem.

Proclamation of the above to be made once a week up to Easter.

24 Feb., 15 Edward IV. [A.D. 1475-6], came John Wymbysshe, grocer, Robert Duplage, tailor, John Broun, grocer,
and William Machon, "pynner," before the Mayor and
Aldermen, and entered into bond in the sum of 56 marks for
the delivery into the Chamber by the said John Wymbysshe of
the sum of 50 marks and a gilt standing cup and covercle to
the use of Thomas, Martin, Ralph, Robert, and John, sons of
John Wymbysshe, when they come of age, the said money, &c.,
having been bequeathed to them by Thomas Welles, late
draper.[1]

5 March, 16 Edward IV. [A.D. 1475-6], petition by good men
of the Mistery of Horners and the Mistery of Botilmakers to
Robert Basset, the Mayor, and the Aldermen, in the Court of
the lord the King in the Chamber of the Guildhall, praying
that—inasmuch as their several Crafts had become so distressed
and impoverished that they were no longer able to bear the
charges imposed upon them on behalf of the King or the City
—the members of both Crafts might be treated as Brethren,
" and occupie and joyne togeder aswell in all thinges to be
borne or doone w^tin the saide Citee by Commaundement of yor
saide lordshipe and Maistershippes for any matier towchyng
oure saide soveraigne lord the Kyng or elles the saide Citee as
in observyng and kepyng goode Rule and Guydyng concernyng the occupacion and werkmanship of the saide Craftes
accordyng to their ordenaunces entred in the Yeldhall," &c.

Their petition granted.

12 March, 17 (16 ?) Edward IV. [A.D. 1475-6], came good men
of the Mistery of Pursers before Robert Basset, the Mayor,
Ralph Verney, Knt., John Yonge, Knt., William Edwarde,
John Tate, Robert Drope, Bartholomew James, Knt., Thomas
Stalbroke, Knt., Richard Gardyner, William Heriot, John
Broune, Thomas Bledlowe, Edmund Shaa, and Thomas Hille,
Aldermen, and showed how, in the first year of the reign of
King Edward III., the Wardens and Fellowship of the Craft had

---

[1] Margin. 22 Sept., 10 Henry VII.
[A.D. 1494], came the above orphan
Ralph Wymbyish, and acknowledged
satisfaction for money accruing to
him by the death of the above John
and Robert his brothers.

complained to the Mayor and Aldermen of frauds practised in the working of leather,[1] viz., " calves skynnes raised and fresed on the bak, which thane were sold for bukkes lether, shepe skynnes were raised and frised on the bak and were sold for gotes lether, and Roes lether and also lambe skynnes were raised and fresed on the bak and were solde for cheverel, which lether thus wrought and counterfeted at that time was died and coloured by the leþ'diers of the saide Citee into divers Colours ; and before that tyme it was used commonly of suche false and untrue lether for to make purses and poyntes and other divers things concerning the said Craft and so put to sale unto the grete hurte and disceite of the Kinges liege people ; For it is not unknowen that if purses and poyntes be made of shepes lether or of lambes lether thus wrought and counterfeted if thei take any maner wete thei must of necessite wexe harde and breke onsonder ; which deceytes, sotilties and Fraudes were than wele considred, and at that tyme it was provided enacted and ordeigned that no man' poyntes from that tyme furthe shuld be made of suche counterfete lether ; Nor that no leþ'dier shulde dye no man' of lether so counterfeted by the which diyng and colouryng the knowelege shuld be alterate or chaunged And thereto at that same tyme the saide leþ'ediers were sworn uppon a booke before the Maire and Aldremen at that tyme being, and beside that the same lether so wrought and counterfeted shuld be forfated and utterly w^toute any Redempcion brent And more over it was ordeigned and enacted that no maner of purses nor poyntes shuld be made to be sold but of suche lether as it mought utterly be knowen and so to be solde for such as it was and for none other in any wise."

They complain that the ordinances then made are not observed and that more frauds than ever were being perpetrated. There were, moreover, many foreigners in the City "from divers countreis of this Realme," Glovers and Pursers, who commonly made false and untrue purses, "for if thei make

---

[1] Cf. ' Cal. Letter-Book E,' p. 223.

purses of dere is lether the pursettes and henges to the same purse be made of shepes lether or elles of other counterfete lether which pursettes and henges will not endure half the tyme that the purse will last, and if thei make quarterd purses thei make the lether of the same quarterd purse to be to shorte and w^t holes or other defaultes therein which defaulte thei set it downward to the bottom of the same purse, and howe be it that the same purses be never so defectif when the pursettes be thereover and sowed thereuppon the defaulte is hid, and thus the biers of all suche manere purses been utterly defrauded and deceived   Ayenst the which deceytes no correccion nor punysshment is had, and so by the forsaid Foreyns the said deceites sotilties and fraudes continuelly usyng the Freemen of the same Craft of pursers here w^{t}in the said Citee been all most utterly distroied."

They prayed therefore a remedy by certain articles in form as set out.[1]   Their prayer granted.

Fo. 118.
Presentacio
Thome Bate-
man capell'i
ad Eccl'iam
p'och Sc'e
Margarete
Patens.

Letter from Robert Basset, the Mayor, to Thomas [Kempe], Bishop of London, presenting Thomas Bateman, chaplain, for admission as Rector of the Church of St. Margaret " Patens," *loco* Sir Walter Muschamp, deceased.[2]   Dated 3 April, 16 Edward IV. [A.D. 1476].

Fo. 118 b.
De lud' Tenis'
Closshyng et
Cailyng
p'hibit' sub
pena.

3 April, 16 Edward IV. [A.D. 1476], ordinance by Robert Basset, the Mayor, and the Aldermen forbidding the exercise of " tenis," " cloisshe " playing or " cailes," indoors or out of doors, under penalty of 40s. and imprisonment for six days.

Proclamacio
de eodem etc.

The above to be proclaimed three several days in manner prescribed.

Custod'
pueror' Will'i
Aleyn aur'
orphan' Civi-
tatis.

25 April, 16 Edward IV. [A.D. 1476], came Nicholas Carlile, Roger Spenser, Richard Cheyne, goldsmith, and John Harrys, goldsmith, before the Mayor and Aldermen, and entered into

[1] Printed in Black's ' History of the Company of Leathersellers,' pp. 38-9. The most important article is one granting to the Wardens of the Mistery of Pursers the right of search for counterfeit leather and leather purses, and of presenting defaults before the Mayor and Aldermen.

[2] In 1479 Bateman exchanged livings with Thomas Houghton, Vicar of Blean, co. Kent. *Vide infra*, fo. 145 b.

bond in the sum of 20 marks for payment into the Chamber by the said Nicholas of a like sum to the use of John, Robert, Johanna, and Margaret, children of William Aleyn, late goldsmith, when they come of age or marry.[1]

John Mondue of Stratford atte Bowe condemned to the pillory for having sold at the "Cartes" in the Chepe certain loaves of bread that were deficient in weight. [No date.]

Fo. 119.
Judi'um Pillor' pro Vendico'e panis deficien in pond'.

Agnes Deyntee of Northhawe convicted of having sold divers dishes of butter which appeared to be good outside, but "w'in stuffed and medled w' corrupte and olde butter not wholesome for mannys body," and condemned by the Mayor and Aldermen to stand under the pillory with some of the dishes about her neck for half an hour, and then to quit the City.[2]

Judicium Pill' pro vendico'e butiri corrupt' et insalubr'.

28 April, 16 Edward IV. [A.D. 1476], came Richard Wither, John Rokke, haberdashers, John Snowe and Richard Wynter, goldsmiths, before the Mayor and Aldermen, and entered into bond in the sum of £20 for payment into the Chamber by the said Richard Wither of a like sum to the use of Henry, son of William Hill, late haberdasher, on his coming of age.

Custod' Henrici filii Will'i Hill haberdasher.

9 May, 16 Edward IV. [A.D. 1476], another bond entered into by the above[3] in the sum of £20 for the payment of a like sum to the use of Richard, son of the above William Hille, on his coming of age.

Fo. 119 b.
Custod' Ric'i filii Will'mi Hill hab'-dassher.

At a Common Council held on Friday 17 May, 16 Edward IV. [A.D. 1476], in the presence of Robert Basset, the Mayor, Humphrey Starkey the Recorder, William Edward, William Taillour, Knt., Robert Drope, Humphrey Hayford, Bartholo-

Exon'acio tenencium de Blietheburgh etc de theolonio etc.

---

[1] Margin. 10 March, 9 Henry VII. [A.D. 1493-4], came John, the above orphan, and acknowledged satisfaction for the said 20 marks, his brother Robert and his sisters Johanna and Margaret being dead.

[2] Fabyan (p. 665) mentions this and the foregoing case, remarking that "this Mayer [Robert Basset] dyd sharpe correccion upon the bakers for makyng of lyght brede, in so much that he set dyverse upon the pyllory among the which in the moneth of......John Mondue, baker, was there punysshed..... and a woman named Agnes Deyntie was also there punysshed for sellyng of false myngyd butter."

[3] Here, however, Richard Wynter is described as *girdler*.

mew James, Knt., Richard Gardyner, Thomas Stalbroke, Knt., William Heriot, William Stokker, Knt., John Broune, Robert Billesdone, Thomas Bledlowe, Thomas Hille, Edmund Shaa, Robert Colwiche, and Hugh Brice, Aldermen, it was agreed that the inhabitants of the manor of Blitheburgh, co. Suff., being of the ancient demesne of the Crown, be discharged from toll as contained in letters patent dated 22 April, 15 Edward IV. [A.D. 1475], and here recorded.

Fo. 120.
Presentacio Mag'ri Thome Asshby ad Eccl'iam p'ochialem Sc'i Petri sup' Cornhull London'.

Letter from Robert Basset, the Mayor, and the Aldermen to Thomas [Kempe], Bishop of London, presenting Thomas Asshby, S.T.B., for admission to the Rectory of St. Peter's, Cornhill, vacant by the death of Master Hugh Damelet. Dated 11 May, 16 Edward IV. [A.D. 1476].

Custod' pueror' Ric'i Awbrey haber-dassher etc.

29 May, 16 Edward IV. [A.D. 1476], came John Aleyn, goldsmith, Richard Twigge, mercer, Richard Swan, skinner, and Richard Bodeley, grocer, before the Mayor and Aldermen, and entered into bond in the sum of £280 for payment into the Chamber by the said John Aleyn of certain specified sums of money to the use of Richard, William, Margaret, Alice, and Alice junior, children of Richard Awbrey, late haberdasher, when they come of age or marry.

Fo. 120 b.
Custod' pueror' Joh'is Dey cutler orph' Civitatis etc.

17 July, 16 Edward IV. [A.D. 1476], came Margaret Dey, widow, Hugh Cloptone, Richard Hulle, mercers, and John Toker, cutler, before the Mayor and Aldermen, and entered into bond in the sum of £143 5s. 8d. for payment into the Chamber by the said Margaret of a like sum to the use of Robert and Isabella, children of John Dey, late cutler, when they come of age or marry.

Fo. 121.
Custod' pueror' Will'i Pounde sen' carnificis.

17 July, 16 Edward IV. [A.D. 1476], came Thomas Sonnyf, "tiler," William Stephyns, Robert Broke, bakers, and Robert Walpole, "bruer," before the Mayor and Aldermen, and entered into bond in the sum of 80 marks for payment into the Chamber by the said Thomas of a like sum to the use of William Pounde, junior, John Pounde, senior, John Pounde, junior, Richard Pounde, Giles Pounde, and Robert Pounde, sons of William Pounde, senior, late butcher, when they reach

the age of 24 years, and of Margaret, daughter of the same, when she reaches the age of 16 or marries.[1]

19 July, 16 Edward IV. [A.D. 1476], came John Pikton, Thomas Burgoyn, Nicholas Alwyn, Richard Haynes, mercers, before the Mayor and Aldermen, and entered into bond in the sum of £143 5s. 8d. for payment into the Chamber by the said John Pikton of a like sum to the use of Richard and John, sons of John Dey, late cutler, when they come of age or marry.

Fo. 121 b.

Custod'
pueror' Joh'is
Dey cultell'
orphan' Civi-
tatis.

18 July, 16 Edward IV. [A.D. 1476], William Hubert, baker, condemned to stand on the pillory for making bread that was deficient in weight.

Fo. 122.

Jud'm Pillor'
super Will'm
Hubert pro
panc deficient'.

6 Sept., 16 Edward IV. [A.D. 1476], came good men of the Mistery or Art of Bakers into the Court of the lord the King in the Chamber of the Guildhall, before Robert Basset, the Mayor, and the Aldermen, and presented a petition to the following effect :—

Ordinaciones
Pistorum.

That every livery-man of the Fraternity obey the summons of the Mayor, and every brother attend the burial of a brother or sister of the Fraternity, under penalty.

That every brother pay his quarterage of 3d.

That the Master and Wardens shall not present any one to the Chamberlain for admission to the freedom by redemption until they have called into counsel others who have been Masters and Wardens in order to learn if he be of "able condicions or not."

That no brother rebuke any member of the Fellowship by "fasyng,"[2] "brasyng,"[3] making affray or otherwise, under penalty.

That no member enhance the price of wheat.

---

[1] Margin. 28 Jan., 9 Henry VII. [A.D. 1493-4], came John Pounde, senior, one of the orphans, and acknowledged satisfaction for the above sum of 80 marks, his sister and brothers having died.

[2] Effronting or showing a bold face, a term still used in the United States of America.

[3] Using effrontery. Cf. "brazen-faced "; "to brazen it out."

That the Masters render account of money and jewels received by them on entering office to the new Masters at the end of their term of 3 years, and that the Wardens render their accounts yearly.

That no apprentice be made free without its being reported to the Master and Wardens.

That an assize of bread of members of the Fellowship be made at least twice a week, and the Mayor be informed of the discovery of bread lacking in weight or unseasonable.

Petition granted.

Fo. 122 b.
Eleccio vice-comitum.

The Feast of St. Matthew [21 Sept.], 16 Edward IV. [A.D. 1476], in the presence of Robert Basset, the Mayor, Humphrey Starky the Recorder, Ralph Verney, Knt., William Taillour, Knt., John Tate, Robert Drope, Humphrey Hayford, Thomas Stalbroke, Knt., Bartholomew James, Knt., William Heriot, William Stokker, Knt., Robert Billesdone, John Broun, Thomas Bledlowe, Edmund Shaa, Thomas Hille, Richard Rawson, Robert Colwiche, and Hugh Brice, Aldermen, and very many Commoners summoned to the Guildhall for the election of Sheriffs—William Horne, salter, was elected one of the Sheriffs of London and Middlesex by the Mayor, and Richard Rawson, mercer, was elected the other Sheriff by the Commonalty.

Fo. 123.

The same day William Philippe, goldsmith, was elected Chamberlain of the City for the year ensuing ; William Galle and Henry Bumpstede were elected Wardens of the City Bridge ; John Broune, William Stokker, Knt., Aldermen, and Robert Hille, goldsmith, John Warde, grocer, Henry Colet, mercer, and John Stodard, tailor, Commoners, were elected Auditors of the account of the Chamberlain and Wardens in arrear.

Afterwards, viz., on the eve of St. Michael [29 Sept.], the said Sheriffs were sworn at the Guildhall, and on the morrow of the said Feast were presented, admitted, &c., before the Barons of the Exchequer.

"Forasmoche as Sir John Chaundeler Preest and Sir John Silbard oþerwise called Banbury of their propre confession bene lawfully atteint that thei on Monday at night last passed in the parissh of Aldermary of London lay in bed wᵗ oone Johan Bawdewyn and hir flesshly knowe. Therefore it is awarded that no maner of persone from hensfurþe Reteyne ne kepe nor Receive the same John and John nor any of theym in any maner of service nor salarye wᵗin the libertie of this Citee uppon payne of Forfaiture of the double salary to theym or any of theym in any maner wise to be yoven."[1]

Proclamacio
fᶜᵃ super
Joh'em Chaun-
deler Capellᵐ
captᵉ in adul-
terio etc.

The above proclamation made Thursday, 26 Sept., 16 Edward IV. [A.D. 1476].

25 Oct., 16 Edward IV. [A.D. 1476], Robert Broun, "in-holder," discharged by the Mayor and Aldermen from serving on juries, &c., owing to increasing age and blindness.

Exon'acio
Rob'ti Broun
Inholder ab
assis'.

Sunday the Feast of Translation of St. Edward [13 Oct.], 16 Edward IV. [A.D. 1476], in the presence of Robert Basset, the Mayor, the Prior of Christchurch, Ralph Josselyn, Knt., Ralph Verney, Knt., John Yonge, Knt., William Taillour, Knt., William Hamptone, Knt., John Tate, Robert Drope, Humphrey Hayford, Bartholomew James, Knt., Thomas Stalbroke, Knt., Richard Gardyner, William Heriot, William Stokker, Knt., Robert Billesdone, John Broune, Thomas Bledlowe, Edmund Shaa, Thomas Hille, and Robert Colwiche, Aldermen, and an immense Commonalty summoned to the Guildhall for the election of a Mayor—Ralph Josselyn, Knt., was elected for the year ensuing.

Eleccio
Maioris.

Afterwards, viz., on the Feast of SS. Simon and Jude [28 Oct.], the said Mayor was presented, admitted, &c., before the Barons of the Exchequer.

29 Oct., 16 Edward IV. [A.D. 1476], came Richard Muston, Thomas Unton, Thomas Kippyng, and Christopher Colyns, drapers, before the Mayor and Aldermen, and entered into bond in the sum of £52 10s. for the payment into the Chamber by the said Richard Muston of a like sum to the use of

Custodᵈ Eliza-
beth' Gregory
filie Rob'ti
Gregory
merceri.

---

[1] Cf. 'Cal. Letter-Book I,' p. 286 ; 'Memorials,' p. 567, note.

L

Elizabeth, daughter of Robert Gregory, late mercer, when she comes of age or marries.

Fo. 123 b.
Custod' Eliza-
beth' Gregory
filie Rob'ti
Gregory mer-
ceri.

1 Dec., 16 Edward IV. [A.D. 1476], came John Petite, Edward Bowdon, Thomas Vandernak, John Polyngton, goldsmiths, and John Pelet, skinner, and entered into a similar bond for the same purpose as the foregoing.

Fo. 124.
Ordinac' con-
c'nen' allutar'
et les Coblers.

Petition of the "Coblers" of the City of London to the following effect :—

That 44 Cobblers (whose names could be disclosed), then householders in the City, may be allowed to continue their occupation according to ordinances made *temp*. Richard Whityngton, Thomas Knolles, and John Frenssh,[1] Mayors of London, and that their number be not increased.

That every such householder of the occupation of Cobblers shall have two servants in their shop, viz., a man and a child, and no more (the child not to exceed the age of 16 years), without disturbance by the Cordwainers.

That if any of the said 44 Cobblers leave the City for debt or other cause, his shop shall not be occupied by nor his stuff disposed of to another Cobbler.

That no Cobbler make "no newe shoon ne sole no old Galages," nor "vampay any botes nor boteux w^t soles of newe lether," under penalty.

That whenever the Cobblers appoint new Governors of their occupation, notification be made to the Wardens of the Cordwainers, and the new Governors be sworn before the Mayor to observe the laws and customs of the City and the ordinances aforesaid, and inform the Wardens of the Cordwainers of any infringement.

That they shall make no assemblies of more than 8 persons without permission of the Mayor, under penalty, according to an Act made by Common Council, 24 Sept., 13 Edward IV. [A.D. 1473].

[1] See 'Cal. Letter-Book H,' p. 425; 'Cal. Letter-Book I,' p. 96.   [2] Journal 8, fo. 61 b.

The above petition granted by Ralph Josselyn, Knt. and Mayor, and the Aldermen, 19 Feb., 16 Edward IV. [A.D. 1476-7].

Form of oath to be taken by the Governors of the Cobblers for the due observance of rules made *temp*. Richard II. and Henry IV., &c.

Fo. 124 *b.*
Sacr'm Gubernator' Pictaciar' London'.

6 March, 17 Edward IV. [A.D. 1476-7], ordinance by Ralph Josselyn, Mayor, and the Aldermen that the executors of a tenant-at-will, according to the custom of the City, ought to have a half-year's notice if the yearly value of the tenement exceed 40s., and, if less, a quarter's notice, like a tenant for life.

Fo. 125.
Q'd execut' post mortem testator' et tenent' ad voluntatem debent h'ere talem premunico'em qualem testator' in vita h'erent.

11 March, 17 Edward IV. [A.D. 1476-7], ordinance by the same that, by ancient custom, if a defendant in his own person in foreign attachment, or at the instance of some other person in his own absence, at the discretion of the Mayor for the time being, do put in security (*imponat securitatem*), whether in the Mayor's Court or Sheriffs' Court, although there be other actions pending against the same defendant in either of those Courts, the said defendant shall not be bound, provided he be not a prisoner, to put in security for other actions, &c.

De securitat' capiend' in Forinseco attachiamento in absenc' defend'.

The same day another ordinance by the same that, by ancient custom of the City, a defendant in a bill of *scire facias* upon foreign attachment in any Court of the City, immediately after he has appeared in plea of that bill and shall have pleaded, shall be bound to find sureties and pledges in the Court where the bill is being prosecuted to answer the plaintiff in the said bill until the plea of that bill be determined, according to the custom of the City, &c.

Si quis pl'it-averit sup' scire fac' in forins' attach' debet invenire securitat'.

Certain fishmongers of "Flisshyng" and "Alkmer" in "Celand" convicted of having brought barrels of herring to the City for sale which were "falsly and deceivably pakked that is for to sey thei have laied and pakked in the mustre[1] in

Combust' Allec' false. et fraudilent' paccat'.

---

[1] In the sample. Fr. *moustre*, that which is shown.

L 2

the endes of the said barrelles goode heryng and w'in corrupte heryng which is poison and unholsome for mans body." Order by the Mayor and Aldermen that the bad fish be burnt, some in Billingsgate Street and the rest in Cheap, and the inhabitants of "Flisshyng" and "Alkmer" and others be warned against sending unwholesome herring and victual, under penalty of being put on the pillory and their fish, &c., burnt.

Fo. 125 b.

Custod'
pueror' Joh'is
Richer male-
maker.

12 April, 17 Edward IV. [A.D. 1477], came Marion Richer, widow, John Fayerford, tailor, Richard Griston, tailor, and Henry Asshbourne, scrivener, before the Mayor and Aldermen, and entered into bond in the sum of £72 5s. 4d. for the delivery into the Chamber by the said Marion of divers sums of money and certain chattels to the use of Agnes, John, Isabella, and Alice, children of John Richer, late "malemaker," when they come of age or marry.

Fo. 126.

Custod'
pueror' Thome
Rawson
mercer.

15 Nov., 14 Edward IV. [A.D. 1474], came Richard Rawson, Thomas Ilome, John Fissher, and John Rawson, mercers, before the Mayor and Aldermen, and entered into bond in the sum of 700 marks for payment into the Chamber by the said Richard of a like sum to the use of Thomas, Margaret, "Amea," Ursula, and John, children of Thomas Rawson, late mercer, when they come of age or marry.

Custod'
pueror' Thome
Rawson
mercer.

10 May, 17 Edward IV. [A.D. 1477], came Christopher Colyns, Robert Brigges, Thomas Unton, Thomas Kippyng, drapers, and John Gybbes, "sherman," before the Mayor and Aldermen, and entered into bond in the sum of £200 for the payment into the Chamber by the said Christopher of a like sum to the use of the above children of Thomas Rawson.

Fo. 126 b.

Custod'
Will'i Mugge
filii Rob'ti
Mugge
Talough-
chaundler.

20 May, 17 Edward IV. [A.D. 1477], came William Chaunce, "stacioner," William Maryner, salter, James Welles, draper, and William Briertone, "stacioner," before the Mayor and Aldermen, and entered into bond in the sum of 20 marks for payment into the Chamber by the said William Chaunce of a like sum to the use of William, son of Robert Mugge, late "taloughchaundler," on his coming of age.

23 May, 17 Edward IV. [A.D. 1477], Hugh Palmer, tailor, discharged by Ralph Josselyn, the Mayor, and the Aldermen from serving on juries, &c., owing to deafness.

Fo. 127.
Exon'acio
Hugonis
Palmer ab
assis'.

At a Common Council held 23 May, 17 Edward IV. [A.D. 1477], ordinance by Ralph Josselyn, Knt. and Mayor, Humphrey Starky the Recorder, William Edward, Robert Drope, Robert Basset, Humphrey Hayford, Richard Gardyner, Bartholomew James, Knt., William Heriot, William Stokker, Knt., John Broune, Robert Billesdone, Edmund Shaa, Thomas Hille, Robert Colwiche, Hugh Brice, and Henry Colet, Aldermen, that a sum of 5 pence should be levied on all householders in the City for payment of a man [in each Ward] to clean the City's ditches; and that two Commoners in each Ward should be elected to receive the money, and pay the labourers' wages by the week, special consideration being given to the poor.

De mundac'oe
Fossat' etc.

Form of precept to the Aldermen on the above.

Precept' super
eodem.

At a Common Council, 12 July, 17 Edward IV. [A.D. 1477], ordinance forbidding the making of "any priveye or sege" over the Walbrook or upon any of the town ditches, and ordering the abatement of those already in existence.

De mundac'
Fossat' de
Walbroke et
de latrin' ib'm
destruend' etc.

Also forbidding "White Tawiers"[1] and others to cast any dung, rubbish, or other filth into the said brook or ditches.

Fo. 127 b.

Robert Cobold, mercer, John Hungerford, draper, John Warde, grocer, William Wykyng, skinner, Robert Hardyng, goldsmith, John Philip, tailor, John Catell, "vynter," and "Edmond" Newman, fishmonger, elected by the Common Council to sell superfluous brick and lime, originally bought by Ralph Josselyn, then Mayor, for repair of the City walls, and reimburse him his expenses.

Concessio fc'a
Rad'o Josselyn
Maiori.

16 July, 17 Edward IV. [A.D. 1477], came Agnes Lok, widow, Thomas Mower, Walter Milson, and John Cole, "curriours," before the Mayor and Aldermen, and entered into bond in the sum of £40 for payment into the Chamber by the said Agnes

Fo. 128.
Custod' Anne
Lok filie Will'i
Lok zonarii.

---

[1] Mention made of the "pittes" [with alum, known also as "Megu-
of the White Tawyers or tanners | cers."

of a like sum to the use of Anne, daughter of William Lok, late girdler, on her coming of age or marriage.

Ordinacio super domibus conduct' sive conducend' apud Leden- hall.

18 July, 17 Edward IV. [A.D. 1477], a "Sessyng" made of Ledenhall by Ralph Josselyn, Knt. and Mayor, Humphrey Starky the Recorder, Ralph Verney, Knt., John Yonge, Knt., William Taillour, Knt., William Edward, William Hamptone, Knt., Robert Drope, Bartholomew James, Knt., Robert Billesdone, John Broun, Thomas Bledlowe, William Stokker, Knt., Edmund Shaa, Thomas Hille, Robert Colwiche, Hugh Brice, "Herry" Colet, and Richard Rawson, Aldermen, viz. :—

. Each of the 8 houses on both sides of Ledenhall, viz., east and west, assessed at 14*d*. weekly.

Each of the 4 houses at both ends, viz., north and south, at 10*d*. ·

Fo. 128 b.

Every occupier of the 4 houses over the Selde shall pay weekly 10*d*. for the two uppermost and 8*d*. for the lower.

Particulars of amount to be paid for warehousing "sarplers"[1] and fodders[2] of lead.

Custod' pueror' Joh'is Randolf mercer'.

31 July, 17 Edward IV. [A.D. 1477], came Robert Erik, girdler, Thomas Graungier, felmonger, John Erik and Richard Erik, upholders, before the Mayor and Aldermen, and entered into bond in the sum of £40 for payment into the Chamber by the above Robert Erik of a like sum to the use of John, Isabella, and Alice, children of John Randolf, mercer, when they come of age or marry.[3]

Fo. 129.

Custod' pueror' Georgii "Knesworth" draper.

3 Aug., 17 Edward IV. [A.D. 1477], came Richard "Crakynthorp," tailor, John Prolle, brewer, Thomas "Crakenthorp," tailor, and Robert Holcome, vintner, and entered into bond in the sum of £34 13*s*. 4*d*. for payment into the Chamber by the said Richard of certain specific sums to the use of John, Thomas,

---

· [1] Bales of wool of an uncertain quantity, but usually half a sack. · But see 'Cal. Letter-Book C,' p. 190, where 21 sarplers are recorded as containing 27 sacks.

[2] Usually, at the present day, 19½ cwt. ('N.E.D.')

[3] Margin. On the 28th Jan., 1 Henry VII. [A D. 1485-6], came Richard Wodelake, haberdasher, who married the above Alice, and acknowledged satisfaction for his wife's patrimony, and for money accruing to her by the decease of her sister Isabella.

William, George, Cecilia, Margaret, Johanna, Elizabeth, and Agnes, children of George " Kneesworth," when they come of age or marry.[1]

19 Sept., 17 Edward IV. [A.D. 1477], John Lety, "powche-maker," discharged by Ralph Josselyn, the Mayor, and the Aldermen from serving on juries, &c., owing to his infirmities.

Fo. 129 b.
*Exon'acio
Joh'is Lety
ab assisis etc.*

20 Sept., 17 Edward IV. [A.D. 1477], Richard Aleyn, tailor, similarly discharged for like cause.

*Exon'acio
Ric'i Aleyn
ab assis'.*

Sunday the Feast of St. Matthew [21 Sept.], 17 Edward IV. [A.D. 1477], in the presence of Ralph Josselyn, Knt. and Mayor, Humphrey Starky the Recorder, Ralph Verney, Knt., John Tate, Robert Drope, Humphrey Hayford, Bartholomew James, Knt., Thomas Stalbroke, Knt., Richard Gardyner, William Heriot, William Stokker, Knt., John Broun, Robert Billesdone, Thomas Bledlowe, Edmund Shaa, Thomas Hille, Robert Colwiche, Hugh Brice, Henry Colet, and Richard Rawson, Aldermen, and very many Commoners summoned to the Guild-hall for the election of Sheriffs—John Stokker, draper, was elected one of the Sheriffs of London and Middlesex by the Mayor, and Henry Colet, mercer, was elected the other Sheriff by the Commonalty.

Eleccio Vice-comitum etc.

The same day William Philippe, goldsmith, was elected Chamberlain for the year ensuing; William Galle and Henry Bumpstede were elected Wardens of the City's bridge; William Stokker, Knt., and Robert Colwiche, Aldermen, John Stodard, tailor, Richard Chawry, salter, Richard Nayler, tailor, and Henry "Dauvers," mercer, Commoners, were elected Auditors of the account of the Chamberlain and Wardens in arrear.

Afterwards, viz., on the eve of St. Michael [29 Sept.], the said Sheriffs were sworn at the Guildhall, and on the morrow of the said Feast were presented, admitted, &c., before the Barons of the Exchequer.

[1] 24 March, 10 Henry VII. [A.D. 1494-5], came the above John, and acknowledged satisfaction for his patrimony and for money accruing to him by the decease of William his brother and Elizabeth and Agnes his sisters.

Custod'
pueror' Nich'i
Hynde
curriour.

2 Oct., 17 Edward IV. [A.D. 1477], came Richard Golofer, Robert Burgeis, mercers, John Clerk and Thomas Norland, grocers, before the Mayor and Aldermen, and entered into bond in the sum of £96 13s. 4d. for payment into the Chamber by the said Richard of the sum of £53 6s. 8d. to the use of Thomas, son of Nicholas Hynde, late " curriour," and £43 6s. 8d. to the use of Isabella, daughter of the same, when they come of age or marry.[1]

Fo. 130.

Eleccio
Maioris.

Monday the Feast of Translation of St. Edward [13 Oct.], 17 Edward IV. [A.D. 1477], in the presence of Ralph Josselyn, the Mayor, the Prior of Christchurch, Ralph Verney, Knt., John Yonge, Knt., William Taillour, Knt., William Edward, William Hampton, Knt., John Tate, Robert Drope, Robert Basset, Humphrey Hayford, Bartholomew James, Knt., Thomas Stalbroke, Knt., William Heriot, Richard Gardyner, John Broun, Robert Billesdone, Thomas Bledlowe, Edmund Shaa, Thomas Hille, Hugh Brice, Richard Rawson, and Henry Colet, Aldermen, and an immense Commonalty summoned to the Guildhall for the election of a Mayor—Humphrey Hayford was elected for the year ensuing.

Afterwards, viz., on the Feast of SS. Simon and Jude [28 Oct.], he was sworn at the Guildhall, and on the morrow was presented, admitted, &c., before the Barons of the Exchequer.

Fo. 130 b.
Exon'acio
Laurenc'
"Wylkynson"
ab assis'.

23 Oct., 17 Edward IV. [A.D. 1477], Laurence " Wilkynson," vintner, discharged by the Mayor and Aldermen from serving on juries, &c., owing to infirmity.

Exon'acio
Joh'is Turnour
ab assisis etc.

24 Oct., same year, John Turnour, draper, similarly discharged owing to deafness.

Combustio
Recium.

27 Oct., same year, proclamation made for all nets of too narrow a mesh used in the Thames to be burnt.

Custod' Ric'i
Banaster filii
Ric'i Banaster
groceri.

The same day came Roger Grove, John Broun, William Godfrey, grocers, and Maurice Moredone, draper, before the Mayor and Aldermen, and entered into bond in the sum of

---

[1] Margin. John Pellet, skinner, who married the above Isabella, | acknowledges satisfaction before Thomas Hille, Mayor [A.D. 1484-5].

£65 13s. 4d. for payment into the Chamber by the said Roger of a like sum to the use of Richard, son of Richard Banaster, late grocer, on his coming of age.

18 Nov., 17 Edward IV. [A.D. 1477], ordinance by Hum- phrey Hayford, the Mayor, Humphrey Starky the Recorder, John Yonge, Knt., William Edward, Robert Basset, Bartho- lomew James, Thomas Stalbroke, Robert Billesdone, Thomas Bledlowe, Edmund Shaa, Thomas Hille, Hugh Brice, Robert Colwiche, Richard Rawson, and Henry Colet, Alder- men, that the Abbot of Waltham Holy Cross and his men and tenants shall be quit of toll and all custom in the City, pursuant to a judgment given and entered on the Rolls of divers customs of the City allowed in an *Iter*, &c.

Fo. 131.

Exon'acio Abb'is de Waltham Se̊e Cruc' etc de Theolonio etc.

10 Dec., 17 Edward IV. [A.D. 1477], came Andrew Tod, mercer, Thomas Dalston, glover, Robert Anore, " bocher," and Richard Stutford, blacksmith, before the Mayor and Aldermen, and entered into bond in the sum of £33 for the delivery into the Chamber by the said Andrew of specific sums of money and certain chattels (comprising a nut and a " Parys cuppe," parcel-gilt) to the use of Marion, Thomas, and William, children of John Rooke, junior, late butcher, when they come of age or marry.[1]

Custod' pucror' Joh'is Rooke junior Bocher.

15 Dec., 17 Edward IV. [A.D. 1477], came good men of the Mistery of Girdlers into the Court of the lord the King in the Chamber of the Guildhall, before Humphrey Hayford, the Mayor, Humphrey Starky the Recorder, Ralph Josselyn, Knt., John Yonge, Knt., William Taillour, Knt., William Hamptone, Knt., Robert Basset, Bartholomew James, Knt., Thomas Stalbroke, Knt., Richard Gardyner, Robert Billesdone, Thomas Bledlowe, Thomas Hille, Richard Rawsone, and Henry Colet, Aldermen, and presented a petition praying that certain articles for governing the mistery might be approved.

Fo. 131 b.

Ordinaco'es Zonarior'.

[1] Margin. 11 Sept., 1478, came | above Marion, and acknowledged Thomas Waren, who married the | satisfaction.

Among the articles (which, for the most part, are of the usual character for the regulation of Guilds) are the following :—

"Also that it shalbe lefull to every persone of the said Craft harnysyng girdils of Sik (silk) or of ledder excedyng not the brede of an half peny to naill all sowdres pendauntes of all suché Girdilles w^t j naill any Acte or Ordenaunce to the contrary made not withstaundyng."

* * *

"Also that every persone of the said Crafte may hold oppene shop and shewe and sell his wares and m'chaundises in the Festes of Seint Barthilmowe Thappostill the Nativite of oure Lady and Seint Thomas Thappostill in the whiche alle other Craftes of this Citee use to uppene their shoppes and shewe and sell theire wares and m'chaundises."

Petition granted.

Fo. 132.
Ordinaco'es de Cobelers.

The same day came good men of the Mistery of "Cobelers" to the Mayor and Aldermen complaining that "Foreyns dwellers w^{t}oute the Fraunches and liberties of this Citee Cobelers and other not beryng any taxe lotte or scotte in the saide Citee daily brynge into the same Citee grete Nombre of Shoes and theym by the doseyne uttre and frely sell at their lib'tie and pleasure whereby the poore lyvyng of your saide Besechers is gretely mynisshed and appaired." They pray therefore that it may be ordained "that the draught of the saide utteraunce and sale of the said shoes so brought by the saide Cobelers and other into this noble Citee mowe be fordone uppon payn of Forfaiture of the same shoes," &c.

Petition granted.

Fo. 132 b.
Presentacio
Roberti Basy
capell'i ad
quandam can-
tariam .v.
cantar' in
capella b'te
Me juxta Guy-
haldam Lon-
don'.

Letter from Humphrey Hayford, the Mayor, and William Philippe, the Chamberlain, to Thomas [Kempe], Bishop of London, presenting Robert Basy, chaplain, for admission to one of the five chantries founded in the Guildhall by Adam Fraunceys and Henry Frowik, vacant by the resignation of Sir John Gregory. Dated 7 Feb., 17 Edward IV., A.D. 1477[-8].

6 Feb., 17 Edward IV. [A.D. 1477-8], came Giles Barbour, fuller, William Chaunte, " stacyoner," William Lucas. " taillour," and Thomas Spenser, fuller, before the Mayor and Aldermen, and entered into bond in the sum of £18 for payment into the Chamber by the said Giles of. a like sum to the use ,of John, son of John " Nicolson," late " stacioner," when he shall come of age.

Custod' Joh'is Nicholson filii Joh'is Nicholson.

10 Feb., the same year, came Richard Marchall, John Mark, William Geffrey, and John Colrede, haberdashers, before the Mayor and Aldermen, and entered into bond in the sum of £15 for payment into the Chamber by the said .Richard of. the sum of £10 to the use of Roger, son of the said Richard Marchall, and £5 to Richard, son of the same, when they shall respectively come of age, the said sums having been bequeathed to them by Roger "Waryng," late tailor.

Fo. 133.

Custod' pueror' Ric'i Marchall haberdassher.

27 Feb., 17 Edward IV. [A.D. 1477-8], ordinance by Humphrey Hayford, the Mayor, Humphrey Starky the Recorder, Ralph Josselyn, Knt., Ralph Verney, Knt., John Yonge, Knt., William Edward, Robert Basset, Bartholomew James, Knt., Richard Gardyner, William Heriot, William Stokker, Knt., Robert Billesdone, Richard Rawson, Edmund Shaa, and Hugh Brice, Aldermen, that the Whitawiers within the liberty of the City shall not exercise their art there, but only outside the liberty, and that Whitawiers living in Suthwerk and Barmondesey strete shall enjoy the freedom of the City, although residing outside, inasmuch as they cannot exercise their art within the same without annoying their neighbours.

Fo. 133 b.

Q'd lez Whitawiers non ex'ceant artem suam infra lib'tatem et licet com'orentur ex'a Civitat' tamen debent gaudere lib'tatem etc.

6 March, 18 Edward IV. [A.D. 1477-8], came John Mynes, mercer, William Whitwey, mercer, Richard Cotys, grocer, and William Brownyng, tailor, before the Mayor and Aldermen, and entered into bond in the sum of £10 for payment into the Chamber by the said John Mynes of a like sum to the use of Roger, son of ...... Hyde (the said sum having been bequeathed to the orphan by Roger "Warenge," late tailor), on his coming of age.

Custod' Rog'i Hyde orph'i Civitatis.

10 March, 18 Edward IV. [A.D. 1477-8], came William Witwange, surgeon, Peter Pekham, John Mathewe, mercers, and John Materdale, tailor, before the Mayor and Aldermen, and entered into bond in the sum of £484 16s. 4d. for the delivery

Fo. 134.

Custod' pueror' Joh'is Dagvile Surgion.

into the Chamber by the said William Witwange of the sum of £133 6s. 8d. and certain chattels to the use of John, Alice, and Thomas, children of John Dagvile, late surgeon, when they come of age or marry.[1]

29 March, 18 Edward IV. [A.D. 1478], came John Wyngar, John Stokes, Thomas Norlond, grocers, and Henry Wyngar, haberdasher, before the Mayor and Aldermen, and entered into bond in the sum of 200 marks for payment into the Chamber by the said John Wyngar of a like sum to the use of John and Elizabeth, children of Robert Tatersale, when they come of age or marry.[2]

Fo. 135.

*Proclamacio
fc'a q'd for-
insecus non
vendat m'can-
dis' alt'i
Forins' nec
circumvaget
in Civit'e cum
rebus venalib'.*

Proclamation to the effect "that no maner of Foreyn take uppon hym to sell to Rataile any maner of m'chaundises w'tin the saide Citee or þe liberties thereof to any maner of Foreyn" contrary to the Act, nor "þt any maner of Foreyn in any maner of wise bere to sell to any maner of persone any maner of m'chaundises in the oppen stretes lanes or waies of þe Citee," under penalty prescribed. [No date.]

*P'sentacio
Mag'ri Joh'is
West capell'i
ad cantariam
sup' ossamenta
mortuor' in
Cimiterio Sc'i
Pauli.*

Letter from Humphrey Hayford, Mayor, and William Philippe, the Chamberlain, to Thomas [Kempe], Bishop of London, presenting Master John West, a notary public [and] chaplain, for admission to the perpetual chantry founded by Roger Beyvyn in the chapel over the bones of the dead in St. Paul's churchyard, vacant by the resignation of Sir John Wright.

6 July, 18 Edward IV. [A.D. 1478], came Robert Halle, John Smert, grocers, William Fuller, "irmonger," and Thomas Champney, "taloughchaundiller," and entered into bond in the sum of £250 for the payment into the Chamber by the said Robert of a like sum to the use of John, son of John Crosby, Knt. and Alderman, late grocer, on his coming of age.

[1] Margin. 6 Aug., 18 Edward IV. [A.D. 1478], came Thomas Call, who married the above Alice, and acknowledged satisfaction for his wife's property.

[2] Margin. 21 Jan., 11 Henry VII. [A.D. 1495-6], came the above John, the orphan, and acknowledged satisfaction for his patrimony and for money accruing to him by the death of Elizabeth his sister.

At a Common Council held 23 July, 18 Edward IV. [A.D. 1478], in the presence of Humphrey Hayford, the Mayor, Humphrey Starky the Recorder, John Yonge, Knt., William Taillour, Knt., Robert Drope, William Hamptone, Knt., Robert Basset, Bartholomew James, Knt., William Heryot, John Broune, Richard Gardyner, William Stokker, Knt., Thomas Hille, Hugh Brice, Richard Rawson, and Henry Colet, Aldermen, it was agreed that, inasmuch as brewers of the City enhance the price of beer against the common weal, foreign brewers should come into the City and there freely sell their beer until further orders.[1]

Fo. 135 b.

Restriccio cujusdam ordinac' brasiat' pro tempore etc.

20 July, 18 Edward IV. [A.D. 1478], William Mynte, "whelewright," discharged by Humphrey Hayford, the Mayor, and the Aldermen from serving on juries, &c., at the request of the Queen, on whose business, as well as that of the Prince, he was daily occupied.

Exon'acio Will'mi Mynte ab assis'.

Monday the Feast of St. Matthew [21 Sept.], 18 Edward IV. [A.D. 1478], in the presence of Humphrey Hayford, the Mayor, Humphrey Starky the Recorder, John Yonge, Knt., William Edward, William Hamptone, Knt., Robert Drope, Robert Basset, Bartholomew James, Knt., Richard Gardyner, Thomas Stalbroke, Knt., William Heriot, William Stokker, Knt., Robert Billesdone, John Broun, Edmund Shaa, Thomas Hille, Robert Colwyche, Hugh Brice, Richard Rawson, and Henry Colet, Aldermen, and very many Commoners summoned to the Guildhall for the election of Sheriffs—Robert Hardyng, goldsmith, was elected one of the Sheriffs of London and Middlesex by the Mayor, and Robert Byfeld, "irmonger," was elected the other Sheriff by the Commonalty.

Fo. 136.

Eleccio Vice comit'.

The same day William Philippe, goldsmith, was elected Chamberlain of the City for the year ensuing ; William Galle and Henry Bumpstede were elected Wardens of the City bridge ; Robert Colwyche, Robert Billesdone, Aldermen, and Richard Chawry, salter, Richard Nailer, tailor, Henry "Davers," mercer, and William Bulstrode, draper, Commoners, were

---

[1] Cf. *infra*, fo. 160 b.

elected Auditors of the accounts of the Chamberlain and Wardens in arrear.

Afterwards, viz., on the eve of St. Michael [29 Sept.], the said Sheriffs were sworn at the Guildhall, and on the morrow of the said Feast were presented, admitted, &c., before the Barons of the Exchequer.

Concessio fc'a Inh'itant' de Fletestrete pro conduct' ib'm h'end' etc.

Petition to the Mayor, Aldermen, and Common Council, on Friday, 25 Sept., 18 Edward IV. [A.D. 1478], by the inhabitants of Fleet Street, for permission to erect two cisterns on the common soil of the City—one to be at the Standard in Fleet Street and the other at Fleet Bridge—pursuant to the will of John Middeltone, late Alderman and executor of Sir William Estfeld, at whose expense water had been brought from Paddington to the aforesaid Standard ; and, further, that the petitioners may be allowed to enjoy the said cisterns and water coming to them for evermore, according to the terms of the will of the said John Middeltone, without interruption.[1]

Petition granted.

Fo. 136 b.

Eleccio Maioris

Tuesday the Feast of Translation of St. Edward [13 Oct.], 18 Edward IV. [A.D. 1478], in the presence of Humphrey Hayford, the Mayor, the Prior of Christchurch, John Yonge, Knt., William Taillour, Knt., William Edward, William Hamptone, Knt., John Tate, Robert Drope, Robert Basset, Bartholomew James, Knt., Richard Gardyner, Thomas Stalbroke, Knt., John Broun, Robert Billesdone, William Heriot, Edmund Shaa, Thomas Hill, Hugh Brice, Thomas Rawson, Henry Colet, and John Warde, Aldermen, and an immense Commonalty summoned to the Guildhall for the election of a Mayor for the year ensuing—Richard Gardyner was elected.

Afterwards, viz., on the Feast of SS. Simon and Jude [28 Oct.], the said Mayor was sworn at the Guildhall, and on

---

[1] Cf. Stow's ' Survey' (ed. Kingsford), ii. 41 : " The inhabitantes of Fleetestreete in the yeare 1478 obtained licence of the Mayor, Aldermen and comminaltie to make at theire owne charges two cesternes, the one to be set at the said standarde [erected in 1471], the other at Fleete bridge for the receit of the wast water ; this cesterne at the standard they builded." See also ' Cal. Letter-Book K,' Introd., pp. 1-li.

the morrow was presented, admitted, &c., before the Barons of the Exchequer.

26 Oct., 18 Edward IV. [A.D. 1478], Robert Wentworth, grocer, discharged by the Mayor and Aldermen from serving on juries owing to deafness, &c.

Exon'acio Rob'ti Wentworth ab assis'.

The same day John Caldebek, grocer, similarly discharged for like cause.

Fo. 137. Exon'acio Johannis Caldebek ab assis'.

27 Oct., the same year, William Wodewarde, goldsmith, discharged from serving on juries, &c., he being over 70 years of age and suffering from divers infirmities.

Exon'acio Will mi Wodewarde ab assis'.

14 Nov., 18 Edward IV. [A.D. 1478], came John Breteyn, salter, John Gybbes, sherman, Richard Burton, goldsmith, and Thomas Curteys, salter, before the Mayor and Aldermen, and entered into bond in the sum of £26 13s. 4d. for payment into the Chamber by the said John Breteyn of a like sum to the use of John and William, sons of Andrew Mason, late salter, when they come of age.

Custod' pueror' Andr' Mason.

12 Nov., 18 Edward IV. [A.D. 1478], ordinance by Richard Gardyner, the Mayor, and the Aldermen that in future, when the church of St. Margaret Patens should become void in law (*infra juris terminum*),[1] four secular clerks of repute within the City or circuit of one mile of the same, approved for their morality and learning, shall be assigned by the Mayor and Aldermen to nominate four persons who should seem most fit for the cure of the church, each nominee being a Professor and Doctor of Sacred Theology or a Bachelor in Theology or Master of Arts, and a secular without other benefice, so that the said Mayor and Aldermen may elect one of the four to reside continuously in the church and faithfully serve it, and thereto be instituted by the Bishop of London.[2]

*Fo. 137 b.
Q'd ad eccl'iam Sc'e Margarete Patens Rector eodem modo eligatur et p'sentet' sicut ad eccl'iam Sc'i Petri sup' Cornhull.*

---

[1] Within the term of the *jus patronatus*, or right of presentation.

[2] Compare a similar ordinance made by the Common Council in 1445 respecting presentation to the church of St. Peter, Cornhill. 'Cal. Letter-Book K,' pp. 310-11.

Judicium
cujusdam qui
perjoravit
pipas conduct'
et furat' fuit
aquam etc.

12 Nov., 18 Edward IV. [A.D. 1478], sentence passed by the Mayor and Aldermen upon William Campion for unlawfully tapping a conduit pipe and bringing water into his house in Fleet Street and elsewhere, viz., that he should be taken out of the Bread Street Compter, where he was confined, and set upon a horse " w^t a vessell like unto a conduyt full of water uppon his hede, the same water Rennyng by smale pipes oute of the same vessell, and that when the water is wasted newe water to be put in the saide vessell ayein " ; and further, that he should be conveyed to divers parts of the City and proclamation made in each place of his misdoing, and finally be brought back to the Compter, there to remain at the will of the Mayor and Aldermen.

Fo. 138.

De officio
clerici Camere.

23 Nov., 18 Edward IV. [A.D. 1478], ordinance by Richard Gardyner, the Mayor, and the Aldermen to the effect that in future John Hert, Clerk of the Chamber, and all other Clerks of the Chamber, should be elected by the Mayor and Aldermen for the time being, and should remain in office during good behaviour ; and further, that no other Clerk in the Chamber of the Guildhall should be keeper of the books, nor record anything therein, nor make the account of the Chamberlain except the Clerk of the Chamber so elected, and that the said John Hert should be Comptroller of the Chamberlain and Clerk of the Chamber as Robert Langford had been.

Eleccio Magr'i
Joh'is Breteyne
in Rectorem
Eccl'ie paro-
chial' Sc'i
Petri sup'
Cornhull.

At a Common Council held on Tuesday, 1 Dec., 18 Edward IV. [A.D. 1478], there being present Richard Gardyner, the Mayor, Humphrey Starky the Recorder, John Yonge, Knt., William Taillour, Knt., William Hamptone, Knt., Robert Drope, Robert Basset, Thomas Stalbroke, Knt., William Heriot, William Stokker, Knt., John Broun, Robert Billesdone, Edmund Shaa, Thomas Hille, Robert Colwiche, Hugh Brice, Richard Rawson, Henry Colet, and Thomas " Home," Aldermen, the following were nominated by four of the most approved Doctors of the City for one of them to be elected Rector of the church of St. Peter upon Cornhulle *loco* Thomas Asshby, deceased, viz., Masters John Breteyn, John Barley, Robert Wrangewishe, Doctors of Theology, and Master Edward

Lupton, Bachelor of Theology. Thereupon John Breteyn of Cambridge was elected on condition he renounced before presentation the benefice he then had.

Letter from Richard Gardyner, the Mayor, and William Philippe, the Chamberlain, to the Dean and Chapter of St. Paul's, presenting Sir John Cheswright, chaplain, for admission to the chantry founded in the said church by Henry "Guleford," vacant by the death of William Wyswale. Dated 2 Dec., 1478.

Fo. 138 b.
P'sentacio
Johannis Ches-
wright capell'i
ad quandam
cantar' in
Eccl' ia Sc'i
Pauli Lond'
fundat' pro
ai'a Henr'
Guleford.

Letters patent appointing John Yonge, Knt. and Alderman, to be Justice for the merchants of Almaine in their house in the City, commonly called *Gildehalla Theutonicorum.* Witness the King at Westminster, 17 Nov., 18 Edward IV. [A.D. 1478].

L're patent'
pro Joh'e
Yonge essena'
Alderman'
Theutonicor'
ap'd le Stile-
yerd.

Letter from the Mayor and Aldermen to Thomas [Kempe], Bishop of London, presenting John Breteyn, Professor of Sacred Theology, for institution as Rector of St. Peter's, Cornhill, vacant by the death of Master Thomas Asshby. Dated 9 Dec., 18 Edward IV. [A.D. 1478].

Fo. 139.
P sentacio
Mag'ri Joh'is
Breteyn ad
Eccl'iam
p'ochialem Sc'i
Petri super
Cornhull.

10 Dec., 18 Edward IV. [A.D. 1478], came John Hawkyns, draper, Milo Ades, Edward Bowdon, and John Polyngton, goldsmiths, before the Mayor and Aldermen, and entered into bond in the sum of £100 for payment into the Chamber by the said John Hawkyns of a like sum to the use of John and Anne, children of Reginald Langdon, late girdler, when they come of age or marry.

Custod'
pueror' Regi-
naldi Lang-
don.

Writ of *habeas corpus cum causa,* addressed to the Mayor, Aldermen, and Sheriffs, touching the detention of William Capell. Witness the King at Wyndesore, 10 Dec., 18 Edward IV. [A.D. 1478].

Fo. 139 b.
Br'e et Return'
ubi dicitur q'd
quidam pro-
palavit verba
obprobriosa in
dedecus Ald'r'i.

Return made to the above by Richard Gardyner, the Mayor, the Aldermen, and Robert Hardyng and Robert Byfeld, the Sheriffs, to the effect that the above William Capell was in custody for vilifying Robert Drope, an Alderman.

Afterwards, viz., on the 22 Dec., the Chancellor remitted the said William Capell to be punished at the discretion of the Mayor and Aldermen.

Fo. 140.
Custod' Joh'is Elys fil' Thome Elys pannar'.

28 Jan., 18 Edward IV. [A.D. 1478-9], came Thomas Wollesby, Henry Skeltone, Richard Fote, and William Edward, drapers, before the Mayor and Aldermen, and entered into bond in the sum of £20 for payment into the Chamber by the said Thomas of a like sum to the use of John, son of Thomas Elys, late draper, when he comes of age.

Fos. 140-1.
Ordinacio Abrocar' in div'sis articulis.

28 Jan., 18 Edward IV. [A.D. 1478-9], articles ordained by the Common Council for regulating Brokers within the City; the first of them restricting their number to 30, of whom at least 18 must be Englishmen born.

Fo. 141.

Form of proclamation thereon.

Fo. 141 b.
Custod' pueror' Joh'is Fenne.

15 Feb., 18 Edward IV. [A.D. 1478-9], came William Stoner, Knt., Roger Tygo, tailor, William Hole, skinner, and Thomas Harward, draper, before the Mayor and Chamberlain, and entered into bond in the sum of £758 19s. $\frac{1}{2}d.$ for payment into the Chamber by the said William Stoner of a like sum to the use of Hugh and Margaret, children of John Fenne, late stock-fishmonger, when they come of age or marry.

Fo. 142.
Custod' pueror' Reginald' Langdon.

16 Feb., 18 Edward IV. [A.D. 1478-9], came Milo "Adys," Edward Bowdone, John Polyngtone, goldsmiths, and John Hawkyns, draper, before the Mayor and Aldermen, and entered into bond in the sum of £100 for payment into the Chamber by the said Milo of a like sum to the use of John and Anne, children of Reginald Langdon, late girdler, when they come of age or marry.

Fo. 142 b.
Exon'acio tenencium Ep'i London' de Stortford in com' Hertf' de Theolonio.

9 March, 19 Edward IV. [A.D. 1478-9], came divers tenants of the Bishop of London from Stortford, co. Herts, before the Mayor and Aldermen, and complained that Robert Byfeld and Robert Hardyng, the Sheriffs, had taken toll of their leather and other goods contrary to the King's writ, dated 7 Feb., 18 Edward IV. [A.D. 1478-9], which they produced.

Thereupon precept was issued to the Sheriffs to restore the toll so taken, and to cease from taking any in future.[1]

10 March, 19 Edward IV. [A.D. 1478-9], came Thomas Hobersty, Walter Milson, Thomas Mower, and John Cole, "curriours," before the Mayor and Aldermen, and entered into bond in the sum of £11 5s. 4d. for delivery into the Chamber by the said Thomas Hobersty of the sum of £10, a feather bed worth 13s. 4d., and three pairs of sheets worth 12s., to the use of Thomas, son of Roger Humfrey, late "curriour," when he comes of age.

Custod' Thome filii Rogeri Humfrey curriour.

10 March, 19 Edward IV. [A.D. 1478-9], came John Clerk, John Stokes, Thomas Norlond, grocers, and Richard Golofer, mercer, and entered into bond in the sum of £675 8s. 7¼d. for payment into the Chamber by the said John Clerk of specific sums of money to the use of Thomas, John, Richard, and Henry, sons of Thomas Bledlowe, late grocer and Alderman, when they come of age.

Fo. 143.

Custod' pueror' Thome Bledlowe Aldr'i.

The same day came John Clerk, William Sandes, Robert Bangill, grocers, and William Fynchamp, mercer, and entered into bond in the sum of £675 8s. 7¼d. for the same purpose as above.

Fo. 143 b.

Custod' pueror' Thome Bledlowe Aldr'i.

16 March, 19 Edward IV. [A.D. 1478-9], came William Ilger, goldsmith, Thomas Lewes, vintner, John Snowe and Ralph Bulkley, goldsmiths, before the Mayor and Aldermen, and entered into bond in the sum of £16 13s. 4d. for payment into the Chamber by the said William Ilger of a like sum to the use of William, Beatrix, Robert, Thomas, John, and Margaret, children of Ambrose Prestone, late "taloughchaundler," when they come of age or marry.

Fo. 144.

Custod' pueror' Ambrosii Prestone Taloughchaundler.

Proclamation by the Mayor to the following effect: "That no labourer, servaunt nor apprentice of any artificer or vitiller or of any other man take uppon hym nor be so hardy to play at Tenys Caill' Clossh foteball or use disyng and Cardyng or other like games w'in this Citee of London or the lib'tie of the same

Fo. 144 b.

Proclamacio fc'a ne quis ludat ad Tenis' Caylyng Clossh-yng pilam pedal' nec aa alios ludos illicit'.

[1] Reference made to a precept which was issued in a similar case in 1375. See 'Cal. Letter-Book H,' p. 5.

M 2

uppon payne of Imprisonment by the space of vj⁰ daies......but that thei use shotyng[1] or other semblable games which be not prohibet nor forboden by the Kynge our soveraign lordes lawes." [No date].

Proclamacio
ſc'a suſ'
ordinac'
abrocarior'.

Proclamation made 28 March, 19 Edward IV. [A.D. 1479], forbidding any one to act as broker unless he be one of the 30 brokers admitted and sworn before the Mayor and Aldermen, pursuant to an ordinance of the Common Council lately made.

Ordinacio
q'd ligna
maremia ad
Rep'aco'em
seu eu'ificac'
ten't' etc. hos-
pitentur apud
Guyhald' et
non alibi.

22 April, 19 Edward IV. [A.D. 1479], ordinance by the Mayor and Aldermen that the Chamberlain store all building material at the Guildhall, and no allowance be made to him in his account for any other storehouse ; that all manner of payments be made in the Chamber, and not by the hands of rent-gatherers ; and that the ale silver[2] be not put in the general account, but in an account by itself, and that the " grete accompte be not letted in no wise therefore as it hath in late daies."

Fo. 145.
Adjurnament'
omnium Cur'
London' pro
tempore causa
pestilencie.

27 April, 19 Edward IV. [A.D. 1479], ordinance by Richard Gardyner, the Mayor, and the Aldermen adjourning the sessions of all Courts in the City before the Mayor or Sheriffs until after Trinity [on account of pestilence[3]].

Ordinacio de
Whitawiers
etc.

20 July, 19 Edward IV. [A.D. 1479], came good men of the Mistery of Whitawyers before the Mayor and Aldermen, and prayed that they might thenceforth be of the Fellowship of Lethersellers, and that all those who then were of the Craft

---

[1] In order to encourage the practice of archery such games as are here mentioned were forbidden in 1477 by Parliament, under the heavy penalty of two years' imprisonment and a fine of £10 for each offence. ' Rot. Parl.,' vi. 188. Reference has already been made (*supra*, p. 22, note 3) to a statute passed in 1472 for enforcing the importation of bow-staves by foreign merchants trading with England. Another statute, passed in 1484, enacted that .for every butt (or tun) of Malmsey or Tyre imported, ten good bowstaves should also be imported, under penalty of a fine. (Stat. I Ric. III., cap. xi.)

[2] A rent or tribute paid yearly to the Mayor by those who sell ale within the City (Halliwell).

[3] Cf. Cotton MS., Vitellius A xvi., fo. 136 : " In this yere [Gardyner, Mayor] was a greate deth, which continued all the yere " (Kingsford's ' Chronicles of London,' p. 188).

of Whitawyers should "chaunge their copies "[1] into the Craft of Lethersellers.[2]

Their petition granted.

The same day it was agreed by the said Mayor and Aldermen that a certain ordinance made in the time of the Mayoralty of Thomas Oulegreve, touching the Art or Mistery of Lethersellers,[3] should be observed, notwithstanding any ordinance afterwards made on petition of the Pursers during the Mayoralty of Robert Basset.[4]

Confirmacio ordinac' conc'nen' les Lethersellers.

30 Aug., 19 Edward IV. [A.D. 1479], came Edmund Worsley, Robert Cobold, mercers, William Pynde, draper, and Giles Dokkyng, " wexchaundiller," before the Mayor and Aldermen, and entered into bond in the sum of £200 for payment into the Chamber by the said Edmund of a like sum of money to the use of Thomas, Elizabeth, and Alice, children of William Neleson, late goldsmith, when they come of age or marry.[5]

Fo. 145 b.

Custod' pueror' Will'i Neleson aur'.

Letter from Richard Gardyner, the Mayor, to Thomas [Kempe], Bishop of London, presenting Sir Thomas Howghton, chaplain, for admission as Rector of the church of St. Margaret Patens, vacant by the resignation of Sir Thomas Bateman by reason of exchange.[6] Dated 6 Sept., 19 Edward IV. [A.D. 1479].

Presentacio Thome Howghton capell'i ad eccl'iam p'ochial' Sc'e Margarete Patens.

20 Sept., 19 Edward IV. [A.D. 1479], ordinance by the Mayor and Aldermen that in future the Bailiff of the Borough of Suthewerk should reside within the borough, and find surety for preserving all the City's liberties within the same.

Fo. 146.

Ordinac' conc'nen' Ballivum de Southwerk.

Tuesday the Feast of St. Matthew [21 Sept.], 19 Edward IV. [A.D. 1479], in the presence of Richard Gardyner, the Mayor, Humphrey Starky the Recorder, William Taillour, Knt., William Edward, Robert Drope, Robert Basset, Bartholomew

Eleccio Vicecom'.

---

[1] See 'Cal. Letter-Book K,' Introd., p. xxxvi.

[2] Petition set out in Black's ' Hist. of the Company of Leathersellers,' p. 38.

[3] *Supra*, pp. 74-5.

[4] *Supra*, pp. 138-40.

[5] Margin. 11 Dec., 14 Henry VII. A.D. 1498], came the above Eliza-

beth and acknowledged satisfaction for her patrimony, as well as for money accruing to her by the death of Alice her sister.

[6] Bateman became Vicar of Blean, co. Kent, by exchange with Houghton. Hennessy's ' Novum Repertorium,' p. cxxv.

James, Knt., Thomas Stalbroke, Knt.; William Stokker, Knt.,
John Broun, Robert Billesdone, William Heryot, Thomas Hille,
Hugh Brice, Richard Rawson, Henry Colet, Thomas Ilame,[1] and
John Stokker,[2] Aldermen, and very many Commoners sum-
moned to the Guildhall for the election of Sheriffs—Thomas
Ilame, mercer, was elected one of the Sheriffs of London and
Middlesex by the Mayor, and John Warde, grocer, was elected
the other Sheriff by the Commonalty.

The same day Milo " Adys," goldsmith, was elected Chamberlain of the City for the year ensuing ; William Galle and
Henry Bumpstede were elected Wardens of the City Bridge ;
Edmund Shaa, Robert Billesdone, Aldermen, William White,
draper, Thomas Cole, skinner, Henry Davers, mercer, and
William Bracebrigge, draper, Commoners, were elected Auditors
of the account of the Chamberlain and Wardens in arrear.

Afterwards, viz., on the eve of St. Michael [29 Sept.], the
said Sheriffs were sworn at the Guildhall, and on the morrow
of the said Feast were presented, admitted, &c., before the
Barons of the Exchequer.

*Admissio
Thome Actone
in officium
ball' i de Suthe-
werk.*

Tuesday the Feast of St. Matthew [21 Sept.], the same year,
Thomas Actone, gentleman, admitted by the Mayor and Aldermen to the office of Bailiff of Suthewerk *loco* Thomas Baker,
deceased ; to hold the said office during good behaviour.

*Recogn' f'a
per Ballivum
de Suthwerk.*

23 Sept., 19 Edward IV. [A.D. 1479], came the above
Thomas Actone, William Bolley, haberdasher, and John Merik,
" stacioner," and entered into bond in the sum of £100 for the
due observance by the said Thomas Actone of the ordinance
recently made touching the office of Bailiff of Suthewerk.

Fo. 146 b.

*Ordinacio pro
nocument'
Bigar' et
carect' apud
Billyngesgate
et Pety Wales
removend'.*

23 Sept., 19 Edward IV. [A.D. 1479], a petition presented to
the Common Council by the inhabitants of Thames Street and
Petiwales,[3] complaining of the common carters of the City
blocking the streets in the neighbourhood of Billingsgate with
their carts in such a way that neither the King nor Queen

---

[1] Ilome, *supra*, p. 160.

[2] Not to be confounded with John
Stokker, Alderman of Langbourn
Ward, who died in 1464.

[3] A part of Thames Street sometimes known as Galley Row, but
more commonly as Petty Wales.
Stow's ' Survey ' (ed. Kingsford), i. 136.

with their retinues, nor the Mayor or Aldermen, nor merchants could without great difficulty make their way in the streets between the church of St. Magnus and the watergate next the Tower of London, and praying that certain regulations for abating the nuisance might be approved.

Petition granted.

The same day Robert Tate, mercer, presented a petition to the Common Council touching a tenement with appurtenances in Tower Street, in the parish of All Hallows Barking, held by him under a lease from the Wardens of London Bridge, and a disputed claim of a quit-rent, and suggesting a mode of settlement.

Fo. 147.

Concessio cujusdam soli p'tinen' Pont' fc'a Rob'to Tate.

Petition granted.

Wednesday the Feast of Translation of St. Edward [13 Oct.], 19 Edward IV. [A.D. 1479], in the presence of Richard Gardyner, the Mayor, the Prior of Christchurch, William Taillour, Knt., William Edward, William Hampton, Knt., Robert Drope, Robert Basset, Humphrey Hayford, Bartholomew James, Knt., Thomas Stalbroke, Knt., William Heriot, John Broun, William Stokker, Knt., Robert Billesdone, Thomas Hille, Richard Rawson, Henry Colet, John Warde, Thomas Ilame, and John Stokker, Aldermen, and an immense Commonalty summoned to the Guildhall for the election of a Mayor for the year ensuing—Bartholomew James was elected.

Fo. 147 b.

Eleccio Maioris.

Afterwards, viz., on the Feast of SS. Simon and Jude [28 Oct.], he was sworn at the Guildhall, and on the morrow was presented, admitted, &c., before the Barons of the Exchequer.

13 Oct., 19 Edward IV. [A.D. 1479], came Henry Bumpstede, William Purchas, Thomas Niche, and William Pratte, mercers, before the Mayor and Aldermen, and entered into bond in the sum of £80 for payment into the Chamber by the said Henry of a like sum to the use of Thomas, son of Ralph Kemp, late mercer, when he attains the age of 27 years, £50 of the said sum having been bequeathed to the said orphan by John Burton, late mercer.

Custod' Thome Kemp fil' Rad'i Kemp.

Fo. 148.

Custod'
pueror' Will'i
Rose irmonger.

15 Oct., 19 Edward IV. [A.D. 1479], came German Manfeld, hatter, Henry Crane, "fletcher," John Umfrey, "bowier," and Peter Caldecote, draper, before the Mayor and Aldermen, and entered into bond in the sum of £40 for payment into the Chamber by the said German of a like sum to the use of Thomas and Clemence, children of William Rose, late "irmonger," when they come of age or marry.

Fo. 148 b.

Ordinacio
scrutiniis
faciend' in
mister' de
lethersellers et
Cirothecarior'.

15 Oct., 19 Edward IV. [A.D. 1479], ordinance *by* the Mayor and Aldermen, that in order to put an end to strife, in future the Leathersellers shall make search in their mistery without the Glovers, and the Glovers in their mistery without the Leathersellers ; and further, that the Leathersellers and Glovers make search of things appertaining to their respective misteries in the mistery of the other, accompanied by a Serjeant-at-Mace, notwithstanding any ordinance to the contrary.[1]

Ordinac' de
Wiredrawers
et Chape-
makers.

15 Oct., 19 Edward IV. [A.D. 1479], came good men of the several Misteries of Wiredrawers and Chapemakers,[2] and presented a petition to the Mayor and Aldermen to the effect that "for asmoche as there is noon sufficiaunt noumbre of iche of the said crafts to chese Wardeyns of theym self to kepe their Rules and Ordenaunces," and each meddled with the other's work, it might be ordained that the two crafts might be made one Fellowship under the name of Wyremongers, and that yearly two Wardens might be chosen who should exercise the right of search, and that apprentices should be bound to the new Fraternity and thereof be made free of the City.

Petition granted.

---

[1] Printed in Black's ' Hist. of the Leathersellers,' p. 39. In 1451 it had been ordained that two Wardens should be respectively chosen by the Leathersellers and the Glovers, and that they should search together for defects in either of their crafts, accompanied by a Serjeant-at-Mace. This procedure, however, appears to have satisfied neither party. See ' Cal. Letter-Book K.' pp. 334-5 ; Black, *op. cit.*, p. 30.

[2] Makers of that part of a buckle by which it is fastened to a strap or belt, usually made of metal. The word appears also as a *verb trans.* Cf. " to chape bokels," *i.e.*, to fit buckles with chapes. ' Cal. Letter-Book K,' p. 199.

8 Oct., 19 Edward IV. [A.D. 1479], ordinance by the Mayor and Aldermen that Thomas Cotton, Keeper of the gaol of Ludgate, shall pay the sum of £6 for the lease of his house near the said gaol for the past five years and no more, inasmuch as he has executed many repairs. Other Keepers to pay 40s. a year for the same and to keep it in repair.

Nota de firma cujusdam domus juxta Ludgate etc.

22 Oct., 19 Edward IV. [A.D. 1479], came good men of the Mistery of Turnours into the Court of the lord the King in the Chamber of the Guildhall, before the Mayor and Aldermen, and presented a petition that certain articles for regulating the Craft might be approved, to the following effect :—

Fos. 149–50.

Ordinacio de les Turnours.

First, that freemen of the Craft, about Whitsuntide, should meet together and choose two Wardens for the two years next ensuing.

That the outgoing Wardens render their account to the new Wardens within a month of their election.

That the Wardens have full power to search and oversee "all maner of Busshell trees, half busshell trees and pekkes, and all other ware and stuf belonging to the Craft."

That a Common Beadle be appointed, to have quarterly for his salary of every freeman of the Craft 4d. more or less, at the discretion of the Wardens and Commonalty.

That fines be imposed for rebuking and chiding members.

That every member taking an apprentice pay to the Common Box 20d.

That no member receive into his service a "foreyn" or one enfranchised in another Craft.

That no member send his wares to be hawked or sold in the streets.

That Wardens failing in their duty be fined 5 marks, one half to go to the Chamber and the other to the Common Box of the Craft.

Petition granted.

23 Oct., 19 Edward IV. [A.D. 1479], John Curate, "fletcher," discharged by the Mayor and Aldermen from serving on juries, &c., owing to his infirmities.

Fo. 150.

Exon'acio Johannis Curate ab assis' etc.

*Exon acio
Will'i Serle
ab assis etc.*
25 Oct., the same year, William Serle, tailor, similarly discharged for like cause.

*Custod
pueror Will'i
Palmer auri-
fabri.*
22 Oct., the same year, came Elizabeth Palmer, widow, John Pake, draper, William Milbourne, "payntour," and Robert Stokker, draper, before the Mayor and Aldermen, and entered into bond in the sum of £300 for payment into the Chamber by the said Elizabeth of a like sum to the use of Matilda and Margaret, daughters of William Palmer, late goldsmith, when they come of age or marry.[1]

*Q'd Bedelli
sint Collector
de la Ale
silver etc.*
26 Oct., 19 Edward IV. [A.D. 1479], ordinance by the Mayor and Aldermen that the Beadle of each Ward should receive for his trouble in receiving the money called " alesilver "[2] 2s. in the pound.

Fos. 150 b–
151 b.
*Ordinacio de
les Pavyours.*
26 Oct., 19 Edward IV. [A.D. 1479], came good men of the Mistery of Pavyours of the City and prayed the Mayor and Aldermen to approve certain ordinances for the regulation of the Craft as set out.[3]

Petition granted.

Fo. 152.
*Ordinacio
Pistor*
9 Nov., 19 Edward IV. [A.D. 1479], petition by good men of the Mistery of Bakers to the Mayor and Aldermen that certain ordinances for the regulation of the Craft formerly made might be duly observed, viz. :—

Ordinance passed anno 7 Henry VI. by the Mayor and Aldermen forbidding bakers to sell to Hucksters more than 13 loaves for a dozen.[4]

Ordinance made anno 15 Henry VI. prescribing certain places where foreign bakers were to stand for sale of bread.[5]

Hallymote.
That the Sheriffs fail not to carry into execution presentments

---

[1] Margin. 13 June, 9 Henry VII. [A.D. 1494], came Robert Wymonde, mercer, who had married the above Matilda, and acknowledged satisfaction for the sum of £150.

[2] *Vide supra*, p. 164, note 2.

[3] The articles are printed in a 'History of the Paviors' Company,' by Charles Welch, F.S.A., from a book of ordinances originally in the possession of the Company, and now in the Guildhall Library, into which they appear to have been transcribed from the record in the Letter-Book.

[4] ' Cal. Letter-Book K,' p. 85.

[5] *Id.*, p. 45.

made by the Hallymote of Bakers held yearly in December at St. Thomas Acon.[1]

Petition granted.

Letter from Bartholomew James, Knt., the Mayor, and Milo Adys, the Chamberlain, to Thomas [Kempe], Bishop of London, presenting Thomas Praty, chaplain, for admission to one of the five chantries founded in the Guildhall Chapel by Adam Fr_nceys and Henry Frowyk, vacant by the resignation of Sir Thomas Fraunceys, priest. Dated 4 Dec., 1479.

Fo. 152 b.
Presentacio Thome Praty capell'i ad quandam cantar' .v. cantar' in capella b'te Marie juxta Guyhald'.

A similar letter from the same to the same presenting William Jonys, chaplain, for admission to one of the same chantries, vacant by the resignation of Robert Basy. Dated 12 Dec., 1479.

Presentacio Will'i Jonys capell'i ad quandam cantar' .v. cantar' in capella b'te M^a juxta Guyhald' London'.

13 Jan., 19 Edward IV. [A.D. 1479-80], came Thomas Wollesby, draper, John Wodeward, "goldwiredrawer," William Chalk, "peautrer," and Alan Broker, goldsmith, before the Mayor and Aldermen, and entered into bond in the sum of £15 for payment into the Chamber by the said Thomas of a like sum to the use of William and Christopher, sons of William Grifithe, deceased, when they come of age.[2]

Fo. 153.
Custod' pueror' Will'i Grifithe.

11 Feb., 19 Edward IV. [A.D. 1479-80], came Thomas Gylmyn, grocer, John Chalk, goldsmith, William Chalk, "peauterer," and Thomas Woodland, sherman, before the Mayor and Aldermen, and entered into bond in the sum of £15 for payment into the Chamber by the said Thomas Gylmyn of a like sum to the use of William, son of John Brodebrigge, late grocer, when he comes of age.

Custod' Will'mi Brodebrigge fil' Joh'is Brodebrigge grocer'.

24 Feb., 19 Edward IV. [A.D. 1479-80], came Richard Knyght, fishmonger, Robert Spayne, scrivener, Thomas Underwode, fishmonger, and [blank], before the Mayor and Alder-

Fo. 153 b.
Custod' pueror' Tho'c Lewes vynter'.

---

[1] Cf. *supra*, p. 100.

[2] Margin. 18 Feb., 16 Henry VII. [A.D. 1500-1], came the above Christopher, and acknowledged satisfaction for his own patrimony, and also for money accruing to him by the death of William his brother.

men, and entered into bond in the sum of £217 14s. for the delivery into the Chamber by the said Richard of the sum of £180 and certain goods and jewels to the use of Edmund, Alice, and Margaret, children of Thomas Lewes, late vintner, when they come of age or marry.[1]

3 March, 19 Edward IV. [A.D. 1479-80], Robert Deynes, an apprentice, who married Elizabeth, daughter of Robert Gregory, deceased, a City orphan, without licence of the Mayor and Aldermen, fined £20, which he brought into Court.[2]

22 March, 20 Edward IV. [A.D. 1479-80], came John Mathewe, John Rypon, mercers, Henry Lee, fuller, and Richard Turnam, " lynendraper," into the Court of the lord the King in the Chamber of the Guildhall, before the Mayor and Aldermen, and entered into bond in the sum of £50 18s. 6d. for the delivery into the Chamber by the said John Mathewe of a sum of £19 16s. 1d. and certain goods and jewels to the use of William, son of William Aleyn, late draper, when he comes of age.

11 April, 20 Edward IV. [A.D. 1480], came Henry Bronde, " cordwaner," Thomas Bukney, " curriour," Geoffrey Spy-ryng, " bruer," and Peter Gretlef, " cordwaner," and entered into bond in the sum of £13 10s. for payment into the Chamber by the said Henry Bronde of a like sum to the use of Katherine and Marion, daughters of Albright Haryson, late cordwainer, when they come of age or marry.[3]

15 April, 20 Edward IV. [A.D. 1480], came Juliana Shosmyth, widow, Richard Chawry, salter, Robert Bradshawe, goldsmith, and John Aunsell, haberdasher, and entered into bond in the sum of 200 marks for payment into the Chamber by the said

---

[1] Margin. 17 June, 1485, came William Dryland, gent., who married the above Alice, and acknowledged satisfaction for his wife's patrimony, and also for money accruing to her by the death of Margaret and Isolda, other daughters of the said Thomas Lewes.

[2] Cf. Cotton MS., Vitellius A xvi.,

fo. 136 b (Kingsford's ' Chronicles of London,' p. 188).

[3] Margin. 14 Jan., 4 Henry VII. [A.D. 1488-9], came Godfrey John-son, who married the above Marion, and acknowledged satisfaction for his wife's patrimony, and for money accruing by the decease of Katherine her sister.

Juliana of a like sum to the use of Roger, Robert, Johanna, Katherine, and Margaret, children of William Shosmyth, late skinner, when they come of age or marry.[1]

5 May, 20 Edward IV. [A.D. 1480], came Margery Wyche, William Rede, "taloughchaundler," John Wynwode, skinner, and William Southous, fuller, and entered into bond in the sum of £4 3s. 4d. for payment into the Chamber by the said Margery of a like sum to the use of Thomas, Petronilla, Katherine, Alice, and Emma, children of Henry Wyche, late " irmonger."

Fo. 155 b.

Custod' pueror' Henr' Wyche irmonger.

13 July, 20 Edward IV. [A.D. 1480], came John Smert, Robert Hall, John Benyngtone, John Brooke, grocers, and Thomas Champney, " taloughchaundler," and entered into bond in the sum of £750 for payment into the Chamber by the said John Smert of a like sum to the use of John, son of John Crosby, Knt., late Alderman and grocer, when he comes of age.

Custod' Joh'is Crosby filii Joh'is Crosby militis.

7 Sept., 20 Edward IV. [A.D. 1480], ordinance by Bartholomew James, Knt., the Mayor, and the Aldermen that in future neither the Brounbakers nor foreign bakers be forced to pay anything to the bakers of white bread, nor to the Mayor for the time being, in part payment of the sum of 40 marks which the said bakers of white bread are accustomed yearly to pay to the Mayor, &c.[2]

Fo. 156.

Q'd les brounbakers exon'ent' a solucione pecunie Maiori etc.

Thursday the Feast of St. Matthew [21 Sept.], 20 Edward IV. [A.D. 1480], in the presence of Bartholomew James, Knt., the Mayor, Humphrey Starky the Recorder, William Taillour, Knt., William Hamptone, Knt., Robert Drope, Robert Basset, Richard Gardyner, William Heryot, Thomas Stalbroke, Knt.,

Eleccio Vicecomit' etc.

---

[1] Margin. 20 Jan., 1 Henry VII. [A.D. 1485-6], came Henry Grene, goldsmith, who married the above Johanna, and acknowledged satisfaction for his wife's patrimony ; on 4 June, 5 Henry VII. [A.D. 1490], came the said Johanna, then a widow, and acknowledged satisfaction for money accruing to her by the decease of Robert her brother, and on 30 Mar.,

10 Henry VII. [A.D. 1495], came William Wiseman, who married the above Katherine, and acknowledged satisfaction for his wife's patrimony, and for money accruing to her by the decease of the said Robert.

[2] Possibly a payment on account of pesage dues, which the Bakers objected to pay in 1450. See ' Cal. Letter-Book K,' p. 358 n.

William Stokker, Knt., John Broun, Robert Billesdone, Hugh Brice, Thomas Hille, Richard Rawsone, Henry Colet, John Stokker, William Horne, John Warde, and Thomas Ilame, Aldermen, and very many Commoners summoned to the Guildhall for the election of Sheriffs—Thomas Danyell, "dier," was elected one of the Sheriffs of London and Middlesex for the ensuing year by the Mayor, and William Bacon, haberdasher, was elected the other Sheriff by the Commonalty.

The same day Milo Adys, goldsmith, was elected Chamberlain of the City for the year ensuing; William Galle, tailor, and Henry Bumpstede, mercer, were elected Wardens of the City's Bridge; Edmund Shaa, Thomas Hille, Aldermen, William Bracebrigge, draper, Thomas Cole, skinner, William White, draper, and Thomas Swan, tailor, Commoners, were elected Auditors of the accounts of the Chamberlain and Wardens in arrear.

Afterwards, viz., on the eve of St. Michael [29 Sept.], the said Sheriffs were sworn at the Guildhall, and on the morrow of the said Feast were presented, admitted, &c., before the Barons of the Exchequer.

Fo. 156 b.

Custod'
'teror' Joh'is
Bremonger
draber.

28 Sept., 20 Edward IV. [A.D. 1480], came Johanna Bremonger, widow, Robert Revell, grocer, William Prune, "taloughchaundler," and John Baker, grocer, before the Mayor and Aldermen, and entered into bond in the sum of £40 for payment into the Chamber by the said Johanna of a like sum to the use of Hugh and Johanna, children of John Bremonger, late draper, when they come of age or marry.

Fo. 157.

Eleccio
Maioris.

Friday the Feast of Translation of St. Edward [13 Oct.], 20 Edward IV. [A.D. 1480], in the presence of Bartholomew James, Knt., the Mayor, the Prior of Christchurch, Humphrey Starky the Recorder, William Taillour, Knt., William Hamptone, Knt., Robert Drope, Robert Basset, Richard Gardyner, Thomas Stalbroke, Knt., William Heryot, William Stokker, Knt., John Broun, Robert Billesdone, Edmund Shaa, Thomas Hill, Hugh Brice, Richard Rawson, Henry Colet, John Warde, Thomas Ilame, Robert Tate, and William Bacon, Aldermen, and an immense Commonalty summoned to the Guildhall for the election of a Mayor for the year ensuing—John Broun was elected.

Afterwards, viz., on the Feast of SS. Simon and Jude [28 Oct.], the said Mayor was sworn at the Guildhall, and on the morrow was presented, admitted, &c., before the Barons of the Exchequer.

7 Nov., 20 Edward IV. [A.D. 1480], ordinance by John Broun, the Mayor, and the Aldermen that in future, in elections of Aldermen by the Wards, there shall be presented no more than two Aldermen, if it happen that any Aldermen be presented ; and if the inhabitants of the Wards in future present more than two Aldermen together with two Commoners in such elections, then their election and presentation shall be void. *De no'ia.o'e et p'sentaco'e Aldi'or' per Wardas.*

10 Jan., 20 Edward IV. [A.D. 1480-1], ordinance by the Mayor and Aldermen that in future bread called " spicebrede," and all other bread, shall not be sold within the City unless it be of just weight and contains the assize. *Q'd null' vendat Spice-brede nisi sit justi ponderis.*

At a Common Council held on Monday, 12 Feb., 20 Edward IV. [A.D. 1480-1], there being present John Broun, the Mayor, Humphrey Starky the Recorder, William Taillour, Knt., William Hamptone, Knt., Robert Drope, Robert Basset, Richard Gardyner, Thomas Stalbroke, Knt., William Heriot, William Stokker, Knt., Robert Billesdone, Edmund Shaa, Thomas Hille, Hugh Brice, Richard Rawson, Henry Colet, John Warde, Thomas Ilame, John Stokker, Robert Tate, William Horn, and William Bacon, Aldermen, the sum of 5,000 marks was granted the King out of " benevolence " for the defence of the realm against the Scots ; and for the more speedy levying of the same, it was agreed that out of each of the 25 Wards there should be elected an efficient man, in order that by the 25 men so elected, together with two persons from each parish, an assessment for the money should be made. It was further ordained that the said 25 men should appoint collectors, who should have power of distress, &c. Provided *Assessio v'''' marc' d'no Regi dat'.*

always that no one should be assessed at less than 5 shillings, and that the poorest should be spared altogether.[1]

Fo. 157 b.   Names of the 25 [*sic*] persons so elected, viz. : Aldrichegate, William Webley ; Algate, Stephen Smyth ; Bassieshawe, Henry Davers : Bisshopesgate, Richard Nailer ; Bradstrete, William White ; Billyngesgate, Thomas Breteyn ; Bredestrete, William Rotheley ; Candilwikstrete, John Mathewe ; Castelbaynard, Thomas Rede ; Chepe, John Marchall ; Crepulgate Within, Thomas Ostriche ; Crepulgate Without, Oliver Causton ; Colmanstrete, Robert Ewell ; Cordwanerstrete, Nicholas Alwyn ; Cornhull, John Hungerford ; Dowgate, Richard West ; Faryngdon Within, William Maryner ; Faryngdon Without, William Galle ; Langbourn, Thomas Kyppyng ; Lymestrete, Edward Stone ; Portsokne, Thomas Dalstone ; Brigge, Edmund Newman ; Towre, William Baldry ; Quenehithe, William Sandes ; Vyntre, Thomas Graunte ; Walbroke, John Clerk.

Juramentum Assessor'.   Form of oath to be taken by Assessors.

Juramentum p'ochianor' assistenc' Assessorib'.   Form of oath to be taken by the parishioners helping the Assessors.

Custod' Margaret' fil' Nich'i Carlile aur'   27 Feb., 20 Edward IV. [A.D. 1480-1], came Richard Burton, John Fawkener, Robert Alcok, and Edmund Shebruk, goldsmiths, and entered into bond in the sum of 10 marks for payment into the Chamber by the said Richard Burton of a like sum to the use of Margaret, daughter of Nicholas Carlile, late goldsmith, when she comes of age or marries.

Fo. 158.

Ordinacio Tegulat'.   14 March, 21 Edward IV. [A.D. 1480-1], came good men of the Mistery of Tylers into the Court of the lord the King in the Chamber of the Guildhall, before John Broun, the Mayor, Humphrey Starky the Recorder, William Hamptone, Knt.,

---

[1] Cotton MS., Vitellius A xvi., fo. 137 : " This yere [20 Edward IV.] was a preste lent and made unto the Kyng of v m[1] markes which was assessed by xxv persones chosyn thrugh the Cite ; that is to say of every ward in London a man, and to theym were assigned of every parisshe ij men. And so by this meanes was the Cite assessid at the said v m[1] markes, which was Repayed the next yere folowyng " (Kingsford's ' Chronicles of London,' pp. 188-9). Cf. Fabyan, pp. 666-7.

Robert Basset, Richard Gardyner, Thomas Stalbroke, Knt., William Heryot, Edmund Shaa, Thomas Hille, Hugh Brice, Richard Rawson, Henry Colet, Thomas Ilame, Robert Tate, and William Wikyng, Aldermen, and made a petition that certain ordinances for the regulation of the Craft[1] might be approved.

Petition granted.

23 March, 21 Edward IV. [A.D. 1480-1], came William Crulle, Thomas Breteyn, "irmongers," John Benyngtone, grocer, and Robert Lulley, "irmonger," and entered into bond in the sum of £80 for payment into the Chamber by the above William of a like sum to the use of John and Johanna, children of Thomas Crulle, late "irmonger," when they come of age or marry.

Fo. 159

Custod' Jueror' Tho'e Crulle irmonger.

7 April, 21 Edward IV. [A.D. 1481], came John Picton, Robert Southwode, and Thomas Bradbery, mercers, and entered into bond in the sum of £758 19s. ½d. for payment into the Chamber by the said John of a like sum to the use of Hugh and Margaret, children of John Fenne, late stockfishmonger, when they come of age or marry.[2]

Fo. 159 b.

Custod' pueror' Joh'is Fenne.

10 April, 21 Edward IV. [A.D. 1481], came John Chester, woolmonger, Dame Agnes Chester, widow, William Broun, draper, and [blank], and entered into bond in the sum of £80 for payment into the Chamber by the above John of a like sum to the use of Dorothy, Elizabeth, Hugh, Thomas, and Alice, children of the said John Chester, when they come of age or marry, the said money having been bequeathed to them by William Chester their grandfather, late skinner.

Fo. 160.

Custod' pueror' Joh'is Chester.

5 June, 21 Edward IV. [A.D. 1481], came good men of the Mistery of Painters before the Mayor and Aldermen, and presented a petition to the following effect :—

Ordinacio Pictorum.

That in future the petitioners may have for the good of the Craft the "halfdele" of the fines and forfeitures in respect of

---

[1] The articles are of the usual kind, relating to meetings of the Fellowship for civic or private business, the taking of apprentices, the Wardens and their right of search, and general behaviour of the members of the Fraternity towards the Wardens and one another.

[2] Margin. Edmund Bam, who married the above Margaret, received his wife's portion *temp.* Hugh Brice, Mayor [A.D. 1485-6].

N

defective work reported to the Chamberlain, the Commonalty having the other "halfdele."

That the Wardens, with an officer assigned by the Mayor, may have the right of search in all matters appertaining to their craft, over foreigners as well as all others of the Craft.

That they may set on work all foreigners approved by the Wardens, without any charge being made to the said foreigners.

Petition granted.

Fo. 160 b.

Ordinac' re-
noval' pro ven-
dicione ser-
visie.

7 June, 21 Edward IV. [A.D. 1481], the ordinance lately made by the Common Council *temp.* William Hamptone, Mayor, touching brewers and the sale of ale and " bere " by foreign brewers, hostelers, cooks, and others residing within the City,[1] to be put into execution.

Fo. 161.

Custod' Rob'ti
Sympson fil'
Rob'ti Symp-
son draper.

18 June, 21 Edward IV. [A.D. 1481], came John Hungerford, William Capell, John Saunder, and John Beauchamp, drapers, and entered into bond in the sum of £1,000 for payment into the Chamber by the said John Hungerford of a like sum to the use of Robert, son of Robert Sympson, late draper, when he comes of age.

Custod'
Kat'ine fil'
Will'i Draiton
Paisteler.

19 June, 21 Edward IV. [A.D. 1481], came Thomas Cole, William Marteyn, and George Grenested, skinners, and entered into bond in the sum of £40 for payment into the Chamber by the said Thomas of a like sum to the use of Katherine, daughter of William Draiton, late " pastiller," when she comes of age or marries.

Fo. 161 b.

Custod'
tueror' Rob'ti
" Middilton "
cissor'.

19 June, 21 Edward IV. [A.D. 1481], came William White, draper, Roger Barlowe, tailor, William Holme and [*blank*], drapers, and entered into bond in the sum of £126 13s. 4d. for payment into the Chamber by the said William White of divers sums to the use of Johanna, Anne, Margaret, Katherine,

---

[1] Referring, probably, to an ordinance of the Common Council held on the 24th Sept., 1473. See Journal 8, fo. 60.

Thomas, and James, children of Robert Middelton, late tailor, when they come of age or marry.[1]

26 June, 21 Edward IV. [A.D. 1481], ordinance by John Broune, the Mayor, and the Aldermen that in future the Chamberlain shall provide four torch-bearers on the eves of St. John Bapt. [24 June] and SS. Peter and Paul [29 June][2] at the expense of the Chamber, the same to be clothed in " jaketes " to match the torch-bearers provided by the Mayor for the time being.

Fo. 162.

De portatorib' Torchiar' in Vigiliis Sc'i Joh'is Baptiste etc.

5 July, 21 Edward IV. [A.D. 1481], came John Benyngton, John Smert, John Broke, and Robert Halle, grocers, and entered into bond in the sum of £1,000 for payment into the Chamber by the said John Benyngton of a like sum to the use of John, son of John Crosby, Knt. and Alderman, and late grocer, on his coming of age.

Custod' Joh'is Crosby filii Joh'is Crosby.

The same day came William Cowper, Simon Hogan, drapers, Everard Newchirch, " peautrer," and [*blank*], and entered into bond in the sum of 10 marks for payment into the Chamber by the said William of a like sum to the use of Richard, son of Richard Langley, late draper, when he comes of age.

Fo. 162 b.

Custod' Ric'i Langley fil' Ric'i Langley draper.

10 July, same year came Thomas Bell, " wexchaundiller," John Wyngare, Thomas Crosse, grocers, and John Frere, " bruer," and entered into bond in the sum of £23 6s. 10d. for

Fo. 163.

Custod' pueror' Joh'is Crosse.

---

[1] Margin. 7 April, 22 Edward IV. [A.D. 1482], came William Fox, " taillour," who had married the above Johanna, and acknowledged satisfaction for his wife's patrimony, as well as for money accruing by the decease of Scolastica her aunt and Elizabeth [*sic*] her sister ; 18 June, 14 Henry VII. [A.D. 1499], came Thomas Hunt, draper, who married the above Anne, and acknowledged satisfaction for his wife's patrimony, as well as for money accruing by the decease of Margaret and Elizabeth [*sic*] her sisters ; 7 Oct., 10 Henry VII.

[A.D. 1494], came Thomas Woodward, who married the above Katherine, and acknowledged satisfaction for her patrimony, and on the 6th Nov. of the same year the said Thomas acknowledged satisfaction for money accruing to his said wife by the decease of Margaret and Elizabeth [*sic*] her sisters.

[2] When the Midsummer Watch was held, and the City was given up to bonfires and carousing. See Stow's ' Survey ' (ed. Kingsford), i. 101-3.

N 2

payment into the Chamber by the said Thomas Bell of a like sum to the use of Peter, Johanna, and Margaret, children of John Crosse, when they come of age or marry.

Concessio fc̄a armurar' de quodam solo.

Friday, 27 July, 21 Edward IV. [A.D. 1481], petition presented to the Common Council by Richard Ferne, John Bride and Richard Michell, the Master and Wardens of the Mistery of "Armurers," praying that they may be allowed to enlarge their wharf in the parish of St. Peter near Paul's Wharf by the space of 10 feet, so that it might be made even towards the Thames with the other wharves next adjoining, inasmuch as at every ebb of the river the soil was covered with entrails of beasts and other filth, to the great annoyance of the petitioners and of those using a common stair adjoining the said wharf.

✓

Petition granted.

Fo. 163 b.

Ordinacio fc̄a pro conservac' Pont' London'.

At the same Common Council a petition was presented by the Wardens of London Bridge complaining of the damage done to the great Tower at drawbridge and other arches and piers of the bridge by the vibration caused by "shod carts" passing over, as well as by frequent drawing of the drawbridge, and praying that it may be ordained that in future "no shod cart laden be suffred to passe over the said Brigge[1] nor the said drawebrigge to be drawne but onely for grete necessite and defence" of the City ; and, further, reminding the Council of "the grete and many inconvenientes that have come in tyme passed and daily come to the stadelinges[2] and grounde werks of the same brigge by Petir men[3] laiers of Wilchons[4] and oþere Fisshers liyng almost daily and tidely in tyme of yere atte said stadelinges to the grete hurt of the same," and praying that an act of Common Council recorded in a book marked with the letter I, fo. lvj, forbidding fishing within 20 fathoms of any

[1] Cf. 'Cal. Letter-Book K,' p. 38.
[2] Foundations or starlings. See 'Cal. Letter-Book A,' p. 186 ; 'Cal. Letter-Book H,' p. 278 n.
[3] Or "Peters"—fishermen using nets called "peteresnets." Cf. 'Cal. Letter-Book A,' p. 186 n.
[4] Wilks, Cf. A.-S. *weaican.*

" stadelyng " of the bridge, may be renewed and ratified ;[1] and, lastly, praying that it may be enacted that no ship lying at Fresh Wharf or elsewhere on the east side of the Bridge shall cast any anchor in the " Goleis " and " Stadelynges " under the Bridge nor within 20 fathoms of the same.

Petition granted.

Friday the Feast of St. Matthew [21 Sept.], 21 Edward IV. [A.D. 1481], in the presence of John Broun, the Mayor, Humphrey Starky the Recorder, William Taillour, Knt., William Hamptone, Knt., Robert Drope, Robert Basset, Richard Gardyner, Thomas Stalbroke, William Heriot, Robert Billesdone, Edmund Shaa, Thomas Hille, Hugh Brice, Richard Rawson, John Warde, John Stokker, Robert Tate, William Bacon, William Horn, and William Wikyng, Aldermen, and very many Commoners summoned to the Guildhall for the election of Sheriffs — Robert Tate, mercer, was elected one of the Sheriffs of London and Middlesex by the Mayor, and William Wikyng, skinner, was elected the other Sheriff by the Commonalty.

Fo. 164.

Eleccio Vice com'.

The same day Milo Adys, goldsmith, was elected Chamberlain of the City for the year ensuing ; William Galle, tailor, and Henry Bumpstede, mercer, were elected Wardens of London Bridge ; Thomas Hille, Hugh Brice, Aldermen, William White, draper, John Swan, " taillour," William Martin, " skynner," and William Spark, draper, Commoners, were elected Auditors of the accounts of the Chamberlain and Wardens in arrear.

Afterwards, viz., on the eve of St. Michael [29 Sept.], the said Sheriffs were sworn at the Guildhall, and on the morrow of the said Feast were presented, admitted, &c., before the Barons of the Exchequer.

---

[1] Among the ordinances proclaimed by Richard Whityngton on entering upon the office of Mayor in 1406, and recorded on fo. 56 of Letter-Book I, is the following : " Item qe nulle pesche en Thamise......pres nulle Wharf de Pount de Temple tanque alle Toure de Loundres ne del autre coste du Thamyse par le space de vynt vadme." London Bridge does not appear to be mentioned.

Q'd s'vientes nec valecti vic' vendant s'visiam ad Retall' etc.

Wednesday, 26 Sept., 21 Edward IV. [A.D. 1481], ordinance by the Common Council that the Sheriffs for the time being, and all future Sheriffs, shall not admit to office any serjeant-at-mace or valet, unless such serjeant or valet find surety before admission not to sell ale by retail, the Sheriffs being fined £5 every time they do to the contrary.

Custod' pueror' Joh'is Bodnam wexchaundeler.

28 Sept., 21 Edward IV. [A.D. 1481], came Robert Fletcher, "cowper," William Broun, draper, Richard Eryk, "upholder," and Robert Gowdby, draper, before the Mayor and Aldermen, and entered into bond in the sum of £55 9s. 2d. for the delivery into the Chamber by the said Robert Fletcher of the sum of £40 and certain jewels to the use of John and Isabella, children of John Bodnam, late "wexchaundiller," when they come of age or marry.

Fo. 164 b.

Custod' Thome fil' Ric'i Grene scrivener.

The same day came John Thornton, John Hunter, Thomas Spence, and Thomas Welles, stockfishmongers, and entered into bond in the sum of 20 marks for the payment into the Chamber by the said John Thornton of a like sum to the use of Thomas, son of Richard Grene, late scrivener, when he comes of age.

Fo. 165.

9 Oct., 21 Edward IV. [A.D. 1481], Sir [Thomas[1]] Percy, Prior of Christchurch, sworn before John Broun, the Mayor, and the Aldermen as Alderman of the Ward of Portsokne, and made oath such as other Aldermen are accustomed to make, &c.

Eleccio Maioris.

Saturday the Feast of Translation of St. Edward [13 Oct.], 21 Edward IV. [A.D. 1481], in the presence of John Broun, the Mayor, the Prior of Christchurch, Humphrey Starky the Recorder, William Taillour, Knt., William Hamptone, Knt., Robert Drope, Richard Gardyner, Thomas Stalbroke, Knt., William "Hariot," Robert Billesdone, Milliam Stokker, Knt., Edmund Shaa, Thomas Hille, Richard Rawson, Hugh

---

[1] Supplied by Rev. A. B. Beaven ('Aldermen of the City of London,' p. 181). This appears to be the first instance recorded in the Letter- | Books of a Prior of Christchurch being sworn as Alderman of Portsoken Ward.

Brice, John Warde, John Stokker, William Horn, and Robert
Tate, Aldermen, and an immense Commonalty summoned to
the Guildhall for the election of a Mayor for the year ensuing—
William " Haryot " was elected.

Afterwards, viz., on the Feast of SS. Simon and Jude
[28 Oct.], he was sworn at the Guildhall, and on the morrow
was presented, admitted, &c., before the Barons of the
Exchequer.

15 Oct., 21 Edward IV. [A.D. 1481], came good men of the   *Fos. 165-7.*
Art or Mistery of Masons of the City of London into the Court   *Ordinacio*
of the lord the King in the Chamber of the Guildhall, before   *Lathamorum.*
the Mayor and Aldermen, and prayed that certain articles for
the better regulation of the Mistery might be approved, which
articles were to the following effect :—

That freemen of the said craft, mistery, or science shall, on
the Feast of Holy Trinity or within ten days of the same,
assemble together in some suitable place within the City and
choose two of themselves, being householders, to be Wardens
of the Craft for the two years next ensuing, the said new
Wardens being presented by the old Wardens and 4 or 6
other honest persons of the Craft for approval and sworn in the
Chamber of the Guildhall.

That all money, jewels, goods, and necessaries belonging to
the Fellowship be delivered to the new Wardens, and an
account rendered.

That a freeman who has been duly elected Warden and
refuses to take office be brought before the Mayor or the
Chamberlain as a rebel against his fellowship and forfeit the
sum of 40s. for his disobedience.

That once in every three years the members be clad in a
livery at the discretion of 6 honest persons or more of the
said Craft, such as the Wardens and Fellowship shall appoint
thereto ; and that every one admitted to the livery, and able
to bear the charge thereof, refusing to take it or wear it, be
liable to forfeit the sum of 6s. 8d.

That once in every two years they attend Mass at Christchurch within Aldgate, clad in their livery, and each make

offering of one penny; and afterwards go to their dinner or recreation at a place appointed, accompanied by their wives if they will. Each member to pay 12 pence for his own dinner, and 8 pence for his wife's dinner if present. Any one absenting himself from the said Mass, offering, or dinner, without reasonable cause, to forfeit 3s. 4d.

Provided always that the dinner be kept the year of the election of the new Wardens, and the "clothyng" given the following year.

That every freeman of the Craft shall attend at Christchurch on the Feast of *Quatuor Coronati*[1] [8 Nov.] to hear Mass, under penalty of 12 pence.

That certain days be kept for payment of quarterages, viz., 3 pence a quarter, an extra payment of 2 pence being made towards any recreation provided on those days by the Wardens. Those absenting themselves without reasonable excuse to be liable to a forfeiture of 12 pence.

No one to be admitted into the freedom of the Craft by the Wardens until examined and proved "connyng" therein, under penalty of 40s. Servants and apprentices not to be enticed away from their masters. Brothers of the Craft not to rebuke or revile the Wardens or each other. Lastly, the Wardens to have a right of search, and the oversight and correction of all manner of work appertaining to the science of Masons within the City and suburbs, in conjunction with an officer of the Mayor assigned to them for the purpose.

Petition granted.

Fo. 167.

Ordinacio de Brounbakers.

15 Oct., 21 Edward IV. [A.D. 1481], came likewise good men of the Mistery of Brounbakers before the Mayor and Aldermen, complaining that persons of divers other crafts use the Craft of

---

[1] Or "Four Crowned Martyrs," a title bestowed on four working masons or sculptors who are said to have suffered death at Rome in the reign of Diocletian [A.D. 284-303] rather than make a statue to a heathen god. In consequence of that Emperor's persecution of Christians, the chronological era known as the "Era of Diocletian" was also called the "Era of Martyrs." A lodge of Freemasons exists in London at the present day known as that of the *Quatuor Coronati* (No. 2076).— Conder, 'The Hole Craft and Fellowship of Masons,' p. 44.

Brounbakers to a greater extent than freemen of the Craft, and refuse to obey the Wardens of the Craft in assize and "past," pay no quarterage, neither bear lot nor scot.   They therefore prayed that certain articles for the regulation of the Craft might be approved and recorded to the following effect :—

That every one occupying the Craft of Brounbakers in the City shall obey the Wardens in their search and observe the rules touching the assize and paste, under penalty of paying 6s. 8d.

That every brother or occupier of the Craft pay every quarter day 6d., besides 13d. to the Beadle, and every journey-man 2d.

That bakers of horsbrede[1] shall not entice customers by giving any advantage to them, but only "xviii caste of horsbrede for the doseyn" whilst keeping the assize and paste, under penalty of 20s.

And that no one of the Craft sell thenceforth any "hors-brede" to hucksters to retail, but only to innholders and such as desire it for their own use, under penalty of 6s. 8d.

Petition granted.

The same day came the Wardens and Fellowship of the Mistery of Wyremongers[2] and prayed that certain articles for the regulation of the Craft might be approved and enrolled,[3] to the following effect (*inter alia*) :—

Fos. 167 b-8 b.

Ordinacio de Wyremongers.

That no one of the Craft work anything pertaining to the same upon Saturday nor on the vigil of any double Feast after the last "pele" of evensong rung in the parish church, under penalty of forfeiting 2 pounds of wax or 8 pence for the pound.

That none work on the Feast of St. Clement the Pope [23 Nov.], "but that it be kept and halowed as it is kept and

---

[1] Horse bread was the common artificial food for horses in the Middle Ages. The modern dog biscuit and oil cake for cattle are its nearest equivalent.

[2] A fellowship formed in 1479 by the union of the Chapemakers with the Wyredrawers. See *supra*, p. 168, and note there.

[3] Compare similar ordinances of the Wyresellers (an association of Pynners and Wyremongers) in 1497. *Infra*, fos. 329 *et seq.*

halowed among oþere craftes of the same citee that in their werk occupie fire and water in eschewyng the hurtes that myght come thereby,"[1] under penalty of 3s. 4d.

That no freeman of the Craft "sett any persone awerk nor werk opynly in his shop in the occupacion of wyndyng of Bokils, cuttyng of stones for muldes,[2] scoryng of the same, gravyng of muldes, castyng of metall, or colowryng of the same metall, by the which any persone not enfraunchesed in the same Craft straungier or other not connyng in the same Craft myght lerne it, but if the same persone not connyng aggree w[t] the Wardeyns of the same Craft for the tyme being Except onely the wiffe son doughter or covenaunt servaunte that hath been apprentice in the same Craft," under penalty.

Also that henceforth no person work in the Craft after 9 P.M., to the annoyance of his neighbours with knocking or filing, under penalty of paying one pound of wax to the Guildhall Chapel and one pound to the use of the Craft, or 8 pence for the pound.

Petition granted.

Fo. 168 b.

Vicecom' mortuus et alter loco ejus electus etc.

Be it remembered that on Saturday, 20 Oct., 21 Edward IV. [A.D. 1481], in the presence of John Broun, the Mayor, the Aldermen, the Common Council, the Wardens, and other good men of all the Misteries of the City summoned to the Great Hall of the Guildhall, Richard Chawry, salter, was elected one of the Sheriffs of the City [sic] *loco* William Wykyng, who died the previous day. The same day the said Richard Chawry received the oath according to custom. On the following Monday, viz., 22 Oct., he was presented at Westminster with the pageant of all the barges (*cum apparatu omnium Bargiarum*),

---

[1] Pope Clement, having suffered martyrdom by drowning with an anchor attached to his neck, was chosen patron of metal-workers. A writer in *Notes and Queries*, 2 Sept., 1911, on the connexion between St. Clement the Pope and the Wyredrawers, states that at one time it was the custom to celebrate St. Clement's Day in Woolwich Dockyard "by a procession in which honour was done to an apprentice got up to represent 'Old Clem,' much begging, drinking, and speechifying being connected with the observance."

[2] Moulds.

according to ancient custom in presentations of the City's Sheriffs on the morrow of St. Michael.

"Be it Remembred that the xxiijth day of October the xxjth yere of the Reign of Kyng Edward the iiijth [A.D. 1481] It is accordet by John Broun Maire and the Aldremen of the Citee of London that from hensfurth in the Goyng and Commyng of the Maire to or from Westmynster when he shall take his Othe there shall no disguysyng nor pageoun be used or hadde from the Maires house to the water nor from the water to the Maires house like as it hath been used nowe of late afore this tyme uppon payn of xx *li* to be lost by the Feolashippe that shall hapne to do the contrary hereunto to thuse of the Chambre etc."

Fo. 169.

Disgysyng et pageons prohibit' qn' Maior recepit suum sacr'm etc.

Letter from John Broun, the Mayor, and Milo Adys, the Chamberlain, to Thomas [Kempe], Bishop of London, presenting Master Thomas Aleyn for admission to one of the five chantries founded in the Guildhall Chapel by Adam Fraunceys and Henry Frowyk, vacant by the resignation of Sir Thomas Praty, the last chaplain. Dated 15 Oct., 1481.

P'sentacio Mag'i i Tho^e Aleyn ad quandam Cantar' .v. cantar' in Capella b'te Marie juxta Guyhald' London'.

27 Oct., 21 Edward IV. [A.D. 1481], Thomas Ludbury, "lorymer," discharged by the Mayor and Aldermen from serving on juries, owing to his infirmities.

Exon'acio Thome Ludbury ab assis'.

The same day John Pierson, mercer, similarly discharged for like cause.

Exon'acio Joh'is Pierson ab assis'.

The same day William Dolfynby, "letherseller," similarly discharged for like cause.

Exon'acio Will'i Dolfynby ab assisis etc.

Letter from the King to the Mayor and Aldermen thanking them for having acceded to his request to appoint Nicholas Suthworth to the office of "Garbelershipe"[1] within the City, and, further, for having made him a freeman without charge. The King promises that this appointment to the office of

Fo. 169 b.

L'ra Reg' Edwardi iiij^{ti} q'd Maior et Aldr'i lib'am h'erent elecc' suor' officiariorum.

---

[1] The garbelage of groceries and other commodities. The duty of the Garbler was to see that all drugs and groceries were duly garbled (*i.e.*, picked), and cleansed before sale.

Garbler shall not be drawn into precedent.   Dated at Windsor
Castle, 16 Nov. [A.D. 1481].

Custod' Mar-
garete fil'
Will'i Gardy-
ner draper.

13 Nov., 21 Edward IV. [A.D. 1481], came Robert Fletcher,
" cowper," William White, Thomas Risby, drapers, and John
Plonket, " sherman," before William " Hariot," the Mayor, and
the Aldermen, and entered into bond in the sum of £60 16s. 2d.
for the delivery into the Chamber by the said Robert Fletcher
of a sum of money [amount not recorded] and certain goods in
trust for Margaret, daughter of William Gardyner, late draper,
when she comes of age or marries.[1]

Fo. 170.

Proclamacio
contu Provi-
sores victual-
ium pro hos-
picio Regis.

Writ to the Sheriffs to make proclamation for all persons
who have suffered at the hands of the King's Takers and
Purveyors in taking wheat, wood, &c., to lay their complaint
before the Lords of the Council or the Steward of the King's
Household, the King's will being that none should be prevented bringing wheat and wood to the City, and that any
wheat or other grain taken by the said Purveyors should be
paid for.   No Purveyor to be accepted as such unless he pro-
duce his commission under the Great Seal.[2]   Witness the King
at Westminster, 16 Nov., 21 Edward IV. [A.D. 1481].

Exon'acio
Joh'is Oterton
ab assis'.

27 Nov., 21 Edward IV. [A.D. 1481], John Oterton, " bowyer,"
discharged by the Mayor and Aldermen from serving on
juries, &c., owing to old age.

Custod'
pueror' Ric'i
Sturges pisce-
nar'.

1 Dec., 21 Edward IV. [A.D. 1481], came Richard Suthewell,
esquire, fishmonger, William Purchas, mercer, and Robert
Darlyngton, fishmonger, and entered into bond in the sum of
400 marks for payment into the Chamber by the said Richard
of 250 marks to the use of John, son of Richard Sturges,
late fishmonger, and £100 to the use of Richard, son of the
same, when they respectively come of age.

---

[1] Margin.   30 July, 14 Henry VII.
[A.D. 1499], came John Gardyner,
scrivener, who married the above
Margaret, and acknowledged satisfaction for his wife's property.

[2] For various statutes regulating
Purveyance, see ' Calendar Letter-
Book I,' pp. 288-98 ; ' Cal. Letter-
Book K,' p. 269.

11 Dec., 21 Edward IV. [A.D. 1481], came John Olston, Rector of the church of St. Michael in "Bassyngeshawe," John Materdale, Thomas Shelley, and Ralph Urmestone, church-wardens, Richard Haynes, Henry Davers, Robert Yarome, William Rollesley, William Estone, John Benname, John Martyn, Hervey Stephens, Nicholas Duraunt, and John Baker, parishioners of the same, and entered into bond in the sum of £18 for the payment of a sum of £3 out of every whole fifteenth granted by Parliament to the King, towards the relief of the poorest parishioners, until such sum of £18 be expended.

5 Feb., 21 Edward IV. [A.D. 1481-2], came good men of the Art or Mistery of Lethersellers into the Court of the lord the King in the Chamber of the Guildhall, before the Mayor and Aldermen, and prayed that certain articles for the regulation of the Mistery[1] might be approved, to the following effect (*inter alia*) :—

That no member "tawe" any leather for any one not a free-man of the City and "reciaunt" within the City and suburbs, under penalty prescribed, except that if "any gentilman or any other honest man willyng to have a skynne or ij or iij or half a doseyn tawed for his owne use no man say nay as the Tawier and he may aggree and accorde takyng for the werk-manship þ'eof."

Also that no "foreyn" shall be put to "tawyng of leder," nor to "diyng of leder," nor to "flotyng of brasill," nor to "drawyng out of leder," nor "kepyng stewe to dry lether in when it is died," nor to "w^t thyng," "paryng," "pollyng," nor "cuttyng of poyntes," under penalty.

Also that no one of the Craft thenceforth "sett on, put on, wynde on, nor perse no maner throwes otherwise called aglettes upon any poyntes or laces, that is to say of leder thredde or silk of what colour soever it be, by no candelight."

Petition granted.

---

[1] The articles are fully set out in Black's 'History of the Leather-sellers' (pp. 39-41), but the date is there given as 5 *January*.

Br'e pro tenen-
tib' ville de
Southwold et
Returnum
ejusdem.

Writ *alias* to the Mayor and Sheriffs forbidding the exaction of toll from the men of the vill of Southwold, co. Suff., the said vill having been formerly held by Gilbert de Clare, late Earl of Gloucester and Hereford, as part of the Earldom of Gloucester, and its tenants free of toll.   Witness the King at Westminster, 11 May, 20 Edward IV. [A D. 1480].

Fo. 172 b.

Return made to the above writ to the effect that the Mayor and Sheriffs had always taken toll of men of Southwold coming to the City with merchandise, and that they could not cease from so doing without prejudice to the City's liberties and customs.

Exon'acio
Joh'is Seman
ab assisis.

14 Feb., 21 Edward IV. [A.D. 1481-2], John Seman, " talough-chaundler," discharged from serving on juries, &c., owing to his infirmities.

Custod' Thome
fil' Walteri
Milson cur-
riour.

16 Feb. the same year came Thomas Hobersty, Thomas Mower, John Cole, curriers, and entered into bond in the sum of £10 for payment into the Chamber by the said Thomas Hobersty of a like sum to the use of Thomas, son of Walter Milson, late currier, when he comes of age.[1]

Fo. 173.

Custod' Isabell'
fil' Will'i
Leche.

1 March, 21 Edward IV. [A.D. 1481-2], came Thomas Hiot, John Lokton, John Benet, and Percyvall Wodehous, drapers, and entered into bond in the sum of £20 for payment into the Chamber by the said Thomas of a like sum to the use of Isabella, daughter of William Leche, when she comes of age or marries, the said money having been bequeathed to her by Thomas Hoye, late " joynour."

Custod' Alicie
fil' Will'i
Leche.

The same day came John Chalk, goldsmith, William Chalk, " peauterer," Robert Panteley, goldsmith, and Thomas Awty, cordwainer, and entered into bond in the sum of £20 for pay-ment into the Chamber by the said John Chalk of a like sum to the use of Alice, daughter of William Leche, when she comes of age or marries, the said money having been bequeathed by the above Thomas Hoye.

---

[1] Margin.   17 Oct., 4 Henry VII. [A.D. 1488], came Alice, wife of Thomas Pelham, *alias* Butter, and daughter of the said Walter Milson, and acknowledged satisfaction of the above sum of £10 accruing to her by the death of her brother Thomas, the orphan.

Letter from William " Haryot," Knt. and Mayor, to the Dean and Chapter of St. Paul's, presenting Laurence Botiller for admission to the second of the three chantries founded in the said church for the souls of Sir John Pulteney, Knt., and Sirs William Milford and John Plesseys, former Archdeacons of Colchester. Dated 7 March, A.D. 1481[-2].

Fo. 173 b.

Psentacio Laurenc' Botiller Capell'i ad se'dam cantar' trium cantar' in Eccl'ia Cathedral' Sc'i Pauli London'.

11 March, 22 Edward IV. [A.D. 1481-2], came Alianora Santone, widow, Roger Barlowe, tailor, Stephen Smyth, haberdasher, and Robert Gawdeby, draper, and entered into bond in the sum of £200 for payment into the Chamber by the said Alianora of a like sum to the use of Robert and William, sons of Thomas Santone, late draper, when they come of age.

Custod' vueror' Tho'e Santone draper.

16 April, 22 Edward IV. [A.D. 1482], ordinance by the Mayor and Aldermen that in future no one should be elected or admitted Serjeant-at-Mace to the Mayor for the time being unless he has previously served as Serjeant-at-Mace with one of the Sheriffs.

Fo. 174.

Q'd nemo eligatur in s'vient' Maioris ad clavam nisi prius extit'it s'viens vic' etc.

Afterwards it was ordained by Edmund Shaa, the Mayor [A.D. 1482-3], and the Aldermen that no one should be elected Serjeant-at-Mace to a Mayor unless he had been two consecutive years as Serjeant-at-Mace with one of the Sheriffs.

16 April, 22 Edward IV. [A.D. 1482], came good men of the Art or Mistery of Barbers of the City into the Court of the lord the King in the Chamber of the Guildhall, before William Haryot, Knt. and Mayor, and the Aldermen, and prayed that certain articles might be approved.[1]

Ordinacio Barbitonsor' etc.

Petition granted.

23 May, 22 Edward IV. [A.D. 1482], John Greves, leatherseller, discharged by the Mayor and Aldermen from serving on juries, &c., owing to his infirmities.

Fo. 174 b.

Exon'acio Joh'is Greves ab assis'.

25 May, 22 Edward IV. [A.D. 1482], John Awndernesse, skinner, similarly discharged for like cause.

Exon'acio Johannis Awndernesse ab assis' etc.

[1] The articles, which relate to the taking of apprentices, are set out in Sidney Young's ' Annals of the Barber-Surgeons' (pp. 61-2), but the date has been inadvertently given as 26 April.

Fo. 175.

*Custod' Ed-
mundi Ed-
ward fil'
Will'i Ed-
ward Ald'i.*

10 June, 22 Edward IV. [A.D. 1482], came William Horn, Richard Chawry, Aldermen, Thomas Breteyn, "irmonger," and William Graunt, salter, and entered into bond in the sum of 450 marks for payment into the Chamber by the said William Horn of a like sum to the use of Edmund, son of William Edward, late Alderman, when he comes of age.

*Br'e et Re-
turn' declarens
consuetudinem
etc. pro terr'
et ten' legat' ad
manum mor-
tuam vel alio
modo etc.*

Writ to the Mayor and Aldermen touching a plea at Westminster between John Penford, plaintiff, and Richard Sparowe, defendant, for unlawful entry into certain messuages contrary to the statute 5 Richard II. [cap. viii.], and commanding the said Mayor and Aldermen to make a return as to whether, by the custom of the City, a freeman can devise lands and tenements within the City in mortmain or otherwise, as well by his written testament as by his last will made without writing, whether it be reduced to writing after the death of the devisor and proved, like a nuncupative testament, by ecclesiastical law or not. Witness W[illiam] "Huse"[1] at Westminster, 8 May, 22 Edward IV. [A.D. 1482].

Fo. 175 b.

*Return' br'is
predict'.*

Return made to the above writ by Humphrey Starky the Recorder *oretenus*, according to the custom of the City, to the following effect:—

By the custom of the City every freeman can, and could, devise lands and tenements within the City in mortmain[2] or otherwise, as well by written testament as by his last will without writing, whether such a will be reduced to writing after the decease of the devisor, and be proved by ecclesiastical law like a nuncupative testament, or not reduced to writing and not proved by ecclesiastical law like a nuncupative testament.[3]

*Consuetud'
sup' attach'm
f orincec' reci-
tat' per br'e.*

Writ to the Mayor and Aldermen reciting that a plea had been moved in the King's Court at Westminster between Roger Bourghchier, mercer, plaintiff, and John Colyns, mercer, defendant, for the recovery of a debt of £100, and that a question had arisen whether there existed in the City an

---

[1] "Husse" or "Hussey," Chief Justice of the King's Bench.

[2] By charter 6 March, 1 Edw. III.

[3] Except in the City of London and other places held like it in free burgage, a devise of lands and tenements by a nuncupative will was void.

immemorial custom to the effect that if any plaint of debt be levied or affirmed by any one in the Court of the lord the King, before the Mayor and Aldermen of the City for the time being, in the Chamber of the Guildhall, so that precept be issued to a Serjeant-at-mace of the Mayor and officer of that Court to summon the defendant to appear before the Mayor and Aldermen at the next Court to answer the plaintiff in the said plaint, and the said Serjeant testifies by word of mouth at the next Court that the defendant had nothing in the City whereby he could be summoned, and then the defendant makes default; that thereupon the said Mayor and Aldermen being informed that some other person for some reason was indebted to the defendant to the extent of the sum specified in the plaint or parcel thereof, precept issues to the Serjeant to attach such sum in the hands of the other person, and if the defendant, being summoned to appear at the next Court and three other Courts, makes default, whilst the plaintiff always appears; that at the last of the said four Courts the said Serjeant summons the person in whose hands the money lies to appear at a further Court to show cause why the money should not be delivered to the plaintiff, and that delivery eventually takes place.[1] The Mayor and Aldermen are enjoined to make a return by the mouth of the Recorder, certifying the King as to the existence of such a custom. Witness T[homas] Bryan[2] at Westminster, 13 June, 22 Edward IV. [A.D. 1482].

Return made to the above certifying the custom as above recited.

Fos. 176-6 b.
Return' br'is p'dict' et cons' p'dict' decla- rat'.

Writ of Privy Seal, by authority of Parliament, granting licence to Thomas Danyell, John Belde, John Lewesson, Henry Reynold, Thomas Rede, Thomas Grene, Thomas

Fo. 177.
Carta Tincto- rum.

---

[1] Further particulars of this case and of the custom of foreign attach- ment in the City are set out in the records of the Court of Common Pleas, de Banco Roll, Michaelmas, 21 Edward IV., Roll 404. See

Appendix (No. 29) to the late Maurice Hewlett's Report *in re* The London Joint - Stock Banks *v.* the Mayor, &c., of London (March, 1878).

[2] Chief Justice of Common Pleas.

Warfeld, William Michell, William Hoode, Nicholas Sewall, William Body, Robert Bromptone, and Stephen Ingram, freemen of the Mistery of Dyers of the City, to found and establish a perpetual Fraternity or Guild[1] with two Wardens and a Commonalty of freemen of the Mistery residing within the City; and with the brethren and sisters of freemen of the same Mistery and others who desire to join the said Fraternity or Guild ; and the said Wardens and Commonalty to be one body and Commonalty incorporate in fact and name, capable of acquiring lands, rents, &c., having a common seal, &c. Witnesses, Thomas [Bourchier], Cardinal Archbishop of Canterbury ; R[obert Stillington], Bishop of Bath and Wells and Chancellor ; Thomas [Scott *alias* Rotherham], Bishop of Lincoln and Keeper of the Privy Seal ; George, Duke of Clarence ; Richard, Duke of Gloucester ; Henry Essex, Treasurer of England ; John Wiltes', the Chief Butler ; Thomas Stanley de Staneley, Steward of the King's Household ; William Hastynges de Hastynges, the King's Chamberlain, &c. Dated at Westminster, 2 December, 12 Edward IV. [A.D. 1472].

Fos. 177 b- 178.

Ordinacio Tinctor'.

9 July, 22 Edward IV. [A.D. 1482], came the Wardens and good men of the Art of Dyers of the City before the Mayor and Aldermen, and prayed that certain articles for the regulation of the Craft might be approved.

Among the articles are the following :—

That if any freeman of the Craft leave the City and teach his craft to strangers and then return, he shall be reputed as a " foreyn " and as no freeman, until he agree with the Fellowship of the Craft and buy his freedom through the Chamber of the City.

That the ordinance touching buying and " departing " of woad and receiving of servants recorded in Letter-Book K, fo. cxxxiii[b], *temp.* John Brokley, Mayor, be strictly observed.

Petition granted.

---

[1] From this one would surmise that the Dyers had not existed as a Fraternity or Guild before their actual incorporation as a Company by charter. The same may be said of the charter granted to the Drapers in 1438. See ' Cal. Letter-Book K,' pp. 224-5.

30 July, 22 Edward IV, [A.D. 1482], came Thomas Clifford, scrivener, William Sandes, grocer, John Wylkynson and Walter Clifford, scriveners, and entered into bond in the sum of £11 3s. 4d. for payment into the Chamber by the said Thomas Clifford of a like sum to the use of John, Richard, Edward, William, and Idonea, children of the said Thomas Clifford, when they come of age or marry, the said money having been bequeathed to them by John Sutton, late mercer.

Fo. 178.
*Custod'
pueror' Thome
Clifford.*

3 July, 22 Edward IV. [A.D. 1482], John Eltryngham, "sadler," discharged by the Mayor and Aldermen from serving on juries, &c., owing to his infirmities.

Fo. 178 b.
*Exon'acio
Joh'is El-
tryngham ab
assis'.*

28 Sept., 22 Edward IV. [A.D. 1482], Thomas Fraunceys, "cowper," similarly discharged for like cause.

*Exon'acio
Thome Fraun
ceys Cowper
ab assis' etc.*

Saturday the Feast of St. Matthew [21 Sept.], 22 Edward IV. [A.D. 1482], in the presence of William "Hariot," Knt., Mayor, Humphrey Starky the Recorder, Robert Basset, Richard Gardyner, John Broun, William Stokker, Knt., Edmund Shaa, Thomas Hille, Richard Rawson, John Warde, John Fissher, Thomas "Norlong,"[1] Richard Nailer, John Mathewe, Robert Tate, and Richard Chawry, Aldermen, and very many Commoners summoned to the Guildhall for the election of Sheriffs —William White, draper, was elected one of the Sheriffs of London and Middlesex by the Mayor, and John Mathewe, mercer, was elected the other Sheriff by the Commonalty.

*Eleccio Vice-
com'.*

The same day Milo Adys, goldsmith, was elected Chamberlain of the City for the year ensuing; William Galle, tailor, and Humphrey Bumpstede, mercer, were elected Wardens of the City's Bridge; Hugh Brice, Richard Rawson, Aldermen, William Martyn, skinner, William Spark, draper, John Materdale, "taillour," and Nicholas Alwyn, mercer, Commoners, were elected Auditors of the accounts of the Chamberlain and Wardens in arrear.

Afterwards, viz., on the eve of St. Michael [29 Sept.], the said Sheriffs were sworn at the Guildhall, and on the morrow

---

[1] Northland or Norland, elected Alderman of Bishopsgate Ward in | Nov., 1481 (Beaven, 'Aldermen of the City of London,' i. 35).

.of the said Feast were presented, .admitted, &c., before the Barons of the Exchequer.

Fo. 179.

Q'd subvic'
Midd' ex-
pendat x marc'
per annum etc.

Tuesday, 24 Sept., 22 Edward IV. [A.D: 1482], ordinance by the Common Council that in future every Under-Sheriff of Middlesex appointed by the Sheriffs of London shall reside continually within the City or county of Middlesex, and hold property in fee within the said City or county of the annual value of 10 marks ; and if no one can be found having these qualifications to serve the office of Under-Sheriff of Middlesex, then the Sheriffs of London for the time being shall retain the office in their own hands and execute the duties of the same.[1]

Fos. 179-180.

Ordinacio
contra falsita-
tem et decepc'
pann' lan'.

The same day, a petition made to the Common Council by the Wardens and whole fellowships of the Misteries of Drapers and Taillours reminding the Council of "the grete untrueth falshode and deceite in late daies begonne and nowe daily used in the makyng fullyng drawyng or settyng of lengeth ⁱn the Teyntours Sheryng & powderyng wᵗ Flokkes of wollen cloth in biyng and sellyng of the same aswell wᵗin this Citee or elswhere wᵗin the reame of England ; the makers of the which clothes in thise daies for the more partie make theym full unperfite both in lengeth and in brede contrary to the goode and holesome Statutes of this lond thereof made, and so afterward when thei be bought, being so unperfite many of theym often tymes be shorn and not fully wette before and some of theym after thei be fully wet and shorn than thei be teyntred and drawen in lengeth, which afterward when thei Receive wete of verrey force must shrynk and beside this where some tyme the Shermen have hurte mennys clothes in their werkmanship as in sheryng to lowe and to nygh the threde than thei powdre theym wᶜ Flokkes and thus by thise meanes been the clothes made wrought and handled to the grete hurt and deceite aswell of the King's true liege people as also of all straungiers which here

---

[1] The reason given for the above ordinance is the bad character and poverty of many of those who had been hitherto appointed Under-Sheriffs of Middlesex.

and in oþere londes and contreis usen to bye of the same unto the grete Rebuke and dishonour of all this Realme and also to the full grevous disclaundre of yor saide suppliauntes "—they prayed therefore that certain articles for remedying such abuses might be approved.

They were to the effect (*inter alia*): That no woollen cloth shall in future be shorn, except "cancellyng,"[1] unless it be previously wetted.

That no one dwelling within the City, free or foreign, give cloth to be "teyntered" or shorn to any one out of the franchise of the City.

That all cloth brought to the City for sale shall be sent to Blackwell Hall, and not be harboured elswhere.

That no freeman have or keep any "Teyntour" in his own place or elsewhere, under penalty of £20; that all such "Teyntours" as then existed in such places be removed by Thursday night at the latest; and that no "Teyntour" be made unless ordained at the discretion of the Mayor and Aldermen.

That no cloth "roughed and shorn" within the realm be sold unless the seller deliver it wet and measured by the yard, and the buyer buy it "at wetyng and meatyng," and not otherwise.

That the Masters and Wardens of the Misteries of Drapers, Taillours, Shermen, and Fullers be granted authority to search for faults in their respective Fellowships, and present such faults as they may find to the Chamberlain for the time being.

Petition granted.

Sunday the Feast of Translation of St. Edward [13 Oct.], 22 Edward IV. [A.D. 1482], in the presence of William Haryot, Knt., Mayor, Humphrey Starky the Recorder, William Taillour, Knt., Robert Drope, Robert Basset, Richard Gardyner, John Broun, Robert Billesdone, William Stokker, Knt., Edmund Shaa, Thomas Hille, Hugh Brice, John Warde, Richard Rawson, John Stokker, Robert Tate, William Horn, John Fissher, Richard Chawry, Thomas "Norlong," John Mathewe, and William White, Aldermen, and an immense Commonalty

Fo. 180.
*Eleccio
Maioris.*

---

[1] *Vide supra*, p. 105 n.

summoned to the Guildhall for the election of a Mayor for the year ensuing—Edmund Shaa was elected.

Afterwards, viz., on the Feast of SS. Simon and Jude [28 Oct.], the said Mayor was sworn at the Guildhall, and on the morrow was presented, admitted, &c., before the Barons of the Exchequer.

Fo. 180 b.

Exon'acio Joh'is Snoth al' Kent skynner ab assis' etc.

21 Oct., 22 Edward IV. [A.D. 1482], John Snoth, *alias* Kent, skinner, discharged by William Haryot, Knt., Mayor, and the Aldermen from serving on juries, &c., owing to increasing old age.

Ordinance by the Common Council, Tuesday, 22 Oct., 22 Edward IV. [A.D. 1482], that thenceforth no freeman of the City sell any woollen cloth by retail or otherwise, except by one yard and one inch to the yard, without fraud, &c.

Also that no freeman occupy any tenters for planing woollen cloth (*pro panno lan' equand'*)[1] without the liberty of the City, and that all tenters within the liberty should be destroyed after Christmas next except ten, five of which should be at Fullers' Hall and five at Leadenhall, and that such tenters should be under the management of discreet men chosen by the Mayor and Aldermen.

Also that every freeman have liberty until Christmas next, and no longer, to plane his cloth, notwithstanding an Act formerly made thereon, so that the said cloths be sealed with the seal assigned therefor.[2]

Exon'acio Will'mi Olyver Taillour ab assis' etc.

23 Oct., 22 Edward IV. [A.D. 1482], William Olyver, tailor, discharged by the Mayor and Aldermen from serving on juries, &c., owing to his infirmities.

Exon'acio Laurencii Stokale sadler ab assis' etc.

28 Oct., the same year, Laurence Stokale, saddler, similarly discharged for like cause.

De offic' co'is Paccator'.

Sunday the Feast of Translation of St. Edward [13 Oct.], 22 Edward IV. [A.D. 1482], ordinance by William "Heriot," the Mayor, and the Aldermen that Robert Fitzherbert, the Common Packer, thenceforth take for his labour for the

---

[1] Cf. "to plane nor sette upon the Tayntours." *Infra*, fo. 266.

[2] See Stat. 4 Edward IV. cap. 1. Cf. *supra*, p. 105.

package of every hundred calf-fells (he finding the cords for such packing) the sum of 8 pence.[1]

23 Nov., 22 Edward IV. [A.D. 1482], came Philip Payn, Robert Darlyngton, Robert Coldham, and William Copynger, fishmongers, and entered into bond in the sum of £79 6s. 2d. for the delivery into the Chamber by the said Philip of the sum of £75 and a silver-gilt cup and covercle to the use of Thomas, Henry, and Elizabeth, children of William Seyger, late fishmonger, when they come of age or marry.[2]

Fo. 181.

Custod' pueror' Will'i Seyger.

Writ to the Sheriff of Sussex to make proclamation that, in view of the prevailing scarcity, wheat, malt, rye, beans, peas, oats, and other grain might freely be brought to the City of London (without interception by the King's Purveyors) out of the county of Sussex, provided it be shipped from the ports of Wynchelsee and Chechestre, and surety be given to the King's Customers that the grain would be carried to the City of London and not elsewhere. Witness the King at Westminster, 21 Nov., 22 Edward IV. [A.D. 1482].

Fo. 181 b.

Commissio Regis sup' caristiam frumenti et al' blador'.

A note of similar writs having been sent to the Sheriff of Cornwall for the ports of Plymouth and Fowey; the Sheriff of Devonshire for the ports of Dartmouth and Exmouth; the Sheriff of Southampton for the port of Southampton; the Sheriffs of Somerset and Dorset for the ports of "Pole" and Weymouth; the Sheriff of Kent for the port of Sandwich and its "creeks"; and the Sheriffs of Norfolk, Suffolk, and Lincoln for the port of Boston.

Similar writ to the Sheriff of Surrey set out.

A note of similar writs having been sent to the Sheriffs of Cambridgeshire, Hertfordshire, Bedfordshire, Buckinghamshire, Oxfordshire, Berkshire, and Essex.

Fo. 182.

5 Dec., 22 Edward IV. [A.D. 1482], came the Wardens and good men of the Craft of Bruers into the Court of the lord the King in the Chamber of the Guildhall, before Edmund

Fos. 182-185 b. ✔

Ordinacio Pandoxatorum.

---

[1] In 1474 the amount had been fixed at 4 pence. *Supra*, p. 117.

[2] Margin. 9 May, 2 Henry VII. [A.D. 1487], came Gerard Danyell, who married the above Elizabeth, and acknowledged satisfaction for his wife's property.

Shaa, the Mayor, and the Aldermen, and prayed that certain articles for the regulation of the Craft might be approved to the following effect :—

First, that every person occupying the " craft or feet " of brewing within the franchise make, or cause to be made, good and " hable " ale, according in strength and fineness to the price of malt for the time being ; that no ale after it be " clensed and sett on jeyst "[1] be put to sale or carried to customers until it have fully " spourged "[2] and been tasted and viewed by the Wardens of the Craft or their Deputy, according to the ordinances and customs of the City ; and that the taster allow no ale that is not " holesome for mannys body," under penalty of imprisonment and a fine.

That ale be not sent out in other men's vessels without leave of the owners of the vessels.

That no brewer maintain a " foreyn " to retail his ale within the franchise of the City.

That no brewer entice customers of another occupying the same craft.

That no brewer engage a " Typler "[3] or " Huxster " to retail his ale until he be sure that the said " Typler " or " Huxster " is clearly out of debt and danger[4] for ale to any other person occupying the craft of brewing within the franchise.

That no " Tipler " or Huckster lend, sell, break, or " kutte " any barrel, kilderkin, or ferkin belonging to any other brewer without leave of the owner.

---

[1] "Gyyste," a balk of timber for resting a thing on. (Way's ' Prompt. Parv.')

[2] Fermented. Cf. " Et qe chescun vesselle qest apporte ou amove a ascun bracyne pur emplire, estoise illoeqes un jour et un noet, pleyn de cervoyse pur *espurger* " (' Liber Albus,' i. 359). Cf. Lat. *spumare=* to spurge.

[3] A tippler was one who drank in small quantities, just as a huckster or pedlar dealt in small quantities.

[4] In the preamble to the petition of the Leathersellers in 1481 for ordinances to be approved by the Mayor and Aldermen, objection is made to members of the fraternity taking. more apprentices than they were able to keep or teach, and thus leading them to " endaunger themselves " (*i.e.*, become debtors) to other men. Black's ' Hist. of the Leathersellers,' p. 39.

That every person keeping a house and being a Brother of Bruers and occupying the craft of brewing pay quarterage towards the great charges and cost of the Craft and Fraternity.

That no one of the Craft, whether he be in the livery of the same or not, presume to go and dine at the feasts of the Mayor or Sheriffs when they are presented at Westminster, unless appointed by the Wardens to take the place of one unable to attend.

That every freeman of the Craft obey the summons of the Wardens on all occasions, under penalty of a fine, except for reasonable cause.

That at every third year, on the election of new Wardens of the Craft and Fraternity, the men of the livery shall attend in a new gown and hood and hear Mass at the church of St. Mary in Aldermanbury, or such other place as may be assigned, and also attend the dinner in the Common Hall of the Fraternity; that every such person keep the said livery for the space of 6 years next ensuing for divers assemblies of the Fellowship; that if he fail to attend in his livery on any occasion, without reasonable excuse, he be fined; that if he receive from the Wardens an "example" or "patron" (sample or pattern) of the livery, and so be licensed to provide and buy his cloth for the said livery where he pleases, and the colour of the cloth so bought and provided be not according to the colour of the said "example" or "patron," he be also fined.

That once every quarter all members of the Fellowship attend, on summons, at the Common Hall of the said Craft or Fellowship, to hear read the statutes and ordinances approved and enacted by the Mayor and Aldermen for the good rule of the Craft, in order that no one incur penalties through ignorance of them.

That no brewer take any servant that has not served his time as an apprentice to the craft, and been made a freeman of the City; nor keep in his house at one time more than two or three apprentices at the most; that all such apprentices be first presented to the Wardens in the Common Hall of the

Craft, and by them be publicly examined as to their birth, "clenesse of their bodies, and other certeyn poyntes."

That apprentices be presented to the Wardens by their master before admission to the freedom of the City, so that it may be ascertained whether they have duly served their term; and that no apprentice who has served his term shall become a Chief brewer or Under brewer, and therefore take wages, until certified as able by the said Wardens under penalty prescribed.

That no one buy malt brought to the City by land or water until carried to the "key" or other market places therefor ordained, and there openly overseen and searched by the Wardens of the Craft or their deputy; that the said malt be "clene, swete, drye, and wele made, and not capped in the Sakkes[1] nor Rawdried malte, dank or wete malte, or made of mowe[2] brent barly, belyed[3] malte, Edgrove malte,[4] acrespired[5] malte, wyvell eten malt or medled," to the deceit of the people, upon pain of forfeiture.

That no one buy corn in the market and leave it in the seller's hands with the view of enhancing its price.

That every one bringing malt or "other cornes" to the City for sale bring it to the market places of old time used, and not sell it by "ensample" upon pain of forfeiture.

That no one sell malt, &c., at the markets of Graschirche or Greyfriars before 9 o'clock until the market bells be rung, nor after the hour of 12.0; that immediately after 12.0 the malt, &c., left unsold, be conveyed by the owners to the houses therefor ordained, so that it be clean out of the market by

---

[1] Possibly meaning deceitfully packed in sacks, so as to display good malt at the top.

[2] "Inowe" (?) = enough, sufficiently.

[3] Swollen in the middle of the grain.

[4] Or "edgroue" = germinating (Way's 'Prompt.').

[5] When grain, exposed to wet weather, sprouts at both ends, it is said to *acrospire* (Halliwell). In the treatise of Walter de Biblesworth or Bibbesworth (xiiith century) we find (in connexion with brewing) the following lines :—

E là cochet vostre blée
Taunke seyt ben germée (wel atome or *spired*).
De cele houre appelleras
Brès (malt) ke blée avant nomas.

1.0 P.M., upon pain of forfeiture; that no man sell any malt, &c., in the said markets to any "foreyn" before 11.0 A.M.; and that between 11.0 A.M. and 12.0 P.M. every one may buy at his liberty.

Petition granted.

12 Dec., 22 Edward IV. [A.D. 1482], petition by all the persons enfranchised in the Craft or Mistery of Glovers of the City to the Mayor and Aldermen, setting forth that they had become so impoverished by the number of "foreyns" coming and working at their craft in the City that they were unable to bear the charges of the City as they had hitherto done, and praying that certain articles for the regulation of their craft might be approved. *Fo. 185 b.*

Ordinacio Cirothecarior'.

The articles are to the following effect :—

First, no freeman of the Craft or Mistery nor other person occupying the said craft shall employ any "foreyn" until such "foreyn" has been admitted by the Wardens and paid 6s. 8d. for being set on work ; that the said "foreyn" be subject to the Wardens, and be sworn to obey the rules and ordinances of the Craft.

That no freeman teach another the craft, except he be bound apprentice to the Craft, or else be free of the same, under penalty of 13s. 4d.

That no freeman take more than 2 or 3 apprentices, nor entice any apprentice or servant out of the service of another.

That those taking wages for their work pay quarterage.

That no freeman buy any gloves made in the country, to sell again, until such gloves have been approved by the Wardens.

Petition granted.

20 Dec., 22 Edward IV. [A.D. 1482], came William Redy, Richard Lakyn, Edmund Worsley, mercers, and entered into bond in the sum of £36 for the payment into the Chamber by the said William Redy of a like sum to the use of Elizabeth *Fo. 186.*

Custod' pueror' Thome Warenger.

and Johanna, daughters of Thomas Warenger, when they come of age or marry.[1]

Fo. 186 b.

Custod' Ric'i Wode fil' Ric'i Wode m'cer'.

27 Feb., 22 Edward IV. [A.D. 1482-3], came William Johnson, Nicholas Kirkeby, innholders, and Stephen Gybson, mercer, and entered into bond in the sum of £20 for the payment into the Chamber by the said William Johnson of a like sum to the use of Richard, son of Richard Wode, late mercer, on his coming of age.

Fo. 187.

Custod' pueror' Joh'is Worth talough chaundler.

7 March, 23 Edward IV. [A.D. 1482-3], came Henry Fronte, John Benyngton, grocers, William Prime, " talough chaundler," and John Duklyng, fishmonger, and entered into bond in the sum of £40 for payment into the Chamber by the said Henry Fronte of a like sum to the use of Johanna and Alice, daughters of John Worth, late "talough chaundler," when they come of age or marry.[2]

Fo. 187 b.

Custod' pueror' Nich'i Okerford vynter.

18 March, 23 Edward IV. [A.D. 1482-3], came Thomas Abraham, grocer, John Palmer, fishmonger, and Richard Brent, grocer, and entered into bond in the sum of £52 12s. 1d. for the delivery into the Chamber by the said Thomas Abraham of a sum of £40 and a certain mass (*mass'*) called "plate," valued at £12 12s. 1d., to the use of John and Thomas, sons of Nicholas Okerford, late " vynter," when they come of age.[3]

---

[1] Margin. 14 May, 8 Henry VII. [A.D. 1493], came Nicholas Hatfeld, parish clerk, who married the above Elizabeth and acknowledged satisfaction for his wife's property ; and on the 6th March, 13 Henry VII. [A.D. 1497-8], came Henry Radclif, gentleman, who married the above Johanna, and similarly acknowledged satisfaction.

· [2] Margin. 21 March, 8 Henry VII. [A.D. 1492-3], came John Awstorp, who married the above Johanna, and acknowledged satisfaction for his wife's patrimony, and for money accruing to her by the decease of Alice her sister.

[3] Marginal note to the effect that on the 10th March, 9 Henry VII. [A.D. 1493-4], the above bond became void, inasmuch as Robert Shirborne, Keeper of the Prerogative of the Bishop [*sic*] of Canterbury, signified to the Court of Mayor and Aldermen under his official seal, that as administsator of the above goods he had discharged the above John Palmer.

Anno primo Edwardi V.[1]

22 April, 1 Edward V. [A.D. 1483], came the Wardens and good folks of the Craft of Shermen of the City and prayed that certain articles for the regulation of the Craft might be approved. The articles are to the following effect :—

Fos. 188-9 b.

Ordinacio Tonsor'.

First, that householders of the Craft having more than two apprentices shall take no others until the terms of such apprentices have expired, and afterwards shall have no more than two apprentices, under penalty of a fine.

That a new apprentice may be taken a year before the expiration of the term of one of the two apprentices, and a third apprentice may be taken who has lost his master by death, and been "sett over" to another by the Chamberlain.

That no apprentice after the expiration of his term presume to work " in journey " with any of the Craft until he has satisfied the Wardens and twelve others of the Craft of his ability, and if he fail in this, he shall be put to " such a connyng place of the said craft " as the Wardens and the twelve may assign, there to perfect himself in his work, receiving wages, meat and drink at the discretion of the said Wardens.

That presentation of apprentices to be made freemen in the Chamber be done in the presence of the three Wardens, or at least two of them, under penalty of a fine.

That no one of the Craft employ more journey men or covenant men than four at once, besides his apprentices, without special licence.

That no one of the Craft henceforth shall " flok powder ne stop' deceivably w^t oile or grese " any cloth after shearing thereof, under penalty of the pillory and a fine.

---

[1] Edward IV. had died in Westminster Palace on the 9th April, at the age of 40, the end being accelerated by his riotous mode of living. His corpse lay for some hours exposed in order that the Peers then in London, and the Mayor of London and his brethren, might view it. ' Archæologia,' Vol. lx. Part II., p. 538 (where the date of his death is given as 5 April).

That no man of the Craft, being in the livery or otherwise, leave the Craft for any other Fellowship without licence of the Mayor and Aldermen,[1] under penalty of forfeiting £40.

Petition granted.

Fo. 189 b.

*Proclamac'
contra mere-
trices vagant'
circa Civita-
tem.*

" For to eschewe the stynkyng and horrible Synne of Lechery the whiche daily groweth and is used more than it hath been in daies past by the meanes of Strumpettes mysguyded and idil women daily vagraunt and walkyng aboute by the stretes and lanes of this Citee of London and Suburbes of the same and also repairyng to Taverns and þere private places of the said Citee provokyng many oþere persones unto the said Synne of lechery   Whereby moche people aswell men as women being of theym self weldisposed daily fall to the said myschevous and horrible Synne   To the grete displeasur of Almyghty God and distourbaunce and brekyng of the Kyng our soveraign lordes peas and of the politique guydyng of the Citee aforesaid My lord the Mair and my Maisters the Aldremen streitly chargen and commaunden uppon the King our soveraign lordes behalf that all suche Strumpettes and mysguyded and idill women aswell dwellyng as Resortyng to the said Citee of London or Suburbes of the same departe and w'drawe theym self and in no wise be so hardy to come ayen Resorte or abide w'in the said Citee or libertie uppon payn þerefore ordeigned and that no persone w'in the same Citee and libertie eide comfort nor receive any suche mysguided and ill disposed women uppon þe payne therefore lymyted and ordeigned, straitly chargyng constables and all oþere officers of the said Citee to arrest all suche mysguyded and idill women as been aforerehersed where so ever thei shalbe founde w'in the same Citee and to brynge theym to one of the Countours there to abide the punysshment and correccioun of the lawe for suche mysdoers ordeigned."   [No date.]

4 May, 1 Edward V. [A.D. 1483], came William Boket, haberdasher, William Purchace, Roger Bowcer, and Thomas Hore, mercers, and entered into bond in the sum of £280 for

---

[1] See ordinance, *infra*, fo. 199.

payment into the Chamber by the said William Boket of a like sum to the use of Bartholomew, Johanna, Agnes, Elizabeth, Juliana, Alice, and Anne, children of Richard Baret, late haberdasher, when they come of age or marry.[1]

27 May, 1 Edward V. [A.D. 1483], Thomas Diker, tailor, discharged by Edmund Shaa, the Mayor, and the Aldermen from serving on juries, &c., owing to his infirmities.

Fo. 190.

Exon'acio Thome Diker ab assis' etc.

Tuesday, 3 June, 1 Edward V. [A.D. 1483], petition to the Common Council by the inhabitants of the parish of St. Giles without Cripplegate setting forth that John Middelton, executor of William Estfeld, late Knight and Alderman, had conveyed water from Hybery to the said parish on condition that the inhabitants should make a sufficient cistern and conduit to receive the said water, and that the inhabitants had accordingly made such a cistern at great cost.[2] They therefore prayed the Common Council to ordain that the said cistern and water might become vested in them for evermore, subject to the right of every inhabitant of the City to take water from the said cistern at will, and that the repair of the cistern, pipes, &c., should be made at the cost of the City, as in the case of other cisterns and conduits.

Fo. 190 b.

Concessio fc'a Inhabitant' de p'och' Sc'i Egidii extra Crepulgate etc pro conductu ib'm h'end' etc.

Their prayer granted.

Petitions by the Mayor and citizens to the Duke of Norfolk, Steward of England, praying that they may be allowed to execute the customary services at the Coronation of Richard III. and Anne his consort.[3]

Fo. 191.

---

[1] Margin. Acquittances by John Bolley, haberdasher, who married the above Johanna, for his wife's patrimony, and also for money accruing by the decease of Agnes, Elizabeth, and Anne, her sisters.

[2] "Some small distance from the east end of this church [St. Giles, Cripplegate] is a water Conduit, brought in pypes of leade from Highbery by John Middleton, one of the Executors to Sir William Eastfield, and of his goodes ; the inhabitants

adioyning castelated it of their owne costes and charges, about the yeare 1483." Stow, 'Survey' (ed. Kingsford), i. 300.

[3] The petition is practically in the same form as that made on the occasion of the Coronation of Edward IV., and recorded *supra*, pp. 5-6. Edward V. had been deposed on the 25th June, 1483, and died (murdered in the Tower) in the following August.

Here follows a record to the effect that the lord Richard III., King of England, and Dame Anne his consort, were crowned at Westminster, 6 July, in the first year of their reign, and on the day of the coronation of the said King and Queen, after the banquet was finished, at which Edmund Shaa, the Mayor, and the Aldermen, and certain citizens chosen by the Common Council to attend upon the Chief Butler of England according to custom were honourably and graciously treated, the said Mayor, after the banquet as aforesaid, offered the King wine in a gold cup with gold ewer (*fiola*) full of water to temper the wine, and after the King had taken the wine the said Mayor retained the cup and ewer for his own use.[1] Likewise the said Mayor, after the said banquet, offered wine to the Queen in a gold cup with gold ewer of water, and after receiving the wine she gave the cup and ewer to the Mayor pursuant to the privileges, liberties, and customs of the City of London on such occasions.[2]

Fo. 191 b.

The names of the citizens elected by the Common Council to attend the Chief Butler of England, viz., Henry Cote, goldsmith, John Tate, mercer, William Sandes, grocer, William Spark, draper, John Swan, tailor, Thomas Ostriche, haberdasher, William Maryner, salter, Richard Knyght, fishmonger, John Pasmer, skinner, Thomas Breteyn, "irmonger," Roger Forde, vintner.

Exon'acio Joh'is Fissher Aldr'i ab officio suo etc.

John Fissher, Alderman, discharged by the Mayor and Aldermen from serving as Alderman or any other office, he consenting to give the sum of 400 marks towards the repair of the Cross in Chepe and other City works. Dated 31 July, 1 Richard III. [A.D. 1483].

---

[1] This cup has inadvertently been mistaken in 'London and the Kingdom' (i. 323) for another cup, set with pearls and other precious stones, which the King, sitting crowned in " le Whitehawle " at dinner, gave to the Mayor and Aldermen on the Feast of Epiphany [6 Jan., 1483-4] for the use of the Commonalty in the Chamber of the Guildhall. Journal 9, fo. 43.

[2] Set out in printed report to the Common Council on Coronations, 18 Aug., 1831. It is also printed in Nicholl's 'Account of the Ironmongers' Company,' pp. 42-3.

31 July, 1 Richard III. [A.D. 1483], came good men of the Mistery of "Inholders" into the Court of the lord the King in the Chamber of the Guildhall, before Edmund Shaa, Knight and Mayor, and the Aldermen, and presented a petition praying that certain ordinances for the better regulation of the Mistery might be approved.

Fos. 191 b-
192 b.

*Ordinacio ae
Inholders.*

The ordinances are to the following effect:—

That people resorting to the City, with their horses or without, be lodged in open inns, having signs hanging out, in open streets, and not in private and "pety hostryes," under penalty prescribed.

That a "botell" of hay weigh 5 lb. of troy weight as of old.

That the Wardens of the Craft have the right of search for horsebread "deceivably medled," baked, or made, being accompanied by an officer of the Mayor when searching without their Fellowship.

That oats and beans brought to the City for sale be brought to the open markets, and not harboured in houses or inns.

That no brown-bread baker, baking horsebread or any other bread, keep any inn or horse to livery, on pain of forfeiting 40s.

That no innkeeper suffer any foreign horsebread to be brought into his house or "colour" it by any of his guests.

Their petition granted.

Sunday the Feast of St. Matthew [21 Sept.], 1 Richard III. [A.D. 1483], in the presence of Edmund Shaa, Knight and Mayor, the Prior of Christchurch, Thomas Fitz William the Recorder,[1] Robert Drope, Robert Basset, Richard Gardyner, John Broun, William "Haryot," Thomas Stalbroke, Thomas Hille, Robert Billesdone, Hugh Brice, Richard Rawson, Henry Colet, John Stokker, John Warde, Robert Tate, William Horn, Richard Chawry, Thomas "Northlond," William White, and John Mathewe, Aldermen, and very many Commoners summoned to the Guildhall for the election of Sheriffs—Thomas "Norlond," grocer, was elected one of the Sheriffs for the City of London and Middlesex by the Mayor, and William Martyn, skinner, was elected the other Sheriff by the Commonalty.

Fo. 192 b.

*Eleccio vice-
comit'.*

[1] Elected 19 June, 1483. Journal 9, fo. 26 b.

P

The same day Milo Adys, goldsmith, was elected Chamberlain of the City for the year ensuing; William Gall, tailor, and Henry Bumpstede, mercer, were elected Wardens of the City Bridge; Richard Rawson, Henry Colet, Aldermen, John Materdale, tailor, Nicholas Alwyn, mercer, William Capell, draper, and William Purchas, mercer, Commoners, were elected Auditors of the accounts of the Chamberlain and Wardens in arrear.

Afterwards, viz., on the eve of St. Michael [29 Sept.], the said Sheriffs were sworn at the Guildhall, and on the morrow of the said Feast were presented, admitted, &c., before the Barons of the Exchequer.

Fo. 193.
Custod' Thome Roller fil' Th' Roller groceri.

26 Sept., 1 Richard III. [A.D. 1483], came Thomas Walker, Thomas Eyre, Richard Rowlowe, and John Maykyn, grocers, and entered into bond in the sum of 100 marks for payment into the Chamber by the said Thomas Walker of a like sum to the use of Thomas, son of Thomas Roller, late grocer, when he comes of age.

Fo. 193 b.
Eleccio Maioris.

Monday the-Feast of Translation of St. Edward [13 Oct.], 1 Richard III. [A.D. 1483], in the presence of Edmund Shaa, Knight and Mayor, the Prior of Christchurch, Thomas Fitz William the Recorder, Robert Drope, Robert Basset, Richard Gardyner, John Broun, William "Haryot," Robert Billesdone, Thomas Hille, Richard Rawson, Hugh Brice, John Stokker, Robert Tate, Richard Chawry, John Warde, William White, William Horn, John Mathewe, Robert Hardyng, Thomas "Norlond," and William Martyn, Aldermen, and an immense Commonalty summoned to the Guildhall for the election of a Mayor for the year ensuing—Robert Billesdone was elected.

Afterwards, viz., on the Feast of SS. Simon and Jude [28 Oct.], he was sworn at the Guildhall, and on the morrow was presented, admitted, &c., before the Barons of the Exchequer.

Ordinac' de lez fre Journey- men art' de Fullers etc.

12 Dec., 1 Richard III. [A.D. 1483], petition by free journey-men of the Art of Fullers to the Mayor and Aldermen praying them to ordain that thenceforth no one using the Craft of Fullers shall employ "foreyns" so long as freemen are

available for work, under penalty, seeing that so many free journeymen of the Craft were unable to obtain work owing to the influx of "foreyns."

Their petition granted.

Tuesday, 13 Jan., 1 Richard III. [A.D. 1483-4], ordinance by the Common Council that no one shall sell ale by retail within the liberty of the City unless he be free of the same ; also that the ordinance made 11 Oct., 11 Henry VI. [A.D. 1432], touching brewers and vendors of ale by retail, and enrolled in Letter-Book K, fo. cxi [b], be strictly observed.

7 March, 1 Richard III. [A.D. 1483-4], came Richard Adif, James Fitte, John Hede, and Richard Lynley, tailors, and entered into bond in the sum of £40 for the delivery into the Chamber by the said Richard Adif of a sum of £20 and certain goods and chattels to the use of Mary, daughter of Richard Bele, late butcher, when she comes of age or marries.[1]

Custod' Marie fil' Ric'i Bele carnificis.

Letters patent incorporating the freemen of the Mistery or Art of Wexchaundelers. Dated 16 Feb., 1 Richard III. [A.D. 1483-4].

Fo. 194 b. Carta de les Wexchaundelers.

Letters patent appointing Richard Gardener, Alderman of the City, to be a Justice for the speedy settlement of disputes among the merchants of the Steelyard. Dated 28 Feb., 1 Richard III. [A.D. 1483-4].

L're patent' pro Ric'o Gardener essend' Alderman' theutonicor' apud le Stileyerd.

1 April, 1 Richard III. [A.D. 1484], came good men of the Art of Brewers into the Court of the lord the King in the Chamber of the Guildhall, before Robert Billesdone, the Mayor, and the Aldermen, and presented a petition praying (*inter alia*) that "no maner of persone of what craft condicion or degree he be occupying the craft or fete of bruyng of ale w'in the saide Citee or libertie thereof from hensfurth occupie or put or do or suffre to be occupied or put in any ale or licour whereof ale shalbe made or in the wirkyng and bruyng of any maner

Fos. 195-195 b. Ordinac' Pandoxat' etc.

---

[1] Margin. 11 March, 9 Henry VII. [A.D. 1493-4], came Robert Hawkyns, hatter - merchant, who married the above Mary, and acknowledged satisfaction for his wife's property.

of ale any hoppes herbes or other like thing but onely licour malt and yeste," under penalty prescribed.

Their petition granted.

Fos. 195 b-196.

Concordia facta int' Cissores et Pelliparios London'.

10 April, 1 Richard III. [A.D. 1484], award by Robert Billesdone, the Mayor, and the Aldermen in a dispute between the Masters, Wardens, and Fellowships of Skinners and Tailors as to order of precedence in civic processions, to the effect that the Master and Wardens of the Skinners should invite the Master and Wardens of the Tailors to dine with them every year at their Common Hall on the vigil of Corpus Christi if they then make an "oppen dyner," and that the Master and Wardens of the Tailors should yearly invite the Master and Wardens of the Skinners to dine with them on the Feast of the Nativity of St. John the Baptist if they then keep an "oppen dyner" at their Common Hall; and, further, that the Skinners should take precedence in processions over the Tailors one year, and the Tailors over the Skinners the following year, except that when an Alderman of either Company should happen to be Mayor, his Company should take precedence during his Mayoralty over all other Companies, according to ancient custom.[1]

Fos. 196 b-198.

Ordinacio de lez Fletchers.

11 May, 1 Richard III. [A.D. 1484], petition by good men of the Art of Fletchers to the Mayor and Aldermen for the better regulation of the Craft, and praying (*inter alia*):—

"That all suche persones as ben admitted allowes w'in the said craft shall have and take from hensfurth for their labour for the werkmanship and makyng of thise thinges underwriten after the Rate ensuyng that is to sey for the makyng of c beryng shaftes[2] of seasonable Tymber well and clenly made w' cros nokked[3] skynned[4] and sered[5] xiiij*d*. ; for makyng of c of

---

[1] The award is set out *verbatim* in the late Mr. Wadmore's 'Account of the Skinners' Company'(pp. 7-8), from the Company's archives. Some years later the Skinners claimed that the award was limited to civic processions, and did not affect "general goings and assemblies," but in January, 1521, the Court of Aldermen ruled otherwise. Repertory 5, fo. 166 b.

[2] Or "carrying" shafts; heavy shafts, used for long distance.

[3] Notched.

[4] Peeled (?).

[5] Varnished.

the best beryng shaftes well and clenly cros nokked after the best maner and skynned and sered as is aforesaid xvj*d*. ; for the makyng of c merke arrowe shaftes[1] well and clenly made after the forme aforesaid xx*d*. ; and for the makyng of c boltes well and clenly made after the best forme and after the maner aboverehersed " [*blank*].

" That no maner persone of the said Craft from hensfurth sette nor do to be sette more of any manere of artelery uppon any stall wyndowe stok or stulp than ij sheefs."

That any one proved to be a " piker " or " imbesiller " of anything belonging to the Craft be put out of the Craft, and not received back except he find convenient surety for good behaviour.

" That no maner persone of the said Craft from hensfurth bere or carye to any Faire market or any other place nerrer unto the Citee of London than xxx myle at lest any maner Chaffer belongyng to the same Craft to sell, and that all suche Chaffer as shall be caried or borne by any persone of the same Craft to any Faire market or other place xxx myle from London or more or it goo oute of this Citee be overseen and serched by the Wardeyns of the said Craft for the tyme being that it be made of goode and seasonable stuf and hable for the King's people to occupie."

Their petition granted.

14 May, 1 Richard III. [A.D. 1484], came Thomas Hoberthorn, grocer, William Leyfeld, cutler, Ralph Petyt, " inholder," and Thomas Shaa, cutler, and entered into bond in the sum of £18 3*s*. for the delivery by the said Thomas Hoberthorn of the sum of £14 and a carriage and four horses valued at £4 3*s*. to the use of Roger, son of William Clopham, when he comes of age.

Fo. 198.

Custod' Rogeri Clopham fil' Will'i Clopham

5 August, 2 Richard III. [A.D. 1484], came John Parowe, Richard Lemman, bakers, William Smyth, salter, and Robert Dunlyng, brewer, and entered into bond in the sum of £40 for the payment into the Chamber by the said John Parowe of the

Fo. 198 b.

Custod' Agnet' filie Will'i Underwode Pistor'.

---

[1] Lighter shafts for shooting at a mark.

sum of £38 6s. 9d. to the use of Agnes, daughter of William Underwode, late baker, when she comes of age or marries.

Fo. 199.

Q'd null' fiat
transmutacio
ab una Arte in
aliam sine
consensu
Maioris et
Aldr'or' etc.

27 August, 2 Richard III. [A.D. 1484], ordinance by the Mayor and Aldermen, in order to avoid dissensions that are likely to arise between the Misteries, that thenceforth no one shall be translated from one Art to another without the consent of the Mayor and Aldermen.

Custod'
pueror' Joh'is
Bremonger
draper.

3 Sept., 2 Richard III. [A.D. 1484], came John Wynnesbury, draper, William Hamlyn, " talughchaundler," Nicholas Violet, " wexchaundler," and John Ledys, fishmonger, and entered into bond in the sum of 10 marks for payment into the Chamber by the said John Wynnesbury of a like sum to the use of Thomas and John, sons of John Bremonger, late draper, when they come of age.

Custod'
pueror' Will'i
Abell ir-
monger.

3 Sept., 2 Richard III. [A.D. 1484], came Elizabeth Denys, widow, Thomas Parker, "irmonger," Thomas Clerk, brewer, and Henry Ungle, "wodmonger," and entered into bond in the sum of £52 9s. 7d. for payment into the Chamber by the said Elizabeth of a like sum to the use of John, Richard, Sibel, Stephen, and Henry, children of William Abell, late " irmonger," when they come of age or marry.[1]

Fo. 199 b.

Custod'
pueror' Joh'is
Bodnam wex-
chaundeler.

9 Sept., 2 Richard III. [A.D. 1484], came John Herford, baker, Thomas Bowier, Thomas Broughton, drapers, and Nicholas Grewell, vintner, and entered into bond in the sum of £40 for payment into the Chamber by the said John Herford of a like sum to the use of John and Isabella, children of John Bodnam, late " wexchaundler," when they come of age or marry.[2]

Fo. 200.

Custod' Alicie
fil' Will'i
Whitwey
merc'.

16 Sept., 2 Richard III. [A.D. 1484], came John Picton, Ralph Potter, Thomas Wolley, and Richard Thornell, mercers, and entered into bond in the sum of £200 for payment into the Chamber by the said John Picton of a like sum to the use of

[1] Margin.   7 Feb., 5 Henry VII. [A.D. 1489-90], came William Matlowe, alias Clerk, who married the above Sibel, and acknowledged satisfaction for his wife's patrimony.

[2] Margin.   26 July, 4 Henry VII. [A.D. 1489], came Audoen (Owen) William, who married the above Isabella, and acknowledged satisfaction for his wife's property.

Alice, daughter of William Whitwey, late mercer, when she comes of age or marries.

17 Sept., 2 Richard III. [A.D. 1484], came Richard White-hede, John Skipwith, drapers, Henry Warfeld, dyer, and John Martyn, " bowier," and entered into bond in the sum of £66 for payment into the Chamber by the said Richard of a like sum to the use of Everard, Alice, Elizabeth, and Elena, children of Robert Bolsore, late tailor, when they come of age or marry.[1]

Fo. 200 b.

*Custod'
pueror' Rob'ti
'Bolsor' cissor'.*

Tuesday the Feast of St. Matthew [21 Sept.], 2 Richard III. [A.D. 1484], in the presence of Robert Billesdone, the Mayor, the Prior of Christchurch, Thomas Fitz William the Recorder, Richard Gardyner, John Broun, William Heriot, Edmund Shaa, William Stokker, Thomas Hille, Hugh Brice, Richard Rawson, Henry Colet, John Stokker, Robert Tate, Richard Chawry, John Mathewe, Robert Hardyng, William White, Thomas Breteyn, Thomas " Northlond," William Martyn, and Richard Chester, Aldermen, and very many Commoners summoned to the Guildhall for the election of Sheriffs—Thomas Breteyn, " irmonger," was elected one of the Sheriffs of the City of London and Middlesex by the Mayor, and Richard Chester, skinner, was elected the other Sheriff by the Commonalty.

Fo. 201.

*Eleccio Vice-
comit'.*

The same day William Purchas, mercer, was elected Chamberlain of the City for the ensuing year ; William Galle, tailor, and Henry Bumpstede, mercer, were elected Wardens of the City Bridge ; Henry Colet, John Stokker, Aldermen, William Capell, draper, William Purchas, mercer, Hugh Pemberton and Roger Barlowe, tailors, Commoners, were elected Auditors of the accounts of the Chamber and Wardens in arrear.

Afterwards, viz., on the eve of St. Michael [29 Sept.], the said Sheriffs were sworn at the Guildhall, and on the morrow of the said Feast were presented, admitted, &c., before the Barons of the Exchequer.

---

[1] Margin. 17 Jan., 7 Henry VII. [A.D. 1491 - 92], came William Grantham, who married the above Alice, and acknowledged satisfaction for money accruing to his wife by the death of Elizabeth her sister.

*Custod' Ric'i
filii Joh'is
Kirkeby aur'.*
9 Oct, 2 Richard III. [A.D. 1484], came Elizabeth Kirkeby, widow, Richard Odyam, draper, Henry Vavisour, "brasier," and John Hede, tailor, and entered into bond in the sum of 500 marks for the delivery into the Chamber by the said Elizabeth of the sum of 400 marks and certain jewels to the use of Richard, son of John Kirkeby, late goldsmith, when he comes of age.

Fo. 201 b.

*Exon'acio
Joh'is Haw-
mond joynour
ab assis' etc.*
12 .Oct., 2 Richard III. [A.D. 1484], John Hawmond, "joynour," discharged by the Mayor and Aldermen from serving on juries owing to infirmities.

*Ordinac' Car-
nificum.*
The same day came good men of the Mistery of Butchers into the Court of the lord the King in the Chamber of the Guildhall, before Robert Billesdone, the Mayor, and the Aldermen, and presented a petition praying that certain articles for the better regulation of the Craft might be approved.

Among them are the following :—

"That no maner persone enfraunchised of the said Craft dwellyng w^tin this Citee or libertie of the same from this tyme forward hire any other persone of the same Craft oute of any suche lese or pasture as he holdeth w^toute the fraunches of this Citee as long as the holder þereof is in will and be of power to occupie it," under penalty prescribed.

That the Wardens be authorized to search for "all maner boores and hogges brought hider here to be sold or occupied, and all such boores and hogges as thei fynde mesels or oþerewise unholesom for mannys body frely to sease theym and forfeit theym and dampne theym to be cast awey."

Their petition granted.

Fo. 202.

*Eleccio
Maioris.*
Wednesday the Feast of Translation of St. Edward [13 Oct.], 2 Richard III. [A.D. 1484], in the presence of Robert Billesdone, the Mayor, the Prior of Christchurch, Robert Drope, Richard Gardyner, John Broun, William Heriot, Edmund Shaa, Thomas Hille, William Stokker, Richard Rawson, Henry Colet, John Stokker, Hugh Brice, Robert Tate, Richard Chawry, William Horne, Thomas " Northlond,"

William White, William Martyn, John Swan, Robert Hardyng, Thomas Breteyn, and Richard Chester, Aldermen, and an immense Commonalty summoned to the Guildhall for the election of a Mayor for the year ensuing—Thomas Hille, Alderman, was elected.

Afterwards, viz., on the Feast of SS. Simon and Jude [28 Oct.], he was sworn at the Guildhall, and on the morrow was presented, admitted, &c., before the Barons of the Exchequer.

15 Nov., 2 Richard III. [A.D. 1484], proclamation made of John Nevell being condemned to stand on the pillory on three different days for having forged a bill, whereby John Auberey of "Garnesey" purported to bind himself to William Talbot of Bristowe in the sum of £13 13s. 4d., for the purpose of himself appropriating the money.

Fo. 202 b.
Judicium
pillor' pro fals'
bill' controfact'
etc.

Wednesday, 15 Dec., 2 Richard III. [A.D. 1484], ordinance by the Common Council that the following clause should in future be inserted in Wardmote commissions :—

Nova claus'
posita in com'-
issione pro
Wardemot'.

"Furthermore we charge and commaunde you that ye suffre no huxsters of ale or Bere to dwell w'in your Warde but suche as bene Fremen or Frewomen of this Citee and of goode fame and disposicion and that thei fynde sufficient Suertie bounde unto the Chamb'leyn of London for the tyme being to be of goode disposicion and guydyng and suffre no misrule nor unlawfull gammes to be had used or exercised w'in their houses and that every nyght betwene Mighelmasse and Easter thei Shitte and Sparre their doores at the hour of ix⁰ of the clok and suffre no persone but theym self their wiffes childern or servauntes to drynk or be logged w'in their said houses after the said hour, and that from the Feast of Easter unto the Fest of Mighelmasse thei shitte and sparre in their said doores at the hour of x of the clok in the nyght and suffre no persones to drynk or to be logged within their said houses after the said hour other than be aboverehersed And that thei shall suffre no maner person to ete nor drynk w'in their said houses any Sondaies in the yeere unto the tyme that high masse be doon at their parissh Chirches.

Provis' fact'
pro Inholders
et Paistelers.

" Also it is accorded in the saide Common Counsell that the acte aboverehersed shall not be hurtyng nor hyndryng unto the Inholders and Paistelers Fremen of the Citee of London as for etyng and drynkyng within their houses uppon Sondayes afore parisshe masse be doon etc."

Fo. 203.
Vicecom' mor-
tuus et alter
loco ejus
electus.

Monday, 7 Feb., 2 Richard III. [A.D. 1484-5], in the presence of Thomas Hille, the Mayor, the Aldermen, the Common Council, the Wardens, and other good men of all the Misteries summoned to the great hall of the Guildhall, Ralph Astry, fishmonger, was elected one of the Sheriffs of the City *loco* Richard Chester, late one of the Sheriffs, who had died the day before.

Afterwards, viz., on the Thursday following, he was sworn at the Guildhall, and on Friday, the 11th Feb., was presented at Westminster with a pageant of all the barges, as of old accustomed in the presentation of Sheriffs[1] on the morrow of St. Michael. And the said Ralph Astry could not be presented sooner because at the time of his election he was at Southampton.

Custod' Ric'i
Fowler fil'
Joh'is Fowler
carnific'.

19 Feb., 2 Richard III. [A.D. 1484-5], came Richard Rowlowe, Thomas Walker, Richard Dunce, grocers, and Robert Hervile, mercer, and entered into bond in the sum of £20 for payment into the Chamber by the said Richard Rowlowe of a like sum to the use of Richard, son of John Fowler, late butcher, when he comes of age.

Fo. 203 b.
Custod' Mar-
garete fil'
Will'i Gardy-
ner draper.

22 Feb., 2 Richard III. [A.D. 1484-5], came James Wilford, tailor, Roger Acherley, Thomas Risby, Robert Gawdeby, drapers, and entered into bond in the sum of £60 16s. 2d. for the delivery into the Chamber by the said James of a sum of money and certain goods to the use of Margaret, daughter of William Gardyner, late draper, when she comes of age or marries.

---

[1] Cf. *supra*, p. 186. A recent ordinance forbade any pageant between the Mayor's house and the riverside on the occasion of his going to Westminster to be sworn into office. *Supra*, p. 187.

Wednesday, 23 Feb., 2 Richard III. [A.D. 1484-5], ordinance by the Common Council that Sheriffs of London for the time being shall receive nothing for arrest by writ of Constables, Beadles, Jurors, or other officers of the City, provided they lawfully and faithfully execute their duties, and for the execution of their duties be prosecuted and vexed at common law, &c.

Ordinacio fact' pro constabular' et al' officiar' pro arrestac' fact' racione officior' suor'.

23 Feb., 2 Richard III. [A.D. 1484-5], came good men of the Art of "Purcers" into the Court of the lord the King in the Chamber of the Guildhall, before Thomas Hille, the Mayor, and the Aldermen, and prayed that certain articles for the government of the Craft approved in the 1st year of Edward III.[1] and the 16th year of Edward IV.[2] might be enforced, and that certain other articles might be approved, to the effect (*inter alia*)—

Fos. 204-5.

Ordinacio Bursarior'.

That the employment of apprentices and foreigners be regulated.

That the Wardens of the Leathersellers and the Wardens of the "Purcers" jointly search for all manner of defaults, as well of the leather whereof purses are made as of the workmanship and making of the said purses.

"That no maner Freman no Foreyn occupying the same occupacion take uppon hym to bere aboute erly or late any maner of ware or Stuf for to sell concernyng the said Craft or occupacion from Inne to Inne from hous to hous or from stall to stall in hustremustre[3] for to sell," under penalty prescribed.

Their petition granted.

22 March, 2 Richard III. [A.D. 1484-5], came Thomas Grafton, Richard Aunsham, Reginald Asshe, mercers, and Thomas Barnwell, fishmonger, and entered into bond in the sum of £80 for payment into the Chamber by the said Thomas Grafton of a like sum to the use of George and John,

Fo. 205.

Custod' pueror' foh'ts Garstanger grocer i.

---

[1] Cf. 'Cal. Letter-Book E,' p. 223.
[2] Cf. *supra*, pp. 138-40.

[3] Huckster-muster, *i.e.*, peddling with samples.

sons of John Garstanger, late grocer, when they come of age.

Fos. 205 b–
206 b.
*Ordinacio
Abrocar' in
divers' articu-
lis.*

Monday, 21 March, 2 Richard III. [A.D. 1484–5], ordinances by the Common Council for the regulation of Brokers.[1] Their number not to exceed twenty-six, &c.

Ordinance by the same Common Council forbidding the use of carts "shodde" with long and square-headed nails injurious to the pavement, and ordering that all carts be thenceforth "shodde" with flat nails according to the sample preserved in the Chamber of the Guildhall.

2 April, 2 Richard III. [A.D. 1485], came Reginald Rutter, Thomas Nicolson, dyer, and Thomas Boughan, sherman, and entered into bond in the sum of £80 for payment into the Chamber by the said Reginald of a like sum to the use of Dorothy, Hugh, Thomas, and Alice, children of John Chester, skinner, when they come of age or marry.[2]

26 April, 2 Richard III. [A.D. 1485], came Richard Elryngton, William Sybson, Richard Batte, and Robert Goldby, drapers, and entered into bond in the sum of £105 6s. 8d. for the delivery into the Chamber of the sum of £100 10s., together with a standing cup called "the Norwiche cuppe" and a mazer (*murra*) with the figure of St. Peter in "le prynte,"[3] to the use of Elizabeth, daughter of Richard Eryk, late upholder, when she comes of age.

---

[1] Very similar to the ordinances of 1452 recorded in 'Cal. Letter-Book K,' pp. 350-2. The number of Brokers then, however, was limited to twenty.

[2] Margin. 14 May, 10 Henry VII. [A.D. 1495], came Robert Reynold, who married the above Dorothy, and acknowledged satisfaction for his wife's patrimony, and also for money that had accrued to her by the deaths of the above Hugh, Thomas, and Alice.

[3] "In the bottom of almost every mazer is to be found a circular medallion, known in the fourteenth and early fifteenth century inventories as a *founce*, or *frounce*, a word of obscure origin, but probably connected with the Latin *fundus*. This name occurs till about 1450, when the medallion is termed the *print*, sometimes the *boss*, names which continue in use till the Reformation." See paper on 'English Medieval Drinking Bowls called Mazers,' by W. H. St. John Hope, F.S.A., *Archæol.*, vol. l.

3 June, 2 Richard III. [A.D. 1485], came Hugh Pemberton, Thomas Cotton, Stephen Janyns, tailors, and Robert Ripon, fishmonger, and entered into bond in the sum of £920 for the payment into the Chamber by the said Hugh of a like sum to the use of Robert, Valentine, Hugh, Thomesina, Alice, and Johanna, children of Richard Nailer, late Alderman,[1] when they come of age or marry.[2]

Fo. 208.

Custodia pueror' Ricardi Nailer nuper Aldr'i.

Commission by the Mayor appointing Thomas Penticost and Nicholas Dyse of Mortlake to search for nets used in the Thames that were of unlawful assize and to see that the seasons for fishing for various kinds of fish were duly observed, in the following terms :—

Fo. 208 b.

Commissio fact' cert' persouis pro conservacione aque Thamis'.

" First that all the Nettes and other Engynnes aswell weres as other ordeyned for fysshyng in the water of Thamys betweene London brigge and Yenlade on thestside of the same brigge of London be of the largenes of ij ynches thrughout atte leste in the Masshe aswell Peter Nettes[3] as other And that the hacches of the said Weres be of the largenes of ij Inches betwene the Staves of the same, except it shall be lefull to them that Fysshe with grete Nettes or Peter Nettes for takyng of Smeltes or Goions[4] to Fysshe from the Fest of Candilmas unto Fest of Thannunciacion of oure Lady in lent than next comyng with the said Nettes, the Masshes of the same grete Nettes in the Bosom[5] and the Codde[6] beyng of the largenes of an Inche atte leste and the residue of the same grete Nettes to be of the largenes of ij Inches in the Masshe and no straiter And the saide Peter Nettes to be of the

---

[1] Of Tower Ward, *ob.* 1483.

[2] Acknowledgment of satisfaction by Robert Bifeld, who married the above Thomesina ; by Walter Robert, who married the above Alice ; and Richard Coulpepyr, who married the above Johanna. The above Valentine recorded as having died.

[3] See 'Cal. Letter - Book A,' pp. 186-8, where many of the ordinances which follow are also recorded.

[4] Gudgeons.

[5] According to Riley (Glossary, 'Lib. Cust.') this represents some kind of broom used in fishing ; if so, it is difficult to understand how it could be possessed of meshes.

[6] A pouch attached to a net, known as cod-net, often weighted with a stone to keep the net low in the water.

largenes of an Inche atte leste by all the same season   And the
same Nettes for smeltes in no other season to be occupied and
used   And that no Salmon betaken between the Nativitee of
oure lady and the day of Seint Martyn [11 Nov.]   And that
thengendre nor the Frye of Salmon betaken at any tyme of
the yeer   Also that no lamprons ne lampreys betaken from the
Midd' of the moneth of Aprill unto the Midd' of the moneth of
August than next folowyng   Nor that any Dac[es] betaken at
anytime from the xv day of bifore [*sic*] the Fest of Thannunciacion of oure lady in lent ne xv daies next after the same Fest
Nor any Roches betaken xxv daies next before the day of
Seint Marke [25 April], nor xv daies after   Also that no kipper
salmon[1] betaken at any tyme of the yeer.   Also that the Nettes
called Codde Nettes which shalbe occupied from Candilmas
[2 Feb.] unto Fest of thannunciacion of oure lady in lent and no
lenger be of an Inche in largenes in the Masshe atte the
leste and no straiter.   And also that the Nettes called Pridde
Nettes[2] be not occupied but from viij daies before the Fest of
Seint Mighell unto the Fest of Seint Martyn and no lenger
Also that Nettes called Trenkes be of the largenes of ij Inches in
the Masshe of the fore part and an Inche and half large and
no straiter in the Masshe of the later part of the same,[3] the
which nettes shalbe occupied from Seint James day [25 July]
unto Fest of Thannunciacion of our lady in lente   And that
thise maner Nettes after folowing be not occupied that is to
sey Shotnet Shofnet[4] Kyddel purce Nette nor castyng Nette[5]

---

[1] A salmon after spawning was
known as a kipper, and "kipper
time" was a close season for salmon
fishing (Webster).

[2] Probably nets for taking mud
lampreys or "prides" (Halliwell).
Cf. Riley's Glossary, 'Lib. Cust.,'
ii. 753. In 1511 the "Pryde net"
or "Pryt" was also known as a
"Kype," a destroyer of fry, and
serving for nothing else but the
taking of lamperns. Journal 14,
fo. 111.

[3] Cf. 'Cal. Letter-Book K,'
pp. 6-7.

[4] For the probable meaning of
these terms see Gloss., 'Lib. Cust.,'
p. 711, *s.v.* 'Chotnet' and 'Chofnet.'

[5] Cf. "That no person shall use......
any net called a Purse-net or Casting-
net," under penalty prescribed.—
'Rules and Ordinances for the
Fisheries in Thames and Medway,'
made by the Court of Aldermen,
4 Oct., 1785 (printed 1827), p. 10.

in no tyme of the yeer Nether that no Wases[1] lambes[2] Stakes nor any other unlawfull Engynnes be occupied w'in the water of Thamys ne any grounde be enhaunced[3] in the said water of Thamys by the meane of legges or otherwyse at any tyme of the yeer contrary to the statutes and ordenaunces therfor ordeigned." Dated 11 June, 2 Richard III. [A.D. 1485].

Similar commissions were sent to the following, viz., to William Kyng of Lambeth, Thomas West, Thomas Wodall of "Putneth," Thomas Jen', John Colyns of Hamersmyth and Fulham, Thomas Clerk, William Rasour of Cheswyk, Robert Bowrer, Richard Michell of Braynford, William Warde, Thomas Fissher of Istylworth, John Grace, John Heyward of Petersham, Edward Blakamore, John Wyther of Tuddyngton, Richard Staunton of Kyngeston, Robert Sparke of Dytton, William Upton, Richard Grenewyche of Hampton, Richard Nortriche, John Nortriche of Walton, Thomas Colyns, Thomas Sheperton of Sheperton, Thomas Buntyng, William Dyk', John Harrys, William A Wode of Stepneth, William Shipman, John Chirchman, William Leyn, John Alexsaunder of Westham, William Clerk, John Horne, Richard Bardone, Thomas Ledys, William Cheyne of Barkyng, William Soudder, Richard Alexsaunder of Wolwyche, John Graung,' William Sampson, Robert Burbild, Richard Danyell of Eryth.

Fo. 209.

Another commission appointing Robert Lylly and Garard Hasten to survey'fishing in the Thames in similar terms to the above. Dated 11 June, 2 Richard III. [A.D. 1485].

Fos. 209-9 b.
It'm commissio fact' pro eadem causa.

Another commission appointing John Stretende and Thomas

Fo. 210.

---

[1] Some kind of unlawful engine for catching fish, but its precise character uncertain. The oath to be taken (*temp.* Eliz.) by the Water-bailiff of the Thames contained the following clause : " Also ye shall knowe no Weares, Rysynges, *Wazes*, nor other noysaunce in the waters aforesaide, eyther sett or made, then is accordyng with the lawes of this Cytye, but you shall put yo' endevor to drawe them up, destroye them and avoyde them."

[2] "That no person shall use any Weels, called a *lomb* or mill-pot, or any other device or engine."—*Ibid.*

[3] Corresponding to "Rysynges" in the oath of the Water-bailiff.

Crippe of the towns of Alhalowen and St. Mary,[1] co. Kent, to survey fishing in the waters of Yenlade and Harsyng.[2]

13 June, 2 Richard III. [A.D. 1485], came the Master, Wardens, and good men of the Craft of Cutlers into the Court of the lord the King, before Thomas Hille, Knt., Mayor, and the Aldermen, and presented a petition praying (*inter alia*) :—

That the number of apprentices to be taken by any person occupying the Craft be limited as prescribed, and that their terms of service be set over or sold only by licence of the Master and Wardens of the Craft, and by the advice of the Chamberlain of the City for the time being.

That the hours of work as prescribed be observed, and that no work be done after those hours by candle light, "except Furbyng and glasyng," nor any man "portraie gylde drawe vernyssh shave Burnysshe ne police in any wyse before or after the houres aforesaid."

That no one occupying the Craft set or cause to be set any "laten pomell uppon any gilt blade," under penalty.

That no man occupying the Craft "put oute or delyver to be made or wrought oute of the Fraunchises . . any maner woodeknyfes; hangars, whynyerdes Trenchour Knyffes, Fyles Syngles Peres Knyfett' oyster Knyfes, Bodekenes," nor other thing appertaining to the Craft ; nor colour nor set on work any foreigner within or without the franchise.

That all work be done in open shop or house and not in secret, and that no one occupying the Craft "take or have any partyng Felowe without licence . . nor that any suche partyng Felowes occupie any hous shoppe or chambre or any place togider as partie Felowes in the saide Crafte or occupie any Tole or Instrument perteynyng to the saide Crafte as Feleaux, but that all suche persones, forasmoche as they be not of habilitie to take hous and shoppe of theym self, by the discrecion of the Maister and Wardeyns of the same Crafte be

---

[1] Near Yantlet Creek.
" Horsing, co. Kent.   Cf. 'Rules | and ordinances, for Fisheries in Thames,' &c., p. 24.

put unto service unto suche tyme as they been of Power to take hous or shoppe uppon theym self," under penalty.

That no freeman occupying the Craft within the City depart thence and teach the Craft outside the City. Any one so doing and returning to the City to be reputed as a "foreyn."

The penalty of 6s. 8d. ordained *temp.* John Hadley, Mayor [A.D. 1393–4], for disobedience to the rules of the Craft[1] to be raised to 13s. 4d.

Their petition granted.

Wednesday the Feast of St. Matthew [21 Sept.], 1 Henry VII. [A.D. 1485],[2] in the presence of Thomas Hylle, the Mayor, the Prior of Christchurch, Thomas Fitzwilliam the Recorder. Richard Gardyner, John Broun, William Heryot, Edmund Shaa. William Stocker, Richard Rawson, Henry Colet, Hugh Bryce, John Stocker, Robert Tate, William Horn, William White. William Martyn, John Swan, Robert Hardyng, John Tate. Thomas Breteyn, and Ralph Astry, Aldermen, and very many Commoners summoned to the Guildhall for the election of Sheriffs—John Tate,[3] Alderman and mercer, was elected one of the Sheriffs of the City of London and Middlesex by the Mayor, and John Swan, tailor and Alderman, was elected the other Sheriff by the Commonalty.

Fo. 212.

Eleccio Vice-comitum.

The same day William Purches, mercer, was elected Chamberlain of the City for the year ensuing; William Galle. tailor, and Simon Harrys, grocer, were elected Wardens of the City bridge; Robert Tate, Alderman, Richard Chawry, Alderman, Hugh Pemberton, Roger Barlowe, tailors, John Pykeryng, mercer, and John Fenkell, draper, Commoners, were elected Auditors of the accounts of the Chamberlain and Wardens in arrear.

---

[1] ' Cal. Letter-Book H,' p. 140.

[2] On the 22nd August the battle of Bosworth had been fought, and King Richard killed. On the 31st the Common Council prepared to give the new King a fitting reception, and voted him a present of 1,000 marks. Its proceedings are duly entered in the Journal of the day (Jour. 9, fo. 84-86 b), but the Letter-Book records nothing.

[3] Not to be confounded with John Tate (*supra*, pp. 55-56, &c.), who died in 1479 (Beaven).

Afterwards, viz., on the eve of St. Michael, the said Sheriffs were sworn at the Guildhall, and on the morrow of the said Feast were presented, admitted, &c., before the Barons of the Exchequer.

A graunte made by co'en Councill to sergeants and yeomen of the Shereffes to sell ale.

Friday, 23 Sept., 1 Henry VII. [A.D. 1485], came the Serjeants and Yeomen of the City before the Common Council, there being present Robert Drope *locum tenens* (of the Mayor),[1] Richard Gardyner, John Broun, Edmund Shaa, William Stocker, Hugh Brice, Richard Rawson, John Warde, Robert Tate, William Horne, William White, William Martyn, John Swan, John Tate, Thomas Breteyn, and Ralph Astry, and presented a petition praying that an Act and ordinance by the Council forbidding such officers to sell ale so long as they held office[2] might be annulled, on the ground (*inter alia*) that of late they had suffered great cost and charges as well by watches by day and night as otherwise.[3]

Their petition granted.

Fo. 212 b.

Eleccio Will'i Stocker in Maiorem Civitat'.

24 Sept., 1 Henry VII. [A.D. 1485], at a Common Council— attended by a multitude of Commoners, the Prior of Christ-church, the Recorder, [Richard] Gardyner, [John] Broun, [Edmund] Shaa, [John] Warde, Robert Tate, [William] White, [William] Horne, [William] Martyn, [John] Swanne, John Tate, [Ralph] Astry—William Stocker, Knt., and John Warde, Aldermen, were nominated by the Commonalty that one of them might be elected Mayor of the City for the residue of the year, viz., from the said 24th day of September until the morrow of SS. Simon and Jude [28 Oct.] then next ensuing, in place of Thomas Hille, Knt., late Mayor, who died on the 23rd Sept. last. Of these the said William Stocker was elected Mayor for the residue of the year, and was sworn the same day in the Guildhall; and afterwards, viz., on Monday, the 26th

---

[1] Thomas Hille, the Mayor, had died that day of the sweating sickness, although it is recorded that this plague did not visit London before the 27th Sept. Vitellius, A xvi., fo. 141 (Kingsford's 'Chronicles of London,' p. 193).

[2] *Supra*, p. 182. Cf. 'Cal. Letter-Book H,' pp. 209-10.

[3] When uncertainty prevailed in the City as to the issue of the battle of Bosworth.

Sept., the said William Stocker was presented at the Tower of London before the Lieutenant there, by writ of the lord the King according to charter, and was there sworn.

Afterwards, viz., on the 28th day of the same month, the said William Stocker died and went the way of all flesh.[1]

29 Sept., 1 Henry VII. [A.D. 1485], at a Common Council—attended by a multitude of Commoners, the Prior of Christchurch, [John] Broun, [John] Warde, [William] Horne, [Hugh] Brice, Robert Tate, [Ralph] Astry, [John] Swanne—John Warde and William Horne were nominated by the Commonalty for one of them to be elected Mayor for the residue of the year, viz., from the Feast of St. Michael until the morrow of SS. Simon and Jude next ensuing, in place of William Stocker, late Mayor, who had died on the 28th Sept. last. Of these John Warde was elected Mayor for the residue of the year, and on the same day was sworn Mayor up to the Feast of SS. Simon and Jude [28 Oct.].

Afterwards, viz., on the morrow of St. Michael, he was presented, together with the two newly elected Sheriffs, before the Barons of the Exchequer, and was admitted. The same day the Mayor had no banquet, but attended a banquet of the Sheriffs, because of the shortness of time.[2]

At a Common Council held on Saturday, 1 Oct., 1 Henry VII. [A.D. 1485], there being present the Mayor, the Prior of Christchurch, Thomas Fitzwilliam the Recorder, John Broun, William White, John Mathew, Ralph Astry, John Swanne, and John Tate, Aldermen—John Hawgh was elected one of the Under-Sheriffs by the said Mayor, Aldermen, and Common Council[3] *loco* John Watno, deceased.

Fo. 213.

Eleccio Joh'is Hawgh in vnum subvicecom' Civitat' London'.

Letter from John Warde, the Mayor, and William Purchas, the Chamberlain, to Thomas [Kempe], Bishop of London, presenting John Norhander, chaplain, for admission to one of the five chantries founded in the Guildhall Chapel by Adam

P'sentacio d'ni Joh'is Norhander ad caut' in capella b'te Marie juxta Guihald'.

---

[1] He too died of the sweating sickness, like his predecessor in office.

[2] It is not clear whether the Mayor gave no banquet because he had so short a time to prepare one or because he had been elected to fill the office only for a short time.

[3] Cf. *supra*, pp. 35-36 n.

Frauceys and Henry Frowyk, vacant by the death of Sir John Cotes. Dated, under the seals of the Mayoralty and the Chamberlain, 5 Oct., A.D. 1485.

Eleccio Maioris.

Thursday the Feast of St. Edward [13 Oct.], 1 Henry VII. [A.D. 1485], in the presence of John Warde, the Mayor, the Prior of Christchurch, Thomas Fitzwilliam the Recorder, Robert Drope, Richard Gardyner, John Broun, Robert Billesdone, Hugh Brice, Robert Tate, Richard Chawry, John Mathewe, William White, William Martyn, Ralph Astry, John Swan, and John Tate, Aldermen, and an immense Commonalty summoned to the Guildhall for the election of a Mayor for the year ensuing—Hugh Brice was elected.

Afterwards, viz.,' on the Feast of SS. Simon and Jude [28 Oct.], he was sworn at the Guildhall, and on the morrow was presented, admitted, &c., before the Barons of the Exchequer.

Fo. 213 b.

Q'd valecti Maioris et Cam'e possint eligi in servientes Maioris.

8 Nov., 1 Henry VII. [A.D. 1485], ordinance by Hugh Brice, the Mayor, and the Aldermen that the Yeomen of the Mayor and the Chamber may be elected Serjeants of the Mayor for the time being, or of the Chamber, any ordinance to the contrary notwithstanding.[1]

Q'd Maior et Aldr'i ac Concil' Civitatis dum modo sederint in Cur' interioris Cam' re non discooperiant capit' sua nisi etc.

Also, in order to avoid infirmities which daily occur from uncovering the heads of the Mayor, Aldermen, and Council of the City when they sit in Court, as well as to save trouble and time (*quam alia tedia et dispendia temporum*), it was agreed the same day by the Mayor and Aldermen that neither the Mayor, Aldermen, nor any of the Council, so long as they sat in the Court of the Inner Chamber, should uncover their heads (except for paying respect to strangers) under penalty of forfeiting one penny as often as they acted to the contrary.

Q'd duo custod' assignentur pro conduct' de Fletestrete et Aldermanbury.

21 Nov., 1 Henry VII. [A.D. 1485], ordinance by the Mayor and Aldermen that two Wardens be assigned by the Mayor for the time being for the conduits of Fletestrete and Aldermannebury, viz., one for each.

[1] See ordinance of 1483. *Supra*, p. 191.

At a Common Council held on Friday, 16 Dec., 1 Henry VII. [A.D. 1485], Thomas Butside was elected Coroner of the City *loco* John Grene,[1] deceased.

Eleccio Thome Butside in Coronatorem.

17 Dec., the same year, Dionisius Burton, tailor, discharged by Hugh Brice, the Mayor, and the Aldermen from serving on juries, &c., owing to his infirmities.

Exon'acio Dionisii Burton ab assisis.

19 Jan., 1 Henry VII. [A.D. 1485-6], came Richard Dunce, John Broke, Richard Noneley, Benedict Trotter, grocers, before the Mayor and Aldermen, and entered into bond in the sum of £100 for payment into the Chamber by the said Richard Dunce of a like sum to the use of Robert, son of William "Thomson," at the age of 24, the said money having been bequeathed to the said Robert by John Parys, late "peautrer."

Custodia pueror' [sic] *Will'mi* " *Thompson*'

The same day came Richard Dunce, John Broke, Richard Noneley, and Benedict Trotter, grocers, and entered into bond in the sum of £100 for payment into the Chamber by the said Richard Dunce of a like sum to the use of John and Margaret his children when they come of age or marry.

Fo. 214.

Custodia pueror' Ric'i Dunce.

False nets condemned to be burnt by " my lord Maire[2] and my Maisters Thaldermen " as a warning to those fishing in the Thames with unlawful nets. [No date.]

Fo. 214 b.

Proclamacion for Nettes.

Coal sacks deficient in measure condemned to be burnt " by my saide lorde Maire and my Maisters thaldermen." [No date.]

Proclamacion for Cole sackes.

4 April, 1 Henry VII. [A.D. 1486], came Katherine White, widow, Henry Somer, haberdasher, John Devereux, " plommer," and William Grey, fuller, and entered into bond in the

Custod' pueror' Joh'is White Carpenter.

---

[1] John Grene is recorded as having been appointed City Coroner by the Common Council on the 1st October, 1485 (Journal 9, fo. 88 b), and appears to have been the first Coroner appointed by that body since the office fell into the hands of the civic authorities, pursuant to the charter of Edward IV., dated 20th June, 1478, after the execution of Anthony Woodville, 2nd Earl Rivers, and Chief Butler of England. A vigorous attempt had been made in 1435 to assert a right to the Coronership by the City by refusing to admit the King's nominee for the deputy-coronership, but it was of no avail. See 'Cal. Letter-Book K,' pp. 186-7.

[2] This is an earlier instance of the use of the title " Lord Mayor " than hitherto supposed. Cf. ' Cal. Letter-Book K,' p. 243 n.

sum of £30 for payment into the Chamber by the said Katherine of a like sum to the use of Agnes, Elizabeth, and Johanna, daughters of John White, late carpenter, when they come of age or marry.

Fo. 215.

For clensyng of stretys.

6 April, 1 Henry VII. [A.D. 1486], ordinance by the Common Council that thenceforth distresses taken for non-payment of fines imposed for negligence in cleansing the streets, &c., should be sold by the Chamberlain if not redeemed within a year and the fines paid, the Chamberlain retaining out of the proceeds the sums due, and keeping the residue to the use of the owners of the distresses.

Fo. 215 b.

An orden-aunce by Co'en Councell that the gownes of sergeauntes shuld be a foote above the hemme [sic].

"FORASMOCHE as the Sergeauntes and yomen bothe of the Maire Shireffes and Chamberleyn of the Citee of London yeerely have their lyverey at the Festes of Cristmas and Pentecost and thereof make their gownes soo longe and so syde[1] that they may not do service in this Citee if nede required as they shuld doo. Therfor it is ordeigned in this Comune Councell that no sergeaunt nor yoman of the said Citee shall make any lyverey gowne geven unto hym by the Maire Shireffes or Chamberleyn of the same Citee any sydder, but the hemme of the same gowne be a foote above the soole of the Foote upward uppon peyne of losyng of their offices.

"ALSO it is ordeigned and enacted in the same Comune Counceill that no Freman be made by Redempcion freely without any thyng payng within the Citee of London at the Request of any persone,[2] but it be by thassent of the Comune Counceill."

Custod' pueror' [sic] *Thome Pelham.*

11 May, 1 Henry VII. [A.D. 1486], came Simon Stephenson, Richard Stukeley, John Hylle, drapers, and Roger Barlowe, tailor, before the Mayor and Aldermen, and entered into bond in the sum of 100 marks for payment into the Chamber by the said Simon of a like sum to the use of Johanna, daughter of

[1] "Side," applied to dress, also means long "side-coats "=long coats worn by children, "side-sleeves "= hanging sleeves (Nares).

[2] The custom of nobles and courtiers soliciting the freedom of the City for their humbler friends and servants became a great abuse. See 'Analytical Index to Remembrancia,' *s.v.* ' Freedom.'

Thomas Pelham, late "sherman," when she comes of age or marries.[1]

Tuesday, 23 May, 1 Henry VII. [A.D. 1486], ordinance by the Common Council prescribing the size of various kinds of fish[2] to be taken in the Thames and exposed for sale, and ordering that immature fish taken be put back into the river.

Fo. 216.

For takyng of Fisshe in Thamys.

The same day came Hugh Acton, John Stodard, Henry Clowgh, and John Spereman, tailors, and entered into bond in the sum of 80 marks for payment into the Chamber by the said Hugh of a like sum to the use of Johanna and Agnes, daughters of Richard Elys, late tailor, when they come of age or marry.

Custod' pueror' Ric'i Elys.

13 June, 1 Henry VII. [A.D. 1486], came John Atkynson, "talughchaundeler," Thomas Colyn, fishmonger, Thomas Watt, draper, and Nicholas Partriche, before the Mayor and Aldermen, and entered into bond in the sum of £16 19s. 5d. for payment into the Chamber by the said John Atkynson of a like sum to the use of Richard, son of Robert Hudgrave, late scrivener, when he comes of age, the said money having been bequeathed to the said Richard by Johanna Hudgrave his grandmother.

Fo. 216 b.

Custod' pueror' [sic] Rob'ti Hudgrave.

27 June, 1 Henry VII. [A.D. 1486], came Matilda "Frosten," widow, Roger Mone, Henry Clough, tailors, and Hugh Colstonsok, fuller, and entered into bond in the sum of 400 marks for payment into the Chamber by the said Matilda of a like sum to the use of Robert, John, Grace, and Agnes, children of Robert "Frosten," late "stacioner," when they come of age or marry.[3]

Fo. 217.

Custodia pueror' Rob'ti "Froston."

---

[1] Margin. 22 May, 7 Henry VII. [A.D. 1492], came Robert Frende, skinner, who married the above Johanna, and acknowledged satisfaction.

[2] The fish specified are barbel, flounder, roach, dace, pike, and tench.

[3] Margin. 27 Oct., 11 Henry VII. [A.D. 1495], acknowledgment of satisfaction by William Marsam, who married the above Agnes; and on 14 April, 23 Henry VII. [A.D. 1508], the above John acknowledged satisfaction for his patrimony at the house of the Blackfriars, being prevented from coming into Court for fear of arrest. The above Grace is recorded as being dead anno 23 Henry VII.

Fo. 217 b.   18 June, 1 Henry VII. [A.D. 1486], the guardianship of William, Martin, Katherine, and Johanna, children of Martin Blundell, late fruiterer, and of Johanna his wife, committed by the Mayor and Aldermen to William Robynson, "bruer," together with a certain brew-house and contents in the parish of St. Mary Somerset, to the use of the said orphans, pursuant to their father's will.

Fo. 218.   Schedule of utensils belonging to the above brew-house,[1] viz.:—

A "bruyng ketyll of coper with a courbe of waynscot"; a "masshe fatte[2] with a lowse[3] botom and a tappe trowe[4] of ledde"; a "wort fatte"; two "kelers[5] for wort"; three gutters of Tree; three "stotyng Baskettes of wykers and vj Roders of Tree";[6] three "hande ketils" of brass; two "sesterns of ledde for licoure"; a "fyrehoke," a "rake," and a "pyke" of iron; twenty little "Tubbes" for yeast; a little "messhe Tubbe," a "water Tubbe," and a "Flete";[7] a "clevyng axe"; a "Fanne"; a "stepyng sestern" of lead; twenty-four "kilderkyns"; a malt mill with all apparel; a "Bere dray" with two pair "wheles"; and a "Blacke haire for a kiln."[8]

---

[1] A similar schedule of utensils of a brew-house is recorded, under date 1335, in Letter-Book E, and is set out in Riley's ' Memorials,' p. 194.

[2] Mash-vat.

[3] Loose.

[4] Tap-trough.

[5] Coolers.

[6] Wooden rudders.

[7] Float.

[8] The schedule of 1335 contains one "heyr" for a kiln (*pro torell*). In the treatise of Walter de Biblesworth (thirteenth century) we find (in connexion with brewing) the phrase *pur ensechier au toral (kulne)*. Riley mistakes *torell* for *tonell*, and translates the word "tuns," suggesting that "heyr" may mean high (*hey*). This is wrong. The true explanation of the connexion of a "blacke haire" with a kiln has been discovered by the kind assistance of Mr. John Hodgkin, to whom the editor had occasion to acknowledge his great indebtedness in the previous Calendar. He has pointed out that in two Vocabularies of the fifteenth century the Latin term *cilicium* is translated "hayre" or "hare"; and that both terms denoted a hair or felt cloth, placed in this instance in a kiln for malting purposes. See Wright's ' Vocabularies,' pp. 200, 233. That "heire" or "heyre" by itself may signify a hair-cloth or hair-shirt is seen furthermore in Langland's ' Piers the Plowman ' (ed. Skeat, i. 130, 131):

" She shulde unsowen hir serke and sette there an heyre
To affaiten her flesshe."

2 July, 1 Henry VII. [A.D. 1486], the guardianship of Thomas, Fo. 218 b.
Henry, Margaret, and Elizabeth, the surviving children of John
Sygar,[1] late fishmonger (his wife Margaret and his son William
being dead), together with tenements in the parish of St. Mary
Magdalen at the old fish-market, at the corner of the lane
called "Lamberdesham"[2] and elsewhere, committed by the
Mayor and Aldermen to Philip Payne, fishmonger, on his
entering into a bond in the sum of £100.

Thursday, 6 July, 1 Henry VII. [A.D. 1486], ordinance by Fo. 219.
the Common Council that thenceforth no stranger should make · *Brocage*
any bargain in the City without paying brokerage for the same *money.*
to the Fellowship of Brokers, under penalty.

Letter from the Mayor and Chamberlain to the Dean and *Presentacio*
Chapter of St. Paul's presenting Sir John Beneakir, chaplain, *Joh'is Beneakir etc.*
for admission to the chantry of Henry Guldeford, vacant by
the resignation of Sir John Chesewright, the last chaplain.
Dated 4 Aug., A.D. 1486.

29 Aug., 1 Henry VII. [A.D. 1485], "Henry" Filberd, tailor, *Exon'acio "Joh'is" Filberd ab assis'.*
discharged by the Mayor and Aldermen from serving on
juries, &c., owing to deafness, &c.

31 Aug., 2 Henry VII. [A.D. 1486], came good men of the *Ordinacio de Marbelers.*
Craft of Marblers, and presented 'a petition to the Mayor and
Aldermen praying that certain ordinances for the better government of their Craft might be approved, among them being the
following :—

"That every persone occupying the said Crafte within the
Fraunchise of the saide Citee that maketh any Stone-werk of
Marbyll, laton' werke or coper werk belongyng or perteynyng
to the same Crafte not sufficient wherethurgh the same werke
of Stone laton' or coper is or shalbe by the Wardeyns of the
same Crafte for the tyme beyng presented and forfaited to the
said Chambre shall pay and make fyne in money the iiij part
of every stone so forfaited after the rate of the price that it

---

[1] His will, dated 22 Dec., 1455,   [2] "Lambardes Hill" (Stow).
enrolled in the Court of Husting.
See 'Cal. of Wills,' ii. 534.

coste as the byer thereof shall confesse and also shall pay and make fyne for every pounde of laton' or coper werke forfaited as it is aforesaid iiij*d*. to be applied and devided in maner and fourme abovesaide."

Their petition granted.

The same day came the Wardens and Fellowship of the "Fruterers" of the City, and prayed that the "Fruterers," freemen of the City, may be allowed to stand with the foreign fruiterers in the market-places as freely as they did before the making of the ordinance anno 3 Edward IV. [A.D. 1463], *temp.* Thomas Cooke, Mayor.[1]

Their prayer granted.

7 Sept., 2 Henry VII. [A.D. 1486], came Thomas Parker, "iremonger," John Smert, grocer, Roger Bartlot, "iremonger," and Thomas Stone, "wexchaundeler," and entered into bond in the sum of £137 6s. for payment into the Chamber by the said Thomas Parker of a like sum to the use of Richard, Sibil, Stephen, and Henry, children of William Abell, late "irmonger," when they come of age or marry, the said money having been bequeathed to them by Elizabeth Denys, widow, mother of the said children.[2]

20 Sept., 2 Henry VII. [A.D. 1486], came Thomas Wynnam, John Hille, John Jak', drapers, and John Smyth, stockfish-monger, and entered into bond in the sum of £380 for the payment into the Chamber by the said Thomas Wynnam of a sum of £330 6s. 8d. to the use of Robert, son of Thomas Hille, Knt. and Alderman, deceased,[3] when he comes of age.

Thursday the Feast of St. Matthew [21 Sept.], 2 Henry VII. [A.D. 1486], in the presence of Hugh Brice, the Mayor, Thomas Fitzwilliam the Recorder, John Broun, John Warde, Henry Colet, John Mathew, Robert Tate, William Martyn, William

---

[1] *Supra*, pp. 32-4.

[2] Margin. 7 Feb., 5 Henry VII. [A.D. 1489-90], came William Matlowe, *alias* Clerke, who married the above Sibil, and acknowledged satisfaction for money bequeathed to his wife by Elizabeth Abell, *alias* Denys, her mother.

[3] Alderman successively of Cordwainer and Cheap Wards. *Ob.* 23 Sept., 1485 (Beaven).

White, Robert Hardyng, Ralph Astry, John Percyvall, William Remyngton, John Fenkell, Ralph Tilney, Hugh Cloptone, John Swan, and John Tate, Aldermen, and very many Commoners summoned to the Guildhall for the election of Sheriffs—John Percyvall, tailor, was elected one of the Sheriffs of the City of London and Middlesex by the Mayor, and Hugh Cloptone, mercer, was elected the other Sheriff by the Commonalty.

The same day William Purches, mercer, was elected Chamberlain of the City for the year ensuing; William Galle, tailor, and Simon Harrys, grocer, were elected Wardens of the City bridge; Robert Tate, Richard Chawry, Aldermen, John Pykeryng, mercer, William Sparke and Robert Fabian, drapers, and Thomas Fabian, mercer, were elected Auditors of the accounts of the Chamberlain and Wardens in arrear.

Afterwards, viz., on the eve of St. Michael, the said Sheriffs were sworn at the Guildhall, and on the morrow of the said Feast were presented, admitted, &c., before the Barons of the Exchequer.

Monday, 25 Sept., 2 Henry VII. [A.D. 1486], petition by the Common Council to the Mayor and Aldermen praying that an Act of Common Council made *temp.* William Gregory, Mayor, touching the number of Clerks, &c., in the service of the Sheriffs,[1] may be varied, and that thenceforth each Sheriff should employ no more than a Secondary with his clerk, a clerk of the paper, and four other clerk-sitters; that these should be freemen of the City, except the Secondary's clerk; that they should be appointed by the Mayor and Aldermen, and not be removed except by authority of the same. Any Sheriff acting to the contrary to incur a penalty of £100. *For Clerkes of the Countour[?].*

The same enacted accordingly.

Letter from the Mayor and the Chamberlain to Thomas [Kempe], Bishop of London, presenting Richard Toteriche, chaplain, for admission to one of the five chantries founded in the Guildhall Chapel by Adam Fraunceys and Henry Frowyk, vacant by the resignation of Master Thomas Aleyn. Dated Sept., A.D. 1481 [*sic*], anno 2 Henry VII. [A.D. 1486]. *Fo. 222.*

Presentacio Ric'i Toteriche capellani ad quandam kantar' .v. cantar in capell' b'te Marie juxta Guyhald' Londoñ'.

---

[1] See 'Cal. Letter-Book K,' pp. 345-7.

Tuesday, 3 Oct., 2 Henry VII. [A.D. 1486], ordinance by the Common Council that the following Secondaries and Clerks in the Compters of the Poultry and Bread Street, who were late "sitters" in the same, shall continue in office during good behaviour, notwithstanding the Act of the 25th Sept. last limiting their numbers, viz. :—

In the Poultry Compter, Henry Wodecok, Secondary, Edmund Taseburgh, Clerk of the paper, Thomas Squyer, Robert Colson, John Love, Thomas Bradshaagh, Humphrey Burley, Hugh Plesyngton.

In the Bread Street Compter, Henry Assheborne, Secondary, William Horwell, Clerk of the paper, William Carewe, Antony Normavyle, John Rothewell, Robert Erham, Thomas Toly, Richard Massam.

Provided always that vacancies be not filled up until there be but four clerks sitting in the said Compters, and after that the ordinance of the 25th Sept. last to be observed for evermore.

Fo. 222 b.

For amercia-
ment' to be
levied of
Straungiers
for noun
apparance in
Enquestes.

3 Oct., 2 Henry VII. [A.D. 1486], the amount of fines imposed on strangers for failing to attend inquests in causes between strangers and denizens pursuant to Stat. 28 Edward III., cap. xiii. (*De medietate linguæ*), ordered by the Common Council to be enhanced in proportion to the number of defaults; the original amount of fine payable, being limited to 3 pence, proving insufficient to compel appearance, new fines are imposed extending from 3 pence to 20 shillings, with power of distress.

Fo. 223.

Custodia
pueror' Joh'is
Benet nuper
Civis et pann'.

5 Oct., 2 Henry VII. [A.D. 1486], came Richard Geffrey, tailor, John Carlyll, grocer, Thomas Bonde, fishmonger, and Richard Hille, tailor, before the Mayor and Aldermen, and entered into bond in the sum of £154 for payment into the Chamber by the said Richard Geffrey of a like sum to the use of John, Edward, and William, sons of John Benet, late draper, when they shall come of age ; the said money being, in part, their patrimony, and, in part, legacies by Agnes Brewes their grandmother and Richard Swalowe their uncle.

11 Oct., 2 Henry VII. [A.D. 1486], came Henry Coote, Thomas Wode, Gilbert Belamy, and John Swerder, goldsmiths, and entered into bond in the sum of £700 for payment into the Chamber by the said Henry Coote of a like sum to the use of Thomas, Robert, Richard, John, Emmota, William, and Antony, children of Robert Cartleage, late goldsmith, when they reach the age of 24 or marry.[1]

Fo. 223 b.

Custodia pueror' Roberti Cartleage.

Friday the Feast of St. Edward [13 Oct.], 2 Henry VII. [A.D. 1486], in the presence of Hugh Brice, Knt., Mayor, the Prior of Christchurch, Thomas Fitzwilliam the Recorder, John Broun, Robert Billesdone, John Warde, Henry Colet, Robert Tate, Richard Chawry, William White, John Martyn, Robert Hardyng, John Tate, Ralph Astry, William Remyngton, John Fenkell, Ralph Tylney, John Percyvale, and Hugh Cloptone, Aldermen, and an immense Commonalty summoned to the Guildhall for the election of a Mayor for the year ensuing— Henry Colet was elected.

Fo. 224.

Eleccio Maioris.

Afterwards, viz., on the Feast of SS. Simon and Jude [28 Oct.], the said Mayor was sworn at the Guildhall, and on the morrow was presented, admitted, &c., before the Barons of the Exchequer.

23 Oct., 2 Henry VII. [A.D. 1486], John Crichefeld, goldsmith, discharged by the Mayor and Aldermen from serving on juries owing to ill-health.

Exon'acio Joh'is Crichefeld ab assisis.

26 Oct., 2 Henry VII. [A.D 1486], Roger Dorsyngton, tailor, similarly discharged owing to divers infirmities affecting his head.

Exon'acio Rog'i Dorsyngton ciss' ab assisis.

27 Oct., 2 Henry VII. [A.D. 1486], William Dockyng, cordwainer, similarly discharged owing to deafness.

Exon'acio Will'i Dockyng allutar' ab assisis.

The same day John Scull, goldsmith, was similarly discharged owing to divers infirmities.

Fo. 224 b.

Exon'acio Joh'is Scull ab assisis.

1 Nov., 2 Henry VII. [A.D. 1486], came Thomas Grafton, mercer, Richard Nonneley, grocer, Thomas Lute, "gentilman,"

Custodia pueror' Thome Hille milit'.

[1] Margin. 26 Sept., 5 Henry VII. [A.D. 1489], the above Emmota recorded as dead, and on 11 Feb., 16 Henry VII. [A.D. 1500-1], the above John recorded as having entered a Religious House.

and Reginald Asshe, mercer, and entered into bond in the sum of £140 for payment into the Chamber by the said Thomas Grafton of a like sum to the use of Agnes, Elizabeth, Robert, Edward, Johanna, and Alice, children of Thomas Hille, Knt., late Alderman, when they come of age or marry.[1]

Fo. 225.

Custodia Joh'is Austeyn filii Laurencii " Austyn."

9 Nov., 2 Henry VII. [A.D. 1486], came Randolph Austeyn, Richard Hawk, Stephen Russell, and John Wayte, " Foundours," and entered into bond in the sum of £13 3s. 10d. for payment into the Chamber by the said Randolph of a like sum to the use of John, son of Laurence " Austeyn," late barber, when he comes of age.

7 Dec., 2 Henry VII. [A.D. 1486], ordinance by Henry Colet, Knt., Mayor, Thomas FitzWilliam the Recorder, John Warde, Hugh Brice, Robert Tate, Richard Chawrye, William White, William Martyn, John Swan, John Tate, William Capell, Hugh Cloptone, John Percyvale, John Mathew, Aldermen, that every Alderman in his Ward receive and take the verdicts and indentures of their Wardmote inquests before coming to the Guildhall " uppon Munday next after the xii day,"[2] bringing with them the said indentures and verdicts on the said Monday, but leaving at home the said inquests, in order to avoid the danger arising from the presence of large numbers attending the Hall in connexion with the inquests.

Fo. 225 b.

Tharticles for Bakers to be kept in their Halymote.

" ALSO forasmoche as in the Halymote of Bakers holden the Sonday before the Fest of Seint Thomas thappostle[3] before the Maire and Shireffes of the saide Citee at Seint Thomas of Acres

---

[1] Margin. 12 July, 12 Henry VII. [A.D. 1497], the above Alice recorded as dead. 27 Nov., 14 Henry VII. [A.D. 1498], came Ralph Lathom, goldsmith, who married the above Elizabeth, and acknowledged satisfaction for his wife's property.

[2] Monday after the Feast of Epiphany [6 Jan.], otherwise " Plow Monday." See 'Cal. Letter-Book H,' p. 276 n.

[3] As to the dates on which the four principal Halimotes in a twelve-month had been customarily held, *vide supra*, p. 100, note. In 1382 the Bakers complained of having to attend Halimotes twice a year before the Mayor and Sheriffs at the church of St. Thomas de Acres, under penalty of a fine ; and it was then agreed by the Common Council that those who attended one of the Halimotes should not be fined, but those who attended neither should be fined 42 pence. See 'Cal. Letter-Book H,' p. 207.

divers articles and charges have been leyde unto the saide bakers the which in tymes passed have not be observed and kept nor as yet be ne may be conveniently kept and observed Wherethurgh the saide bakers yeerely have ronne in perjurie to the grete jeoperdie of their Soules Therefore the saide vij day of Decembre and yeer abovesaid it is aggreed by the saide Mair and Aldermen that the saide articles shalbe voide and in noe wyse leyde unto the charge of the saide bakers at the day and place aforesaid and that in stede and place of the same articles thise articles underwreten shalbe leyd unto their charge at the day and place abovesaid.

" First, that the saide Bakers shall by their saide othes truely enquere and present if any Baker bake any Brede to be solde except Horsebrede otherwise than ij or iiij lofes for j*d.* or oon lofe for j*d.* of wheten brede at all tymes of the yeere except ayenst and in the tyme of Cristemas that every Baker shall mowe bake peny lofes or ij peny lofes or above of gretter pryce of white brede ; and if any Baker doo the contrary that they shall by their said othes present it."

That they shall inquire and truly present any baker found forestalling or regrating wheat.

That they shall present any baker found baking any bread to be sold that was not wheaten bread " not medled with other cornes," and any brown baker baking white bread to be sold.

Thursday, 1 Feb., 2 Henry VII. [A.D. 1486-7], ordinance by the Common Council—there being present Henry Colet, Knt., Mayor, Robert Billesdone, John Warde, Hugh Brice, William Horn, Richard Chawry, John Mathewe, William White, Ralph Astry, William Martyn, William Remyngton, Ralph Tilney, William Capell, John Percyvall, and Hugh Cloptone, Aldermen—that Master John Archer, Rector of the church of St. Mary de Wolchirch, and his successors shall receive yearly the sum of 4 marks from the Wardens of London Bridge for offerings due for the lower part of the Stocks, where fishmongers and butchers sell their victuals. An agreement to

Nota iiij^{or} *marc' solut' Rectori b'te Marie Wolchurche pro les Stockes per Custod' Pont' London'.*

be drawn up to that effect, Master William Chaunte acting on behalf of the City.

Fo. 226.

For dilatory plees no more to be used.

The same day ordinance by the Common Council that no Attorney or Pleader in the Courts of the Mayor or Sheriffs shall thenceforth plead any false plea or any untrue dilatory plea, or allege any matter other than that which they have good reason to believe to be true, under pain of losing their office ; and further, that it shall be lawful for every Attorney and Pleader, on the first day of appearance in the said Courts, to have an " imparlans "[1] unto the next Court day and no longer, in order to communicate with their clients, and to learn the truth of the matter with which they are dealing, as of old accustomed. Provided always that the ministers of the said Courts take nothing for recording the said " imparlans."

For goyng to Feyres etc.

The same day ordinance by the Common Council forbidding freemen of the City thenceforth to send their wares to any Fair or Market within the realm for the next seven years, under penalty of £100, inasmuch as such a course tended to the impoverishment of the City, and was injurious to those living in the country owing to the bad quality of the wares sent for sale.[2]

Fo. 226 b.

Custodia Joh'is Rawson filii Thome Rawson.

1 Feb., 2 Henry VII. [A.D. 1486-7], came Richard Lacon, Edmund Worsley, William Westone, and William Redy, mercers, and entered into bond in the sum of 500 marks for payment into the Chamber by the said Richard of a like sum to the use of John, son of Thomas Rawson, late mercer, when he comes of age.

Fo. 227.

Custodia Katerine Higson filie Rogeri Higson sadler.

8 Feb., 2 Henry VII. [A.D. 1486-7], came John Payntour, Thomas Eyre, Thomas Goldsmyth, grocers, and John Eryk, upholder, and entered into bond in the sum of 100 marks for payment into the Chamber by the said John Payntour of a like

---

[1] *Imparlance :* time given by a Court to *imparle* or consult with one's client as to mode of action.

[2] On the 14th March the Common Council ordered that the execution of the ordinance should be postponed until Michaelmas. *Infra*, pp. 242, 245. It was eventually annulled by the Parliament which met 9 Nov., 1487. Stat. 3 Henry VII., ca p. ix.

sum to the use of Katherine, daughter of Roger Higson, late saddler, when she comes of age.[1]

8 Feb., 2 Henry VII. [A.D. 1486-7], the charter of the Mistery of Bakers of the City allowed by Henry Colet, Knt., Mayor, and the Aldermen, and ordered to be recorded, provided the aforesaid Bakers do nothing, by virtue of the charter, contrary to the liberty of the City. *Fo. 227 b.*

The aforesaid charter of incorporation granted to the Bakers, dated 22 July, 1 Henry VII. [A.D. 1486].[2] *Carta Pistorum.*

21 Feb., 2 Henry VII. [A.D. 1486-7], came the Wardens and other good men of the Mistery of Carpenters into the Court of the lord the King in the Chamber of the Guildhall, before Henry Colet, the Mayor, and the Aldermen, and presented a petition praying that certain ordinances[3] as set out for the regulation of the Craft might be approved. *Fos. 228-31. Ordinacio de Carpenters.*

Their prayer granted.

7 March, 2 Henry VII. [A.D. 1486-7], came John a More, fishmonger, John Morley and Richard Morley, "talughchaundelers," and Thomas Tabilion, "bruer," and entered into bond in the sum of £53 2s. 6d. for payment into the Chamber of a like sum [*ends abruptly*]. *Fo. 231 b.*

---

[1] Margin. 11 March, 14 Henry VII. [A.D. 1498-9], came John Halle, grocer, who married the above Katherine, and acknowledged satisfaction for his wife's patrimony.

[2] In the return made by the Company to the Livery Companies Commission of 1884 (iii. 28) this charter is wrongly ascribed to Henry VIII

[3] The articles, which are of considerable length, will be found set out in an "Historical Account" of the Company of Carpenters, by Edward Basil Jupp and William M. Pocock, F.R.I.B.A. (ed. 1887), pp. 344-53. They have been transcribed from the Letter-Book, but the transcript is sadly deficient in literal accuracy. One of the article is distinctly noticeable as revealing the formation of a temporary Court of Assistants. It is to the effect that on Friday of every week the Master and Wardens should thenceforth call such of the Fellowship as they might think fit "to assemble at their saide Common Halle there for to have communicacion aswell for the supportacion and continuance of the good Rules and ordenaunces of the said Crafte as for the reformacion repressyng and punysshement of Rebellious or mysdoers ayenst the same Rules and ordenaunces or any of theym."

R

Fo. 232.

Wednesday, 14 March, 2 Henry VII. [A.D. 1486-7], ordinance by the Common Council that a former ordinance forbidding attendance at Fairs[1] be suspended until Michaelmas next.

*Custodia
pueror' Joh'is
Thomas
merceri.*

27 March, 2 Henry VII. [A.D. 1487], came Nicholas Barly, skinner, John Gordon, "armurer," Richard Tolle, and...... tailor, before the Mayor and Aldermen, and entered into bond in the sum of £130 for payment into the Chamber by the said Nicholas of a like sum to the use of Alice and John, children of John Thomas, late mercer, when they come of age or marry.

Fos. 232 b-34.

*Ordinacio
Fullonum.*

27 March, 2 Henry VII. [A.D. 1487], came the Wardens and other good men of the Art or occupation of Fullers before the Mayor and Aldermen, complaining of the low estate into which the Craft had fallen owing to the lax system of apprenticeship, the excessive influx of foreigners, and the want of proper supervision of work, and prayed that certain articles for the better regulation of the Craft might be approved, to the following effect.—

First, that no time-expired apprentice nor other person of the Craft set up shop or "wirkynghous" within the City or liberty before being "enhabled" by the Wardens and four other honest householders of the Fellowship "councellyng" and assistant to them; and that the person so "enhabled" pay 20d. to the use of the Fellowship.

That every apprentice be of "good disposicion and of free and true stocke and kynrede born," and be approved by the Wardens.

That no one having more than four apprentices take another apprentice until the terms of all the apprentices, above the number of four, be fully expired, under penalty of £10; but those having only four apprentices may take another a year before the expiration of the term of one of the four to fill his place.

That no "foreyn" be set on work in the Craft after Michaelmas next.

That the Wardens have a right of search.

---

[1] *Supra*, p. 240.

That one half of all penalties be to the use of the Commonalty and the other to the use of the Craft.

Their prayer granted.

2 April, 2 Henry VII. [A.D. 1487], came Edward Grene, John Milles, Thomas Fyssher, mercers, and William Grene, tailor, before the Mayor and Aldermen, and entered into bond in the sum of £80 for payment into the Chamber by the said Edward of a like sum to the use of John, Margaret, Edward, and Elizabeth, children of John Grene, late "lynnendraper," when they come of age or marry.

Fo. 234.

Custodia pueror' Johannis Grene

Royal Proclamation.

Fo. 234 b.

For forged and feyned tales.

"FORASMOCHE as many of the Kyng oure Sov'aign lordes Subgiettes been disposed daily to here fayned contrived and forgied Tydynges and tales and the same Tidynges and Tales nether dredyng god nor his highnes uttre and tell agayn as though they were true to the grete hurt of divers of his Subgiettes and to his grevous displeasure Therefore in eschewyng of suche untrue and forgied tydynges and tales the Kyng oure saide sov'aign lord straitly chargeth and commaundeth that no maner persone what so ever he be utter nor telle any suche tydynges or tales but he brynge forth the same persone the which was auctor and teller of the said tidynges or Tales uppon payne to be sette on the pillorie there to stande as long as it shalbe thought convenient unto the Maire baillef or other officer of any Citee burgh or towne where it shall hapne any suche persone to be taken and accused for any suche tellyng or reaportyng of any suche tidynges or tales Ferthermore the same our sov'aign lord straitly chargeth and commaundeth that all Maires Bailiffes and other officers diligently serche and enquire of all suche persones Tellers of suche tydynges and tales not bryngyng forth thauctor of the same and theim sette on the pillorie as it is abovesaid.[1] [No date.]

---

[1] This proclamation was probably issued in April, 1487, when rumours were afloat that the Earl of Warwick, son of the late Duke of Clarence, had escaped from the Tower; whereas in reality he remained in safe custody whilst being impersonated by Lambert Simnel, a bright lad of obscure origin, who succeeded in getting his title to the Crown acknowledged by the Irish.

Fo. 235.

*Custodia
Joh'is Suth-
worth filii
Randulphi
Suthworth.*

29 May, 2 Henry VII. [A.D. 1487], came John Symson or Sympson, John Berell, grocers, Hugh Cawode, mercer, and Richard Kyng, grocer, and entered into bond in the sum of £60 for payment into the Chamber by the said John Symson of a like sum to the use of John, son of Randolph Suthworth, late grocer, when he comes of age.

Fos. 235 b–
236 b.

20 July, 2 Henry VII. [A.D. 1487], petition by the Wardens and good men of the "Art or occupation" of Barbours of the City that certain articles[1] for the regulation of their "Crafte or Science" may be approved.

Their prayer granted.

Fo. 236 b.

*Eleccio Vice-
comitum.*

Friday the Feast of St. Matthew [21 Sept.], 3 Henry VII. [A.D. 1487], in the presence of Henry Colet, Knt., Mayor, the Prior of Christchurch, Thomas Fitzwilliam the Recorder, John Broun, Robert Billesdone, John Warde, William Horne, Richard Chawry, John Mathewe, Robert Tate, William White, Ralph Astry, William Remyngton, John Fenkell, John Tate, John Swanne, William Capell, John Percyvale, Hugh Cloptone, and William Isaac, Aldermen, and very many Commoners summoned to the Guildhall for the election of Sheriffs—John Fenkell, Knt., draper, was elected one of the Sheriffs of the City of London and Middlesex by the Mayor, and William Remyngton, fishmonger, was elected the other Sheriff by the Commonalty.

The same day William Purches, mercer, was elected Chamberlain of the City for the year ensuing; Simon Harrys, grocer, and John Tutsam, draper, were elected Wardens of London Bridge; Richard Chawrye, John Mathewe, Aldermen, William Sparke, Robert Fabian, William Haryot, drapers, and Thomas Bullesdone, skinner, Commoners, were elected Auditors of the accounts of the Chamber and Wardens of the City Bridge in arrear.

Afterwards, viz., on the eve of St. Michael [29 Sept.], the said Sheriffs were sworn at the Guildhall, and on the morrow of

---

[1] The articles have been set out (from the Letter-Book) in Sidney | Young's 'Annals of the Barber-Surgeons,' pp. 63-5.

the said Feast were presented, admitted, &c., before the Barons of the Exchequer.

Another proclamation reminding citizens that the ordinance of 1 Feb. last forbidding their attending country fairs and markets had been suspended until Michaelmas.[1]

A proclamacion for goyng to faires.

29 Sept., 3 Henry VII. [A.D. 1487], came Johanna "Blakham," widow, Robert Duplage, James Grene, and Richard Joskyn, tailors, and entered into bond in the sum of £100 for payment into the Chamber by the said Johanna of a like sum when Margaret, daughter of Thomas Blakham, late fishmonger, comes of age or marries.

Fo. 237.

Custodia Margarete filie Thome "Blakeham."

Saturday the Feast of St. Edward [13 Oct.], 3 Henry VII. [A.D. 1487], in the presence of Henry Colet, Knt., Mayor, the Prior of Christchurch, Thomas Fitzwilliam the Recorder, John Broun, Knt., Edmund Shaa, Knt., Robert Billesdone, Knt., Hugh Brice, Knt., John Warde, William Horne, Richard Chaury, John Mathewe, William White, John Swan, Ralph Astry, John Tate, John Percyvale, Hugh Cloptone, Ralph Tynley, William Isaac, John Fenkell, Knt., and William Remyngton, Aldermen, and an immense Commonalty summoned to the Guildhall for the election of a Mayor for the year ensuing—William Horne, Knt., was elected.

Fo. 237 b.

Eleccio Maioris.

Afterwards, viz., on the Feast of SS. Simon and Jude [28 Oct.], he was sworn at the Guildhall, and on the morrow was presented, admitted, &c., before the Barons of the Exchequer.

19 Oct., 3 Henry VII. [A.D. 1487], came John Heron, mercer, Thomas Creme, draper, and Richard Adyff, tailor, and entered into bond in the sum of £206 for payment into the Chamber by the said John Heron of a like sum to the use of Alice, Johanna, and Elizabeth, daughters of John Mustell, late mercer, when they come of age or marry.[2]

Custodia pueror' Joh'is Mustell merceri.

---

[1] *Vide supra*, pp. 240, 242. Marginal note "annulled by auctorite of Parliament."

[2] Margin. In Nov., 1498, and March, 1500, Thomas Shripley (?), who married the above Alice, and Nicholas Aleyn, who married the above Elizabeth, came and acknowledged satisfaction for their wives' patrimony, as well as for money accruing by the decease of the above Johanna their sister.

Fo. 238.
Exon'acio Joh'is Belle Scissoris.

25 Oct., 3 Henry VII. [A.D. 1487], John Belle, tailor, discharged by the Mayor and Aldermen from serving on juries, &c., owing to deafness.

Custodia Margarete filie Mathei Woodeward.

14 Dec., 3 Henry VII. [A.D. 1487], came John Peke, Thomas Exmewe, goldsmiths, John Cornyssh, saddler, and John Briteyn, salter, and entered into bond in the sum of £25 for payment into the Chamber by the said John Peke of a like sum to the use of Margaret, daughter of Matthew "Wodward," late goldsmith, when she comes of age or marries.

Fo. 238 b.

14 Dec., 3 Henry VII. [A.D. 1487], ordinance by William Horne, Knt., Mayor, and the Aldermen, that Wardens of the Misteries should thenceforth make no ordinances in their Misteries unless the same be approved by the Mayor and Aldermen for the time being, &c., and thereupon Wardens of divers Misteries brought in their books of ordinances that had not been approved by the Court of Aldermen, and those ordinances were cancelled, and the leaves of the books on which they were recorded were cut out (*abscisa*), &c.[1]

Custodia Hugon' Fenne filii Joh'is Fenne.

9 Jan., 3 Henry VII. [A.D. 1487-8], came Richard Welles, Hugh Broun, mercers, William Broun and John Pasmer, skinners, and entered into bond in the sum of £379 9s. 6¼d. for payment into the Chamber by the said Richard of a like sum to the use of Hugh, son of John Fenne, late stockfishmonger, when he comes of age.[2]

[1] It would be interesting to know whether the books of any of the Livery Companies bear witness to mutilation having taken place about this time. It is recorded that in 1490 the Saddlers prayed the Court of Aldermen to approve of a new set of ordinances to take the place of those which had been *cancelled* for want of authorization. *Vide infra*, fo. 280. There are other instances in the Letter-Book of new ordinances taking the place of ordinances which had hitherto regulated various Fraternities without the Court's authority, but the latter are not specifically recorded as having been cancelled.

[2] Margin. 28 June, 8 Henry VII. [A.D. 1493], it is recorded that the above Hugh had died under age, and that satisfaction for the above money had been acknowledged by John Fenne his brother, and Edmund Bamme, who married Margaret his sister.

18 Jan., 3 Henry VII. [A.D. 1487-8], came Henry Brian, Thomas Quadryng, mercers, Thomas Eyre, John Payntour, grocers, and entered into bond in the sum of £400 for payment into the Chamber by the said Henry of a like sum to the use of Elizabeth and Alice, daughters of Richard Rawson, late mercer and Alderman, when they come of age or marry.[1]

Fo. 239.

Custodia
pueror' Ric'i
Rawson
Aldermanni.

19 Jan., 3 Henry VII. [A.D. 1487-8], came William Sybson, junior, draper, Thomas Eyre, grocer, Peter Watson, draper, and John Crane, "upholster," and entered into bond in the sum of £100 for payment into the Chamber by the said William of a like sum to the use of Thomas, Philippa, Margaret, Beatrix, and Anne, children of John Gardyner, when they come of age or marry.

Fo. 239 b.

Custodia
pueror' Joh'is
Gardiner.

22 Jan., 3 Henry VII. [A.D. 1487-8], came Richard Herlywes, grocer, William Jeffrey, haberdasher, William Campion, grocer, and Robert Hille, grocer, and entered into bond in the sum of 100 marks for payment into the Chamber by the said Richard of a like sum to the use of Margaret, daughter of William Benet, late grocer.[2]

Fo. 240.

Custodia Margarete filie
Will'i Benet

The same day came Robert Creket, John Snoryng, William Coppynger, and Philip Payne, fishmongers, and entered into bond in the sum of £225 17s. 2d. for payment into the Chamber by the said Robert of a like sum to the use of John and Walter, sons of John Heynes, draper, when they come of age.

Fo. 240 b.

Custodia
pueror' Joh'is
Heynes drap'.

---

[1] Margin. 11 July, 14 Henry VII. [A.D. 1499], came John Fox, mercer, who married the above Elizabeth, and Godfrey Darrald, merchant of the Staple of Calais, who married the above Alice, and acknowledged satisfaction for their wives' patrimony.

[2] A marginal note records that the above recognizance was annulled by order of the Court, and that the said Richard was enjoined to give the sum of 10 marks to William Milbourne, the Chamberlain, for the repair of the Guildhall. Milbourne was elected Chamberlain in Sept., 1492 (*infra*, fo. 294 b) : *ob.* 12 July, 1506.

[3] A marginal note, under date Dec., 9 Henry VII. [A.D. 1493], mentions the above orphans as having died.

Fo. 241.

*Custodia
pueror' Steph'i
Gibson mer-
cer'.*

21 Feb., 1 [*sic*] Henry VII. [A.D. 1485-6], came John Redy, mercer, John Hille, draper, William Heton and William Redy, mercers, and entered into bond in the sum of £500 for payment into the Chamber by the said John Redy of a like sum to the use of John, Thomas, William, Margaret, Juliana, and Stephen, children of Stephen Gybson, late mercer, when they come of age or marry.[1]

Fo. 241 b.

*Custodia
pueror' Will'i
Rowse merceri.*

12 Feb., 3 Henry VII. [A.D. 1487-8], came Richard Hadley, grocer, John Clement, goldsmith, William Campion, grocer, and John Corbet, sherman, and entered into bond in the sum of £200 for payment into the Chamber by the said Richard of a like sum to the use of Robert, Elena, William, John, Agnes, Alice, Margaret, Margery [*sic*], and Richard, children of William Rowse, late mercer, when they come of age or marry.[2]

Fo. 242.

*Custod'
Johanne fi.'
Johannis
Wheteley.*

13 Feb., 3 Henry VII. [A.D. 1487-8], came John Wheteley, grocer, James Smyth, fishmonger, Thomas Masse, writer of court-letter, and Thomas Dawne, tallow-chandler, and entered into bond in the sum of £20 for payment into the Chamber by the said John of a like sum to the use of Johanna, daughter of John Wheteley, grocer, when she comes of age or marries.[3]

Fos. 242 b-244.

*Ordinacio de
" Grey-
tawiers."*

5 March, 3 Henry VII. [A.D. 1487-8], came the Wardens and good men of the Mistery of " Graytawiers "[4] of the City into

---

[1] Margin. 8 July, 9 Henry VII. [A.D. 1494], came Thomas Belle, mercer, who married the above Margaret, and on 31 Aug., 19 Henry VII. [A.D. 1503], came John Garard, draper, who married the above Juliana, and acknowledged satisfaction for their wives' patrimony.

[2] A marginal note under date 28 Jan., 9 Henry VII. [A.D. 1493-4], mentions the above Robert, William, John, Richard, Agnes, and Alice, as being dead, and Thomas Balam, grocer, who married the above Elena, as acknowledging satisfaction for his wife's property. On the 30th Aug., 18 Henry VII. [A.D. 1502], came Reginald Reynold, who married the above Margaret, and acknowledged similar satisfaction.

[3] Margin. 18 Nov., 21 Henry VII. [A.D. 1505], came John Pratte of Brandonferry, who married the above Johanna, and acknowledged satisfaction for the said sum.

[4] Tanners of grey leather, in contradistinction to " Megucers," or whitetawyers (using alum in their work), and " Matri-tawyers," or tanners using madder. See ' Memorials,' p. 85 n. ; ' Cal. Letter-Book H,' p. 152 n.

the Court of the lord the King in the Chamber of the Guildhall, before the Mayor and Aldermen, and prayed that certain ordinances for the better regulation of their Mistery[1] might be approved.

Their prayer granted.

12 March, 3 Henry VII. [A.D. 1487-8], came William Weston, Hugh Cawode, mercers, John Gawsem, "vynter," and Walter Smert, skinner, and entered into bond in the sum of £300 for payment into the Chamber by the said William of a like sum to the use of Elizabeth, daughter of Roger Arnold, late haberdasher, when she comes of age or marries.

Fo. 244.

Custodia Elisabeth' filie Rog'i Arnold.

Proclamation by order of the Mayor and Aldermen for all those who have suffered from " unlawful and ungodly contractes and unclene bargains " of usury and " fals chevesaunce," to lay their complaint before the Mayor and other Commissioners appointed to hear and determine such complaints, and justice should be done.[2]

Fo. 244 b.

A proclamacion for usury.

28 March, 3 Henry VII. [A.D. 1488], came Dame Elizabeth Hille, widow, Ralph Tilney, Alderman, William Hille, Richard Hille, and John Hille, grocers, and entered into bond in the sum of £1,885 12s. 4d. for payment into the Chamber by the said Dame Elizabeth of a like sum to the use of Agnes, Elizabeth, Johanna, Robert, Edward, and Alice, children of Thomas Hille, Knt., late Alderman, when they come of age or marry.[3]

Fo. 245.

Custodia pueror' Thome Hille milit'.

---

[1] The ordinances chiefly relate to the election of Master and Wardens and their right to oversee work, the number of apprentices to be allowed, the employment of journeymen, the setting up house or shop, and general obedience to the Master and Wardens for the time being.

[2] A proclamation to similar effect is recorded *circ.* 1455-6 ; ' Cal. Letter-Book K,' p. 374.

[3] Margin. 13 Dec., 6 Henry VII. [A.D. 1490], came John Croke, draper, who married the above Agnes, and acknowledged satisfaction for his wife's patrimony ; 20 Jan., 6 Henry VII. [A.D. 1490-1], came Ralph Lathom, who married the above Elizabeth, and acknowledged satisfaction for his wife's patrimony, and, later, for money accruing to her by the death of Alice her sister.

Fos. 245 b-
247.

*Ordenaunce
for kepyng of
prisoners with-
in Newgate.*
Ordinances of the Common Council held on Friday, 19 April,
3 Henry VII. [A.D. 1488], touching the custody of prisoners in
Newgate, Ludgate, and the Compters, the same to be inscribed
on tables as follows[1] :—

Fos. 247-8.
Ordinances and Rules concerning the keeping and demeaning
of the prisoners within Ludgate, the first ordinance being as
follows :—

"FORASMOCHE as the Gaole of Ludgate is called a free
prison, and so longe tyme hath been called and halh of olde
tyme been ordeyned for the ease of fremen and frewomen of
this Citee[2] It is ordeigned that all Fremen and frewomen
of this Citee for almaner accions and causes for the which
they owne to be imprisoned treson and Felony oonely
except shalbe committed unto the Gaole of Ludgate there
to abide unto they be lawfully delivered And that no
foreyns for any maner cause be committed to the same
gaole Provided alway that it shalbe lefull to the Maire or
the Maire and Aldermen for the tyme beyng to sende any
Freman or Frewoman to the prison of Newgate for their
chastisement."

Fos. 248-9.
Ordinances and Rules concerning the keeping and demeaning
of the prisoners within the Compters.

Fos. 249-
251 b.

*Ordinacio de
Cowpers.*
16 April, 3 Henry VII. [A.D. 1488], came the Wardens and
good men of the Mistery of " Cowpers " before the Mayor and
Aldermen, and prayed that certain ordinances for the better
government of the Mistery might be approved.[3]

Their prayer granted.

---

[1] These ordinances follow closely
other ordinances promulgated in 1431
and 1463. See 'Cal. Letter-Book K,'
pp. 124-7 ; and *supra*, pp. 40-3.

[2] Cf. *supra*, p. 42 n. ; 'Cal.
Letter-Book I,' p. 215 ('Memorials,'
p. 673).

[3] Set out in Firth's ' Hist. Memor.
of the Coopers' Company,' pp. 17-23.
A clause imposing a fine of 40s. a
barrel on Coopers using unmarked
and unlawful barrels was amended in
1491 and the fine reduced to 20d.
Infra, fo. 285.

28 April, 3 Henry VII. [A.D. 1488], ordinance by the Common Council that tanned leather brought to the City for sale shall be brought " wholly " to the seld at the Ledenhall,[1] so that it may be viewed and assayed by seven persons specially appointed, viz., 3 Cordwainers, 2 Girdlers, and 2 Curriers, or by (at least) three, viz., one from each of the said Crafts; and, further, that well tanned leather and falsely tanned leather be distinguished by " markes and signes of iron."[2]

Fo. 251 b.

An orde-naunce for tanned Lether to be brought to the selde at Ledenhall.

26 April, 3 Henry VII. [A.D. 1488], came the Wardens and good men of the Art or occupation of " Plommers " before the Mayor and Aldermen, and prayed that certain articles for the better rule of the Craft might be approved.[3]

Their prayer granted.

Fos. 252-253 b.

Ordinacio de Plommers.

26 April, 3 Henry VII. [A.D. 1488], came good folk of the Crafts of " Powchemakers," " Galeggemakers,"[4] and " Patyn-makers," enfranchised by the name of " Powchemakers," before the Mayor and Aldermen, and prayed that certain ordinances[5] for the good rule of the said Craft might be approved, to the following effect :—

Fo. 254.

Ordinacio de Powche-makers.

---

[1] An ordinance had been passed in 1438 that all leather brought to the City for sale should be lodged for the purpose of assay in a seld situate to the north of the Guildhall. In 1443 that seld was ordered to be closed and another found to take its place. It appears that the Leaden-hall was then made to provide the necessary accommodation. See 'Cal. Letter-Book K,' pp. 285-6. In 1370 Adam Lovekyn obtained an order from the Court of Aldermen that foreign tanners should bring their wares to his seld known as Tanners' seld in Friday Street for purpose of assay and sale. See 'Cal. Letter-Book G,' p. 260.

[2] Set out in Black's ' Hist. of the Leathersellers,' pp. 118-19. In 1412 it was ordained that all tanned leather was to be taken to the " selds of old appointed," and the number of Assayers was to be eight, six, or (at least) four. See 'Cal. Letter-Book I,' p. 100.

[3] The articles are of the usual kind, relating chiefly to Wardens searching for false weights and bad work, the taking of apprentices, the marking of " sowder " so that the maker may be identified, the tools to be provided by journeymen working in the Craft, the amount of quarterage to be paid, &c.

[4] Makers of *galoches* either of leather or wood. The latter (makers of *galoches de feust*) were placed by the Mayor and Aldermen in 1400 under the supervision of the Pouch-makers. See ' Cal. Letter-Book I, p. 9.

[5] See Black's ' Hist. of the Leather-sellers,' pp. 119-20.

That no work be done on Sundays or Double Festival days.

That no member go to any Fair outside the City with any ware belonging to the Craft unless it be first examined by the Wardens to see if it be well made.

That the Wardens be authorized to oversee all work made by members of the Craft, to wit "Belows," Lanterns, Sconces, Bags, and "Powches," wheresoever found.

That one-half of all fines go to the Chamberlain and the other half to the use of the Craft.

Their prayer granted.

Fos. 254 b-
255 b.

*Ordinacio de
Purcers.*

The same day came the Wardens of the Craft of "Purcers" complaining to the Mayor and Aldermen that whereas the search of all manner of purses had formerly been made by the said Wardens, such search had recently been undertaken by the Wardens of the Craft of "Powchemakers," who searched all manner of bags and "powches" with the "purces" belonging thereto, although they exercised only the "Fete of makyng of Sconces, Bowgettes, Patens, Males, and Belows," and thus great dissension and debate had arisen. They therefore pray that certain articles[1] for the better regulation of the Craft may be approved, to the following effect:—

That no purses of leather put to sale be lined thenceforth with "lynnen clothe as [*sic*] roten clothe, paper," or other kind of cloth, but only with leather, under penalty.

That the Wardens may elect every two years four able persons of the Craft to have a view and oversight of all things concerning the honour and profit of the same Craft.

That no one be presented to the Chamberlain by a member of the Craft for admission to the Freedom of the City without being sworn by the Wardens immediately after admission to obey the rules and ordinances of the Craft.

That no member admit any one into the Craft by way of redemption until he be approved by the Wardens and the aforesaid four persons.

---

[1] See Black's 'Hist. of the Leathersellers,' pp 120-2.

That a solemn Mass be yearly kept at the Grey Friars within Newgate on Trinity Sunday, and that every brother shall offer a penny and every sister a halfpenny.

That on the decease of any brother or sister "all suche Torches as be belongyng to the same Crafte be at buryall to brynge the body honestly to therthe."

"Also it is ordeigned the day and yeere abovesaid by the Maire and Aldermen to pacifie the stryfe and debate the which was late moved betwix the Fealishippe of the Purcers and Powchemakers for the Serche of bagges and powches that the Wardeyns of the said Fealiship of Purcers for the tyme beyng shall have the serche of alman' purces not joyned nor annexed to any bagge or pouche And the Wardeyns of the said Crafte of Powchemakers for the tyme beyng shall have the Serche of alman' bagges and powches with purces joyned and annexed unto the same."

Their prayer granted.

13 June, 3 Henry VII. [A.D. 1488], came the Master, Wardens, and good men of the Craft of "Wexchaundelers" before the Mayor and Aldermen, and prayed that certain articles for the good order of the Craft might be approved, to the following effect:—

Fos. 255 b-256 b.
Ordinacio de Wexchaunde-lers.

That due obedience be paid to the Master and Wardens.

That no member of the Craft make, or cause to be made, "any torches, quarerrers,[1] prykettes,[2] Sises,[3] Chambre morters,[4] Tapers, Candelles, nor Imagery but of good and hable wexe and sufficient wyke, that is to say not puttyng thereto any Rosen, Code,[5] Turpentyne ne Talowe whereby the Kynges liege people may be deceyved," under penalty prescribed.

---

[1] Square torches used at funerals. Cf. *cierges squarres*, Letter-Book G, fo. 283 ('Memorials,' p. 359).

[2] Wax candles for placing on a perk or spike of metal (Riley).

[3] Great candles?

[4] Candles used at funeral obsequies r "mortuaries." Cf. will of John de Wyngeffeld proved and enrolled in the Court of Husting in 1361, where he desires to be buried in church with nine *tapres* and five *morters* of wax. 'Cal. of Wills,' ii. 48.

[5] Cobbler's wax (Riley).

That no member " occupie any prynte mark or seale to marke their ware with but oonely suche as the Maister and Wardeyns of the saide Crafte have imprynted in wexe before theym and put both it and the name of the owners in the Indenture therefore ordeigned and made." Default in marking wax put to sale to be punished by fine.

No " foreyn " or alien to be set on work in the Craft.

Young men who refuse to work for reasonable hire or wages to be brought by the Wardens before the Mayor or Aldermen to be punished as vagabonds.

Their prayer granted.

Fos. 256 b-257 b.

Ordinacio de Netmakers.

The same day came good men of the Craft of Netmakers of the City before the Mayor and Aldermen, and prayed that certain articles for the better government of the Craft might be approved, to the following effect :—

That once a year two Wardens be elected who shall have power to search and oversee all manner of work belonging to the Craft.

No member to take any apprentice that has not been presented to and approved by the Wardens.

No member to put any foreigner to work without licence of the Wardens.

One-half of fines, forfeitures, and penalties to be applied to the use of the Chamber and the other to the use of the Craft.

Their prayer granted.

Fo. 257 b.

Ordinacio de Lez Pynners.

3 July, 3 Henry VII. [A.D. 1488], came good men of the Mistery of " Pynners " before the Mayor and Aldermen, and complained that the Fellowship of the Craft enfranchised within the City had become greatly impoverished by the presence of " foreyns," who not only took away the living and sustenance of themselves, their apprentices and servants, but paid nothing towards the relief of the poor members of the Craft. They prayed, therefore, that such " foreyns," when presented to the Masters of the Craft for the purpose of being allowed to work, should be made to pay a sum of 3*s.* 4*d.*, one-half to be applied to the use of the Chamber and the other to the use of the Craft. They further prayed that an ordinance forbidding all

work by night and on certain days might be amended so far as to allow every freeman of the Craft, their servants and apprentices, to work at all times from 5 A.M. from Michaelmas until 8 P.M. until Lady Day [*sic*], excepting Saturdays and the Vigils of Double Feasts "after none rongen,"[1] as formerly excepted.

[Result not recorded.]

5 July, 3 Henry VII. [A.D. 1488], came the Wardens and other good men of the Art or Mistery of " Hatt' merchauntes " before the Mayor and Aldermen, and prayed that certain articles for the better government of the Craft might be approved, to the following effect :—

Fos. 258-259 b.

Ordinacio de Hatt' merchauntes.

That a Common Beadle for summoning the Commonalty be appointed.

That no member thenceforth keep open house or shop " to make an open shewe of any maner wares concernyng the said Crafte or Mistere nor hange outeward in to the stretes any maner of the said Wares to selle any Sonday in the yeere nor any Fest whereof the vigill is commaunded by the chirche to be fasted nor uppon Cristmas day nor the two days next followyng nor the two dayes next folowyng the Festes of Ester and Whitsontyde,"[2] under penalty prescribed.

That apprentices be presented to the Wardens on entering service and on becoming freemen.

That every member of the Craft attend a Mass, &c., on the eve of St. James, Ap. [25 July], and the Sunday after Lammas Day [1 Aug.] for the souls of the " Brethern " and " Sistern " of the Craft deceased, under penalty prescribed.

That the Wardens be elected every two years on the Feast of St. James aforesaid.

---

[1] In or about 1435 the Girdlers complained that " noone " was sometimes rung at 11 o'clock, sometimes at 12, and sometimes at 1 P.M., and thus caused discord. See 'Cal. Letter-Book K,' p. 198.

[2] We may possibly here find a better explanation of the term " Double Feasts " than that given in ' Cal. Letter-Book K,' p. 198 n.

That any one being duly called to be of the clothing or livery and refusing pay 20s.

Their prayer granted.

Fo. 259 b.
*Ordinacio
Cultellarior*. 18 July, 3 Henry VII. [A.D. 1488], came the Master and Wardens of the Craft and Mistery of Cutlers of the City before the Mayor and Aldermen, bringing with them their book of ordinances pursuant to a recent order, the said ordinances not having yet been duly authorized by the Court,[1] and prayed that they might have and enjoy the same by authority of the Court like as they had used and enjoyed them by their own authority and common assent. The ordinances are to the following effect :—

That every freeman of the Mistery, being in the clothing, shall pay quarterly four pence to the Master and Wardens for their search, and every freeman not being of the clothing, and occupying a shop, two pence.

That every "allowe" or "covenant servant" of any of the Fellowship who withdraws himself from his master's service, by night or day, or lies out of his Master's house without licence, shall pay to the Master and Wardens for the time being the value of a week's wages towards the maintenance of the poor men of the Craft; and every master who permits a servant to leave his house and fails to report the matter shall pay 3s. 4d., one-half to the use of the Chamber and the other for the maintenance of poor craftsmen.

That every freeman of the Craft pay yearly to the Clerk of the Craft 20d., if he has served as Master, and 12d. if he has been Warden; and that those of the Clothing shall pay 8d., and those not of the Clothing 4d.

Their prayer granted.

Fos. 260-1.
*Ordinacio de
Paynters*. The same day came good men of the Mistery of "Paynters" before the Mayor and Aldermen, complaining that they had become so impoverished by the influx of foreigners that they could not bear the charges of the City as heretofore, and prayed that certain articles for the

---

[1] *Vide supra*, p. 246.

better rule of the Craft might be approved, to the following effect :—

That no member of the Craft "take any assay of any persone that shalbe his apprentice above a moneth day at the fermest," but that the same apprentice shall be bound and presented to the Wardens by his master, who shall pay for the apprentice 20*d*. to the common box.

Unruly apprentices to be reported to the Wardens.

An apprentice to appear before the Wardens and four honest men of the Craft at the end of his term, in order to be examined as to his qualifications. " And if it so be [that he be found not qualified] that the said Wardeyns, and the iiij men assigne the same persone as a Covenaunt man to an honest man of the same crafte not by the day woke moneth nor quarter but by the space of an hoole yeere And that the same persone shall chose his maister hym self whether he wilbe with his old Maister orelles with a newe And that the Wardeyns shall make his covenaunt so as the Maister may live And the said servaunt may have his lernyng."

The above Wardens and four men to them assigned to search and oversee all manner of work belonging to the Craft.

Every one of the Clothing or Livery to pay yearly 4*d*. towards " Barge hyre " to wait upon the Mayor and Sheriffs when they go to Westminster, &c., and those not of the Clothing, 2*d*.

The Wardens to cause these ordinances to be read twice a year, and to incur a penalty of 13*s*. 4*d*. for neglect of their duties.

Their prayer granted.

18 July, 3 Henry VII. [A.D. 1488], came good men of the Art or Mistery of "Curriours" of the City before the Mayor and Aldermen, and prayed that certain articles for the better rule of the Craft might be approved, to the following effect :—

Fo. 261 b.
Ordinacio de Curriouis.

Any one refusing to undertake the duties of Warden to incur a penalty of 40*s*.

The Wardens to have the right of search, and any work they find defective by default of the worker they are to help and

s

amend, when possible, at the cost of the worker ; if impossible of amendment, the work is to be forfeited, and brought into the Chamber of the Guildhall, there to be judged according to the laws of the City.

No member to set on work any person of the Fellowship who had wilfully refused to obey the ordinances of the Craft, under penalty.

No member to attempt to sell any work untruly wrought.

Any member having a grievance against another to lay the matter before the Wardens before going to law.[1]

The Wardens and Fellowship to meet at the four quarter days to see that the ordinances have been observed.

One-half of all fines, forfeitures, and penalties to go to the Chamber of the City, and the other half to the use of the Fellowship.

Their prayer granted.

Fos. 262-263 b.

Ordinacio de " Bowyers."

The same day came the Wardens and good men of the Art or Mistery of "Bowiers" of the City before the Mayor and Aldermen, and prayed that certain articles for the better rule of the Craft might be approved, to the following effect :—

That penalties as prescribed might be imposed on those not appearing when summoned by the "Bidell" of the Craft.

Fines to be imposed for working on Saturday or the Vigil of any "double" Feast after " none " rung.

That servants and "allowes" be not enticed away from their masters.

That Wardens be elected every two years about the Feast of Michaelmas.

That every householder of the City using the Craft pay quarterly 3*d*. to the common box for the maintenance of a light before "the Rode and Seint George" in the Chapel of St. Thomas on London Bridge.

No member of the Craft to deliver to any enfranchised Fletcher any bows to sell in the country, but a Fletcher may have 3 or 4 bows for his own use and disport.

---

[1] Margin :—*nota contra co'em legem.*

No freeman of the Craft to open a shop without licence of the Wardens.

No freeman to work beyond the franchise of the City except by the King's authority, but in cases where any "Chaffer" has become soiled on its way to fair or market, the owner of the "Stuf" may clean it again.

A penalty of 6s. 8d. to be paid by any one refusing the office of Warden.

Their prayer granted.

29 July, 3 Henry VII. [A.D. 1488], came good men of the Craft of "Wolmen" and "Wollepackers" of the City before the Mayor and Aldermen, and prayed that certain articles for the better rule of the Craft might be approved, to the following effect :— *Fos. 263 b- 264 b.*

Ordinacio de Wolmen et Wollepackers.

That on the 3rd May, yearly [sic], there shall be elected a Master and two Wardens to be Rulers of the Craft for the space of two years [sic].

No foreigner to be set on work so long as a freeman or freeman's apprentice can be obtained, and no apprentice to be set on work when a freeman can be obtained, under penalty of 20s.

No member of the Craft to have more than two apprentices at a time, except it be a child of 14 years of age at the most.

Wardens neglecting their duties to pay 40s.

Their prayer granted.

Proclamation by the Mayor and Aldermen forbidding the casting of refuse into the Thames, and commanding "that no maner persone Fyssher nor other drawe any Nette betwene Ratclyff Mille or Wapping Mille westward toward London brigge nor from London brigge unto the Nasshe[1] ayenst the Bysshop of Derehams place[2] uppon the payne that may falle thereof. Also that no maner persone fysshe in the said water *Fo. 264 b.*

Proclamacio pro retib' et sordibus non projiciendis in Thamisia.

---

[1] Naze ?
[2] "Durham house builded by Thomas Hatfielde, Bishop of Durham." The site is the present Adelphi. Stow's 'Survey' (ed. Kingsford), ii. 99, 373.

of Thamyse with any maner Nette from the temple brigge[1] unto the toure of London nygh any wharf on bothe sydes of the same Thamyse by the space of xx fadom'[2] Also that no maner persone fysshe in the said water with any Castyng Nettes or Angles or with any maner Nettes but yf they holde thassise uppon payne of Imprisonament of their bodies and losyng of the said Nettes and Angles and the Fysshes taken with the same and also the same Nettes and Angles to be brent in Chepe."

The proclamation, further, notifies the appointment of John Petite, grocer, as overseer of the Thames from London Bridge westward, and Robert Lilly as overseer from London Bridge eastward. Moreover, butchers are forbidden to cast any " inwardes of Bestes " into the river, " but if they be cutte in to small pecys."[3] [No date.]

Fo. 265.

Presentacio Will'i Tande Capellani ad secundam Cantar' etc. in eccl'ia Sc'i Pauli.

Letter from William Horne, Knt., Mayor, to the Dean and Chapter of St. Paul's, presenting William Tande, chaplain, for admission to one of the three chantries founded in St. Paul's for the souls of Sir John de Pulteney, William Milford, and John Plesseys, late Archdeacons of Colchester, vacant by the resignation of Laurence Botiller. Dated 6 Sept., A.D. 1488.

Exon'acio Will'i Ussher ciss' ab assisis.

10 Sept., 4 Henry VII. [A.D. 1488], William Ussher, tailor, discharged by the Mayor and Aldermen from serving on juries, &c., owing to his divers infirmities and blindness.

Eleccio Vice-comitum.

Sunday the Feast of St. Matthew, Ap. [21 Sept.], 4 Henry VII. [A.D. 1488], in the presence of William Horne, Knt., Mayor, Thomas Fitzwilliam, Knt., Recorder, John Broun, John Warde, Robert Tate, John Tate, William White, William Martyn, John Swan, Ralph Astry, John Percyvale, Ralph Tilney, William Isaac, John Broke, John

---

[1] This was no more than a pier or jetty which the owners of the Temple were bound to maintain on the river-side, as found by inquisition made in 1360. 'Memorials,' p. 306. Similarly we find " Lambeth Bridge " mentioned by writers long before the erection of a real bridge at Lambeth in 1863. *Vide supra*, p. 48 n. We are reminded of the old landing stairs and ferry by the present Horse-ferry Road.

[2] Cf. *supra*, pp. 180-181 n.

[3] See regulations of 1472 touching butchers. *Supra*, p. 104.

Fenkell, and William Remyngton, Aldermen, and very many Commoners summoned to the Guildhall for the election of Sheriffs — William Isaac, draper, was elected one of the Sheriffs of the City of London and Middlesex by the Mayor, and Ralph Tylney, grocer, was elected the other Sheriff by the Commonalty.

The same day William Purches, mercer, was elected Chamberlain of the City for the year ensuing ; Simon Harrys, grocer, and John Tutsam, draper, were elected Wardens of the City's Bridge ; John Mathewe, William White, Aldermen, William Heryot, draper, Thomas Bullesdon, skinner, Walter Povy, tailor, and William Stede, grocer, Commoners, were elected Auditors of accounts of the Chamber and Wardens in arrear.

Afterwards, viz., on the eve of St. Michael [29 Sept.], the said Sheriffs were sworn at the Guildhall, and on the morrow of the said Feast were presented, admitted, &c., before the Barons of the Exchequer.

1 Oct., 4 Henry VII. [A.D. 1488], came the Wardens and good men of the Art or Mistery of Fullers of the City before the Mayor and Aldermen, and prayed that certain articles for the better regulation of the Craft might be approved, which articles are to the following effect :—

Fos. 265 b. 266 b.

Ordinacio de Fullers.

That no member of the Craft henceforth go to the dinners or feasts of the Mayor or Sheriffs unless bidden by an officer of the Mayor or Sheriffs, or by the Wardens, under penalty of paying the sum of 3s. 4d. ; one-half of the same to the use of the Chamber and the other of the Craft.

No member to employ more than 6 workers in the Craft at once.

No member to take as a servant, "allowe," or apprentice, any one born beyond the sea.

No member to put out cloth to "burle,"[1] "pyke," or

---

[1] To pick the burrs or burls from the surface of woollen cloths. Dyer, 'The Fleece,' Book III., has :—

"Soon the clothier's shears
And *burler's* thistle, skim the surface sheen."

"rowe"[1] by any one except a brother admitted and a householder of the same Craft.

Any member having a journeyman or covenant man to "make a clere rekenyng" with him on his departure.

No member to set cloth upon the "tayntours" on Sundays, Our Lady Days, or Principal Feasts.

No member to take any "Chaffer" or ware for his workmanship.

No member to take cloth "to plane[2] nor sette uppon the Tayntours without it be of his owne rowyng," in order to avoid strife and variance that often arose between the owner of the cloth and the worker that "roweth" the same, "as it may be evidently shewed."

No member to bring cloth to the mill to be "thycked"[3] until the Wardens have seen the cloth and found it suitable for the "thyckyng."

No journeyman nor servant "allowes" to leave his master's service without reasonable cause of sickness, lack of meat or drink, or non-payment of wages.

The same not to haunt the stews side nor the "kayles" nor any other riotous game or play.

That no member of the Craft make, or cause to be made, any affray upon the Stair appertaining to the Craft nor at their "Tayntours."

Their prayer granted.

---

[1] To rough cloth with card or teasel, a process which took place over a "perch." Cf. "Sheringe with broade sheres or rowinge at the perche."—Will of Richard Hilles enrolled in the Court of Husting, 1588. 'Cal. of Wills,' ii. 713.

[2] Cf. "panno equando," *supra*, p. 198.

[3] That is to say, *fulled*. Fr. *fouler*, to tread, full or *thicken* cloth. The old method of fulling cloth was to tread it with the feet, "hence come our surnames of Fuller, Walker, and Tucker, fullers being known as walkers or tuckers from walking on or kneading the cloth when under treatment" ('Drapers' Dict.'). Among the deceits mentioned in a statute of Edward VI. (Stat. 5 & 6 Edw. VI. c. 6) as practised by clothworkers was taking cloth out of the mill before it was "full thicked." Cf. "No thycker of the same Crafte (Hurers) thicke no ware to no straunge man or woman." *Infra*, p. 264. Cf. Stat. 22 Edw. IV. c. 5.

2 Oct., 4 Henry VII. [A.D. 1488], came the Wardens and other good men of the Art or Mistery of Hurers of the City before the Mayor and Aldermen, and brought in certain unauthorized ordinances for the government of the Craft, pursuant to an order of the Court,[1] for approval, to the following effect :— Fos. 266 b-269. *Ordinacio de Hurers.*

That every one, within the Livery of the Craft and without, shall attend Mass on summons by the Beadle in the Lady Chapel annexed to the parish church of " oure lady Berkyng," and offer 1*d.*, under penalty of forfeiting a pound or half a pound of new wax according to his being in the Livery or not.

That every two years, after celebration of the Mass in the said chapel on the day of the Nativity of Our Lady [25 March], the whole Fellowship shall meet in some convenient place and elect two new Wardens, and those who refuse office, without reasonable cause, shall pay 40*s.*

That every 3 or 4 years, if thought necessary, a new clothing of livery be provided, and the names of those who refuse to receive it be presented by the Wardens and " the twelve "[2] of the Fellowship, for the time being, to the Mayor and Aldermen for correction after their discretion.

That four times a year, viz., within 14 days after Christmas, Easter, Midsummer, and Michaelmas, the Fellowship shall meet, and every brother pay his quarterage of 4 pence, under penalty of forfeiting a pound or half a pound of new wax according as he be in the Livery or not.

That apprentices be presented to the Wardens and be English born.

·" That no man of the saide Crafte egge entice ne purloyne in to his service any other mannes servaunt of the same Craft tyll his maister and he be aggreed," under penalty of 40*s.*

" That no persone or persones of the same Crafte go into Foreyns houses for to wirke nor in to no straunge places for to teche the science of the saide Crafte," under similar penalty·

---

[1] *Supra*, p. 246.

[2] Not previously mentioned. Here we are reminded of a " Court of Assistants."

That if any member take any work to a stranger to be worked " he make therof a good ende hymself or elles do it to be made among the Freemen Brethern and true wirkers of the saide Crafte," under penalty of 20s.

That no " thycker " of the Craft " thicke " any ware to a strange man or woman " which can make no good ende thereof," or " put it to dresse " to any but brethren of the Craft, or true workers of the same, under penalty of 6s. 8d.

Any one discovering " the Counceill lefull " of the Craft to forfeit 10s.

That no member implead another without licence of the Wardens, so long as he can get justice within the Craft.

That no apprentice out of his term take a house to work in until he be " assaied " by the Wardens as to his " connyng to work sufficiently."

That no freeman of the Fellowship set an alien to work or to buy or sell in his shop, under penalty of 6s. 8d.

That disputes between masters and servants touching work or wages be referred to the Wardens.

That upon every default done contrary to the ordinances distress shall be taken by the Wardens and kept 40 days. If it be not then redeemed, the said Wardens and " the twelve " shall cause the same to be valued and sold, and return the surplus (if any), after recovering the amount of fine, to the owner.

That Wardens proved to be remiss in their duties forfeit 6s. 8d. for every neglect.

The above articles (*inter alia*) approved and ordered to be recorded.

Fo. 269 b.

*Eleccio
Maioris.*

Monday the Feast of Translation of St. Edward [13 Oct.], 4 Henry VII. [A.D. 1488], in the presence of William Horne, Knt., Mayor, Thomas Fitzwilliam, Knt., Recorder, Richard Gardyner, John Broun, Knt., Robert Billesdone, Knt., John Warde, Henry Colet, Knt., Robert Tate, Richard Chawry, William White, John Mathewe, William Martyn, John Tate, John Fenkell, Knt., William Remyngton, John Percyvale, Knt., John Swan, William Capell, Knt., John Broke, William

Isaac, and Ralph Tilney, Aldermen, and an immense Commonalty summoned to the Guildhall for the election of a Mayor—Robert Tate was elected.

Afterwards, viz., on the Feast of SS. Simon and Jude [28 Oct.], he was sworn at the Guildhall, and on the morrow was presented, admitted, &c., before the Barons of the Exchequer.

1 Oct., 4 Henry VII. [A.D. 1488], came the Wardens and other good men of the Art of "Corsours" of London before the Mayor and Aldermen, complaining of the lack of ordinances to govern their Craft, and praying that they would approve of ordinances to the following effect:— *Ordinacio de Corsours.*

That yearly on Saint "Loes"[1] day the Wardens be chosen as rulers and governors of the Craft.

That members pay a quarterage of 4*d*.

That members not attending on summons forfeit 4*d*.

The articles approved.

2 Oct., 4 Henry VII. [A.D. 1488], came the Wardens of the Art of "Lorymers" before the Mayor and Aldermen, and brought in their book of ordinances pursuant to an order of the Court,[2] and prayed that the same might be approved, to the following effect:— *Fos. 270-271 b.* *Ordinacio de Lorymers.*

That no member of the Craft work on any "Saturday vigill even" or "any other Festivall even" after "none" rung in his parish church, under penalty, except "vernysshyng," "burnysshyng," and "bosyng,"[3] and work no longer than from 5 A.M. until 7 P.M. between Michaelmas and Lady Day.

That when any brother or sister happens to die, freemen of the Craft shall come in their "most honest clothyng" to the parish church of the deceased to *dirige,* and on the morrow to a Mass of *Requiem,* under penalty in case of default without reasonable excuse ; and that every such brother or sister—"if they in their lyfe paied well and truly their quarterages and other charges" of the Craft—shall within

---

[1] St. Louis. A church in Paris dedicated to St. Giles and St. Loe.

[2] *Supra,* p. 246.

[3] Embossing.

8 days of their decease have 30 masses sung for them by one of the four Orders of Friars, at the cost of the Fraternity.

That if a member of the Craft of "good guydyng and conversacion falls to povertie by goddes sonde[1] and hath no thynge to helpe hym self with all that than he shall have wokely a Reward of the co'en boxe of the same Crafte that is to say he that hathe been Wardeyn of the said Crafte shall have wokely xd and he that hathe not been Wardeyn shall have wokely vijd And if any suche persone so havyng suche Almes of the said Crafte dye that than his burying to be paid for of his owne goodes if he be of power and elles to be paied and borne at the charge of the said Crafte."

That apprentices be not enticed out of the service of their masters, and that no apprentice out of his term set up shop until he be made a freeman of the Craft, and that every apprentice at the first opening of his shop pay 12*d.* towards the maintenance of the Craft.

That no member take any journeyman or "allowes" except by the year.

That all disputes be referred to the Wardens before any other steps be taken.

That no member disclose any lawful matter or communication touching the Fellowship, under penalty.

That any one using high and "owterageous" language at meetings and not keeping silence at the bidding of the Wardens shall forfeit a pound of wax.

That no member of the Craft renew or cause to be renewed any old ware belonging to himself to sell the same again as new ware, under penalty; but he may varnish and amend anything pertaining to the Craft for another person.

That the Wardens shall have the right of search and seize badly wrought works and bring them to the Guildhall.

---

[1] God's visitation. Cf. 'Piers Plowman' (ed. Skeat), i. 239 :—
" Blynde men and bedreden and broken in here membres

And ale poure pacientes *a-payed of godes sonde* " (resigned to God's visitation).

" Also that no persone of the said Crafte hereafter tynne any olde werke belongyng to the said Crafte for to selle that is to say Bittes Steroppes or any other thynge except the thinges that been hable to bere the fylyng as Frensshe Bittes the which bene hable to bere the tynnyng uppon payne to lose at every tyme that any suche persone so dothe a pounde of wexe."

One-half of all fines and forfeitures to be to the use of the Chamber of the Guildhall, and the other to the use of the Commonalty of the Craft.

The above articles approved.

18 Nov., 4 Henry VII. [A.D. 1488], came William Grene, John Lee, tailors, William Brikles, grocer, and Edward Grene, mercer, before the Mayor and Aldermen, and entered into bond in the sum of £200 for payment into the Chamber by the said William Grene of a like sum to the use of Elizabeth, daughter of Stephen Traps, late tailor, when she comes of age or marries.

Fo. 272.

Custodia Elizabeth filie Steph'i Traps.

3 Dec., 4 Henry VII. [A.D. 1488], came John Grey de Noryell, co. Beds, yeoman, John Rock, haberdasher, Robert Setcole, " Foundour," William Kyrfote, grocer, and John Robynson, stockfishmonger, and entered into bond in the sum of £40 for the payment by the said John Grey to David, son of William Waren, late tailor, when he comes of age, of the sum of £36 in respect of the issues of a certain tenement in the parish of All Hallows in Bredestrete, which tenement had been devised by Roger Waren, late tailor, to William, the father of David, in tail male ; and in the event of the decease of the said David under age for the payment of the said money to Elizabeth Waren, sister of the said David.

Fos. 272-272 b.

Custodia David Waren' filii Will'i Waren' Cissoris.

29 Jan., 4 Henry VII. [A.D. 1488-9], came John Broke, Alderman,[1] John Storke, William Curle, grocers, and Thomas Bullesdone, skinner, and entered into bond in the sum of £1,373 2s. 11¼d. for payment into the Chamber by the said

Fo. 273.

Custodia pueror' Thome Breleyn Aldr'i.

---

[1] A Grocer ; he had recently been elected Alderman of Farringdon | Ward Within : he was Sheriff 1489-90.

Alderman of a like sum to the use of William, Johanna, Juliana, Matilda, and Elizabeth, children of Thomas Breteyn, late Alderman,[1] when they come of age.[2]

Fo. 273 b.

Custodia Thome Edward filii Will'i Edward groceri.

29 Jan., 4 Henry VII. [A.D. 1488-9], came Margery Edward, widow, Philip Edward, grocer, Richard Hille, tailor, and Alexander Hedlam, upholder, and entered into bond in the sum of £110 for payment into the Chamber by the said Margery of a like sum when Thomas, son of William Edward, late grocer, comes of age or marries.

Custodia pueror' Johannis Gardyner Cissoris.

17 Feb., 4 Henry VII. [A.D. 1488-9], came John Hardy, John Barnarde, Alexander Bassyngthwayte, tailors, and John Sympson, dyer, and entered into bond in the sum of £66 for payment into the Chamber by the said John Hardy of a like sum to the use of John and Margaret, children of John Gardyner, late tailor, when they come of age or marry.

Fo. 274.

Custodia pueror' Thome Hewetson Cissoris.

19 Feb., 4 Henry VII. [A.D. 1488-9], came William Worthyngton, draper, James Fitte, tailor, Thomas Pays, draper, and John Haddesley, girdler, and entered into bond in the sum of £64 13s. 4d. for payment into the Chamber by the said William of a like sum to the use of John, Peter, Henry, William, Thomas, and Margaret, children of Thomas Hewetson, late tailor, when they come of age or marry.[3]

Fo. 274 b.

Custod' Joh'is filii Thome Riche merceri.

23 March, 4 Henry VII. [A.D. 1488-9], came Thomas Croke, skinner, Richard Croke and John Croke, drapers, and Richard Thornell, mercer, and entered into bond in the sum of £100 for payment into the Chamber by the said Thomas Croke of a

---

[1] Ironmonger; elected Alderman of Aldersgate Ward in Nov., 1483; *ob.* 1485. (Beaven.)

[2] Margin. 4 Oct., 12 Henry VII. [A.D. 1496], came William Esyngton, gentleman, who married the above Johanna, and acknowledged satisfaction for his wife's patrimony.

[3] Margin. 10 July, 20 Henry VII. [A.D. 1505], came the above Henry, orphan, and acknowledged satisfaction for his patrimony, as well as for money accruing to him by the death of the above John, Peter, Thomas, and Margaret; and on 5 Feb., 21 Henry VII. [A.D. 1505-6], came the above William and did likewise.

like sum to the use of John, son of Thomas Riche, late mercer, when he comes of age or marries.

16 July, 4 Henry VII. [A.D. 1489], came Richard Stewarde, Richard Cock', William Hamlyn, Thomas Piers, "tallughchaundelers," and Philip Leycok, "hurer," and entered into bond in the sum of £36 11s. 8d. for payment into the Chamber by the said Richard Stewarde of a like sum to the use of Walter and Thomas, sons of Richard Alpe, late "tallughchaundler," when they come of age or marry.

Fo. 275.

Custod' pueror' Ric't Alpe Tallugh'.

John Spicer condemned to stand on a pillory for being a "common bawde." [No date.]

Fo. 275 b.

Judicium Pillorie pro quodam pronuba.

Elizabeth Judela (Indela ?), convicted of being a "common bawde," to be led from prison to the Pillory in Cornhill with "mynstralcye," with a "rayhode" on her head and a white rod in her hand,[1] and there the cause to be proclaimed, and then to be conveyed through Chepe to Newgate, and to avoid the City, "but if[2] she laufully behold in prison by sum laufull accion." [No date.]

Judicium cujusdam Co'is pronube.

Thomas Elys, "dawber," condemned by "my lord the Maire" and the Aldermen to stand on the pillory for forging a bond purporting to bind John Walshe to him in the sum of £10. [No date.]

Fo. 276.

Judicium pillorie pro fabricacione unius fict' obligacionis.

Monday the Feast of St. Matthew [21 Sept.], 5 Henry VII. [A.D. 1489], in the presence of Robert Tate, Mayor, Thomas Fitz William the Recorder, Robert Billesdone, John Warde, Henry Colet, William Horne, Richard Chawry, William White, William Martyn, John Tate, John Swanne, John Percivall, William Remyngton, William Capell, William Isaac, and Ralph Tilney, Aldermen, and very many Commoners summoned to the Guildhall for the election of Sheriffs—William Capell, Knt., draper, was elected one of the Sheriffs of the City of

Eleccio Vicecomit'.

---

[1] See ordinance of 1382. 'Cal. Letter-Book H,' p. 189; 'Liber Albus,' i. 459.

[2] Unless. Cf. 'Piers Plowman' (ed. Skeat), i. 316, 368.

London and Middlesex by the Mayor, and John Broke, grocer, was elected the other Sheriff by the Commonalty.

[The election of a Chamberlain not recorded.]

Simon Harrys, grocer, and John Tutsham, draper, elected Wardens of London Bridge ; William White, William Martyn, Aldermen, Walter Povy, tailor, William Stede, grocer, Richard Swan, skinner, and Thomas Boterell, draper, Commoners, were elected Auditors of the accounts of the Chamber and Wardens in arrear.

Afterwards, viz., on the eve of St. Michael [29 Sept.], the said Sheriffs were sworn at the Guildhall, and on the morrow of the said Feast were presented, admitted, &c., before the Barons of the Exchequer.

Fos. 276-
276 b.

Custodia
pueror'
Johannis Pasy
tallugh'.

23 Sept., 5 Henry VII. [A.D. 1489], came Stephen Hunt, grocer, John Frensshe, baker, Thomas Barry, "brwer," and Gilbert Wilson, "brwer," and entered into bond in the sum of £14 13s. 4d. for payment into the Chamber by the said Stephen of a like sum to the use of Peter, Katherine, and Margaret, children of John Pasy, late "tallughchaundler," when they come of age or marry.

Fo. 277.

Eleccio
Maioris.

Tuesday the Feast of Translation of St. Edward [13 Oct.], 5 Henry VII. [A.D. 1489], in the presence of Robert Tate, the Mayor, Thomas Fitz William the Recorder, the Prior of Christchurch, John Broun, Knt., Robert Billesdone, Knt., John Warde, Hugh Brice, Knt., Henry Colet, Knt., William Horne, Knt., Richard Chawry, John Mathewe, William White, William Martyn, Ralph Astry, John Tate, John Percyvale, Knt., William Remyngtone, John Fenkell, Knt., William Isaac, Ralph Tilney, William Capell, Knt., and John Broke, Aldermen, and an immense Commonalty summoned to the Guildhall for the election of a Mayor for the year ensuing—William White was elected.

Afterwards, viz., on the Feast of SS. Simon and Jude [28 Oct.], he was sworn at the Guildhall, and on the morrow was presented, admitted, &c., before the Barons of the Exchequer.

Letter from Robert Tate, the Mayor, and William Purches, the Chamberlain, to Master Richard Lychefeld,[1] Doctor of Laws, Canon Residentiary in the Cathedral Church of St. Paul, and Warden of the spiritualities of the City and diocese of London, the Bishopric being vacant,[2] presenting Sir William Stodard, chaplain, for admission to a chantry in the Chapel over the bones of the dead in St. Paul's Churchyard, vacant by the death of Sir John West, the last chaplain. Dated 27 Oct., A.D. 1489.

Presentacio Will'i Stodarde Capell'i ad cantariam in Capella sup' ossament' mortuor' in Cimiterio Eccl'ie Cathedralis Sc'i Pauli London'.

9 Nov., 5 Henry VII. [A.D. 1489], Thomas Hawes, haberdasher, discharged by William White, the Mayor, and the Aldermen from serving on juries, &c., owing to his infirmities.

Exon'acio Thome Hawes ab assisis.

20 Nov., 5 Henry VII. [A.D. 1489], came John Wolston, Thomas Laman, Thomas Wode, and John Dudley, "bochers," and entered into bond in the sum of £10 for payment into the Chamber by the said John Wolston of a like sum to the use of Thomas and Agnes, children of Thomas Wolston, late butcher, when they come of age or marry.[3]

Fo. 277 b.

Custod' pueror' Thome Wolston Carnific'.

11 Dec., 5 Henry VII. [A.D. 1489], came Edward Grene, mercer, Oliver Warner, William Grene, tailors, and Robert Palmer, barber, and entered into bond in the sum of £136 19s. 9¾d. for payment into the Chamber by the above Edward of a like sum to the use of Margery, daughter of Thomas Graunt, late vintner, when she comes of age or marries.

Fo. 278.

Custodia Margerie filie Thome Graunt vinitar'.

Letters patent appointing John Percevale, Knight and Alderman, to be justice to the merchants of the Guildhall of the Teutonics for the speedy recovery of debts and hearing of pleas in cases where the Sheriffs and Mayors may be unable to determine such matters from day to day. Witness the King at Westminster, 25 Jan., 5 Henry VII. [A.D. 1489-90].

Fo. 278 b.

L're patentes d'ni Regis fact' Johanni "Percyvale" militi ad essend' Aldr'm Theutonicor' abud le Stylyerde etc.

---

[1] Archdeacon of Middlesex ; *ob.* 27 Feb., 1496-7 ; buried in St. Paul's (Newcourt, 'Rep.,' i. 81).

[2] Thomas Kemp, Bishop of London, had died on the 28th March, 1489, and his successor, Richard Hill, was not consecrated until the following November, although elected to the See in August.

[3] Margin. 7 April, 10 Henry VII. [A.D. 1495], John Long, "bocher," becomes a surety *loco* Thomas Wode, deceased.

Fos. 278 b-
279 b.

*Ordinacio dez
Foundours.*

2 April, 5 Henry VII. [A.D. 1490], came the Wardens and other good men of the Art or occupation of "Foundours" praying that certain articles[1] for the rule of the Craft might be approved, to the following effect:—

That every member obey the summons of the Beadle, under penalty, unless "he be letted by meltyng or other lefull causes."

That every brother of the Clothing pay a quarterage of 3 pence, every householder keeping a shop and not of the Clothing 2 pence, and every journeyman a penny for the "fyndyng of light, kepyng of masses, buryng of poore brethern," and other deeds of alms.

That members attend Mass for all the Brotherhood on the Feast of the Assumption [15 Aug.], in the church of St. Laurence, Jewry, or other place appointed, and there make offering, under penalty.

That no brother out of the Clothing take more than one apprentice at a time except by special permission, and no brother who is of the Clothing take more than two apprentices at a time; that a Warden or ex-Warden have three apprentices and no more, and one who has been Upper Warden no more than four.

That apprentices be "right lymmed."

That every brother going to a fair shall show his ware before it be packed to the Wardens for approval.

Petition granted.

Fo. 279 b.

*Eleccio Vice-
comitum.*

Tuesday the Feast of St. Matthew [21 Sept.], 6 Henry VII. [A.D. 1490], in the presence of William White, the Mayor, Thomas Fitz William the Recorder, John Broun, Robert Billesdon, John Warde, Henry Colet, William Horn, Robert Tate, Richard Chawry, John Mathewe, William Martyn, Ralph Astry, John Swanne, John Tate, Hugh Cloptone, John Percyvale,

---

[1] The articles are much to the same effect as those recorded in 1456. See 'Cal. Letter-Book K,' pp. 375-6. They will be found printed from the Letter-Book in Williams's 'Annals of the Founders' Company' (pp. 10-12), but the date is wrongly given as 4 Henry VII., 1489, and "right lymmed" (in connexion with apprentices) has been misread "right bounde."

William Remyngton, John Broke, William Capell, Henry Cote,[1] and Robert Revell, Aldermen, and very many Commoners summoned to the Guildhall for the election of Sheriffs—Henry Cote, goldsmith, was elected one of the Sheriffs of the City of London and Middlesex by the Mayor, and Robert Revell, grocer, was elected the other Sheriff by the Commonalty.

[The election of Chamberlain not recorded.]

Simon Harrys, grocer, and Christopher Elyot, goldsmith, were elected Wardens of London Bridge; William Martyn and John Swanne, Aldermen, Richard Swanne, skinner, Thomas Boterell, draper, Richard Hawkyns, draper, and John Pasmer, skinner, Commoners, were elected Auditors of the accounts of the Chamberlain and Wardens in arrear.

Afterwards, viz., on the eve of St. Michael [29 Sept.], the said Sheriffs were sworn at the Guildhall, and on the morrow of the said Feast were presented, admitted, &c., before the Barons of the Exchequer.

Wednesday the Feast of Translation of St. Edward [13 Oct.], 6 Henry VII. [A.D. 1490], in the presence of William White, the Mayor, the Prior of Christchurch, Thomas Fitz William the Recorder, John Broun, Knt., Robert Billesdone, Knt., John Warde, Henry Colet, Knt., William Horne, Knt., Robert Tate, Richard Chawry, John Mathewe, William Martyn, John Swan, John Tate, William Remyngton, William Isaac, John Percyvale, Knt., Robert Revell, and Henry Cote, Aldermen, and an immense Commonalty summoned to the Guildhall for the election of a Mayor for the year ensuing—John Mathewe was elected. *Eleccio Maioris.*

Afterwards, viz., on the Feast of SS. Simon and Jude [28 Oct.], he was sworn and admitted, and on the morrow was presented, accepted, &c., before the Barons of the Exchequer.

6 Oct., 6 Henry VII. [A.D. 1490], came the Wardens and other good men of the Art or occupation of Saddlers of London before the Mayor and Aldermen, and showed that, whereas in times past ordinances had been made for the rule of the Craft that had not been authorized within the City, they had brought *Fos. 280-281 b.* *Ordinacio Sellarior'.*

---

[1] Mentioned for the first time. Spelt "Coot," *infra*, p. 279.

T

in their book of ordinances before the Mayor and Aldermen, as commanded, and those that were not authorized had been cancelled;[1] and thus they had been left without ordinances wherewith to govern the Craft. They prayed, therefore, that certain ordinances might be approved, to the following effect:—

That the Wardens and Fellowship shall yearly attend Mass on the Feast of the Assumption [15 Aug.], in the church of St. "Faystres,"[2] in their last livery, and in the afternoon of the same day be at a *Dirige,* and on the morrow at a *Requiem* for the souls of deceased members of the Craft.

That on the same Feast four new Wardens be elected, and brought within a month, by the old Wardens and 4 or 6 of the most honest persons of the Craft, to the Guildhall to be sworn.

That any member admitted, by the Wardens and 8 persons of the Fellowship "to theym assistent," to the Clothing (or Livery) and refusing it, without reasonable excuse, shall pay for his disobedience 13s. 4d.

That any member of the Clothing wishing to take a "patron" of the cloth to buy his gown cloth as he will shall pay for the same "patron," towards the priest's and beadle's gowns, 16d., and shall bring the cloth before the Wardens, in order that they may see whether the colours be "like," under penalty; and he that is admitted into the Clothing shall pay, according to custom, an ounce of silver or a spoon of silver,[3] to the value of 4d.

That any one admitted by the Wardens and by the 8 persons "to theym assistent" to be a brother or sister of the Craft, the

---

[1] *Supra*, p. 246.

[2] St. Vedast, Foster Lane.

[3] The gift of spoons on such occasions was very general in livery companies, and specimens of them may be seen at the present day in the Guildhall Museum. Apprentices to the Basket-makers, on obtaining their freedom, were called upon to present their company with a silver spoon, the spoon in many cases being stamped with the initials of the donors. See 'Records of the Basket-makers' Company,' recently edited by H. H. Bobart, the clerk of the Company, pp. 106-7. Many of the spoons so presented appear to have been destroyed in the Great Fire, whilst those of a later date have been sold. The Pewterers' Company also sold many of their spoons (Welch, 'History of the Pewterers' Company,' ii. 6).

brother shall pay 13s. 4d. and the sister 6s. 8d. for the benefit of the poor of the Craft; " and if it hapne any suche brother or sister or any other housholder of the saide Craft the whiche before hath kept the gode Rules of the same Craft and also have payed their duetes of xiijd. yerly falle herafter in povertie by the visitacion of God than the said brother sister or housholder shalbe refresshed of the comon boxe by the discrecion of the Wardeyns and of the forsaid viij persones to theym assistent."

That an aggrieved member submit his complaint to the Wardens before taking action, and that no member maintain any quarrel between members of the Craft until the Wardens have given licence to the parties to go to law, under penalty of 5s. to the augmentation of the alms of the Craft.

That no member entice away a "Custumer beyng in dette afore tyme to any other persone of the same Crafte," under penalty of 20s.

That no one disclose any matter touching the welfare of the Fellowship which might cause strife or debate.

That no member attend feasts of the Mayor or Sheriffs, or any other Feast " where any greate assemble of people shalbe," unless invited or ordered.

That servants or "allowes" working by the year or quarter shall receive their wages within a month of the expiration of the quarter.

That such workers shall give their masters a month's warning before leaving.

That no journeyman work in chambers or privy places to avoid examination of his work, under penalty of 3s. 4d.

That the taking of apprentices be regulated as directed.

That the Wardens have full power of search, and that all works wrought to deceive the buyer " as stuff belongyng to the same Crafte the whiche is daily sette uppon upholsters stalles to selle and brought by Foreyns unto the Citie that the said stuffe so unlafully wrought may some of it be fynable and some may utterly be forfeit " ; and that any one opposing such search pay 10s.

T 2

That four Auditors be appointed yearly, and any one refusing the office pay 3s. 4d.

That on election day the whole of the Clothing shall choose 8 persons, of which the Wardens shall elect 4, to be Wardens for the year ensuing.

That the Wardens and Renters hereafter render their account by Michaemas Day next after their leaving office.

That one half of all fines, forfeitures, and penalties remain to the use of the City's Chamber, and the other to the use of the Fellowship.

Their petition granted.

Fo. 281 b.

Custodia pueror' Rob'ti Godewyne pannar'.

23 Nov., 6 Henry VII. [A.D. 1490], came Johanna Godewyne, widow, Robert Fitzherbert, draper, Laurence Ailmer, draper, and William Hampton, "powchemaker," and entered into bond in the sum of £400 for payment into the Chamber by the said Johanna of a like sum to the use of Richard, Robert, William, and Margery, children of Robert Godewyne, late draper, when they come of age or marry.[1]

Fo. 282.

Judicium Cristine Houghton co'is pronube et meretric'.

21 Oct. [A.D. 1490], " Crystyne " Houghton, *alias* Stone, having been convicted as a common " bawde " and common " strumpet," ordered to void the City, and, having been found again therein, is condemned to be set on the pillory for an hour on two several days, and then be committed to prison for a year and a day.

Fo. 282 b.

Custodia pueror' Will'i Dolphynby letherseller.

9 Dec., 6 Henry VII. [A.D. 1490], came Richard Barbour, Richard Harpham, John Parys, and William Pyerson, " lethersellers," and entered into bond in the sum of £220 for payment into the Chamber by the said Richard Barbour of a like sum to the use of Nicholas, Anne, Margaret, Johanna, and Alice, children of William Dolphynby, when they come of age or marry.[2]

---

[1] Margin. 22 Dec., 12 Henry VII. [A.D. 1496], came Robert Moumford, draper, who married the above Margery, and acknowledged satisfaction for his wife's patrimony.

[2] Margin. 12 March, 8 Henry VII. [A.D. 1492-3], came John Brampton, who married the above Johanna, and acknowledged satisfaction for his wife's patrimony; and on the 21st May, 15 Henry VII. [A.D. 1500], came Ralph Broun, leatherseller, who married the above Alice, and did likewise.

16 Dec., 6 Henry VII. [A.D. 1490], came John Awode, felmonger, Robert Byfeld, "iremonger," John Hirst, tailor, and
John Hille, glover, and entered into bond in the sum of £37 for
payment into the Chamber by the said John Awode of a like
sum to the use of Katherine, daughter of John Wode, late
glover, when she comes of age or marries.[1]

12 Feb., 6 Henry VII. [A.D. 1490-1], came Robert Adlyn, John
Tate, mercers, Thomas Bullesdon, skinner, and Robert Bifeld,
"iremonger," and entered into bond in the sum of £140 for payment into the Chamber by the said Robert Adlyn of a like sum
to the use of Robert, Thomas, and Elizabeth, children of
Robert Lulley, late "iremonger," when they come of age or
marry.[2]

Thursday, 24 Feb., 6 Henry VII. [A.D. 1490-1], in the presence
of John Mathewe, the Mayor, the Aldermen, the Common
Council, the Wardens, and other good men of all the Misteries
of the City summoned to the Great Hall of the Guildhall, Hugh
Pemberton, tailor, was elected one of the Sheriffs of the City
loco Robert Ryvell, who had died the previous day. And the
same Hugh was sworn the day of his election; and afterwards,
viz., on the 2nd March next following, he was presented before
the Lieutenant of the Tower pursuant to the King's writ
thereon.

25 Feb., 6 Henry VII. [A.D. 1490-1], came Thomas Rathbone,
draper, Robert Okeborne, mercer, William Rothwell, mercer,
and Ralph Huet, skinner, before the Mayor and Aldermen, and
entered into bond in the sum of £100 for payment into the
Chamber by the said Thomas of a like sum to the use of John,
Reginald, Matthew, Elizabeth, Peter, Arnold, and John [sic],

Fo. 283.

*Custodia
Katerine
filie Joh'is
Wode glover.*

*Custodia
pueror' Rob't
Lulley ire-
monger.*

Fo. 283 b.

*Vicecom'
mortuus et
alter loco suo
electus est.*

*Custodia
pueror' Rogeri
Gerveys
Cissoris.*

---

[1] Margin. 7 June, 6 Henry VII.
[A.D. 1491], came Richard Wilde,
salter, who married the above Katherine, and acknowledged satisfaction
for his wife's patrimony.

[2] Margin. 19 Nov., 16 Henry VII.
[A.D. 1500], came the above Robert,
the orphan, and acknowledged satisfaction for his patrimony, and also
for money accruing to him by the
death of the above Thomas and
Elizabeth.

children of Roger Gerveys, tailor, when they come of age or marry.[1]

" By the King

" To our trusty and welbeloved the Maire and Shireffes of oure Citie of London.

" Trusty and welbeloved we grete you wele   And where as we late directed unto you oure especialle l'res willyng and desiryng you by the same to suffre suche galeymen as with smalle merchaundises bene repaired from theire galey to oure Citie of London to make uttraunce and sale of the same in shoppes and other places as they have custumably done herebefore as they say   It is so as ye knowe wele that at your late beyng with us for this matier we desired the Right reverend fadre in God the bisshop of Excestre Keper of our prive seelle to have communicacion with you and to take som Resonable endetherin not repugnaunt unto the fraunchises and liberties of our saide Citee   Whereunto ye were confourmable   Wherfore we wolle and desire you seyng that they be comen so ferre with theyr saide merchaundises and have as they sey paied theyr custumes for the same   Ye wille for this season suffer theym to make sale of theyr said merchaundises as they have done of tyme passed yeving unto theym a certeyn tyme and season to make their said uttraunce and not to passe or excede the same   And that ye wille thus do at this tyme in avoiding thexclamacion and daily pursuyt that they make unto us in this behalf as we trust you   Yeven under our signet at our palois at Westm' the xiiij[th] day of Feverier " [A.D. 1490-1].

4 March [A.D. 1490-1], pursuant to the above letter, it was agreed by the Mayor and Aldermen that the " Galymen " who were then in the City should be permitted to sell their small wares, viz., glass and such like, in their accustomed shops, on condition their wares were exposed for sale before Pentecost

---

[1] Margin. 11 Feb., 17 Henry VII. [A.D. 1501-2], the above Reginald acknowledged satisfaction for his patrimony and for money accruing to him by the decease of John and John [sic] his brothers and Elizabeth his sister; and on 23rd Nov., 24 Henry VII. [A.D. 1508], the above Peter acknowledged satisfaction for his patrimony and money accruing by the decease of the above John, Matthew, Arnold, John [sic], and Elizabeth.

next, under penalty of forfeiting the same if found in open shops after the eve of Pentecost (*post illam vigiliam*).

26 March, 6 Henry VII. [A.D. 1491], came John Kyrkeby, "taillour," William Maryner, salter, Henry Warfeld, dyer, and Richard Childe, dyer, and entered into bond in the sum of £220 for payment into the Chamber by the said John of a like sum to the use of William, son of Walter Stalworth, late tailor, when he comes of age or marries.

Fo. 284 b.

Custodia Willi Stalworth filii Walteri Stalworth Cissoris London'.

22 March, 6 Henry VII. [A.D. 1490-1], came the Wardens and other good men of the Art or occupation of "Coupers" and presented a petition praying that the penalty of 40s. imposed on "Coupers" during the Mayoralty of Sir William Horne for using unmarked and unlawful barrels[1] may be reduced to 20d., and that the Wardens may have right of search, &c.

Their prayer granted.

Ordinacio des " Cowpers."

24 March, 6 Henry VII. [A.D. 1490-1], Thomas Hardy, grocer, discharged from serving on juries, &c., owing to his infirmities.

Fo. 285.
Exon'acio Thome Hara ab assisis etc

At a Common Council held on Friday, 15 April, 6 Henry VII. [A.D. 1491], there being present John Mathewe, the Mayor, Thomas Fitz William, Knt., the Recorder, John Broun, Knt., Hugh Brice, Knt., Henry Colet, Knt., William Horne, Knt., William White, William Martyn, Ralph Astry, John Swan, Hugh Cloptone, William Remyngtone, William Isaac, Henry Coot, and Hugh Pemberton, Aldermen, and an immense Commonalty, it was ordained :—

Fo. 285 b.

That if William Purches, the Chamberlain, will advance a sum of money out of his own property for the benefit of the conduit, it shall be repaid him out of the revenues of the Chamber by yearly instalments.

Also that thenceforth, at the election of a Chamberlain of the City, two good men shall be nominated by the Mayor and Aldermen to the Commonalty, for them to elect one of them as Chamberlain for the year ensuing and none other.[2]

Modus eligend' Camerarium.

---

[1] *Vide supra*, p. 250 n.
[2] There is nothing recorded in subsequent elections to show that this or the next ordinance was carried into execution.

Modus eligend'
custodum
Pontis
London'.

Also that at the election of Wardens of London Bridge four discreet men shall be nominated by the Mayor and Aldermen to the Commonalty, for them to elect two and no others.

Nota pro novo
conductu apud
" Grasse-
chirchestrete."

Also that licence be given to Dame Elizabeth Hille, widow of Thomas Hille, Knt. and Alderman, to turn up the soil on the public way of "Graschurchstrete" for the purpose of a conduit.[1]

Consuetudo
certificata q'd
terre et tene-
menta infra
London' ex-
istenc' sunt
legabilia tam
per cives etc.
quam per alios
quoscumque
etc.

Writ to the Mayor and Aldermen touching a plea of debt at Westminster between John Ernley, plaintiff, and Thomas Garth, late of Boxtede, co. Essex, Esquire, and commanding the said Mayor and Aldermen to make a return as to the custom of lands and tenements in the City being capable of being devised by others than citizens and freemen of the City. Witness T. Bryan. at Westminster, 31 Jan., 6 Henry VII. [A.D. 1490-1].

Fo. 286.

Consuet' certi-
ficata per
Thomam Fitz
William
militem Re-
cordatorem
ejusdem Civi-
tat' de terris
et ten'tis per
testament'
legat' in eadem
Civit'.

The custom of the City thereon certified by the mouth of Thomas Fitz William the Recorder, to the effect that in the said City a custom had never existed for lands and tenements to be capable of being devised only by citizens and freemen of the City, but a custom had always existed for lands and tenements in the City to be capable of being devised by others holding them, as well as by citizens and freemen of the City, by their testaments.[2]

At a Common Council held on Saturday, 30 July, 7 Henry VII. [A.D. 1492], there being present the Mayor, the Recorder, [John] Broun, [Hugh] Brice, [John] Warde, [William] Horne, R[obert] Tate, [William] White, [William] Martyn, [John] Swan, J[ohn] Tate, [John] Percyvale, [William] Remyngton, [John] Fenkell, [Ralph] Tilney, [William] Isaac, [William] Capell, [Henry] Cote, [Hugh] Pemberton, Sheriffs[3]—Thomas

---

[1] "Thomas Hill, grocer, maior 1485, caused of his goods the Conduit of Grasse Streete to be builded." Stow, 'Survey' (ed. Kingsford), i. 110.

[2] On the other hand, only freemen could devise in mortmain. Calthrop's 'Ancient Customs and Usages of the City,' 1670, pp. 103-4; Bohun's 'Privilegia Londini,' 1723, p. 210. Cf. *supra*, p. 192.

[3] There is some mistake here. Neither Cote nor Pemberton was Sheriff at this time. Probably the date of the Common Council should be 30 July, 6 Henry VII. [A.D. 1491].

Marwe, "gentilman," was admitted to the office of Common Pleader of the City *loco* Thomas Frowyke.

20 Aug., 6 Henry VII. [A.D. 1491], came Thomas Bledlowe, "gentilman," Thomas Galle, "taillour," John Lee, "taillour," and John Harop, "tallughchaundeler," and entered into bond in the sum of £60 12s. 6d. for payment into the Chamber by the said Thomas Bledlowe of a like sum to the use of Richard, Henry, and John, sons of Thomas Bledlowe, late grocer, when they come of age or marry.[1]

Fo. 286 b.

Custodia pueror' Thome Bledlowe Civis et groceri.

Wednesday the Feast of St. Matthew [21 Sept.], 7 Henry VII. [A.D. 1491], in the presence of John Mathewe, the Mayor, Thomas Fitz William, Knt., the Recorder, John Broun, Knt., John Warde, Hugh Brice, Knt., William Horne, Knt., Robert Tate, William White, William Martyn, John Swanne, John Tate, Hugh Cloptone, John Percivale, Knt., William Remyngton, Ralph Tilney, William Isaac, Henry Cote, and Hugh Pemberton, Aldermen, and very many Commoners summoned to the Guildhall for the election of Sheriffs—Thomas Wood, goldsmith, was elected one of the Sheriffs of the City of London and Middlesex by the Mayor, and William Broun, mercer, was elected the other Sheriff by the Commonalty.

Eleccio Vicecom'.

Simon Harrys, grocer, and Christopher Eliot, goldsmith, were elected Wardens of London Bridge.

The same day William Purches, mercer, was elected Chamberlain of the City; John Swanne and John Tate, Aldermen, Richard Hawkyns, draper, John Pasmer, skinner, Bartholomew Rede, goldsmith, and Richard Wither, haberdasher, Commoners, were elected Auditors of accounts of the Chamber and Wardens in arrear.

Afterwards, viz., on the eve of St. Michael [29 Sept.], the said Sheriffs were sworn at the Guildhall, and on the morrow

[1] Margin. 22 Dec., 11 Henry VII. | of the orphans, recorded as being [A.D. 1495], the above Richard, one | dead.

of the said Feast were presented, admitted, &c., before the Barons of the Exchequer.

[*N.B.   The whole of folio 287 torn out and missing.*]

Fo. 288.

Custodia pueror'......Bufford Civis et merceri.

24 Nov., 7 Henry VII. [A.D. 1491], came Thomas Rede, "paynter," Thomas Pays, skinner, William Dryclough, grocer, and Robert Penson, skinner, and entered into bond in the sum of £22 6s. 8d. for payment into the Chamber by the said Thomas Rede of a like sum to the use of Elizabeth, daughter of [William[1] ?] Bufford, late mercer, when she comes of age or marries.

Fo. 288 b.

Custodia pueror' Roberti Ryngbell groceri.

· 16 Dec., 7 Henry VII. [A.D. 1491], came Giles Grevell, Peter Joy, William Sparke, George Bulstrode, and Richard Close, drapers, and entered into bond in the sum of £520 for payment into the Chamber by the above Giles of a like sum to the use of Margaret, Alice, Thomasina, and Leticia, children (*pueri*) of Robert Ryngbell, late grocer.[2]

Fo. 289.

Custodia pueror' Will'i Chalke.

16 Dec., 7 Henry VII. [A.D. 1491], came Thomas Nutson, draper, John Lynley, fishmonger, Richard Hayman, "barbour," William Campe, scrivener, and entered into bond in the sum of 20 marks for payment into the Chamber by the said Thomas Nutson of a like sum to the use of Ralph and William, sons of William Chalke, late "peauterer," when they come of age.

Custodia pueror' Johannis Gregory.

16 Dec., 7 Henry VII. [A.D. 1491], came Robert Pauntley, goldsmith, Robert Fabian, draper, Richard Telyff and Thomas Prayers, goldsmiths, and entered into bond in the sum of £40 for payment into the Chamber by the above Robert Pauntley of a like sum to the use of Bartholomew and Elizabeth, children of John Gregory, when they come of age.

---

[1] The name is not filled in. There is recorded, however, a William Bufford, mercer, who had a *wife* named Elizabeth in the year 1482. Hust. Roll 212 (29).

[2] Margin. 1 July, 16 Henry VII. [A.D. 1501], came Edward Lymryk, who married the above Thomasina, and William Hynde, mercer, who married the above Alice, and acknowledged satisfaction for the patrimony of their respective wives; 26 Feb., 21 Henry VII. [A.D. 1505-6], came William Nevile, "taillour," who married the above Leticia, and did likewise.

A deed whereby Sir John Fortescue,[1] Knt., grants licence to Hugh Cloptone, the Mayor, the Commonalty, and their successors, at their will and pleasure, to dig and break ground, where and as oft as need shall require, in a close called the " Mewes close,"[2] and in all other of his closes, lands, and tenements, as well arable as " unarable," in the county of Middlesex, as may be necessary for the conveyance of water by conduit-pipes or otherwise to the City; and also in a close called the " Covent Gardyn," held by the grantor for a term of years under the Abbot of Westminster; the said licence to continue as to the " Mewes close," &c., for a term of 180 years; and as to the close called the " Covent Gardyn " so long as the grantor, his heirs and successors, shall continue to have interest therein, without the grantees paying anything, and without making any compensation to tenants, fermors, or occupiers, other than they have been accustomed to do or make in time past. Dated 4 Dec., 7 Henry VII. [A.D. 1491].

Fo. 289 b.

Carta Joh'is Fortescue milit' facta Civitati etc. pro Conductu.

Indenture of lease by Sir John Fortescue, Knt., to Sir John Broune, Knt. and Alderman, Sir Robert Billesdone, Knt. and Alderman, John Warde, Alderman, Sir Hugh Brice, Knt. and Alderman, Sir William Horne, Knt. and Alderman, William White, Alderman, William Purches, mercer, John Smart, grocer, William Bracebrigge, draper, Richard Swan, skinner, Richard Knight, fishmonger, and Richard Graunte, salter, their executors and assigns, of " a medowe called the Conducte mede with a particion in the middes of the same, whiche medowe lieth beside the newe house of the Conducte of Tybourne in the countie of Middelsex abuttyng in brede towardes the North uppon the Kynges highwey ledyng to Londonward viij Roddes and a half of assise every Rodde conteynyng in lenght xvj fote and a half, and uppon the Westside next therto is a grete

Fo. 290.

Indentura inter Joh'em Fortescue militem et Civitat' pro conduct' ducend' ad Civitat' predictam etc.

---

[1] Known as Sir John Fortescue, junior, of Punsborne (or Ponnysbourne, a manor near Hatfield). His wife was Alice, a daughter of Sir Geoffrey Boleyn, Alderman of the City, and Mayor in 1457-8.

[2] Near Charing Cross, so called from the King's falcons having at one time been kept and " mewed " there.

broke of watyr Rennyng called Aybroke and uppon the
Estside next thereto lieth ij closes of the same Sir John Fortescue
whiche John Hardy and John Butteler occupie, also an angle of
the said medowe called the Conducte Mede abutteth upon a
lane called Suglane uppon thest and in brede there twenty
Roddes and a yerde after the mesure aforewriten   Also the
Conducte mede abutteth uppon the close of the said Sir John
Fortescue that John Hardy aforewriten occupieth and uppon
the lande belongyng to Seynt James in the Feld upon[1] the
Southside and in brede there fivescore Roddes and two after
the measure aforsaid, and the said Conduct mede is in
leynght fro the North to the South with the particion aforsaid
sevenscore Roddes and three after the measure aforesaid Alle
which Conducte mede as is nowe hedged diched and closed
one Miles Clifton cordwaner late occupied and nowe Thomas
Duffe Inholder occupieth and holdeth of the same Sir John
Fortescue.''

All of which meadow called the Conduit Mead, together with
another close with a well therein adjoining, the said Sir John
Fortescue lets to the said Sir John Broune and others aforesaid
for a term of 180 years from Michaelmas last, at an annual rent
of £4, reserving power of distress and re-entry in case of
default, and saving always to the Mayor and Commonalty
such interest as they have in the said lands for the conveyance of water to the City.   Dated 21 Dec., 7 Henry VII.
[A.D. 1491].

Fos. 290 b-
    291 b.

Ordinacio dez
Payntours.

16 Dec., 7 Henry VII. [A.D. 1491], came the Wardens and
other good men of the Art or occupation of " Payntours " before
the Mayor and Aldermen, complaining of the members of the
Craft becoming impoverished by the influx of " foreyns,' who
bear neither scot nor lot nor other charge, and prayed that
certain articles might be approved, to the following effect :—

That no freeman of the Craft henceforth employ a foreigner
when he can get a freeman equally capable and " as gode
chepe.''

[1] St. James, Piccadilly.

That every one using the Craft pay a quarterage of 8 pence towards the great charges of the Craft, and that every person so paying quarterage shall pay nothing for his supper at the Common Hall on quarter-days, nor for barge hire when the Craft shall wait upon the Mayor or Sheriffs when they go to Westminster to take their oath, or for "fechyng in" of the King or Queen or of the Prince when it shall happen by water or by land.

That the ordinance lately authorizing the Wardens to make search for badly wrought work[1] may be amended so as to authorize the Wardens to present to the Chamberlain for the time being the names of those who obstruct the said Wardens in carrying out their search.

That a workman not finishing a work according to contract, without reasonable excuse, lose 6s. 8d., one half to the use of the Chamber and the other to the use of the Craft.

Brothers of the Craft to help one another in time of need.

Petition granted.

19 Jan., 7 Henry VII. [A.D. 1491-2], came John Hille, Simon Stephenson, and John Bettes, drapers, and William Redy, mercer, and entered into bond in the sum of £16 8s. 11d. for payment into the Chamber by the said John Hille of a like sum to the use of William, son of Richard Kelet, late "pulter," when he comes of age.

Fo. 291 b.

Custodia Will'i Kelet filii Ric'i Kelet civis dum vixit et pulter London'.

15 March, 7 Henry VII. [A.D. 1491-2], came Richard Hadley, grocer, Richard Bromale, "joynour," John Colet, mercer, and John Clement, goldsmith, and entered into bond in the sum of £125 8s. 8d. for payment into the Chamber by the said Richard Hadley of a like sum to the use of Roger, son of John Skirwith, late "letherseller," when he comes of age.

Fo. 292.

Custodia Rogeri Skirwith filii Joh'is Skyr-with lether-seller.

At a Common Council held on Thursday, 15 March, 7 Henry VII. [A.D. 1491-2], there being present the Mayor, the Recorder, [John] Broun, [Hugh] Brice, [Henry] Colet, [William] Horne, [William] White, [John] Mathewe, [William] Martyn, John Tate, [John] Percyvale, [John] Swanne, [John]

---

[1] See articles of 1488. *Supra*, pp. 256-7.

Fenkell, [William] Capell, [Henry] Cote, [Hugh] Pemberton, and both Sheriffs, it was agreed that the matter concerning the profits of John Hert's office should be directed by the Court of the Mayor and Aldermen.

Fo. 292 b.

Also that thenceforth all those who entered into bond for orphans' goods should be bound yearly in the Council Chamber of the Guildhall on Monday next after Mid-Lent Sunday,[1] to the intent that it may appear to the Mayor and Aldermen whether the persons so bound were alive or dead and were living within the City or not.

Custodia pueror' Joh'is Hervy carnificis.

29 March, 7 Henry VII. [A.D. 1492], came William More, "bocher," William Hoppy, "bruer," William White, "foundour," and Thomas Rowlande, "tiler," and entered into bond in the sum of £30 for payment into the Chamber by the above William More of a like sum to the use of Thomas, Nicholas, and Elena, children of John Hervy, late butcher, when they come of age or marry.[2]

Fo. 293.

Letter from Hugh Cloptone, the Mayor,[3] and Thomas Fitz William, Knt., the Recorder, to Richard [Hill], Bishop of London, presenting Thomas Forman, chaplain, for admission to a chantry in the Chapel of the Blessed Mary near the Guildhall for the soul of Roger Depeham, vacant by the death of Richard Spillesbury. Dated 18 May, 7 Henry VII. [A.D. 1492].

Ordinario dez Surgeons.

28 Feb., 7 Henry VII. [A.D. 1491-2], came the Wardens and other good folk of the Fellowship of Surgeons enfranchised in the City, "not passyng in noumbre of viii persones," before the

---

[1] The fourth Sunday after Shrove Tuesday, and the third Sunday before Easter. Otherwise known as "Mothering Sunday," from the custom of visiting one's parents on that day, a custom that arose from the procession to the Mother Cathedral Church for the purpose of making oblations.

[2] Margin. 25 Sept., 8 Henry VII. [A.D. 1492], came John Flynt, who married the above Elena, and acknowledged satisfaction for his wife's patrimony, as well as for money accruing to her by the decease of the above Nicholas her brother.

[3] His election was probably recorded on folio 287, which has been torn out.

Mayor and Aldermen, and presented a petition praying that, in consideration of their small number, they might continue to be discharged from serving as Constables and from any office "beryng any armure," as well as from juries, &c., as they had been accustomed time out of mind ; and further, to continue to have the search of all "foreyns" using the "feate of Surgery in the City."[1]

Petition granted.

17 April, 7 Henry VII. [A.D. 1492], ordinance by Hugh Cloptone, the Mayor, Sir Thomas Fitz William the Recorder, Sir John Broun, Knt., Sir William Horne, Knt., Robert Tate, John Mathewe, Richard Chawry, William Martyn, John Tate, Sir John Percivale, Knt., Sir William Capell, Knt., Sir John Fenkyll, Knt., William Remyngton, Rauf Tilney, John Broke, Henry Cote, and Hugh Pemberton, Aldermen, that John Hert, the Clerk of the Chamber, should thenceforth receive for his labour as follows, viz.: of every new freeman 12d. ; for every translation 2s. ; for setting over of an apprentice 2s. ; for every judgment 8d. ; for every copy taken out for any freeman 6d. ; and the sum of 46s. 8d. bequeathed to the Clerk of the Chamber for the time being, viz., by Master Reynwell 40s., by Master Philpot 3s. 4d., and by Master Carpenter 3s. 4d. ; and his liveries. Furthermore, that the said John Hert should have under him a clerk, who should have meat and drink with the Mayor for the time being, and 26s. 8d. for wages out of the Chamber, also his clothing and all profits for making searches in the Chamber.

Fo. 293 b.

De officio clerici camere.

19 July, 7 Henry VII. [A.D. 1492], came James Smyth, Thomas Lighton, Richard Bur, and Philip Seman, fishmongers,

Custodia pueror' Will'i Crompe pisc'.

---

[1] Set out at some length in D'Arcy Power's 'Memorials of the Craft of Surgery,' pp. 79-81. In 1514 the Wardens, &c., of the Surgeons, "not passyng in nombre xij persones," petitioned Parliament to similar effect, and their petition was granted (Stat. 5 Henry VIII. cap. 6). By the Act of 1745 (Stat. 18 George II. c. 15), which made the Barbers and Surgeons of London two separate bodies, surgeons were specially exempted from the several offices of constable, scavenger, overseer of the poor, and all parish, ward, and leet offices, as well as from serving on any jury or inquest. The Barbers were not thus exempted by the Act.

and entered into bond in the sum of 50 marks for payment into the Chamber by the above James of a like sum to the use of Hugh, William, Margaret, and Margery, children of William Crompe, when they come of age or marry.

Fo. 294.

Presentacio dn'i Thome Addyngham capell'i ad secundam cantariam trium cantariar' in eccl'ia Sc'i Pauli London'.

Letter from Hugh Cloptone, the Mayor, to the Dean and Chapter of St. Paul's, presenting Thomas Addyngham, chaplain, for admission to the second of the three chantries founded in the said church for the souls of Sir John Pulteney and of William Milford and John Plesseys, late Archdeacons of Colchester, vacant by the resignation of Sir William Tande, the last chaplain.   Dated 26 July, A.D. 1492.

Fo. 294 b.

Presentacio Edwardi Champflour capell'i ad cantariam sanctar' Katherine et Margarete in eccl'ia Sc'i Suthini [sic].

Letter from the same to Richard [Hill], Bishop of London, presenting Edward Champflour for admission to a chantry founded at the altar of SS. Katherine and Margaret in the church of St. " Swithun " for the soul of Roger Depeham, vacant· by the removal of Sir Robert Simond, the last chaplain.   Dated ...... 7 Henry VII.

Ordinance by a Common Council held on Thursday, 6 Sept., 8 Henry VII. [A.D. 1492], that every freeman brewing beer or ale without the franchise of the City may sell the same to retailers or otherwise, any ordinance to the contrary[1] notwithstanding.

Eleccio Vicecom' Civitatis London'.

Friday the Feast of St. Matthew [21 Sept.], 8 Henry VII. [A.D. 1492], in the presence of Hugh Cloptone, the Mayor, Thomas Fitz William, Knt., the Recorder, John Broun, Knt., Hugh Brice, Knt., William Horne, Knt., Robert Tate, William White, William Martyn, John Tate, John Percyvalle, Knt., William Remyngtone, William Isaac, Ralph Tilney, John Broke, Henry Cote, Hugh Pemberton, and William Purches, Aldermen, and very many Commoners summoned to the Guildhall for the election of Sheriffs—William Purches, Alderman and mercer, was elected one of the Sheriffs of the City of London and Middlesex by the Mayor, and William Welbeke

---

[1] Cf. ordinances of 1360 and 1382, 'Cal. Letter-Book G,' pp. 123-4; 'Cal. Letter-Book H,' p. 184 ; 'Liber Albus,' i. 360.

(or Welbeck), Alderman[1] and haberdasher, was elected the other Sheriff by the Commonalty.

The same day William Melborne, "peyntour," was elected Chamberlain of the City ; Thomas Bullesdone, skinner, and Robert Weston, mercer, were elected Wardens of London Bridge ; John Tate and William Remyngtone, Aldermen, Bartholomew Rede, goldsmith, Richard Wither, haberdasher, William Sparke, draper, and William Hert, tailor, Commoners, were elected Auditors of the accounts of the Chamber and Wardens in arrear.

Afterwards, viz., on the eve of St. Michael [29 Sept.], the said Sheriffs were sworn at the Guildhall, and on the morrow of the said Feast were presented, admitted, &c., before the Barons of the Exchequer.

24 July, 7 Henry VII. [A.D. 1492], came the Wardens and other good men of the Mistery of English " Wevers " before the Mayor and Aldermen, and prayed that certain articles might be approved and placed on record, to the following effect :—

Fos. 295-296 b.

Ordinacio dez Englisshe Wevers.

That no member revile or rebuke any of the Bailiffs of the Craft, under penalty of fine and imprisonment.

That every member of the Craft attend on summons at a place prescribed on certain quarter-days and bring in and deliver to the Bailiffs their " lome fermes " for the King's duty,[2] or otherwise agree with the Bailiff for the same, under penalty of forfeiting 3*s.* 4*d.* every quarter, one half to the Chamber and the other to the Craft ; and, further, pay quarterage of 2*d.*, or make agreement, under penalty of 12*d.*

---

[1] Recently elected Alderman of Broad Street Ward, but the date of his election does not appear to be recorded (Beaven).

[2] In 1422 the Woollen-Weavers claimed to have the survey of the work of all weavers by virtue of their paying a certain ferm to the King for every loom. 'Cal. Letter-Book I,' pp. 271-2. When the Weavers were summoned at the *Iter* of 1321 to show by what authority they claimed to have their Guild, they stated (*inter alia*), *quod nullus habeat utensilium de officio inter eos nisi testificetur pro bono et fideli et habeat unde sustinere possit firmam Regis* (' Liber Custumarum,' i. 416).

U

That on the decease of a brother every person in the livery being warned to come to his burial, *Dirige*, and Mass and comes not, without reasonable excuse, shall forfeit 8*d.*

That every person of the livery who disobeys a summons to attend general processions shall forfeit 12*d.*

That the Bailiffs of the Craft and the Wardens of the Guild make search, every six weeks, of all manner of workmanship appertaining to the Craft, as of the "heldes"[1] and "slaies" or "slayes"[2] occupied in the same, and notify any default they find to the workers and owners of the same, so that it be rectified by the time of the next search; and if not rectified, that then the said Bailiffs, by the advice of the said Wardens and of six or eight of the Fellowship who have been Bailiffs, shall impose a fine upon such workers and owners at their discretion.

That the Bailiffs be experienced in the craft, and that one be a woollen weaver and the other a linen weaver, according to ancient ordinance; and that the Wardens of the Craft be elected by the Bailiffs for the time being, with the advice of former Bailiffs.

That every three years the Fellowship shall have a new livery or clothing; that the Bailiffs for the time being, together with six or eight of the Fellowship who have served as Bailiffs, shall buy a whole cloth or more for the livery; and that every one of the livery shall go and fetch of the same a gown cloth at a reasonable price, and, if he like not the cloth, that he take a "scantlon"[3] thereof and pay a fine of 12*d.*, and buy his gown at his pleasure.

That if a Bailiff cause a freeman to be made "of the Chamber" or "of the Charter" for love or favour, he shall pay for the same freeman 6*s.* 8*d.* to the use of the Craft, and a silver

---

[1] Probably identical with "healds," *i.e.*, small cords looped in the middle through which the yarns are drawn and separated. See 'N. E. D.,' *s.v.* 'Heddle.'

[2] Combs "to divide the threads of the warp, and press close the weft." —John James, 'Hist. of Worsted Manufacture in England' (1857), p. 14.

[3] Fr. *échantillon*, a pattern.

spoon of the value of 4*s*., after the old custom and usage of the Craft.[1]

That if any householder of the Craft set on work or " colour any foreyn " as a free journeyman, and present him not within 14 days to the Bailiffs, nor pay the duties for him of old accustomed, viz., a penny a week, the same to lose 6*s*. 8*d*.

That any of the Craft convicted of purloining any manner of yarn, woollen or linen, or other goods, shall forfeit for the first time 13*s*. 4*d*., and for a second offence forfeit his looms to the behoof of the King's ferm.

That no householder of linen weavers take any woollen yarn to weave unless he can work it himself and have " gere " wherewith to work it, under penalty prescribed.

That no man of the Craft take any "chayne"[2] of another man's warping without leave of the Bailiffs.

That the whole Fellowship attend church on the Feast of the Assumption [15 Aug.] to hear Mass and make offering, and that those in the clothing shall attend a Requiem on the morrow for the Brethren and Sisters of the Craft who had " past to godde," under penalty in case of default.

That all of the livery, and householders out of the livery, shall come to the dinner at the place and hour assigned ; and every Bailiff shall pay 16*d*., those in the clothing 12*d*., and every householder out of the clothing 8*d*.

That no Bailiff thenceforth " take no suyte ayenst any persone in the Guildhall of this Citie nor in any other Court of the Kyng with the godes of the said Crafte for myspendyng of the same " without the advice of 12 or 8 persons who have served as Bailiffs, under penalty of £10.

That the Bailiffs bring in their accounts at the time and in the manner prescribed, and that when in office they faithfully levy all fines and penalties, and distrain for the same when necessary.

Petition granted.

---

[1] See note *supra*, p. 274.

[2] Technical term for the longitudinal threads in a woven fabric, otherwise the warp. 'N.E.D.,' *s.v.* 'Chain.'

Fo 296 b.

At a Common Council held on Tuesday, 25 Sept., 8 Henry VII. [A.D. 1492], Robert Harryson admitted by the Mayor and Aldermen to be General Attorney of the Commonalty of the City to answer for the citizens drawn into a plea in the county of Lancaster, he receiving yearly 26s. 8d. out of the Chamber, and a ray gown (*togam stragulatam*) at Christmas of the rank of a gentleman (*ad sect' gen'os'*).

Fo. 297.

Custodia pueror' Henr' Faryngdon.

2 Oct., 8 Henry VII. [A.D. 1492], came William Bailly, Henry Chalender, Robert Levendale, and John Stokes, draper, and entered into bond in the sum of £15 for payment into the Chamber by the said William Bailly of a like sum to the use of John, Hugh, and Cristiana, children of Henry Faryngdon, late fuller, when they come of age or marry.

Fos. 297 b-298 b.

Carta clericor' paroch' London'.

Letters of Privy Seal of King Edward IV. reciting letters patent dated 8 Feb., 27 Henry VI. [A.D. 1448-9], incorporating the Fraternity of Parish Clerks of the City, on condition that they maintained two chantry priests to pray for the good of his soul and others in the Chapel of St. Mary near the Guildhall, a condition which the Fraternity, through poverty, being now unable to fulfil, it is hereby discharged from the maintenance of one of the two priests. Dated at Westminster, 10 July, 15 Edward IV. [A.D. 1475].[1]

Fo. 298 b.

Eleccio Maioris.

Saturday the Feast of Translation of St. Edward [13 Oct.], 8 Henry VII. [A.D. 1492], in the presence of Hugh Cloptone, the Mayor, Thomas Fitz William, Knt., the Recorder, John Broun, Knt., John Warde, William Horne, Knt., William White, John Mathewe, William Martyn, John Tate, William Remyngton, John Percyvale, Knt., William Isaac, John Fenkell, Knt., Henry Cote, John Broke, Hugh Pemberton [Aldermen], William Purches, and William Welbeke, the

---

[1] In 1443 an arrangement had been come to between the Parish Clerks and the civic authorities by which, in return for certain concessions, the Clerks agreed to maintain *one* chantry priest in the Guildhall Chapel ('Cal. Letter-Book K,' pp. 290-1). Henry VI. (we are told) raised the number to two (see Stow, 'Survey,' ed. Kingsford, i. 170, 273-4), but these proved in course of time to be beyond the means of the Fraternity to keep up.

Sheriffs, and an immense Commonalty summoned to the Guild-hall for the election of a Mayor for the year ensuing—William Martyn was elected.

Afterwards, viz., on the Feast of SS. Simon and Jude. [28 Oct.], he was sworn at the Guildhall, and on the morrow was presented, admitted, &c., before the Barons of the Exchequer.

23 Oct., 8 Henry VII. [A.D. 1492], came John Clerke, tailor, John Draiton, grocer, John Wright, tailor, "Cutbert" Richard-son, fuller, and Richard Hogekyns, fuller, and entered into bond in the sum of £30 for payment into the Chamber by the said John Clerke of a like sum to the use of John and Elizabeth, children of David Johnson, late tailor, when they come of age or marry.

Fo. 299.

Custodia pueror' David Johnson cissoris.

20 Nov., 8 Henry VII. [A.D. 1492], came William Fitz William, tailor, John Spryng, fuller, Richard Warham, tailor, and William Fouler, dyer, and entered into bond in the sum of £64 for payment into the Chamber by the said William Fitz William of a like sum to the use of John, son of John Hardy, late tailor, when he comes of age.

Fo. 299 b.

Custod' pueror' [sic] Joh'is Hardy cissoris.

11 Dec., 8 Henry VII. [A.D. 1492], came Dame Elizabeth Hille, widow, Richard Hille, gentleman, John Storke and John Hille, grocers, and entered into bond in the sum of 500 marks for payment into the Chamber by the said Elizabeth of a like sum to the use of Robert, son of Thomas Hille, Knt., late grocer and Alderman of the City,[1] when he comes of age.

Fo. 300.

Custodia Roberti Hille filii Thome Hille militis.

20 Feb., 8 Henry VII. [A.D. 1492-3], came the Wardens and other good men of the Art or Mistery of "Lethersellers" before the Mayor and Aldermen, and prayed that it might be ordained that thenceforth every man and woman of the Craft keeping a "mansion" should be assessed by the Wardens at 12 pence a year for their quarterage, and every member not of the livery at 8 pence, for the relief of the poor and other charges of the Craft, under penalty in case of default.

Fo. 300 b.

Ordinacio de lez lether-sellers.

---

[1] Alderman successively of Cord-wainer and Cheap Wards; knighted 1484 or 1485; ob. 23 Sept., 1485. (Beaven.)

Also that no freeman of the Craft or "occupiyng the ware perteynyng to the same Craft" place such ware in any inns, taverns, alehouses, or other place for sale, but sell it in open shop or in his house or in open standing in a convenient place, under penalty of forfeiture of all such ware.[1]

Their prayer granted.

Fo. 301.

Custodia Henrici Lymnour filii Thome Lymnour.

1 March, 8 Henry VII. [A.D. 1492-3], came Richard Lilbourne, gentleman, John Hede, tailor, Richard Taillour, sherman, John Hyndson, gentleman, and entered into bond in the sum of £70 for payment into the Chamber by the said Richard Lilbourne of a like sum to the use of Henry, son of Thomas Lymnour, late mercer, when he comes of age.

Fo. 301 b.

Custodia Ric'i Turnour filii Ric'i Turnour lynyndraper.

5 March, 8 Henry VII. [A.D. 1492-3], came Robert "Hertishorne," Edward Dronyke (Drouyke?), Thomas Pole, tailors, and Robert Turnour, "peauterer," and entered into bond in the sum of £13 6s. 8d. for the delivery into the Chamber by the said Robert "Hertishorne" of a like sum, together with a ring, 12 silver spoons, a feather bed, and appurtenances, to the use of Richard, son of Richard Turnour, late "lynyndraper," when he comes of age.

Custodia Alic' Gyles filie Laur' Gyles.

12 March, 8 Henry VII. [A.D. 1492-3], came Marion Gyles, widow, John Pasmer, skinner, Thomas Eyre, grocer, and Richard Stutfold, "blaksmyth," and entered into bond in the sum of £73 5s. for payment into the Chamber by the said Marion of a like sum to the use of Alice, daughter of Laurence Gyles, late "berebruer," when she comes of age or marries.

Fo. 302.

Forfait brede.

16 April, 8 Henry VII. [A.D. 1493], ordinance by the Mayor and Aldermen that all bread hawked about the City for sale should be forfeited to the Chamber and be disposed of at the discretion of the Chamberlain, and not by the Sheriffs.

Foreyn Bakers shalle not put to sale brede within the City after xij of the clock upon payn of forfaiture of the same.

Also it was ordained by the same Mayor and Aldermen that no foreign baker should thenceforth put to sale any bread within the City or liberties after the hour of 12 noon, under pain of forfeiting the said bread to the use of the Chamber if taken and presented by an officer of the Chamber; if taken

---

[1] See Black's ' History of the Leathersellers,' p. 122.

and presented by freemen bakers, one half of the forfeiture shall go to the Craft of freemen bakers and the other to the Chamber ; and, further, that all foreign bakers bringing bread to the City in carts shall remove their carts by noon, on penalty of *imprisonment and fine*.[1]

2 July, 8 Henry VII. [A.D. 1493], came Richard Golofer, Richard Feldyng, mercers, George Bulstrode, William Nightyngale, drapers, and Thomas Shenton, grocer, and entered into bond in the sum of £506 11s. 5d. for payment into the Chamber by the said Richard Golofer of a like sum to the use of John, Richard, and Henry, sons of Thomas Bledlowe, late grocer and Alderman,[2] when they come of age or marry.[3]

Fo. 302 b.

*Custodia
pueror' Thome
Bledlowe.*

21 May, 8 Henry VII. [A.D. 1493], came the Wardens and other good men of the Art or Mistery of Skinners and presented a bill or supplication to the Mayor and Aldermen, complaining that journeymen, freemen of the Craft, were unable to obtain work owing to the great influx of strangers and foreign journeymen, and praying that it may be enacted as follows :—

Fo. 303.

*Ordinacio
dez Skynners.*

" That no straunger nor foreyn herafter take upon hym thoccupacion of the said Craft of Skynners nor take nor occupye any house or chaumbre and therin dwelle or sojourne with any persone within the said Citee or liberties aforesaid upon payn of 6s. 8d., the one half therof to the Chamberleyn of London to thuse of the said Citee and that other half to the Felauship of Skynners," and, further, that they be not set on work by freemen.

Their prayer granted.

24 Sept., 9 Henry VII. [A.D. 1493], came the Wardens and other good men of the Art or Mistery of " Berebruers," before the Mayor and Aldermen, and presented a petition to the following effect :—

Fos. 303 b-4.

*Ordinacio dez
Berebruers.*

That two persons submitted to them may be admitted as Wardens of the Fellowship for the ensuing year, and be sworn

---

[1] Cf. *infra*, p. 301.

[2] Alderman of Farringdon Ward Without ; removed to Dowgate ; *ob.* 1478 (Beaven).

[3] 1 July, 10 Henry VII. [A.D. 1495], the above Richard Bledlowe, brother of Thomas [*sic*], recorded in margin as being dead.

in the Court of the Guildhall, called the Mayor's Court, to rule the Craft and see that its ordinances are observed; and that henceforth the Rulers and Governors of the Fellowship before going out of office, calling unto them 6 or 8 honest members, shall choose Rulers and Governors for the following year; that any one so chosen and refusing to take office shall forfeit 40s., one half to go to the Chamber and the other to the use of the Fellowship.

That no one of the Craft send any wheat, malt, or other grain for brewing to the mill to be ground, nor put any hops in the brewing unless it be clean and sweet, under penalty of 20s.

That the said Rulers, with an officer of the Chamber appointed for the purpose, shall search all manner of hops and other grain four times a year or more, and taste[1] and assay all beer, as well as survey all vessels used for beer.

That no member take or "embesille" the vessels belonging to another member, under penalty.

That no member take into his service any one who had been proved by the Fellowship to be an "untrue or a deceyvable servaunt in myscoryng or mystailling" between his master and his customers.

"Also that every persone of the said Feaulisship herafter uppon a lefulle warnyng to hym geven appere at an houre and place to hym assigned by the Rulers and Governors of the same Craft for the tyme beyng to thentent to comon' [*commune*] of and in such causes and nedes as shalle concerne the gode Rule of the said Crafte and the comon' profite of this Citee and none other," under penalty.

That the Rulers and Governors duly report to the Chamberlain the result of every search within 14 days.

---

[1] Officers known as Ale Conners are appointed yearly by the Livery in Common Hall at the present day, and are paid their "ancient salaries" of £40 out of the "City's cash." According to the form of oath ad- ministered to them in the 15th century, they were bound to "make their taste" of ale whenever required by brewer or brewster, in order to ascertain its quality. See 'Cal. Letter-Book D,' pp. 10 n., 201-2.

That they render their accounts to the new Rulers within a month of going out of office.

Their petition granted.

Saturday the Feast of St. Matthew [21 Sept.], 9 Henry VII. [A.D. 1493], in the presence of William Martyn, the Mayor, Thomas Fitz William, Knt., the Recorder, John Broun, Knt., John Warde, William Horne, Knt., Robert Tate, William White, Ralph Astry, John Tate, William Remyngton, John Percivale, Knt., Ralph Tilney, William Capell, Knt., John Broke, Henry Cote, Hugh Pemberton, William Welbeke, and William Purches, Aldermen, and very many Commoners summoned to the Guildhall for the election of Sheriffs—Robert Fabian, draper, was elected one of the Sheriffs of the City of London and Middlesex by the Mayor, and John Wynger, grocer, was elected the other Sheriff by the Commonalty.

Fo. 304 b.

Eleccio Vice com'.

The same day William Milbourne, painter, was elected Chamberlain of the City ; Christopher Eliot, goldsmith, and Simon Harrys, grocer, were elected Wardens of London Bridge ; William Remyngton and John Percivale, Aldermen, William Sparke, draper, William Hert, tailor, Laurence Ailmer, draper, and Richard Nonneley, grocer, Commoners, were elected Auditors of the accounts of the Chamber and Wardens in arrear.

Afterwards, viz., on the eve of St. Michael [29 Sept.], the said Sheriffs were sworn at the Guildhall, and on the morrow of the said Feast were presented, admitted, &c., before the Barons of the Exchequer.

10 Oct., 9 Henry VII. [A.D. 1493], Nicholas Bacheler, draper, discharged by the Mayor and Aldermen from serving on juries, &c., owing to deafness and other infirmities.

Exon'acio Nicholai Bacheler ab assisis.

Sunday the Feast of Translation of St. Edward [13 Oct.], 9 Henry VII. [A.D. 1493], in the presence of William Martyn, the Mayor, Thomas Fitz William the Recorder, John Broun, Knt., John Warde, Hugh Brice, Knt., William Horne, Knt., Robert " Horne " [Tate ?], William White, John Mathewe, Richard Chawry, Ralph Astry, John Tate, William Remyngton,

Eleccio Maioris.

John Percivale, Knt., William Capell, Knt., John Broke, Hugh Pemberton, William " Purche," and William Welbeke, Aldermen, and an immense Commonalty summoned to the Guildhall for the election of a Mayor for the year ensuing—Ralph Astry was elected.

Afterwards, viz., on the Feast of SS. Simon and Jude [28 Oct.], he was sworn and admitted at the Guildhall, and on the morrow was presented, admitted, &c., before the Barons of the Exchequer.

3 Oct., 9 Henry VII. [A.D. 1493], came the Wardens and other good men of the Art or Mistery of Curriours before the Mayor and Aldermen, and presented a petition, showing that

Fos. 305-6.
Ordinacio dez Curriours.

it had been ordained *temp.* Robert Drope, Mayor [A.D. 1474-5], that all tanned leather brought to the City should be brought to the Leadenhall, there to be searched and marked by seven honest persons of the Crafts of " Cordwaners," " Curriours," and " Girdilers," or by three persons of the said Crafts, viz., one of each, which ordinance is enrolled in the Guildhall,[1] and hitherto has been duly observed, but that now foreign " Curriours " dwelling without the City daily buy leather of country tanners insufficiently tanned, " which causeth the same Tanners to embesille and absent theym self from the said Citee and make their marketts without, and for thentent they wille not be serched accordyng to the said acte and ordenaunce they selle there for 20*d.* or 2*s.* better chepe in a dyker of lether than other welle serched and marked is solde and bought within this Citee." They prayed, therefore, that it might be ordained that any one buying or occupying any leather not marked and searched at Leadenhall shall forfeit the same and incur a fine.

Also that no leather that has been searched and marked be given to one dwelling out of the City to " cory " or dress, but only to freemen curriers living within the City and willing to work it at a reasonable price.

---

[1] Probably referring to the ordinance of 1488, when Horne, and not Drope, was Mayor. *Supra,* p. 251.

That the number of apprentices taken by members of the Craft be limited as prescribed, viz., that no one who had been Master or Warden should take more than three apprentices; that no one of the Clothing who had not been Warden should take more than two; and no one out of the livery should take more than one.

That no servant of the Craft leave the City to work in the country so long as he can find work in the City, without licence of the Wardens and of his master.

That the articles ordained *temp.* Sir William Horne, Knt., be amended so far as to impose a penalty upon those guilty of producing bad work, towards defraying the expenses of the Wardens in every search made.

That all members attend upon summons by the Beadle, under penalty of forfeiting a pound of wax or 6 pence for the pound.

Their petition granted.

21 Nov., 9 Henry VII. [A.D. 1493], came Richard Bromale, "joynour," William Rothewelle, Robert Purches, mercers, and John Axe, dyer, and entered into bond in the sum of £125 for payment into the Chamber by the said Richard Bromale of a like sum to the use of Roger, son of John Skyrwith, late leatherseller, when he comes of age.

Fo. 306.

Custodia Rogeri Skyr-with filii Joh'is Skyr-with letherseller.

Letter from William Martyn, Mayor, to the Dean and Chapter of St. Paul's, presenting Thomas Carver, chaplain, for admission to the second of the three chantries founded for the souls of Sir John Pulteney and Sirs William Milforde and John Plessys, Archdeacons of Colchester, vacant by the resignation of Sir Thomas Addyngham. Dated 2 Oct., A.D. 1493.

Fo. 306 b.

Presentacio Thome Carver capellani ad secundam cantariam trium canta-riarum in eccl'ia Sc'i Pauli London' per Joh'em Pulteneymilit' nuper fundat'.

13 Dec., 9 Henry VII. [A.D. 1493], came John Griffith, "wyredrawer," Thomas Davy, tailor, Thomas Eyre, grocer, and William Calberd, grocer, and entered into bond in the sum of £60 for payment into the Chamber by the said John Griffith of a like sum to the use of Robert, Mary, and Johanna,

Custodia pueror' Thome Story pelli-parii.

children of Thomas Story, late skinner, when they come of age or marry.

Fo. 307.

*Custodia
Joh'is Suth-
worth fil'
Rad'i Suth-
worth.*

28 Jan., 9 Henry VII. [A.D. 1493-4], came William Suthworth, Richard Kyng, John Draiton, and Geoffrey Cobbe, grocers, and entered into bond in the sum of £60 for payment into the Chamber by the said William Suthworth of a like sum to the use of John, son of Ralph Suthworth, late grocer, when he comes of age.

Fo. 307 b.

*Custodia
pueror'
Johannis Pace
tallugh-
chaundler.*

The same day came William Wymonde, dyer, Thomas Wymonde, fuller, William Proude, draper, and William Skydmore, mercer, and entered into bond in the sum of £15 for payment into the Chamber by the said William Wymonde of a like sum to the use of Peter, Katherine, and Margaret, children of John Pace, late "tallughchaundeler," when they come of age or marry.

Fo. 308.

*Custodia
Will'i filii
Henrici
Nevile
iremonger.*

20 Feb , 9 Henry VII. [A.D. 1493-4], came John Nicholas, tailor, William Huntyngfeld, fuller, John Welforde, cordwainer, and Roland Byrde, "iremonger," and entered into bond in the sum of £5 for payment into the Chamber by the said John Nicholas of a like sum to the use of William, son of Henry Nevile, late "iremonger," when he comes of age.

Fo. 308 b.

*Confirmacio
Thome
Butside et
Henrici
Wodcok
Secundar'
in* [sic].

18 Feb., 9 Henry VII. [A.D. 1493-4], ordinance by Ralph Astry, Knt., the Mayor, Thomas Fitz William, Knt., the Recorder, John Broun, John Warde, Hugh Brice, Knt., William Horne, Knt., Robert Tate, William White, John Mathewe, William Martyn, Knt., John Tate, John Percyvale, Knt., John Fenkell, Knt., William Remyngton, William Isaac, Ralph Tilney, William Capell, Knt., John Broke, Henry Cote, Hugh Pemberton, William Welbeke, and William Purches, Aldermen, sitting in full Court in the Inner Chamber of the Guildhall, that Thomas Butside[1] and Henry Wodecok, the Secondaries in the two Compters[2] of the City, shall thenceforth remain in office under the authority of the Court of Mayor and Aldermen during good behaviour, and shall not be removed therefrom

---

[1] Elected Coroner of the City in 1485. *Vide supra*, p. 229.

[2] Situate, one in the Poultry and the other in Bread Street (later, in Wood Street).

except by authority of the said Court, and then only for reasonable cause.[1]

6 March, 9 Henry VII. [A.D. 1493-4], came William "Wystowe," John Auncell, Richard Aubrey, John Haryngton, haberdashers, and William Lilly, "brouderer," and entered into bond in the sum of £40 for payment into the Chamber by the said William "Wistowe" of a like sum to the use of John, Robert, and Johanna, children of John Hertyngton, late saddler, when they come of age or marry.[2]

Fo. 309.

Custodia
pueror' Joh'is
Hertyngton
sellar'
London'.

Letter from Ralph Astry, the Mayor, to the Dean and Chapter of St. Paul's, presenting Nicholas Wyllys, chaplain, for admission to the second of the three chantries founded in that church for the souls of Sir John Pulteney, Knt., and Sirs William Milford and John Plesseys, Archdeacons of Colchester, vacant by the death of Thomas Carver. Dated 23 June, A.D. 1494.

Fo. 309 b.

Presentacio
Nich'i Wyllys
ad secundam
cantar' trium
cantar' in
eccl'ia Sc̄i
Pauli
London'.

25 June, 9 Henry VII. [A.D. 1494], came the Wardens and other good men of the Art or Mistery of Whitebakers, and prayed that a certain penalty might be imposed on foreign bakers who failed to remove their carts by a certain hour as prescribed *temp.* Sir William Martyn, Mayor, " as there is none other payn assessed nor lymyted but only the forfaiture " (of the bread).[3] They further prayed that their Wardens might have the search and oversight, under the Mayor for the time being, of the assize of all foreign bread brought into the City for sale,

Ordinacio des
Whitebakers.

---

[1] In 1441 the Common Council had ordained that thenceforth Under-Sheriffs (the nature of whose office was akin to that of the Secondaries) should not be removable, but remain in office during good behaviour, the reason assigned for this change being that frequent removals caused great expense and inconvenience. See ' Cal. Letter-Book K,' p. 257. See also ordinance of 1486, *supra*, pp. 235, 236.

[2] Margin. 10 Dec., 22 Henry VII. [A.D. 1506], came John Blakwood, " merchant haberdasher," who married the above Johanna, and acknowledged satisfaction for his wife's patrimony.

[3] The ordinance *temp.* Martyn, Mayor, as recorded *supra*, p. 295, will be seen, however, to have expressly imposed a penalty of *imprisonment* and *fine* on such defaulters, whereas the penalty for selling bread at unlawful hours was *forfeiture*.

inasmuch as foreign bakers brought and sold bread made of evil and unwholesome paste, and passed it off as bread made by the petitioners.

Their prayer granted.

15 July, 9 Henry VII. [A.D. 1494], came Agnes Austeyn, widow, Henry Somer, haberdasher, John Austeyn, fishmonger, and Thomas Turke, fishmonger, and entered into bond in the sum of £80 for payment into the Chamber by the said Agnes of a like sum to the use of Johanna and Katherine, daughters of John Austeyn, late fishmonger, when they come of age or marry.

20 July, 9 Henry VII. [A.D. 1494], came the Wardens and good men of the Art or Mistery of Tailors before the Mayor and Aldermen, and complained that freemen journeymen of the Craft were unable to obtain work owing to the influx of "persones aswelle aliaunt' straungiers as Foreyns journeymen"; and further, that a great number of strangers "botchers" infested the City, each keeping daily in his house three or four strangers occupying the same handicraft, to the great prejudice of the King's liege subjects, who would gladly undertake the work if the strangers were not there; and this contrary to the statute of Richard III. passed in restraint of strangers.[1]

They pray therefore "that it may be enacted and entred of Recorde......as is entred for the Crafte of Skynners[2] that no straunger nor foreyn herafter takyng upon hym the said occupacion of Taillours take nor occupie any house shop or Chamber and therin dwell or sojourne w^t any persone within the said Citee or libertie of the same upon payn to forfait at every default 6s. 8d. the one half therof to the Chamberleyn of London to thuse of the said Citee and the other half therof to the said Feaulisship of taillours."

Also that no one occupying the Craft employ any journeyman unless he be a freeman of the City.

Their prayer granted.

[1] Stat. 1 Ric. III. cap. ix. [A.D. 1484].

[2] *Supra*, p. 295.

Sunday the Feast of St. Matthew [21 Sept.], 10 Henry VII.
[A.D. 1494], in the presence of Ralph Astry, Knt., the Mayor,
Thomas Fitz William, Knt., the Recorder, John Broun, Knt.,
John Warde, Hugh Brice, Knt., William Horne, Knt., Robert
Tate, William White, William Martyn, Knt., Richard Chawry,
John Tate, John Percyvale, Knt., William Remyngton, John [sic]
Isaac, John Broke, Hugh Pemberton, William Purches, William
Welbeke [Aldermen], and both Sheriffs, and very many Com-
moners summoned to the Guildhall for the election of Sheriffs—
Nicholas Alwyn, mercer, was elected one of the Sheriffs of
the City of London and Middlesex by the Mayor, and John
Warner, senior, armourer, was elected the other Sheriff by the
Commonalty.

William Milbourne, citizen and painter, was elected City
Chamberlain for the year ensuing; Christopher Elyot, gold-
smith, and Simon Harrys, grocer, were elected Wardens of
London Bridge; John Percivale, Knt., and John Fenkell,
Aldermen, Laurence Ailmer, draper, Richard Noneley, grocer,
Nicholas Mattok, fishmonger, and Nicholas Nynnys, tailor,
Commoners, were elected Auditors of the accounts of the
Chamber and Wardens in arrear.

Afterwards, viz., on the eve of St. Michael [29 Sept.], the
said Sheriffs were sworn at the Guildhall, and on the morrow
of the said Feast were presented, admitted, &c., before the
Barons of the Exchequer.

Letter from Ralph Astry, Knt., the Mayor, and Thomas
Fitz William, Knt., the Recorder, to Richard [Hill], the Bishop
of London, presenting Richard Upton, chaplain, for admission
to the chantry founded at the altar of SS. Katherine and
Margaret in the church of St. Swithun for the soul of Roger
Depeham, vacant by the resignation of Sir Edward Champflour,
the last chaplain. Dated under the seals of the Mayoralty
and of the Recorder......Henry VII. ......

9 Oct., 10 Henry VII. [A.D. 1494], came Nicholas Alwyn, John
Picton, mercers, William Heryot, draper, and John Mille,
mercer, and entered into bond in the sum of £590 and 7¼d.
for payment into the Chamber by the said Nicholas of a like

sum to the use of Richard and Johanna, children of Henry "Cantlow," late mercer, when they come of age or marry.[1]

Fo. 312.

Eleccio Maioris.

Monday the Feast of Translation of St. Edward [13 Oct.], 10 Henry VII. [A.D. 1494], in the presence of Ralph Astry, Knt., the Mayor, Thomas Fitz William, Knt., the Recorder, John Warde, Hugh Brice, Knt., William Horn, Knt., Robert Tate, William White, John Mathewe, Hugh Cloptone, William Martyn, Knt., Richard Chawry, William Remyngton, John Percyvale, Knt., William Isaac, John Fenkell, Knt., Ralph Tilney, William Capell, Knt., John Broke, Henry Cote, Hugh Pemberton, William Purchas, William Welbeke [Aldermen], and both Sheriffs, and also an immense Commonalty summoned to the Guildhall for the election of a Mayor—Richard Chawry was elected for the year ensuing.

Afterwards, viz., on the Feast of SS. Simon and Jude [28 Oct.], he was sworn at the Guildhall, and on the morrow was pre_ sented, admitted, &c., before the Barons of the Exchequer.

Custodia Elisabeth' Eryke filie Ricℹ Eryke upholder.

22 Jan., 10 Henry VII. [A.D. 1494-5], came Robert Cryket, William Copynger, Nicholas Mattoke, and William Barde, fishmongers, and entered into bond in the sum of £105 6s. 8d. for payment into the Chamber by the said Robert Cryket of a like sum to the use of Elizabeth, daughter of Richard Eryke, late upholder, when she comes of age or marries.[2]

Fo. 312 b.

Exon'acio Thome Barnard pellip' ab assisis etc.

Mandamus to the Mayor and Sheriffs for the discharge of Thomas Barnard, skinner, from serving on juries, &c., if he be over 70 years of age. Witness the King at Westminster, 16 Feb., 10 Henry VII. [A.D. 1494-5].

Fo. 313.

Exon'acio Joh'is Jenyns Whitebaker.

Similar mandamus for the discharge of John Jenyns, whitebaker. Witness the King at Westminster, 14 Feb., 10 Henry VII. [A.D. 1494-5].

---

[1] Margin. 13 July, 12 Henry VII. [A.D. 1497], came Oliver Wood, who married the above Johanna, and acknowledged satisfaction for his wife's patrimony.

[2] Margin. 30 March, 15 Hen. VII. [A.D. 1500], came Robert Creket, junior, who married the above Elizabeth, and acknowledged satisfaction for his wife's patrimony.

19 March, 10 Henry VII. [A.D. 1494-5], came Thomas Bradbury, George Bradbury, mercers, Christopher Elyot, goldsmith,
and Richard Thornell, mercer, and entered into bond in the
sum of £362 14s. 5d. for payment into the Chamber by the
said Thomas Bradbury of a like sum to the use of John, James,
Elizabeth, and Dionisia, children of Thomas Bodley, late tailor,
when they come of age or marry.

*Custodia
pueror' Thome
Bodley Cis-
soris.*

The same day came Edward Waren, "tallughchaundler,"
Richard Dean, skinner, Thomas Piers and John Brown,
tallow-chandlers, and entered into bond in the sum of £40 for
payment into the Chamber by the said Edward Waren of a
like sum to the use of Thomas and Margaret, children of
Richard Morley, late tallow-chandler, when they come of
age or marry.[1]

Fo. 313 b.

*Custodia
pueror' Ric'i
Morley.*

16 July, 10 Henry VII. [A.D. 1495], came Margaret Reynolde,
widow, John Broun and Christopher Hawe, mercers, and
Bartholomew Rede, goldsmith, and entered into bond in the
sum of 500 marks for payment into the Chamber by the said
Margaret of a like sum to the use of Elena, Johanna, Richard,
Margaret, Ralph, and Mary, children of John Reynolde, late
mercer, when they come of age or marry.[2]

Fo. 314.

*Custodia
pueror' Joh'is
Reynolde......
merceri.*

6 Aug., 10 Henry VII. [A.D. 1495], came the Wardens and
other good men of the Art or Mistery of White Bakers before
the Mayor and Aldermen, and complained that whereas certain
places had been assigned to foreign bakers for the sale of bread
anno 15 Henry VI., as recorded in the " boke of K,"[3] and it had
been ordained that bread of Stratford should not be hawked in

Fo. 314 b.

*Ordinacio
dez White
Bakers.*

---

[1] Margin. On the 17th May,
14 Henry VII. [A.D. 1499], came
Thomas Lauryman (Lamyman ?),
cutler, who married the above Margaret, and acknowledged satisfaction
for his wife's patrimony.

[2] Margin. 30 Aug., 18 Henry VII.
[A.D. 1502], came Nicholas Lambert,
who married the above Johanna, and
William Jones, mercer, who married

the above Elena; on the 19th Oct.,
24 Henry VII. [A.D. 1508], came
Richard Long, mercer, who married
the above Margaret ; and on the
18th July, 23 Henry VII. [A.D. 1508],
came Thomas Powell, who married
the above Mary, and acknowledged
satisfaction for the patrimony of their
respective wives.

[3] See ' Cal. Letter-Book K,' p. 45.

X

the streets, and that the carts of foreign bakers should be removed from their standing by noon, under penalty[1]—it was now the custom for foreign bakers of Stratford to bring with them certain spare horses besides their cart horses to carry and hawk their bread in every part of the City, to the great prejudice of the Fellowship of White Bakers of the City. It had been proved, moreover, that such bread was lacking in weight and " unsesonable of past," to the great deceit of the King's people. They pray therefore that it may be decreed that thenceforth no foreign baker of Stratford shall bring any spare horse into the City for the purpose aforesaid.

Their prayer granted.

Fo. 315.
Ordinacio Barbitonsor'.

6 Aug., 10 Henry VII. [A.D. 1495], came the Wardens and other good men of the Art or Mistery of Barber-Surgeons (*Barbitonsorum Sirurgic'*) before the Mayor, and prayed that the following article might be approved and recorded :—

" Also if any persone of the said Crafte be duely warned and somoned to come to the burying of any other persone of the same Crafte and cometh not to the place to hym appoynted within thour lymyted at his said Somons, every suche persone without a lawfull and a reasonable [excuse] shalle pay at every tyme that he so failleth iij*s*. iiij*d*. the one half therof to thuse of the Chaumber of the said Citee and the other half to thalmes of the said Craft &c."

Their prayer granted.

Fo. 315 b.
Ordinacio dez Brouderers.

2 Sept., 11 Henry VII. [A.D. 1495], came good men of the Art or Mistery of " Brouderers " before the Mayor and Aldermen, and presented a petition to the following effect :—

That in order to avoid certain " inconveniences " that had arisen in the Craft, " and to thentent also that the ornamentes of Goddes Churche and all other thynges made in the said Crafte myght be truely wrought, and the Crafte duely ordred and so contynued," they would ordain that thenceforth all persons using the Craft within the City and suburbs who shall " wyrke any maner of broudered werke as floures ymages or

---

[1] *Vide supra*, pp. 294, 301.

orfrays to be sette uppon velwet satyne and damaske shall
make the same floures ymages or orfraies of fyne gold fyne
silver and right silke and of none other stuff countrefeit and the
same wirke shall sette with right silke upon payn of xl*s.* for
every pece of werke so made to the contrary."

"Also that almaner persones usyng the said Crafte as is
aforseid shall sette no maner coper Golde lukes[1] golde or other
countrefeit gold or stuff but only upon satyn of bruges[2] Sarcenet[3]
tarteron[4] Worsted tewke[5] Fustian, taffata[6] bustean[7] and Chamlet[8]
and not uppon Right velvet right satyne nor damaske upon
peyne of all suche werk to be putt to fyre and brent or elles to
be yeven to poure Churches or Chapelles after your discrecion
And over this it wolde please you for execucion of the premisses
to graunt unto the Wardeyns of the saide Crafte of Brouderers
and to their successors associat jointly to gider with theym ij
mercers expert in the said Crafte the same mercers to be
assigned by the Wardeyns of the Crafte of the mercery for the
tyme beyng and with a Serjaunt of the Chambre power and
auctorite at all convenient seasons when they shalle thynke
expedient for to serche and oversee all maner broudred werke
aswell within the Citee as the Suberbes of the same and alle
suche werke as they shall finde unsufficient and made of
deceyvable stuff or wrought contrary to the ordenaunce above
expressed to take and present to your said Chambre there to be
discussed as the value therof requireth and accordyng the
Importaunce of this your Acte Also to ordeigne enacte and
establisshe that all Copes vestmentes and tunecles made within
this Citee kepe their fulle Shappe in leynth and brede after a
lawfull assise of olde accustumed upon peyne of xx*s.* for every
Cope Vestment and tunecle made to the Contrary "—one half

---

[1] Gold of Lucca ?

[2] Bruges.

[3] Or sarsnet, a stuff of silk, so called from having been first made by Saracens, probably in Spain.

[4] Tartaryn, a costly mediæval stuff, the character of which cannot now be traced.

[5] A kind of buckram.

[6] Or taffety, a light silk stuff.

[7] Bustian, a kind of fustian (Drapers' Dict.).

[8] Possibly a material made of camel's hair.

thereof to be to the use of the Chamber, and the other half
to go equally to the boxes of the Crafts of Mercers and
" Brouderers."

" A Cope to holde in leyngth vij quarters of a yerde kepyng
his compas rounde about."

" A cheseble to holde in leingth a yerde and half and in
brede a yerde and a quarter."

" A tunecle to holde in leyngth a yerde and a quarter and in
brede a quarter."

Also that no freeman of the City occupying " broudery " set
any foreign " brouderer " to work except with the approval of
the Wardens of " Brouderers " for the time being, under penalty.

Their petition granted.

Fo. 316.   16 Sept., 11 Henry VII. [A.D. 1495], came the Wardens and
Ordinacio dez other good men of the Art or Mistery of Bakers before the
Bakers London'. Mayor, and presented a petition praying :—

That no foreign cart of Stratford bringing bread to the City
for sale be allowed to stand elsewhere than in the places accustomed,[1] nor bread be sold after noon, under penalty.

That no foreign baker of Stratford carry bread on horse
or man's back to houses unless the bread has been sold at
the markets and in market time.[2]

Petition granted.

Fo. 316 b.   Monday the Feast of St. Matthew [21 Sept.], 11 Henry VII.
Eleccio Vic'. [A.D. 1495], in the presence of Richard Chawry, Mayor, Robert
Sheffelde the Recorder,[3] John Broune, Knt., John Warde,
Hugh Brice, Knt., Henry Colet, Knt., Robert Tate, William
White, William Martyn, Knt., John Tate, William Remyngton,
John Percyvale, Knt., John Fenkell, Knt., William Isaac, Ralph
Tilney, Henry Cote, Hugh Pemberton, William Purches,
William Welbecke [Aldermen], and both Sheriffs, and very many

---

[1] See ' Cal. Letter-Book K,' p. 45.
Also *supra*, p. 294.
[2] Cf. *supra*, p. 306.

[3] His appointment not recorded.
M.P. for the City in the Parliaments
of 1497 and 1504 (Beaven).

Commoners summoned to the Guildhall for the election of Sheriffs—Thomas Kneseworth, fishmonger, was elected one of the Sheriffs of the City of London and Middlesex by the Mayor, and Henry Somer, haberdasher, was elected the other Sheriff by the Commonalty; William Milborne, painter, was elected City Chamberlain for the year ensuing; Simon Harrys, grocer, and Christopher Elyot, goldsmith, were elected Wardens of London Bridge; John Fenkell, Knt., William Capell, Aldermen, Nicholas Mattok, fishmonger, Nicholas Ninnys, tailor, William Stede, grocer, and Thomas Creme, draper, Commoners, were elected Auditors of the accounts of the Chamber and of the Wardens in arrear.

Afterwards, viz., on the eve of St. Michael [29 Sept.], the said Sheriffs were sworn at the Guildhall, and on the morrow of the said Feast were presented, admitted, &c., before the Barons of the Exchequer.

Tuesday the Feast of Translation of St. Edward [13 Oct.], 11 Henry VII. [A.D. 1495], in the presence of Richard Chawry, Mayor, Robert Sheffeld the Recorder, John Broun, Knt., John Warde, Hugh Brice, Knt., Henry Colet, Knt., William Horn, Knt., Robert Tate, William White, John Mathewe, Hugh Cloptone, William Martyn, Knt., William Remyngton, John Percyvale, Knt., John Tate, William Isaac, Ralph Tilney, John Fenkell, Knt., John Broke, Henry Cote, Hugh Pemberton, William Purches, and William Welbeke, Aldermen, and an immense Commonalty summoned to the Guildhall for the election of a Mayor—Henry Colet, Knt., was elected.

Fo. 317.

Eleccio Maioris London'.

Afterwards, viz., on the Feast of SS. Simon and Jude [28 Oct.], he was sworn and admitted at the Guildhall, and on the morrow was presented, admitted, &c., before the Barons of the Exchequer.

Writ to all Justices, Sheriffs, Escheators, Bailiffs, &c., forbidding the exaction of toll from tenants, &c., of lands and fiefs belonging to the Prior and Convent of Christchurch, Canterbury. Witness the King at Westminster, 8 Nov., 11 Henry VII. [A.D. 1495].

Carta tenenc' Archi'pi Cantuar' etc.

Fo. 317 b.

*A graunt made
to Robert Gode-
yere mercer of
the offic' of
Pakkershipe
and Gawger-
shippe of the
Citee of
London.*

Grant by a Court of Aldermen held 21 Nov., 11 Henry VII.
[A.D. 1495]—there being present Sir Henry Colet, Knt., the
Mayor, Hugh Brice, Knt., William Horne, Knt., Robert Tate,
William White, Hugh Cloptone, William Martyn, Knt., John
Percivale, Knt., William Isaac, Ralph Tilney, John Broke,
Hugh Pemberton, William Purches, William Welbeke, and
Robert Fabian, Aldermen, in the Inner Chamber of the
Guildhall—to Robert Godeyere, mercer, of the reversion of the
offices of " Pakkership " and "Gawger Shippe "[1] for a term of
21 years after the expiration of a similar term for which the
said offices had formerly been granted to Robert Fitz Her-
bert, draper, and John Fitz Herbert, gentleman.

Fos. 318-
319 b.

*Ordinacio dez
Pastelers etc.*

15 Dec., 11 Henry VII. [A.D. 1495], came the Wardens and
other good men of the Art or Mistery of Pastelers of the City
before the Mayor and Aldermen, and complained that whereas
in time past they had been " of power to have a company of
theym. self in one clothing " and been able to bear the City's
charges, they had now fallen into such poverty, owing to their
being deprived of their living by vintners, brewers, innholders,
and tipplers, that they could no longer appear in one clothing,
nor were able to bear the City's charges, unless speedy remedy
be applied. They prayed therefore that certain articles might
be approved and enrolled, to the following effect :—

That every brother of the Fellowship attend an appointed
church on the Feast of Exaltation of Holy Cross [14 Sept.]
to hear Mass, and make offering of one penny, a brother's
attendance being excused for reasonable cause, but *not* the
offering of a penny. That he also attend on the following
morning to hear a *Requiem* for the souls of all deceased
members.

That every brother, on due warning, attend funerals,
obits, &c., of Brethren and " Sistern " of the Fellowship.

---

[1] The offices of packing all manner
of merchandise and of gauging wine-
vessels (to see if they contained law-
ful measure) were granted (*inter alia*) to the Mayor and Commonalty in
1478 by King Edward IV. for a
sum of £7,000.

That disputes be submitted to the Wardens before action be taken at law.

That the Wardens have authority to search and oversee all manner of dressed victuals in open shops, to see if they be wholesome and also "whether the penyworthes therof be reasonable for the comon wele of the Kynges liege people or not."

That all persons that seethe, roast, or bake victuals for sale in the City pay henceforth such quarterage to the Wardens as freemen had been accustomed to pay in support of the Craft.

That no one thenceforth send any victuals ready dressed about the streets or lanes to be sold, under penalty of forfeiture of the same to the use of poor prisoners in Ludgate and Newgate and fine.

"That no persone nor persones enfraunchised in the said Crafte of Pastelers from hensforth shalle take uppon hym or theym to make any grete Festes......as the Serjauntes Fest the Maires Fest the Shireffes Fest and the Taillours Fest without thadvice of the Wardeyns......to thentent that the Fests of everiche of theym shalbe welle and worshipfully dressed for thonoure of this Citee and also for thonour and proffite of the persones that shalle bere the charges therof," under penalty prescribed.

"That whate persone or persones of the same Crafte that hereafter shall serve the Maire......for the tyme beyng or any of the Shireffes......for the yere of Mairaltie or Shervalte as their householde Coke or Cokes shalle neither in his own propre persone nor by any his servaunt or servauntes by Colour Crafte or otherwise that yere dresse or do to be dressed any Festes brekfastes dyners or Sopers for any Weddynges obites Craftes or otherwise out of the Maire or Sherriffes houses without suche Fest brekefast dyner or Souper be made at the cost and charge of the said Maire and Sherreffes for the tyme beyng to thentent that every man of the same Feaulisshippe may have a competent livyng," under penalty prescribed.

"That from hensforth there shalbe but one shoppe occupied on the Sonday of the said Crafte in Bredestrete and one in Briggestrete to hentent that your Suppliauntes the gode Folkes of the same Craft may serve Godde the better on the Sonday as trew Cristen men shuld do ; and the ij shoppes to be opened by thadvice of the Wardeyns for the tyme beyng that is for to sey one shoppe to be occupied on the Sonday in the one strete and an other shoppe in the other strete and an other persone to occupie and open a shoppe on the next Sonday in the one strete and an other in þe other strete and so alwey one to occupie after an other," under penalty prescribed.

That "if any persone or persones enfraunchised in the said Crafte hereafter make any bill or billes of fare and proporcion for any Fest dyner or Souper by the desire of any persone or persones or elles make covenaunt with any to dresse such Fest dyner or Souper that then none other of the same Craft shall put any suche persone or persones from the makyng and dressyng of the said Fest dyner or Souper," under penalty of 20s.

That every one enfraunchised in the Craft "that herafter shalbe commaunded by the Wardeyns......to bere the Corce of any brother or sister of the same Crafte to burying shall bere the same Corce or Corces to the Churche and to burying without any resistence grudge or geyneseyng of any persone or persones so commaunded upon peyn of iijs. iiijd."

That " if any foreyn or straunger take upon hym to make or dresse any Fest dyner or Souper within the same Citee or liberties therof that thanne it shalbe lefull to the Wardeyns for the tyme beyng with a Serjaunt of the Maires to theym assigned to attache take and arrest any such Foreyn or straunger so makyng any Fest dyner or Souper and to bryng the same Foreyn or straunger to prison and to bide the punysshement of the Maire and Aldermen for the tyme beyng and over that to forfeite at every tyme so doyng 10s. to be divided in maner and forme abovesaid."

That every brother of ability and power shall pay for his quarterage yearly for the priest and clerks and his dinner 4s.

That no freeman of the Craft slander or revile another, under penalty.

That any brother making unreasonable complaint to the Wardens shall forfeit 20 pence.

That no one of the Craft shall from henceforth "make or do to be made upon one day more than ij dyners and one Souper," under penalty of 6s. 8d.

Petition granted.

Writ to the Mayor and Sheriffs to discharge Roger Grove, netmaker, from serving on juries, &c., if he be proved to be over 70 years of age. Witness the King at Westminster, 4 Feb., 11 Henry VII. [A.D. 1495–6].

Fo. 320.
Exon'acio Rogeri Grove ab assisis.

6 Feb., same year, the above Roger Grove discharged accordingly.

Similar writ to the Mayor, Aldermen, and Sheriffs for the discharge of John Gyva, "iremonger," on account of infirmity. Witness the King at Westminster, 28 Jan., 11 Henry VII. [A.D. 1495–6].

Exon'acio Joh'is Gyva ab assisis.

Similar writ to the Mayor and Sheriffs for the discharge of John Taillour if he be found to be over 70 years of age. Witness the King at Westminster, 12 Jan., 11 Henry VII. [A.D. 1495–6].

Exoneracio Joh'is Taillour ab assisis.

5 Feb., same year, the above John Taillour discharged accordingly.

Charter of incorporation of the Cooks of the City. Dated 11 July, 22 Edward IV. [A.D. 1482].[1]

Fo. 320 b.
Carta Cocor' London'.

Writ to the Mayor, Aldermen, and Sheriffs for the discharge of John Burgh, "plomer," from serving on juries, &c., owing to infirmity. Witness the King at Westminster, 4 Feb., 11 Henry VII. [A.D. 1495–6].

Fo. 321.
Exon'acio Joh'is Burgh ab assisis.

The above John Burgh discharged accordingly.

9 Feb., 11 Henry VII. [A.D. 1495-6], came Johanna Bodley, widow, Thomas Warde, mercer, William Butler and William Prat, grocers, and entered into bond in the sum of £100 for

Fo. 321 b.
Custodia pueror' Ric'i Bodley groceri.

---

[1] In the return made by the Company to the Commission of 1884, it is stated that "by an inspeximus charter of George III. it appears that King Edward IV., in the 27th [sic] of his reign," granted the Cooks a charter of incorporation.

payment into the Chamber by the said Johanna of a like sum to the use of "Elias," Elena, and John, children of Richard Bodley, late grocer, when they come of age or marry.[1]

Fo. 322.
Ordinacio dez Curriours.
Petition by John Cordell, John Salter, Richard Colman, Robert Wittam, William Foster, William Ederiche, Thomas Hurloke, William Goldyng, Hugh Filcok, William Olyver, Thomas Maylard, William Cobley, John Johnson, John Turtill, Thomas Maynard, Thomas Crocroft, William Wodelef, Thomas Juster, and Thomas Norres, with other freemen of the Craft of "Curriours," complaining of an ordinance made in the Mayoralty of William Martyn which allowed them (not being in the clothing) to have only one apprentice,[2] and which, if allowed to stand, would compel them and others to leave the City, and praying that it may be enacted that thenceforth they may take three apprentices.

Thereupon it was agreed by the Mayor and Aldermen that every freeman of the Craft might take two apprentices if he could afford to do so. [No date.][3]

Fo. 322 b.
Exon'acio Simonis Hogan ab assisis.
Writ to the Mayor, Aldermen, and Sheriffs for the discharge of Simon Hogan from serving on juries, &c., if he be found to be over 70 years of age. Witness the King at Westminster, 26 Jan., 11 Henry VII. [A.D. 1495-6].

Discharged accordingly.

Exon'acio Joh'is Samay ab assisis.
Similar writ to the Mayor and Sheriffs for the discharge of John Samay *alias* Parker, "foundour." Witness the King at Westminster, 10 March, 11 Henry VII. [A.D. 1495-6].

Discharged accordingly.

Exon'acio Will'i Johnson ab assisis.
Similar writ to the Mayor and Sheriffs for the discharge of William Johnson, fuller. Witness the King at Westminster, 28 Jan., 11 Henry VII. [A.D. 1495-6].

Discharged accordingly.

---

[1] Margin. 13 Jan., 23 Henry VII. [A.D. 1507-8], came the above "Elias" and acknowledged satisfaction for his patrimony, and for money accruing to him by the death of John his brother; and the same day came William Copland, merchant tailor, who married the above Elena, and acknowledged satisfaction for his wife's property.

[2] *Supra*, p. 299.

[3] The concluding paragraph has been inaccurately recorded, but the sense is clear.

Similar writ to the Mayor and Sheriffs for the discharge of John Sponer, "foundour." Witness the King at Westminster, 9 Feb., 11 Henry VII. [A.D. 1495-6].

Discharged accordingly.

Similar writ to the Mayor and Sheriffs for the discharge of William Hamlyn, "tallughchaundler." Witness the King at Westminster, 20 Feb., 11 Henry VII. [A.D. 1495-6].

[Discharge not recorded.]

3 March, 11 Henry VII. [A.D. 1495-6], came John Calson, "taillour," John Betonson, draper, John a Kychen, "taillour," and Richard Frier, "taillour," and entered into bond in the sum of £60 for payment into the Chamber by the said John Calson of a like sum to the use of Richard, Elizabeth, and Alice, children of Richard Dakers, late tailor, when they come of age or marry.[1]

3 March, 11 Henry VII. [A.D. 1495-6], came Richard Holmes, "Fletcher," Benjamin Digby, mercer, John Baynard, goldsmith, and Robert Howdale, goldsmith, and entered into bond in the sum of £25 9s. 9½d. for payment into the Chamber by the said Richard Holmes of a like sum to the use of John and Agnes, children of Robert Holmeby, late "Fletcher," when they come of age or marry.

14 May, 11 Henry VII. [A.D. 1496], came William Lambert, Richard Feldyng, Robert Grene, and Hugh Cloptone, junior, and entered into bond in the sum of £49 9s. 11d. for payment into the Chamber by the said William Lambert of a like sum to the use of William and Agnes, children of William "Tenacres," late mercer, when they come of age or marry.[2]

Fo. 324.
Custodia pue-
ror' Will'i
"Ten-
akres".......
merceri.

[1] Margin. 7 Feb., 18 Henry VII. [A.D. 1502-3], came Stephen Alounde, fuller, who married Alice, and acknowledged satisfaction for his wife's patrimony ; and on the following 17th July further acknowledged satisfaction for money accruing to her by the death of the above Elizabeth her sister.

[2] Margin. 13 Feb., 20 Henry VII. [A.D. 1504-5], came William Dauncy, mercer, who married the above Agnes, and acknowledged satisfaction for his wife's patrimony, as well as for money accruing to her by the death of William her brother.

Fo. 324 b.

Custodia Joh'is filii Thome Nicolson dyer.

17 May, 11 Henry VII. [A.D. 1496], came John Cutte, fishmonger, John Bracebrig, draper, Henry Ivy, sherman, and John Baskervile, tailor, and entered into bond in the sum of £150 for payment into the Chamber by the said John Cutte of a like sum to the use of John, son of Thomas Nicolson, late dyer, when he comes of age.

Fo. 325.

Presentacio Will'i Crane capell'i ad eccl'iam S'ce Margarete "Patens."

Letter from Henry Colet, Knt., the Mayor, to Master Thomas Jean, Doctor of Laws, Canon Residentiary in the Church of St. Paul and Vicar General, the Bishopric of London being vacant,[1] presenting William Crane, chaplain, for admission to the incumbency of the parish church of St. Margaret "Patyns," vacant by the death of Thomas Houghton, the last Rector.[2] Dated 20 May, 11 Henry VII. [A.D. 1496.]

Recogn' xvj libr' per Thomam Bowyer fact' Cam'ar' ad usum Joh'is Bodnam.

17 May, 11 Henry VII. [A.D. 1496], came Thomas Bowyer, draper, and entered into bond in the sum of £16 for payment into the Chamber by the said Thomas Bowyer of a like sum, by instalments as prescribed, to the use of John Bodnam.

Fo. 325 b.

Custodia pueror' Joh'is Uttersall Stacioner.

21 June, 11 Henry VII. [A.D. 1496], came William Johnson, alias Rippon, "bocher," John Wilson, "peauterer," John Maidenwell, "brouderer," and William Hexstall, grocer, and entered into bond in the sum of £26 15s. 4d. for payment into the Chamber by the said William Johnson of a like sum to the use of Margery, Agnes, and Katherine, children of John Uttersall, late "stacioner," when they come of age or marry.

Fo. 326.

Custodia Reginaldi Nicolson filii Thome Nicolson tinctoris.

22 June, 11 Henry VII. [A.D. 1496], came Ralph Bukberd, tailor, John Hert, "gentilman," Thomas Waren, fuller, and Richard Hodgekyns, sherman, and entered into bond in the sum of £150 for payment into the Chamber by the said Ralph Bukberd of a like sum to the use of Reginald, son of Thomas Nicolson, late dyer, when he comes of age.

---

[1] Richard Hill, Bishop of London, had died in February, 1496, and the See remained vacant until the following August, when Thomas Savage was translated to London from Rochester.

[2] Cf. *supra*, p. 165.

6 Sept., 12 Henry VII. [A.D. 1496], came John Hurst, Fo. 326 b.
"gentilman," Bartholomew Somer, haberdasher, Henry Denys, *Custodia Anne*
armourer, and Edmund Burton, draper, and entered into bond *filie Elie*
Alfonse
in the sum of £50 for payment into the Chamber by the said *vinitarii.*
John Hurst of a like sum to the use of Anne, daughter
of Elias Alfonse, late vintner, when she comes of age or
marries.[1]

24 Nov., 10 Henry VII. [A.D. 1494], came Richard Chawry, Fo. 327.
John Broke, Aldermen, Richard Nonneley, grocer, and
William Salford, mercer, and entered into bond in the sum of
£273 5s. for payment into the Chamber by the said Richard
·Chawry of a like sum to the use of Mary, daughter of Richard
Gardyner, late Alderman,[2] when she comes of age or marries.[3]

The same day came Hugh Clopton, William Martyn, Knt., Fo. 327 b.
Aldermen, John Pasmer and Roger Grauntoft, skinners, before
the Mayor and Aldermen, and entered into bond in the sum of
£273 5s. for payment into the Chamber by the said Hugh of a
like sum to the use of Mary, daughter of Richard Gardyner,
late Alderman, when she comes of age or marries.[4]

The same day came Hugh Clopton, William Martyn, Richard Fo. 328.
Chawry, John Broke, Aldermen, Richard Nonneley, William
Salforde, John Pasmer, and Roger Grauntoft, and entered into
a similar bond.

Wednesday the Feast of St. Matthew [21 Sept.], 12 Henry VII. Fo. 328 b.
[A.D. 1496], in the presence of Henry Colet, Knt., the Mayor, *Eleccio Vic'.*
Robert Sheffeld the Recorder, John Broun, Knt., John Warde,
the Prior of Christchurch, William White, Richard Chawry,
John Tate, John Percivale, Knt., William Isaac, John Broke,
William Capell, Knt., Henry Cote, Hugh Pemberton, William
Purches, William Welbeke, Robert Fabyan, Aldermen, and

---

[1] Margin. 4 April, 12 Henry VII.
[A.D. 1497], came John Mounes,
"iremonger," who married the above
Anne, and acknowledged satisfaction
for the said money.
[2] Alderman of Queenhithe, Walbrook, and Bassishaw Wards.

[3] Margin. 16 Dec., 20 Henry VII.
[A.D. 1504], came Giles Alyngton,
Esquire, who married the above
Mary, and acknowledged satisfaction
for his wife's patrimony.
[4] Marginal note to similar effect.

very many Commoners summoned to the Guildhall for the election of Sheriffs—John Shaa, goldsmith and Alderman,[1] was elected one of the Sheriffs of the City of London and Middlesex by the Mayor, and Richard Haddon, mercer, was elected the other Sheriff by the Commonalty.

The same day William Milborne, "payntour," was elected Chamberlain of the City for the year ensuing; Simon Harrys, grocer, and Christopher Eliot, goldsmith, were elected Wardens of London Bridge; William Capell, Ralph Tilney, Aldermen, William Stede, grocer, Thomas Creme, draper, Richard Odyam, draper, and John Peyntour, grocer, Commoners, were elected Auditors of the accounts of the Chamber and Wardens in arrear.

Afterwards, viz., on the eve of St. Michael [29 Sept.], the said Sheriffs were sworn at the Guildhall, and on the morrow of the said Feast were presented, admitted, &c., before the Barons of the Exchequer.

Eleccio Maioris.

Thursday the Feast of Translation of St. Edward [13 Oct.], 12 Henry VII. [A.D. 1496], in the presence of Henry Colet, Knt., the Mayor, Robert Sheffelde the Recorder, John Warde, Robert Tate, William White, John Mathewe, Richard Chawry, John Tate, William Isaac, Ralph Tilney, John Percyvale, Knt., William Capell, Knt., Henry Cote, Hugh Pemberton, William Purches, William Welbeke, Robert Fabyan, Nicholas Alwyn,[2] John Shaa, Aldermen, and an immense Commonalty summoned to the Guildhall for the election of a Mayor—John Tate was elected Mayor for the year ensuing.

Afterwards, viz., on the Feast of SS. Simon and Jude [28 Oct.], he was sworn at the Guildhall, and on the morrow was presented, admitted, &c., before the Barons of the Exchequer.

Custodia pueror' Joh'is Jenyns pistoris.

1 Dec., 12 Henry VII. [A.D. 1496], came George Atclyff, Robert Carvell, mercers, Gerard Danyell, fishmonger, and entered into bond in the sum of £40 [for payment into the Chamber by the said George Atclyff of a like sum to the use of William and Anne, children of John Jenyns, late baker, when they come of age or marry.—*On fo. 332.*]

---

1 Of Bread Street Ward.
2 Alderman successively of Cole-   man Street and Bassishaw Wards. *Ob.* 1506 (Beaven).

2 March, 12 Henry VII. [A.D. 1496–7], came good men of
the Fellowships of Pynners and Wyremongers before the
Mayor and Aldermen, praying that the said Fellowships may
be made one Fellowship of Wyresellers, and that the name of
Pynners and Wyremongers may be annulled; that the brethren
of the same Craft of Wyresellers may yearly elect an
" Umpere " and two Wardens to see its rules and ordinances
observed : and further, that the following ordinances of the
Pynners and Wyremongers, already approved and recorded,[1]
may be applied to the Wyresellers, viz. :—

First, that no one of the Craft work on Saturday or vigil of
double feast after 3 P.M., under penalty of paying 2 pounds of
wax, or else 8 pence the pound.

Also that all freemen of the Craft obey every summons to
assemble together.

That they obey the " Umper " and Wardens, and not revile
one another.

That no one of the Craft hire another out of his dwelling-
house, shop, or standing place at any market or fair.

That no one of the Craft entice a servant away from his
master.

That no freeman of the Craft take any work except in
connexion with other freemen of the Craft without licence of
the " Umpere " and Wardens.

"Also that from hensforth no persone enfraunchised in the
said Crafte wirk or set aworke any persone openly in his shoppe
in the wyndyng of Bokles cuttyng of Stones for moldes scoryng
of the same Gravyng of the moldes castyng of metalles or
colouryng of the same whereby any persone estraunger from the
said Felisship might lerne the said occupacions," &c., under
penalty prescribed.[2]

" That no Foreyn holde house or shoppe......nor bye nor sell
any thing touchyng the saide Crafte unto the tyme he be
examined by the Umpere and Wardeyns......if he be able to

---

[1] Cf. *supra*, pp. 185-6 ; 254-5.   [2] Cf. *supra*, p. 186.

kepe and occupie the said Crafte and also be made Freman of the same Citee."

That no " Foreyn " work in the said occupation until he be presented by a freeman of the Craft to the Umpire and Wardens, and sworn to obey the rules.

* * * *

That unruly members be put out of the Fellowship until such time as they may reform.

"Also that no persone of the said Felisshippe holde oppen shoppe on the Sonday but if any estraunger will bye of his merchaundises on the Sonday he shall cause hym to come to his house and there shewe hym his ware for the ease of travallyng people," under penalty prescribed.

"That no woman beyng foreyn worke nor occupie any thyng belongyng to the said Crafte until she pay a fine of iijs. iiijd."

" That from hensforth no persone worke in the said Crafte as knokkyng filyng or any other noyfulle werke whereby his Neighbours and other the Kynges people myght be noyed or diseased[1] from the Fest of Seynt Michell tharchaungell unto the Fest of the Annunciacion of oure lady but only from thoures of v of the clok in the mornyng unto viij of the clok in the nyght," under penalty prescribed.

" Also that from hensforth it shalbe lefulle to the Umpere and Wardeyns........to make due serche in alle places necessary and convenient......of almaner Wyre almaner Englisshe Pynnes Claspes anlettes[2] paknedilles bokels cheynes Fisshe hokes Stok-cardes and hand cardes [3] and of alle other thynges perteynyng to the said Crafte of Wyresellers."

That members of the Craft shall not hawk or proffer their wares to sell at an inn or elsewhere within the franchise of the City.

---

[1] Dis-eased, to have one's ease disturbed.

[2] Annulets, or little rings.

[3] Toothed instruments for carding wool. In 1356 we find the Card-makers associated with the Pynners ('Cal. Letter-Book G,' pp. 63-4), and in 1386 with the Wyredrawers ('Cal. Letter-Book H,' p. 291).

" That it shalbe lefulle to the said Umpere Wardeyns and Felisshippe to have and kepe their light within the White Friers in Fletestrete ...... there to brenne in thonour of God oure lady Seint Mary Seint James and Seynt Clement[1] and every yeere in the Fest of thassumpcion of our lady there to kepe their masse And on the morowe next ensuyng the same Feste to elect and chose their Umpere and Wardeyns for the yeere then next ensuyng.' The said light and mass to be maintained only in the White Friars, and not elsewhere without permission of the Mayor and Aldermen.

Their prayer granted.

14 March, 12 Henry VII. [A.D. 1496-7], came Dame Margery Astry, widow, Henry " Coles " (Colet?), Knt., Alderman, and William Copynger and Nicholas Mattok, fishmongers, and entered into bond in the sum of £573 10s. 4d. for payment into the Chamber by the said Dame Margery of a like sum to the use of John, son of Robert Rivell, late grocer and Alderman,[2] when he comes of age.

Fo. 331.

Custodia Joh'is Ryvell filii Rob'ti Ryvell Alderman'.

29 April, 12 Henry VII. [A.D. 1497], came Nicholas Barley, skinner, Richard Seman, skinner, John Welles, *pellarius* (skinner?), William Busshe, fishmonger, and Richard Hanchet, skinner, and entered into bond in the sum of £102 2s. 5d. for payment into the Chamber by the said Nicholas Barley of a like sum to the use of Robert and Philippa, children of William Hampton, late " pouchemaker," when they come of age.[3]

Fo. 331 b.

Custodia pueror' Will'i Hampton pouchemaker.

1 Dec., 12 Henry VII. [A.D. 1496], came Thomas Broke, fishmonger, Geoffrey Kent, draper, Thomas Howden, tailor, Alexander Perpoynt, " stokfysshemonger," and John Crowche, fishmonger, and entered into bond in the sum of £47 2s. 9d. for payment into the Chamber by the said Thomas Broke of a

Fos. 332-332 b.

Custodia Juliane filie Johannis Thornetone " stocfisshe-monger."

---

[1] As to the connexion of St. Clement with workers in metal, see note *supra*, p. 186.

[2] Of Farringdon Ward Without. *Ob.* Feb., 1491 (Beaven).

[3] Margin. 20 April, 21 Henry VII. [A.D. 1506], came John God, " taillour," who married the above Philippa, and acknowledged satisfaction for his wife's patrimony.

like sum to the use of Juliana, daughter of John Thorntone, late " stokfisshemonger," when she comes of age or marries.[1]

Fo. 333.

*Custodia
pueror'
Johannis
Halle groceri.*

12 May, 13 Henry VII. [A.D. 1498], came William Alborough, senior, and William Alborough, junior, mercers, William Wykes, grocer, and Roger Halle, grocer, before the Mayor and Aldermen, and entered into bond in the sum of £246 and 22½ pence for payment into the Chamber by the said William Alborough, senior, of a like sum to the use of John and Johanna (*que ad tunc fuit in ventre matris sue*[2]), children of John Halle, late grocer, when they come of age or marry.[3]

Fo. 333 b.

*Custodia
Rogeri Mone
filii Joh'is
Mone.*

7 Sept., 13 Henry VII. [A.D. 1497], came William Miller, " girdeler," George Salle, tailor, James Nube, sherman, Thomas Sutton, mercer, William Geffrey, dyer, and entered into bond in the sum of £14 3s. 4d. for payment into the Chamber by the said William Miller of a like sum to the use of Roger, son of John Mone.[4]

Fly-leaf.

Trade-marks of the following Coopers (*the names of some of them being illegible*), viz., William Tanner, Thomas Assheford, John Blundell, Robert Middelton, Alwine Geradson, Henry W......, Dederic D......, Herman Johnson, Nicholas Smyth, Arnold Osumbrug, John Doys, Herman ......, Arnold Willinson, ... Sconeburgh, Cornelius ......, John Mattelow, Laurence Gilysson, Daniel ......, Simon Claisson, Henry Couper ......, Henry Newey, John Evyngare, William ......, Richard Copelond.

---

[1] Margin. 15 Sept., 18 Henry VII. [A.D. 1502], came Alice Wode, late wife and executrix of the said John Thornton, and showed that the above Juliana had died under age and not married.

[2] The prognostication of the sex of the child *en ventre sa mère* is (to say the least) curious.

[3] Margin. This recognizance void. because another was entered into *temp.* William Remyngton, Mayor, anno 17 Henry VII.

[4] Margin. This recognizance void, because recorded in Letter-Book M, fo. 1.

END OF LETTER-BOOK L.

INDEX.

B

336

Coldham, Robert, 199
Cole, John, 149, 163, 190
—— Thomas, 83, 166, 174, 178
Colet, Henry, mercer, 144
—— Henry, Alderman, &c., 149, 150,
151, 152, 153, 157, 158, 160, 166,
167, 174, 175, 177, 209, 210, 215,
225, 234, 237, 238, 239, 241, 244,
245, 264, 269, 270, 272, 273, 279,
285, 308, 309, 310, 316, 317, 318,
321
—— John, 66
—— —— Agnes, daughter of, wife
of Richard Blisset, 66, 66n.
—— —— Alice, daughter of, wife
of William Whit, 66, 66n.
—— —— Geoffrey, son of, 66
—— —— Johanna, daughter of, 66
—— —— John, son of, 66
—— —— Robert, son of, 66
—— John, mercer, 285
Colman, Richard, 314
—— Robert, 85
Colrede, John, 155
Colsale, Robert, 108
Colson, Robert, 236
"Columbyne," a, as a decoration, 66,
122
Colvyle, John, 103
Colwiche, Colwyche, Robert, City
Chamberlain, 35, 39, 40, 43, 48,
53, 55, 60, 66, 72, 80, 86, 90, 91,
97, 107, 111, 114
—— —— Alderman, 122, 127, 128,
129, 130, 132, 133, 134, 135, 142,
144, 145, 149, 150, 151, 153, 157,
160
Colyn, Thomas, 231
Colyns, Christopher, 145, 148
—— John, 192, 223
—— Robert, 88
—— Thomas, 223
Common Clerk, the, to have the
custody of the City Records, 17;
to account for amercements in
Mayor's Court, 38
Common Hunt:
Stokker, John, 36, 59
Sudbury, William, 36
Common Packer. See Packer and
Gauger.
Common Pleaders:
Frowyke, Thomas, 281
Marwe, Thomas, 280-1
Common Serjeants-at-law:
Baldewyn, John, 36
Bryan, Thomas, 36
Compters, the Secondaries and Clerks
in, to continue in office during good
behaviour, 236, 300-1; ordinances

touching treatment of prisoners in,
250
Comptroller of the Chamberlain, 160
Conduit, from Ludgate to Newgate,
new pipes to be thenceforth re-
paired by the City, 130; money
advanced by the Chamberlain for,
279; licence to turn up soil in
Gracechurch Street for purpose of a,
280; licence granted by Sir John
Fortescue to the Mayor and
Commonalty to break ground on
his property for making a, 283
Conduit Mead granted to the City by
Sir John Fortescue, 283-4
Conduit pipes, punishment for tapping,
160
Conduits, Wardens appointed for, 228
Constantyn, Costantyn, William,
Alderman, 30, 34, 35, 37, 38, 40,
45, 56, 60, 62, 64, 66, 68, 70, 72,
73, 74, 76, 79, 80
Cook, Coke, Thomas, Alderman, &c.,
12, 14, 15, 18, 20, 21, 22, 24, 29,
30, 34, 35, 37, 38, 39, 40, 45, 51,
56, 64, 68, 70, 72, 73, 74, 76n., 94
Cook, William, 1
—— Wolford, M.D., 103
Cooks, Mistery of, ordinances ap-
proved, 129-30; charter of incor-
poration, 313
Coopers, their trade-marks, 1, 322;
Mistery of, ordinances, 250; penalty
for using unmarked barrels by, re-
duced, 279
Coote. See Cote.
Copes, their length prescribed, 308
Copland, William, 314n.
—— —— Elena, wife of, daughter
of Richard Bodley, 314
Copynger, William, 199, 247, 304, 321
Corbet, John, 248
—— William, 6, 9, 20, 94, 101
Corbrande, Corbronde, Thomas, 87
88, 110
Cordell, John, 314
Cordwainers, their composition with
Cobblers, 51; to share fines with
Cobblers, 114
Cordwainer Street, 19
Corffe, Robert, elected Sub-escheator,
81
Corneborowe, Averey, 58
Corn-meters not to pay anything to
the Bailiff of Billingsgate, 87; the
above ordinance revoked, 95
Cornysshe, John, 44, 246
—— Thomas, 113
Corone, Nicholas de, 131
—— —— John, son of, 131

D

F

G

H

to, not to take place without con-
sent of the Mayor and Aldermen,
214 ; unauthorized ordinances cut
out of their books, 246
Mondue, John, 141
Mone, John, 322
—— Roger, son of, 322
Monnyng, Munnyng, Reymund. See
Vawe.
More, William, 95, 286
Moredone, Maurice, 152
"Morkins," 117n.
Morley, John, 241
—— Richard, tallow-chandler, 241,
305
—— —— Margaret, daughter of,
wife of Thomas Lauryman, 305
—— —— Thomas, son of, 305
Mortmain, City custom as to devise
in, 192
Mortymer, John, 35, 60, 110
Motener, John le, 101
"Mothering Sunday," 286n.
Moumford, Robert, 276n.
—— —— Margery, wife of, daughter
of Robert Godewyn, 276
Mounes, John, 317n.
—— —— Anne, wife of, daughter of
Elias Alfonse, 317
Mountford, George, admitted At-
torney in Sheriffs' Court, 61
Mower, Thomas, 149, 163, 190
Mugge, Robert, 148
—— —— William, son of, 148
Munnyng. See Vawe.
Muschamp, Thomas, 6, 34, 38, 55
Mustell, John, 245
—— —— Alice, daughter of, wife of
Thomas Shripley, 245
—— —— Elizabeth, daughter of,
wife of Nicholas Aleyn, 245
—— —— Johanna, daughter of, 245
Muston, Nicholas, 99, 100
—— Richard, 145
Mynes, John, 155
Mynte, William, 157
Mynto, John, 1

N

Nayler, Nailer, Richard, tailor, 151,
157, 176
—— Richard, tailor and Alderman,
195, 221
—— —— Alice, daughter of, wife of
Walter Robert, 221n.
—— Hugh, son of, 221
—— —— Johanna, daughter of, wife
of Richard Coulpepyr, 221n.
—— —— Robert, son of, 221

Nayler, Nailer, Richard, Thomesina,
daughter of, wife of Robert Bifeld,
221n.
—— —— Valentine, son of, 221
Nele, Neele, John, 62
—— William, vintner, 35, 60
Neleson, William, 165
—— —— Alice, daughter of, 165
—— —— Elizabeth, daughter of, 165
—— —— Thomas, son of, 165
Netmakers, Mistery of, ordinances,
254
Nets, false, to be burnt, 152, 229 ;
commissioners appointed to ex-
amine, 221, 223-4
Nevile, Nevell, Henry, ironmonger,
82, 131, 300
—— —— William, son of, 300
—— John, 217
Newchirch, Everard, 179
Newey, Henry, 322
Newgate, water brought from Priory
of St. Bartholomew to, 4 ; ordi-
nance regulating the holding of
Sessions at, 137
Newgate prison, ordinances for better
regulation of, 41-3, 250 ; Sheriffs to
procure a yearly commission for
gaol-delivery at their own cost, 101
Newkyrk, Everard, 78
Newman, Edmund, 49, 95, 149, 176
—— Henry, 88, 110
Newton, Henry, 75n.
—— —— Elena, wife of, daughter
of John Amady, 75n.
Niche, Thomas, 167
Nicholas, John, 300
Nicholas V., Pope, his Bull touching
oblations to curates to be obeyed,
128
Nicholl, John, 131
Nicholson, John, 74, 155
—— —— John, son of, 74, 155
Nicolson, Thomas, dyer, 220, 316
—— —— John, son of, 316
—— —— Reginald, son of, 316
Nightyngale, William, 90, 295
Ninnys, Nynnys, Nicholas, 303, 309
Noneley, Nonneley, Richard, 229,
237, 297, 303, 317
Norfolk (John Howard), Duke of,
207
Norhander, John, chantry priest in
Guildhall Chapel, 227
Norland, Norlond, Thomas, grocer,
152, 156, 163, 209
—— Thomas, Alderman, 195, 197,
209, 210, 215, 216
Norlong, John, 54, 70
—— Thomas, 104

S

T

PRINTED BY JOHN EDWARD FRANCIS, BREAM'S BUILDINGS, CHANCERY LANE, E.C.

CPSIA information can be obtained at www.ICGtesting.com
Printed in the USA
LVOW12s1101140514

385761LV00010B/130/P